STEVE KURTH

ILLUSTRATOR 10

SHOP MANUAL

New Riders

201 West 103rd Street, Indianapolis, Indiana 46290

Illustrator 10 Shop Manual

Copyright © 2002 by New Riders Publishing

International Standard Book Number: 0-7357-1176-3

Library of Congress Catalog Card Number: 2002101601

Printed in the United States of America

First Printing: June 2002

06 05 04 03 02   7 6 5 4 3 2 1

Interpretation of the printing code: The rightmost double-digit number is the year of the book's printing; the rightmost single-digit number is the number of the book's printing. For example, the printing code *02-1* indicates that the first printing of the book occurred in 2002.

Trademarks

Warning and Disclaimer

David Dwyer
Publisher

Stephanie Wall
Associate Publisher

Steve Weiss
Executive Editor

Donnie O'Quinn
Series Editor

Gina Kanouse
Production Manager

Sarah Kearns
Managing Editor

Linda Anne Bump
Senior Acquisitions Editor

Victoria Elzey
Acquisitions Editor

Damon Jordan
Project Editor

Kathy Malmloff
Product Marketing Manager

Susan Nixon
Publicity Manager

Jim Conway
Manufacturing Coordinator

Donnie O'Quinn
Cover Design

Donnie O'Quinn
Interior Design & Layout

Cheryl Lenser
Senior Indexer

Contents at a Glance

Table of Contents

5   Color Controls   85

6   View Controls   89

7   The File Menu   91

CONTENTS

10   The Type Menu   245

13   The Effect Menu   297

CONTENTS

15   The Actions Palette   349

16   The Align Palette   363

17   The Appearance Palette   369

30 The Stroke Palette 485

31 The Style Palette 491

40   The Tab Ruler Palette   559

41   The Variables Palette   563

Preface

Adobe Illustrator 10 is one of the most complex and under-utilized applications in the graphic arts industry today. Since Illustrator 8, the application has steadily changed from Photoshop's little sister into a full-fledged media powerhouse in its own right. Yet most users know a fraction of the application, and fail to grasp the true power of even the basic tools.

That's where this book comes in. Even after you've learned the basics, it's difficult to remember the function of every tool, every palette, and every item of every dialog box of every command. And the newest features: Do they replace old tools? How are they used in conjunction with an existing workflow? Are they really as effective as the marketing reports would have you believe?

This book contains no tutorials. It doesn't hold your hand or strive to entertain you with witty prose. Like you, I use Illustrator for a living. When the clock is ticking, I know you don't want to flip through page after page of unnecessary text for the information you need. I've presented the facts—and only the facts—so you can get in, get out, and get back to work.

The Interface

The main text of this book covers the entire interface of Illustrator 10. Each tool and command receives the following treatment:

Specific Function

A summary of the purpose and function of each item. This section even places seemingly insignificant items into an easy to understand, production-oriented context.

Mistakes to Avoid

A list of complex but avoidable misuses of the software. Since many aspects of Illustrator are so non-intuitive, this section explains the common mistakes—and offers realistic solutions.

Issues to Consider

A list of advice, warnings, guidance, and shortcuts. Illustrator never works in a vacuum, and this section fleshes out an item's relationship with other commands, issues, and techniques.

The Dialog Box

Definitions and recommended settings for each option in every dialog box. Because the real power of Illustrator rests in its on-screen controls, users must understand the cause-and-effect relationship of every setting.

Techniques Appendices

The back of the book contains over 80 step-by-step techniques that range from selection strategies, to dynamic object workflow, to lighting effects. This list further illustrates the most demanding and production-enhancing uses of Illustrator. With a few print-specific exceptions, they represent a core set of skills that you can apply to images for any medium.

Topic Numbering

Every topic in this book is numbered for fast and easy reference. In the main text, the topics also reflect the layout of Illustrator's interface. For example, if a particular issue involves the Transform Each command, a cross reference would appear as follows:

*(For more information, see 9.8, Object: Transform: **Transform Each**.)*

This indicates that in Illustrator, the Transform Each command is found in the Object menu, under the Transform submenu. In the book, the command is the 8th topic listed in Chapter 9; to find it, flip to the Table of Contents to locate the page number, or refer to the footers at the bottom of each page.

Considerable effort was made to include as many cross-references as possible. Each topic contains a "Related Topics" section, which lists the tools, commands, and techniques most commonly encountered when using a specific part of Illustrator.

Macintosh and Windows Commands

Keyboard shortcuts are included for Macintosh and Windows users. Mac keys appear in parentheses, Windows keys appear in brackets. For example:

- (Option) [Alt]-click an item in the Layers palette to select it.
- Choose (Option-Command) [Alt-Control]-B to create a blend from selected paths.

Visit www.newriders.com

On the publisher's Web site, you'll find information about their other books, the authors they partner with, book updates and file downloads, promotions, discussion boards for online interaction with other users and technology experts, and a calendar of trade shows and other professional events. They hope to see you around.

Call or Fax New Riders

You can reach the publisher toll-free at (800) 571-5840; ask for New Riders. If outside the U.S., call 1-317-581-3500 and ask for New Riders. If you prefer, you can fax them at 1-317-581-4663, Attention: New Riders.

Contact the Author

Contact Steve Kurth at *kurth@illustratoranswers.com*. Find updates to this book and additional materials at *www.illustratoranswers.com*.

Acknowledgments

I gratefully acknowledge the assistance of the people who made this book possible: Donnie O'Quinn, who conceived and developed the Shop Manual series; Victoria Elzey, Damon Jordan, and the rest of the staff at New Riders; David Rogelberg and the fine folks at StudioB; Matt LeClair, Tim Plumer, and Greg Heald for their aces technical editing; and the folks at Adobe, especially Mordy Golding and the beta testing team.

I would also like to acknowledge the people who have helped me to this point, including my colleagues Chris Fournier, Randy Hagan, and Ted Darling; my iSET and AGI students and clients (especially those at Verizon, including Mary Tuttle, Brian Fraley, and Martha Elmali). A tip of the pen to authors Matt LeClair and Ted Alspach. Hats off to Dorrie, Rick, the Misol Ha, and her crew. Hellos to my pals at Ethos, especially Judy, Brian, Pete, and Gary. Big hellos to Nancy, David, Jacques, Judy, Linda, Mel, Céilum, Java Imhoff, and Tom Bowman. Special thanks to Mom, Dad, Joel, Beth, Robbie, Katie, Matt.

Dedication

This book is dedicated to Michelle Belanger. Thank you for everything, baby.

Selection Tools

Selection Tools Overview

Selecting objects is a vital part of any Illustrator work session. Selection is the act of nominating an object for modification. Even the slightest change of an object almost always requires that a selection be made first. This means you will be selecting continually in Illustrator. When a selection is made, the items selected are highlighted. The color they are highlighted in corresponds to the layer the items are on. When you first start a document and haven't made any new layers, the default selection color is light blue. When anchor points are selected, they appear as solid boxes. Anchor points that aren't selected on objects that contain a selection display as hollow points.

In some cases, objects may be modified without being selected:

- **If they are on a layer or in a group that is targeted.** Targeting also nominates objects for modification, but differs in that it enables modification of group and layer level styling. *(For more information, see 25.8, Target.)*

- **If a swatch from the gradient, styles, appearance, or brushes palette is dragged onto them.** This changes objects without selecting them.

• **If the definition of an existing attribute changes.** For example, an object filled with a global swatch color may change as the definition of the swatch is altered. Changing the definition of styles, brushes, and symbols commonly alters objects that use those items.

Mistakes to Avoid

Selecting objects for techniques that require targeting. For example, the opacity of a layer affects all of the objects on the layer, but selecting all of the objects on the layer will not give you access to the layer's transparency setting. You would need to target the layer to do that.

Arrow tools and lasso tools use different keyboard modifiers. Adding and subtracting objects to a selection is done differently with the arrow-style selection tools than with the lasso-style tools. Shift-clicking while using the Selection, Direct Selection, and Group Selection tools toggles an object's selection state. When using the Lasso and Direct Select Lasso tools, Shift-clicking adds to a selection but has no deselecting functionality.

Adding Shift at the wrong time. Shift while selecting with the Selection and Direct Selection and Group Selection tools toggles a selection on or off. Shift while dragging or transforming constrains the transformation. Shift-select the objects required. Release the mouse. Then click-drag to transform. Add the Shift key as you drag to constrain.

Trying to transform with the Lasso tools. Unlike their counterparts, the Lasso and Direct Select Lasso tools are pure selection tools. They have no editing functions. To temporarily switch to the Selection or Direct Selection tool (whichever was used last), hold down the (Command) [Ctrl] key.

Accidentally clicking off the object. Clicking an empty part of the document deselects everything.

Issues to Consider

Contextual selection menu. The selection tools feature a contextual menu. Once an object is selected, Illustrator's selection tools can be used to select other objects in front of or behind the selected object. Hold down the (Control) [Right Mouse] button to access the contextual menu. This menu features a Select submenu, which contains the Select Next Object commands. This functionality is partially available through the Select menu. *(For more information see 11.5 Select: Next Object Above.)*

Choosing Edit: Undo recalls the last selection made. Part of the function of the command Edit: Undo is to recall the last selection. That is, if you edit an object, deselect the object and choose Edit: Undo, the edits will be removed and the object will become selected again. If an object is selected but has not yet been modified when you choose Undo, the last modification will be undone and those objects will be selected as well as the current one. This is often used to recall a complex selection.

The presence of selections alters the affect of some tools. Some tools will affect only selected objects if a selection is present. For example, if a selection is made, the Knife tool can only affect the selected objects. If no selection is made, it affects all objects.

Related Topics

11.1   Selection Menu
25.7   Name
25.8   Target

1.2
_____

Selection Tool
Type "V"

Use this tool to select and move objects. Selected objects may also be scaled and rotated using this tool in conjunction with the Bounding Box feature. *(For more information, see 14.22, View Bounding Box.)*

When you click and drag to create a selection, a preview outline extends outward from your starting point. When the mouse button is released, all objects the preview outline touches become selected.

When you click to make a selection, only one object can be selected per click. The cursor must be over a Fill or directly on a path or point to make a selection. Note that if an object has a Fill of None or the document is in Outline mode, no Fill is available to be clicked on. In these cases, click on a path segment, or point to select the object. Click on an empty part of the document to deselect all.

When the cursor is positioned over a selectable object, the cursor display will change to indicate a selection is possible. A solid box next to the Arrow cursor indicates the cursor is positioned over a path or selectable fill. A white box indicates the cursor is positioned over an anchor point.

Mistakes to Avoid

Clicking inside a path in Outline mode. Unlike Preview mode, clicking on the interior of a filled path does not select the object in Outline mode.

Attempting to select individual members of a group. Since a group is an object, this tool selects all of the items in a group with one click. Use the Direct Selection tool or Group Selection to select individual items in a group.

Trying to select points. The Selection tool cannot select specific path segments or points. The Selection tool does change displays to indicate the cursor is over an unselected anchor point, but it can only select objects.

Confusing Selection tool with Free Transform Tool. The Free Transform and the Selection Tool have the same cursor and appear the same when the bounding box is visible. Both can also scale, reflect, and rotate objects. Since they do not behave exactly the same, be certain which tool you are using by checking the toolbox. (Or, set the Status Bar to Current Tool, which enables you to check the lower left corner of the window.)

Issues to Consider

The Use Area Select Preference alters selectable areas. This preference enables objects to be selected by clicking on their Fills. With this preference disabled, an object can only be selected by clicking on a path segment or point. In the disabled setting it is more difficult to select objects, but selections made will always be from points along the object. This may be useful when used in conjunction with View: **Snap to Point**. This preference is checked by default.

Shift toggles selection state. Reverse the selection status of an object by selecting it with the Shift key depressed. Selected objects become deselected; deselected objects become selected.

The Bounding Box may interfere with Snap to Point. In many cases, you may want to position one anchor point atop another. The best way to do this is to click directly on one point and drag it atop the other while using the View: Snap to Point option. The bounding box, while useful for transformation, interferes with this. To move point to point in this way, either disable the bounding box, or use the Direct Selection tool. *(For more information see 14.33 View: Snap to Point.)*

Objects are easily duplicated with this tool. Press the (Option) [Alt] key as you reposition an object to create a copy of the object. This does not work when scaling or rotating an item with this tool.

Modifications with the Selection tool. Consider the following editing options when using the Selection tool:

- **Move.** Selected objects may be moved by Click-dragging from one location in the document to another. Hold down the Shift key after you start dragging to constrain the positioning of the object to the document's default angles Double-click on the Selection Tool to open the Move Dialog box. Hold down the (Option) [Alt] key as you move an item to move a duplicate of the object. *(For more information, see 8.12, Edit: Preferences: General and 9.3, Object: Transform: Move.)*

- **Scale.** When the Bounding Box is visible a wire frame box appears around the selected objects. Click-drag on corner points of the bounding box to scale objects both horizontally and vertically at the same time. Click-drag on a left or right center box to scale horizontally. Click on the top or bottom center point to scale vertically. Add Shift as you drag to constrain the width and height of the objects as you scale. By default, objects will be scaled toward the point opposite the point dragged. For example, if you scale the object by dragging the lower-right corner of the bounding box, the upper right corner of the object would be held in place while the rest of the object was scaled toward that corner. Hold down the (Option) [Alt] key to scale objects about their centers.

- **Rotate.** When the bounding box is visible a wire frame appears around the selected objects. When the cursor is positioned directly on the bounding box near the control points, it becomes a curved double-headed arrow. When this cursor is displayed, Click-drag to rotate the selection about its center. Hold down Shift as you drag to constrain to the default constrain angles. The default angles are applied relative to the object, not the page.

- **Reflect.** When the bounding box is visible a wire frame appears around the selected objects. Reflect an object across an axis by Click-dragging from one control point on the bounding box directly across the object. This can scale the items as well. Reflecting this way is less precise than using other methods since it often involves scaling the objects inadvertently.

1.3

Direct Selection Tool   *Type "A"*

Use this tool to select and move anchor points, direction points, segments, mesh points, and objects. Since the tool can select any or all of an object, it is the highly flexible and frequently used.

When you click and drag to create a selection, a preview outline extends outward from your starting point. When the mouse button is released, all points and segments the preview outline touches become selected. Selected points will be indicated by in the highlight color of the layer. Unselected points will be outlined in the highlight color of the layer but their centers will remain unfilled. Selected segments do not become highlighted in a unique way. You can identify a selected segment if an object is highlighted but the anchor points connected to the segment are not solid.

Issues to Consider

Switching to the Group Selection tool saves time. When used in conjunction with the Group Selection tool, most everyday selection functions can be accomplished with the Direct Selection tool. Use this tool to select complete objects and then release the modifier key to switch back to the Direct Selection tool.

Only one item may be selected per click. When the cursor is positioned over a selectable object, the cursor display will change to indicate a selection is possible. A solid box next to the arrow cursor indicates the cursor is positioned over a path or selectable fill. A white box indicates the cursor is positioned over a point.

Setting Direct Selection tool preferences. The Use Area Select Preference affects the Direct Selection tool. *(For more information, see 8.12 Edit: Preferences: **General**.)*

Once a selection is established, items may be moved by click-dragging them into a new position. Clear or copy selected items as needed. Moving an anchor or mesh point moves all of the segments connected to it as well. Moving a straight line segment repositions the anchor points on either end of it. Moving a curved segment repositions the direction points that control it, but leaves the anchor points in place. Hold down the (Option) [Alt] key when moving an item to duplicate it.

Accessing the Group Selection tool. Hold down the (Option) [Alt] key to temporarily switch to the Group Selection tool.

1.4

Group Selection Tool

Use the Group Selection tool to select group objects and the component members of group objects. The Group Selection arrow selects entire path objects with a single click. If the path is grouped to another path, clicking the path again will select the paths grouped to that object. Since groups may be grouped to groups, sequential clicking will continue to select items along the group chain.

Hold down the (Option) [Alt] key to temporarily switch to the Direct Selection Tool.

Mistakes to Avoid

Attempting to select anchor points with the Group Selection tool. Unlike the Direct Selection tool, this tool cannot select components of a path. Rather, it selects components of a group.

Issues to Consider

The Group Selection tool is invaluable when selecting graphs. Graph objects are essentially an elaborate system of groups. This makes the group selection tool well suited to selecting object series quickly.

1.5

Lasso Tool

Use the Lasso tool to select objects using a freeform selection marquee.

Click-drag with the Lasso tool and a freeform guide follows the cursor. Objects the guide crosses will be selected when the mouse is released. Add the Shift key as you drag to add objects to the current selection. Add the (Option) [Alt] key as you drag to subtract objects from the current selection.

1.6

Direct Selection Lasso Tool *Type "Q"*

Use the Direct Selection Lasso tool to select anchor points, direction points, segments, and mesh points using a freeform selection marquee.

Click-drag with the Direct Selection Lasso tool and a freeform guide follows the cursor. Items the guide crosses will be selected when the mouse is released. Add the Shift key as you drag to add objects to the current selection. Add the (Option) [Alt] key as you drag to subtract objects from the current selection.

1.7

Magic Wand Tool *Type "Y"*

Use the Magic Wand to select objects. Multiple objects may be selected in a single click, based upon their similarity to the object clicked.

To select an object with the Magic Wand tool, click directly on the object with the tool. Any object may be selected in this way. If the object is part of a group, only the item and not the Group is selected.

Additional objects with similar Fills, strokes, stroke weights, opacities and or blend modes will also be selected, depending upon the settings in the Magic Wand palette. *(For more information, see 27.1, The Magic Wand Palette.)*

Add the Shift key as you click to add objects to the current selection. Add the (Option) [Alt] key as you click to subtract objects from the current selection.

Issues to Consider

Object opacity is compared, not actual opacity. The Magic Wand compares the opacity applied to objects, not layers an object is on or the opacity of a Fill or stroke. Thus an object with a 100% opacity on a 10% opacity layer would be selected along with other 100% opacity objects, even though it is mostly transparent because of the layer it is on.

Without Use Area Select, the Magic Wand is limited. If you disable the Use Area Select Preference (in the Edit: Preferences: **General** dialog box), you must click directly on an anchor point to select items. This can be difficult. Even if Use Area Select is activated, you must click directly on anchor points when in Outline mode.

Meshes, symbols, rasters, and envelopes cannot be selected by similarity. These objects may be selected as the initial objects clicked, but are not selected based upon their similarity to other objects.

Object Creation Tools

Pen Tool Suite

Use the tools in this suite to precisely create and edit custom paths. The pen tools utilize an interface that, although initially difficult to master, accords the user with a high degree of control over the creation of paths. Since other popular applications, such as Photoshop, QuarkXPress, FreeHand, Flash, and InDesign also feature pen tools with near identical interfaces, users who learn the pen tool will enjoy productivity benefits in those applications as well.

The most difficult thing about using the Pen tool is placing and controlling direction points. This will require some practice. *(For more information, see C.3, Drawing a Basic Path.)* Using the Pen tools will likely also involve using the Direct Selection tool.

Related Topics
1.3   Direct Selection tool
1.6   Direct Selection Lasso tool
Appendix C, Path & Object Techniques

2.2

Pen Tool

Use the Pen tool to create paths. When using the Auto Add/Delete preference, the Pen tool can also add and remove anchor points from existing selected paths. Paths created by this tool are commonly closed paths. The only way to create an open path with the Pen is to switch to another tool, such as the Selection tool. *(For more information, see 8.12, Edit: Preferences:* **General***)*

The Pen tool can create both anchor and direction points. An anchor point may contain up to two direction points, or "curve handles," each affecting the line segments before and after the anchor point. The direction points may or may not be symmetrical to each other. If no direction points affect it, a segment is said to be straight. Otherwise, it is curved.

To create a straight segment with the Pen tool, click in the document to establish an anchor point. The standard Pen tool cursor will indicate that a new path is to be created by displaying an "x" in the lower right. Reposition the cursor and click a second time. A straight-line segment connects the points. Additional clicks will continue to add anchor points connected by straight segments. Position the cursor atop the initial anchor point and click to close the path. The cursor will change to indicate the path is to be closed by temporarily displaying an "o" in the lower right. All paths created with the Pen tool will behave like this. To leave the path open, consider holding down the (Command) [Ctrl] key on the keyboard to temporarily access the last selection arrow tool used. Click off the object and it will become deselected, leaving the path open.

To create an anchor point that contains direction points, click-drag with the tool. Two symmetrical direction points are pulled out from the anchor point. Do not confuse the direction segments with path segments. Release the mouse to stop dragging the direction points and reposition the cursor. Click again to establish another anchor point. The segment connecting the anchor points will be curved toward the forward direction point of the previous point.

Since direction points are symmetrical by default, the two segments affected by them tend to create smooth curves. To create a curve segment that corners sharply into another curve or becomes straight will require editing the direction points. This can be done as the path is being created.

To draw a curve segment that connects to a straight segment, you will need to delete the forward direction point. To do this, click on the anchor point you have just created with the pen tool. The cursor will temporarily display a small version of the Convert Direction Point Tool next to it. The forward direction point is deleted and will not affect the next anchor point you create. Click again to create another segment.

Once removed, you can reset the forward direction point. Click-drag on the anchor point to reposition both the forward and rear direction points. The two direction points will remain at 180° from each other, but the forward direction point may be set at any distance from the anchor point while the rear direction point retains its original distance.

To create a path that turns sharply from one curve to another (picture the letter "m") you will need to create non-symmetrical direction points. To do this, (Option) [Alt] click-drag the anchor point you have just created with the pen tool. A new, non-symmetrical direction point will be created. Release the mouse to stop dragging the direction point and reposition the cursor. Click to establish a new anchor point. The new segment will be curved based upon the new forward direction point.

Issues to Consider

Anchor points should be positioned in transitional locations in the path. Look at the overall shape of the curve and place anchor points in the middle of those transitions.

Paths with fewer anchor points are easier to handle. They are easier to edit and they print faster. Don't limit yourself, but try to draw paths without unnecessary anchor points. New users often become discouraged with direction points and opt to create long polygons with many points. In the long run it will take less time to learn the tool than to create and edit poorly drawn paths.

Long direction segments create difficult curves. Try to limit the length of a direction segment to a third the distance of the path segment.

Drag direction points in the direction you want the curve to go. If the path if moving up and to the right, drag the curve handle in that direction. Remember that the direction points pull the segment. Don't fight the pull.

The Use Precise Cursors preference affects the Pen tool. If you have activated Use Precise Cursors, the Pen tool will display as crosshairs rather than the pen icon. The Caps Lock key will temporarily activate this preference as well.

2.3

Add Anchor Point Tool

Use the Add Anchor Point tool to add anchor points to paths. This is commonly done to change the shape of a path, or to isolate a part of the path before it is copied or deleted. When the Auto Add/Subtract preference is enabled (in the Edit: Preferences: **General** dialog box), the Pen tool will switch to the Add Anchor point tool automatically whenever it is positioned over a selected path.

To add an anchor point to a path, click directly on a path with the Add Anchor Point tool. Many users select paths prior to adding points. An anchor point will be added to the path in the position clicked. The new anchor point will contain the direction points needed to maintain the shape of the path. Hold down the (Option) [Alt] key to temporarily access the Subtract the Delete Anchor Point tool.

2.4

Delete Anchor Point Tool

Use the Delete Anchor Point tool to delete anchor points from selected paths. This is commonly done to simplify a path, or to change the shape of a path. When the Auto Add/Subtract preference is enabled, the Pen tool will switch to the Delete Anchor Point tool automatically whenever it is positioned over a selected anchor point.

To subtract an anchor point from a path, position the cursor directly on an anchor point with the Delete Anchor Point tool. The path need not be selected to do this, but many users find it easier to locate points for removal with a selection made. The anchor point will be removed from the path and the segments on either side of the anchor point are merged into one segment. This will often change the shape of the path. In this respect the Delete Anchor point is different from deleting an anchor point by hitting the Delete key or choosing Edit: Clear. Deleting an anchor point in that way removes the point and the segments, creating an open path. Hold down the (Option) [Alt] key to temporarily access the Add Anchor Point tool.

Mistakes to Avoid

Accidentally deleting anchor points with Auto Add. If you create an anchor point and then click on it again, when using the Auto Add option, you will delete the point. This is commonly an error committed by users new to the Pen tool who intend to click-drag on an anchor point to create direction points but hesitate.

2.5

Convert Anchor Point Tool

Use the Convert Anchor Point tool to add, edit, and remove direction points.

As with the Add and Delete Anchor Point tools, a selection is not necessary to use the Convert Anchor Point tool. Making a selection first is helpful, though, since it makes it easier to locate the anchor points. Click directly on an anchor point to remove the direction points. Click-drag on an anchor point to create two symmetrical direction points. Click-drag on a direction point to reposition it independently of the other direction point. Hold down the Shift key as you drag to constrain the movement of the cursor to the default constrain angle. Add the (Option) [Alt] key as you use the tool to perform the changes on a duplicate of the anchor point, creating new segments.

Mistakes to Avoid

Inappropriate direction points. Independent direction points are easier to handle, but often result in unwanted corners and creases. Limit the use of them to when your path requires it.

2.6

Type Tool Suite

Use the Type tools to enter text, define type-bounding areas, and to select existing type.

Type in Illustrator is defined as having an orientation (horizontal or vertical) and a kind. The kind is the model by which text flows or is bounded. Type must be either inside a bounding shape (area type), set along a path (path type), or along a straight line oriented about a single point (point type). The Type and Vertical Type tools can be used to define bounding rectangles and establish type orientation points. Both type and the path that acts as its bounding area or baseline are considered a single object and are selected with one click of the Selection tool. Use the Direct Selection tool to select bounding areas and baselines independent of their type blocks.

All of the Type tools select existing text in the same manner regardless of the type's orientation or kind. Click once with any text tool on existing text to establish an insertion point. Drag across characters to select them. The insertion point may be nudged one space using the arrow keys on the keyboard. Add the (Command) [Ctrl] key to nudge the insertion point to the next or preceding word (left and right arrows) or next or preceding paragraph (up and down arrows). To select type as you move the insertion point, (Command-Shift) [Ctrl-Shift] click the arrow keys.

With an insertion point active, position the cursor elsewhere in the text object and Shift-click to select the text up to the point clicked. Double-click to select a complete word and the space that follows it. Double-click-drag (double-click and then drag the mouse before you let up on the second click) to select a series of complete words. Triple-click with any type tool to select an entire paragraph. Triple-click-drag to select a complete sequence of paragraphs.

Issues to Consider

Type may be formatted as an object. Type attributes, such as font and paragraph alignment may be set for entire type objects by selecting them with a selection tool.

An object may be a bounding area or baseline for type, but not both. Objects defined as one of these are not easily switched to the other. Be careful that you are sure you know what you are doing before converting a path to a bounding area or baseline.

Paths converted to type bounding boxes or baselines become part of the type object. When you convert objects to type bounding areas, they become part of the text object. The original objects are set to a fill and stroke of None. When you select area type objects, both the bounding area and the type baselines are highlighted. Selected path type displays an I-beam at the insertion point. To style the bounding object independently of the type, select the path using the Direct Selection or Direct

Select Lasso tool. If the baseline or I-Beam is not visible, you will know that only the bounding object is selected.

Related Topics

10.1   Type Menu
37.1   Character Palette
38.1   MM Design Palette
39.1   Paragraph Palette
40.1   Tab Ruler Palette
Appendix D, Type Techniques

2.7

Type Tool

Type "T"

The Type tool may be used to establish bounding areas for type, to enter text, and to select type. Also, the Type tool can perform the functions of the other type tools when used in conjunction with keyboard shortcuts and commands.

To create horizontally oriented point type, click with the Type tool. Shift-click to create vertical point type. An anchor point is created in the clicked position. As text is entered, it flows in a straight line oriented about the anchor point. Paragraphs will only wrap to the next line in the event that text goes all the way to the end of the pasteboard. Of course, a hard or soft return will force the text to the next line. The baseline of point type is not an editable path as it is in path type.

To establish a bounding rectangle for type, click-drag with the Type tool. Shift-Click-drag to create a bounding area for vertically oriented type. A rectangular wire frame will follow your cursor, indicating the location of the type area when the mouse is released. When the mouse is released, a blinking insertion point will indicate the position type will appear as you type. The type entered into this rectangle will be area type.

The horizontal cross bar of the default Type Tool cursor is called the *hot point.* When the hot point is directly atop a path that is not already a bounding object for type, or a complex object such as a symbol set, a compound path, a mask or a graph, the Type tool toggles to either the Area Type (in the event the path is closed) or Path type tool (in the event the path is open). To switch between the Area and Path Type tools, hold down the (Option) [Alt] key. So, if you want to create path type on a circle (a closed path) position the hot point directly on the path and (Option) [Alt] click. To switch to the Vertical Type tool, hold down the Shift key while clicking to establish type. In this way, the Type tool can be used to create all the various type objects without switching to another tool.

2.8

Area Type Tool

Use the Area Type tools to convert objects to bounding areas for text. Position the hot point of the Area Type tool directly atop a path and click. The object will become a bounding area for type and a blinking insertion point will be displayed. Type blocks which contain more characters than can be contained are indicated with a plus icon in the lower right of the object.

Objects converted to bounding areas for type lose all previous appearance settings and are assigned a black fill and no stroke, which are the default attributes for text. To switch to the Vertical Area Type tool, hold down the Shift key while clicking to establish type.

2.9

Path Type Tool

Use the Path Type tool to convert objects to baselines for text. Position the hot point of the Path Type tool directly atop a path and click. The object will become a baseline for type and a blinking insertion point will be displayed.

Objects converted to baselines for type lose all previous appearance settings and are assigned a black fill and no stroke, which are the default attributes for text. To switch to the Vertical Path Type tool, hold down the Shift key while clicking to establish type.

2.10

Vertical Type Tool

This tool functions the same as the Type tool except that it creates vertically oriented type. Add the Shift key when using to create horizontal type. Type orientation may also be switched using the Type: Type Orientation: **Horizontal** command.

2.11

Vertical Area Type Tool

This tool functions the same as the Area Type tool except that it creates vertically oriented type. It has the same shortcuts as other vertical type tools. *(For more information, see 2.10, Vertical Type Tool).*

2.12

Vertical Path Type Tool

This tool function the same as the Path Type tool except that it creates vertically oriented type. It has the same shortcuts as other vertical type tools. *(For more information, see 2.10, Vertical Type Tool.)*

2.13

Shape Suite

The shape tools, with the exception of the Flare tool, create commonly used closed geometric paths.

Issues to Consider

Numerically defined sizes do not include stroke width. If you create an object at a specific size, the size defined is the size of the path, not the overall size of the shape. This actual size may be larger or smaller due to strokes or appearance applied to the object. This is the case even if the Use Preview Bounds option is activated. *(For more information, see 8.12, Edit: Preferences: **General**.)*

2.14

Rectangle Tool *Type "M"*

Use this tool to create rectangular closed paths. Rectangles may be defined numerically or by eye. To define a rectangle numerically, click anywhere in a document with the Rectangle tool. A rectangle will be created the size specified in the resulting dialog box with its upper-left corner being the point clicked in the document. To define a rectangle numerically about a center point, (Option) [Alt] click in the document with the Rectangle tool.

To define a rectangle by eye, click-drag in the document with the Rectangle tool. A rectangular wire frame will follow the movement of the cursor, indicating where the rectangle will be created when the mouse is released. To drag from the center rather than a corner, hold down the (Option) [Alt] key as you drag. To reposition a rectangle as you are creating it, hold down the spacebar and drag the rectangle into a new position. To create a perfect square, hold down the Shift key as you drag. Hold down the tilde (~) key to create many rectangles at once. These key combinations may be used in conjunction with each other.

Rectangle Options Dialog Box

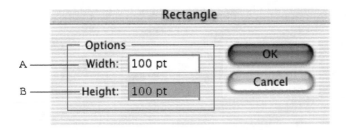

A. **Width**

Use this option to set the horizontal distance the rectangle covers.

B. **Height**

Use this option to set the vertical distance the rectangle covers.

2.15

Rounded Rectangle

Use this tool to create rectangles with rounded corners. The rounded corners are measured in terms of the radius of the circle that would be required to create them.

Except for the addition of corner radius, the tool functions the same as the Rectangle tool. By default, the radius of the rounded rectangle will be the size of the last rounded rectangle created or the Corner Radius value in the General Preferences. To increase the corner radius incrementally as you draw the rectangle, click the Up Arrow key on the keyboard as you drag. Decrease the corner radius incrementally by clicking the Down Arrow on the keyboard as you drag. Set the corner radius to 0 by clicking the Left Arrow on the keyboard as you drag. Set the corner radius to completely rounded (one half of the shorter measure of the rectangle) by clicking the Right Arrow on the keyboard as you drag. The left and right arrows are useful if you want a rectangle that is mostly rounded or straight. Click the arrow and then adjust the radius with the up or down arrows accordingly.

Rounded Rectangle Options

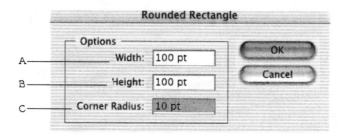

A. Width

Use this option to set the horizontal distance the rectangle covers.

B. Height

Use this option to set the vertical distance the rectangle covers.

C. Corner Radius

Use this option to set the size of the curve used for corners. The size describes the radius of a circle whose arc might be used to create the rounded corner. The measure also describes the distance from the corner of the bounding box of the rounded rectangle to the first anchor point along a side.

2.16

Ellipse Tool

Use this tool to create closed ellipse-shaped paths. Ellipses may be defined numerically or by eye. To define an ellipse numerically, click anywhere in a document with the Ellipse tool. An ellipse will be created the size specified in the resulting Ellipse dialog box with its upper-left corner being the point clicked in the document. The corner of an ellipse is actually the corner of the bounding box of the object. To define an ellipse numerically about a center point, (Option) [Alt] click in the document with the Ellipse tool.

To define an ellipse by eye, click-drag in the document with the Ellipse tool. An oval wire frame will follow the movement of the cursor, indicating where the ellipse will be created when the mouse is released. To drag from the center rather than a corner, hold down the (Option) [Alt] key as you drag. To reposition an ellipse as you are creating it, hold down the spacebar and drag it into a new position. To create a perfect circle, hold down the Shift key as you drag. Hold down the tilde (~) key to create many ellipses at once. These shortcuts may be used in conjunction with each other.

Ellipse Options

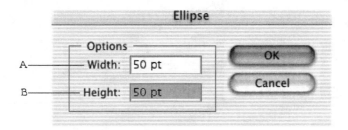

A. **Width**

Use this option to set the horizontal distance the ellipse covers.

B. **Height**

Use this option to set the vertical distance the ellipse covers.

2.17

Polygon Tool

Use the Polygon tool to create polygonal closed paths. Polygons may be defined numerically or by eye. To define a polygon numerically, click anywhere in a document with the Polygon tool. A polygon will be created with the number of sides and the size specified in the resulting Polygon dialog box with its center being the point clicked in the document.

To define a polygon by eye, click-drag in the document with the Polygon tool. A wire frame will follow the movement of the cursor, indicating where the polygon will be created when the mouse is released. Polygons are always created from their center points. To reposition a polygon as you are creating it, hold down the spacebar and drag the polygon into a new position. Increase the number of sides in a polygon as you draw it by clicking the Up Arrow on the keyboard while you drag. Decrease the number of sides in the same manner using the Down Arrow. To create a polygon with a flat (0°) bottom segment, hold the Shift key down as you drag. Create multiple objects as you drag by holding down the tilde (~) key.

Polygon Options Dialog Box

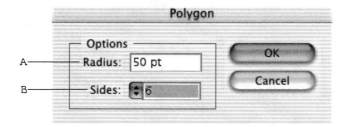

A. **Radius**

Use this option to set the distance from the center of the polygon to the farthest anchor point.

B. **Sides**

Use this option to set the number of sides and anchor points the object has.

2.18

Star Tool

Use the Star tool to create star-shaped closed paths. Stars may be defined numerically or by eye. To define a star numerically, click anywhere in a document with the Star tool. A star will be created the number of points and the size specified in the resulting dialog box with its center being the point clicked in the document. The two radius values refer to the distance to the inner and outer points of the star. The fields may be used interchangeably as the lower value is always the inside radius.

To define a star by eye, click-drag in the document with the Star tool. A wire frame will follow the movement of the cursor, indicating where the star will be created when the mouse is released. To reposition a star as you are creating it, hold down the spacebar and drag the star into a new position. Increase the number of points in a star as you draw it by clicking the Up Arrow on the keyboard while you drag. Decrease the number of points in the same manner using the Down Arrow. To freeze a radius, hold down the (Command) [Ctrl] key as you drag. When a radius is frozen, dragging out increases the other radius, dragging in decreases it. Releasing the (Command) [Ctrl] key frees the radius. In this way you can resize the distance between the radii and resize the star. To create a star with opposite arms at the same angle, hold down the (Option) [Alt] key as you drag. This creates the kind of star seen on the American flag. Hold down the Shift key as you drag to snap the star 0° rotation. Create multiple objects as you drag by holding down the tilde (~) key.

Star Options Dialog Box

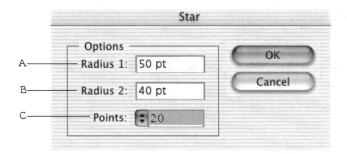

A. **Radius 1**

Use this option to set the distance between the center of the star and the inner anchor points.

B. **Radius 2**

Use this option to set the distance between the center of the star and the outer anchor points. In practice, no real distinction is made between these fields. Whichever field is smaller is the inner radius; the larger field is the outer radius.

C. **Points**

Use this option to set the number of points in the star.

2.19

Flare Tool

Use the Flare tool to create a lens flare effect. Flares consist of center circles; optional rays that extend out from the center circle; a halo surrounds the center; overlapping circles in a line form rings. A flare is a custom object. Once created, you must expand the object to use many standard editing tools on it.

Flares may be defined numerically or by eye. To define a flare numerically, click in the document. A flare will be created using the values you select in the resulting flare dialog box centered about the point you clicked. To apply a flare with the default settings, (Option) [Alt] click where you want the center of the flare.

To create a flare by eye, first click-drag to establish the center, halo, and rays. Reposition the flare while creating it by holding down the spacebar as you drag. Add or subtract rays while creating the flare by clicking the up and down arrows on the keyboard. Press (Command) [Control] as you drag to hold the center of the flare constant. Next, Click-drag to establish the rings. The rings are connected to the center by a linear spine. Add or subtract rings while creating the flare by clicking the up and down arrows on the keyboard. To reset the options in this dialog box to their defaults, hold down the (Option) [Alt] key·to toggle the Cancel button to a Reset button.

To reset the options of an existing flare, select it and double-click on the Flare tool. The Flare Tool Options dialog opens. Reset the options in this dialog box to change the current flare.

All the objects created are set to the Soft blend mode, which is commonly used for lighting effects. For this reason, the flare works best when used in front of other objects, especially darker objects. If part of the flare is exposed against a white background, it will look odd.

Issues to Consider

Flares often print as rasters. By default, flares employ gradients and the Soft blend mode. This commonly results in images that must be printed as raster art. *(For more information, see 7.45, File: Document Setup: Transparency.)*

Flare Tool Options Dialog Box

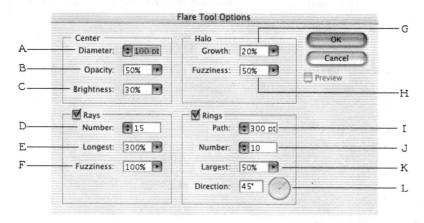

A. **Diameter** (0 to 1000 pts)

This option sets the size of the core circle. The core circle has a gradient fill and is the center point of the rays and the axis about which the smaller circles are offset.

B. **Opacity** (0 to 100%)

This option sets the opacity of the circle immediately behind the core circle. Identify this circle by its multi-stop gradient fill.

C. **Brightness** (0 to 100%)

This option determines the amount of white in the center circle gradient.

D. **Number** (0 to 50)

Use this option to set the total number of rays. Entering 0 is the same as disabling this option. Although rays appear to be a series of segments, the ray is actually a single closed path with many points.

E. **Longest** (0 to 1000%)

Use this to set the distance of the longest ray as a percentage of the average ray length.

F. **Fuzziness** (0 to 100%)

Use this option to blur the ray object. 0% creates a sharp edge, 100% makes it fuzzy.

G. **Growth** (0 to 100%)

Use this option to size the halo as a percentage of the overall flare size.

H. **Halo Fuzziness** (0 to 100%)

Use this option to blur the halo object. 0% creates a sharp edge, 100% makes it fuzzy.

I. **Path** (0 to 1000 pts)

This option sets the distance of the path between the center and the rings

J. **Number** (0 to 50)

This option sets the number of ellipses created as rings.

K. **Largest** (0 to 100%)

Use this to set the size of the largest ring as a percentage of the overall size.

L. **Direction** (0 to 359°)

Use this to set the direction the path and the rings are offset from the center and halo. Set numerically or by using the radius arm.

2.20

Line Tool Suite

With the exception of the Spiral tool, all of the tools in this suite may be double-clicked to establish their default options.

2.21

Line Segment Tool   *Type "\"*

Use the Line Segment tool to create straight open paths with only two anchor points. The segments cannot be continued to form other shapes using this tool. It should only be used when what you want is just a line. Line segments may be created numerically or by eye. To create a line segment numerically, click in the document with the tool. The Line Segment dialog box will appear, allowing you to specify the distance and direction from the initial point clicked the line segment will be. To reset the options in this dialog box to their defaults, hold down the (Option) [Alt] key to toggle the Cancel button to a Reset button.

To create a line segment by eye, click-drag in the document. A straight guide follows the cursor indicating where the segment will be created when the mouse is released. By default, the last used options will be applied to the next object created. Double-click on the tool to change these options before creating a new shape in the document. Hold down the (Option) [Alt] key as you drag to drag from the center of the segment rather than an end. Hold down the Shift key as you drag to constrain the segment to the document's default angles. Hold down the spacebar to reposition the segment as you drag. Create multiple objects as you drag by holding down tilde (~) key.

Line Segment Tool Options Dialog Box

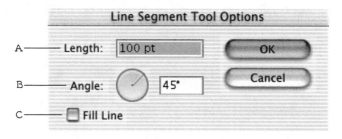

A. **Length** (1–1000 pts)

Use this option to set the distance of the line created.

B. **Angle** (0–360°)

Use this option to set the direction of the line. 0° runs to the right, degrees move counterclockwise from there.

C. **Fill Line**

Use this option to include a fill attribute, if specified, in the line. Lines do not commonly require fills since they are invisible on straight-line segments. Fills may be added to lines later and can be useful in some techniques. For example, applying Object: Path: **Outline Stroke** to a filled line creates the outlines shape and retains the original segment. The segment can then be styled or used as a baseline for type.

2.22

Arc Tool

Use the Arc tool to create open curved segments and curved segments joined by straight lines. Arcs may be created numerically or by eye. To create an arc numerically, click in the document with the tool to call up the Arc Segment dialog box. The shape of the arc is established by the distance the segment travels (the x and y lengths) and the slope of the curve. Slopes are measured from 100, completely convex to –100, completely concave. The slope is driven opposite the Base Along Axis. So a completely convex curve with an X Axis base is the same as a completely concave curve with a Y Axis base. To reset the options in this dialog box to their defaults, hold down the (Option) [Alt] key to toggle the Cancel button to a Reset button.

To create an arc by eye, click-drag with the tool. A guide will follow indicating where the arc will be created when the mouse is released. By default, the last used options will be applied to the next object created. Double-click on the tool to change these options before creating a new shape in the document. Click on the up and down arrows as you drag to increase and decrease the slope of the curve. Hold down the Shift key as you drag to set the x and y axis lengths to the same length. To reposition an arc as you create it, hold down the spacebar. Hold down the (Option) [Alt] key to drag an arc from the center. Create multiple objects as you drag by holding down the tilde (~) key.

Arc Segment Tool Options Dialog Box

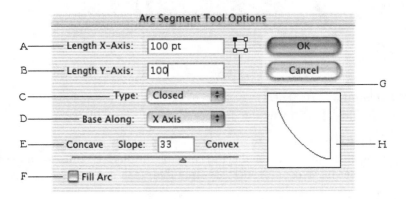

A. **Length X-Axis** (1 to 1000 pts)

Use this field to set the horizontal distance from one end of the arc to the other.

B. **Length Y-Axis** (1 to 1000 pts)

Use this field to set the vertical distance from one end of the arc to the other.

C. **Type**

Arcs may be open paths with two anchor points or closed paths with three. Set this in the Type field. In closed arcs the ends of the curve are connected with a right angle.

D. **Base Along**

Use this field to set the base direction of the arc. The base is the side opposite the curve.

E. **Slope** (-100 to 100)

Use this slider and field to set the depth of the curve of the arc. Slopes are measured from 100, completely convex to –100, completely concave.

F. **Fill Arc**

Use this option to include a fill attribute, if specified. Disabling the option discards fill attributes as new arcs are created.

G. **Bounding Box**

Use this interface to set the orientation of the angle. The wire frame indicates the bounding box of the arc with the highlighted point being the location clicked in the document. Thus the arc will be created in the directions away from the highlighted point.

H. **Preview**

This pane previews the arc options set in this dialog box. It is only visible when setting default options.

2.23

Spiral Tool

Use the Spiral tool to create open spiral paths. Spirals are often used as decorative motifs or as the beginning of more complex work. In versions prior to Illustrator 10, which include the Arc tool, they were used to create open curves quickly by making a spiral with only two points. Spirals may be created numerically or by eye. To create a spiral numerically, click in the document with the tool. The Spiral dialog box opens, allowing you to specify the radius of the spiral, the direction it rotates (Style), the number of line segments the arc has, and the rate at which it curves toward the center (Decay). To reset the options in this dialog box to their defaults, hold down the (Option)[Alt] key to toggle the Cancel button to a Reset button.

To create a spiral by eye, click-drag with the tool. A guide will follow the cursor indicating where the spiral will be created. Click on the up and down arrows as you drag to add or subtract path segments. Adding the (Command) [Ctrl] key as you drag affects the decay of the spiral. Drag away from the initially clicked point to decrease the decay. Drag toward the initial point to increase the decay. This will have the effect of creating more turns of the spiral as you command-drag in, and fewer turns as you command-drag out. Create multiple objects as you drag by holding down the tilde (~) key. Hold down the spacebar as you drag to reposition the object.

Spiral Dialog Box

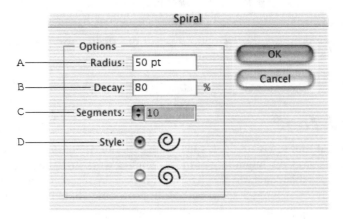

A. **Radius** (0 to 8192 pts)

The radius is the base dimension of the arc. The radius is the distance from the point initially clicked to the edge of the curve. Do not confuse it with the size of the spiral overall. In spirals with a decay of less than 100%, it is the radius of the outer curve of the spiral. In spirals with a decay of greater than 100%, the radius is the size of the inner curve of the spiral.

B. **Decay** (5% to 150%)

Decay is the rate a spiral falls in on itself. A decay of 100% causes the path to fall onto itself, creating a circle.

C. **Segments**

This field sets the number of line segments an arc has. Do not confuse it with the number of arms in the spiral.

D. **Style**

Use these options to set the spiral clockwise or counterclockwise.

2.24

Rectangular Grid Tool

Use the Rectangular grid tool to create a grid of squares, commonly for the purpose of creating guides. The grid is actually a group, consisting of identical, straight open paths at right angles from each other. The group may also be framed with a closed, rectangular path.

Rectangular grids may be created numerically or by eye. To create a grid numerically, click in the document with the tool. The Rectangular Grid Tool Options dialog box opens. To reset the options in this dialog box to their defaults, hold down the (Option) [Alt] key to toggle the Cancel button to a Reset button.

To create a rectangular grid by eye, Click-drag with the tool. A guide will follow your cursor, indicating where the grid will be created. By default, the last used options will be applied to the next object created. Double-click on the tool to change these options before creating a new shape in the document. Hold down the (Option) [Alt] key as you drag to create a grid from its center. Hold down the Shift key as you drag to create a grid with equal width and height. Click the up and down arrow keys on the keyboard as you drag to add and subtract horizontal dividers. Click the left and right arrow keys on the keyboard as you drag to add and subtract vertical dividers. Create multiple grid groups as you drag by holding down the tilde (~) key. Hold down the spacebar as you drag to reposition the object.

Rectangular Grid Tool Options

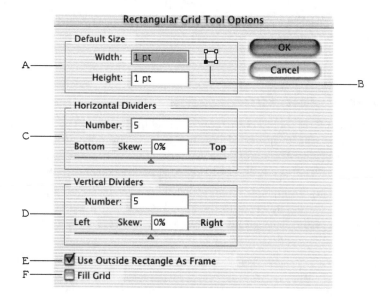

A. Default Size
Use these fields to set the width and height of the grid overall.

B. Bounding Box
The wire frame indicates the bounding box of the grid with the highlighted point being the location clicked in the document. Thus the grid will be created in the directions away from the highlighted point.

C. Horizontal Dividers
Use these fields to set the number of horizontal dividers (open paths) in the grid. The Skew fields determine the rate at which dividers are

distributed. A skew of 0% creates equidistant dividers. Increasing or decreasing the skew amount offsets each subsequent path additionally by the skew percentage. The effect is progressive.

D. **Vertical Dividers**

Use these fields to set the number of vertical dividers (open paths) in the grid. The options are the same as they are for horizontal dividers.

E. **Use Outside Rectangle as Frame**

A bounding rectangle may be created in lieu of the outermost open paths by checking the Use Outside Rectangle as Frame box. In the event that grid objects were given fills, only this rectangle's fill would be visible on screen, as open, straight paths have no internal area.

F. **Fill Grid**

Disable the Fill Line check box to create objects with a Fills of None.

Related Topics
*14.24 View: **Guides***

2.25
_____

Polar Grid Tool

Use the Polar Grid tool to create concentric ellipses with intersecting dividers, commonly for the purposes of creating guides. The polar grid is actually a group, consisting of a series of concentric ellipses (or, alternately, a single compound path) and a group of straight, open, two-anchor-point paths.

Polar grids may be created numerically or by eye. To create a grid numerically, click in the document with the tool. The Polar Grid Tool Options dialog box opens. Use the fields in this dialog box to set the size of the grid (width, height), and the number of dividers in the grid.

To create a polar grid by eye, click-drag with the tool. A guide will follow your cursor, indicating where the grid will be created. By default, the last used options will be applied to the next object created. Double-click on the tool to change these options before creating a new shape in the document. Hold down the (Option) [Alt] key as you drag to create a grid from its center. Hold down the Shift key as you drag to create a grid with equal width and height. Press the Up and Down Arrow keys on the keyboard as you drag to add and subtract concentric dividers. Press the Left and Right Arrow keys on the keyboard as you drag to add and subtract radial dividers. Create multiple grid groups as you drag by holding down the tilde (~) key. Hold down the spacebar as you drag to reposition the object.

Polar Grid Tool Options Dialog Box

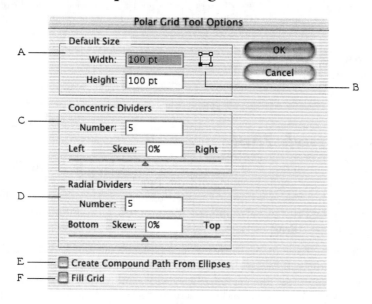

A. **Default Size** (1 to 1000 pts)

The width and height fields describe the size of the largest concentric ellipse.

B. **Bounding Box**

The wire frame indicates the bounding box of the grid with the highlighted point being the location clicked in the document. Thus the grid will be created in the directions away from the highlighted point.

C. **Concentric Dividers** (0 to 999)

Use the concentric dividers field to set the number of additional ellipses created. The Skew fields determine the rate at which dividers are distributed. A skew of 0% creates equidistant dividers. Increasing or decreasing the skew amount offsets each subsequent path additionally by the skew percentage. The effect is progressive.

D. **Radial Dividers** (0 to 999)

Use the Radial Dividers field to set the number of intersecting paths open paths extend from the center of the ellipses. Radials may also be skewed.

E. **Create Compound Path from Ellipses**

Check the Create Compound Path from Ellipses check box to create one compound path from the ellipses instead of a series of simple paths. This is usually done in cases where the ellipses are being used as design elements and not guides.

F. **Fill Grid**

Set the Fills of all of the objects in the grid to None by unchecking the Fill Grid check box.

Related Topics
14.24 View: Guides

2.26

Paintbrush Tool   *Type "B"*

Use the Paintbrush tool to create freeform paths and to edit objects that contain brushes. The paths created with the Paintbrush tool will be styled by default with brushes. Brushes are applied to strokes. There must be a brush available in the brushes palette to use this tool. For more information on the brushes, see 19.1 Brushes Palette.

The Paintbrush tool creates freeform open paths by default. As you draw with the tool, a guide will follow the cursor, indicating where the path will be created. An exception to this occurs when using a calligraphic brush, when the brush stroke will be previewed rather than the path. Since a mouse can be difficult to control, people who use this tool a lot commonly employ a pressure sensitive tablet for greater control over the drawing process. This is an excellent choice, since Illustrator's calligraphic and scatter brushes can respond to pressure from such a tablet.

To create a closed path instead of an open one, hold down the (Option) [Alt] key as you drag. A circle will appear next to the cursor to indicate you are creating a closed path. When you release the mouse, a straight line connects the ends of the path.

With the Paintbrush tool selected, hold down the (Option) [Alt] key to temporarily switch to the Smooth tool. *(For more information, see 2.29, Smooth Tool.)*

Change the behavior of the Paintbrush tool by double-clicking on the tool to open the Paintbrush Tool preferences dialog box.

Paintbrush Tool Options

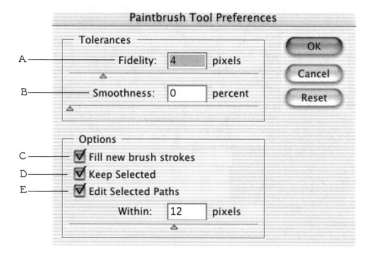

A. Fidelity (.5–20 pixels)

Use the Tolerance section to control how closely the created paths match the movement of the cursor. Fidelity controls how closely the path created matches the cursor. At higher values, subtle changes in the path are disregarded.

B. Smoothness (0–100%)

Smoothness is a tweak applied to the curve drawn with the intent of removing awkward jumps in the line and reduce the number of points needed to define a path. At higher settings, the adjustments made to the path will make it difficult to trace paths accurately. Both of these settings can substantially alter the lines you draw.

C. Fill New Brush Strokes

Disable the Fill New brush strokes check box to create an object with a Fill of None.

D. Keep Selected

Disable the Keep Selected check box to deselect an object immediately upon creation. Only the Paintbrush and Pencil tools have this option. All other objects remain selected upon creation. Disabling Keep Selected makes it harder to edit paths but can be less distracting when creating many shapes.

E. Edit Selected Paths (2–20 pixels)

Use Edit Selected Paths to enable the Paintbrush tool to redraw selected paths. The paintbrush can reshape any path, open or closed, that contains a brush stroke. The paths to be redrawn must be within the specified distance and contain a brush stroke. When using the feature, the Paintbrush will reshape selected paths rather than creating new ones. The reshaping may apply to part or all of a path. For example, you may add to an existing path using this option by click-dragging on one of the end points in the path. The path will continue as you drag. When the cursor is within the established editing range, it will change. The standard brush cursor will lose its usual 'x' and the Precise Cursor will change from an X to a +. *(For more information, see 8.12, Edit: Preferences: **General**.)*

The impact on paths edited in this way are much more dramatic than those created by the Smooth tool. To access the Smooth tool while drawing, hold down the (Option) [Alt] key. For details on the Smooth tool. *(For more information, see 2.29, Smooth Tool.)*

Related Topics
19.1   Brushes Palette
2.29   Smooth Tool
8.7   Define Pattern

2.27
Pencil Tool Suite

Tools in the pencil suite create and edit freeform open paths that are not automatically given a brushstroke. Many users utilize the pencil suite for its simplicity and ease of use. Paths made with the pencil tool are commonly Joined for use as closed paths. *(For more information, see 9.44, Object: Path: **Join**)*

2.28
Pencil Tool   *Type "N"*

Use the Pencil tool to create and edit open freeform paths. To edit the preferences for the tool, double-click on it. The Pencil Tool Preferences dialog box opens. The options here are the same as the ones that govern the Paintbrush tool, except that fills cannot be automatically discarded. *(For more information, see 2.26, Paintbrush Tool.)*

To create a path, click-drag with the tool. A temporary guide follows the cursor, indicating where the path will be created. When you let go of the mouse, an open path is created. Make a closed path instead by holding down the (Option) [Alt] key as you drag. The two ends of the path will be connected by a straight line. A circle will appear next to the cursor to indicate the path will be closed. Edit and continue existing paths in the same manner as the Paintbrush tool. Temporarily access the Smooth tool by holding down the (Option) [Alt] key.

2.29

Smooth Tool

Use the Smooth tool to manually apply smoothness (as in the smoothness settings in the Paintbrush and Pencil tools) to specific parts of a path. The Smooth tool is not intended for making wholesale changes to the shape of a path. You cannot use it to add twists and turns to a path and the resulting path will not exactly represent the path of your cursor. It is intended to simplify the task of manually adjusting anchor and direction points to create an overall smoother, more organic appearance of a path. If you wish to redraw a path completely, consider using the Pencil or Paintbrush tool with the Edit Selected Path option activated.

To edit the preferences for the tool, double-click it. The Smooth Tool Preferences dialog box opens. The options here are the same as the Tolerance preferences that govern the Paintbrush tool. *(For more information, see 2.26, Paintbrush Tool.)*

To use the Smooth tool, first select a path and then click-drag with the Smooth tool. A temporary guide will follow the cursor, indicating the area of the path that will be affected. Upon releasing the mouse, the path will be redrawn. Anchor points may be added or subtracted to the path and direction points will be added to all the anchor points affected. At lower fidelity settings, the path will be more impacted by the motion of the Smooth tool. The higher the smoothness setting, the less angular the resulting path will be. Only one path may be smoothed at a time. If multiple paths are selected, the Smooth tool will affect only the object nearest to the initial point clicked. The Smooth tool cannot affect graphs, symbol sets, meshes, or envelopes.

2.30

Erase Tool

Use the Erase tool to delete portions of a path and to break a path into separate segments. The Erase tool works on any path except graphs, symbol sets, meshes, and envelopes.

To use the Erase tool to break a path, first select the path and then click on the path with the Erase tool. Anchor points are added, and the path splits at the point it was clicked. To delete a portion of a path, click-drag along a selected path. A temporary guide follows the cursor, indicating which portion of the path will be deleted. The Erase tool can only affect one path at a time. Dragging across more than one selected path will only alter the first object dragged across.

Transformation Tools

Transformation Models

Transforming objects is one of the key tasks to be performed in Illustrator. This chapter covers four distinct models for transforming objects; basic transformation, reshaping, free transformation, and liquify.

Basic transformation is used to scale, flip, rotate, and shear objects or points. It is the core model of transformation and is used in almost every Illustrator session. It can be performed using the tools described here and through menus and palettes. The Rotate, Reflect, Scale, and Shear tools use this model and behave in exactly the same way, The Twist tool also uses this model but varies slightly in its behavior from the other tools.

Reshaping is a way of editing individual points on a path while retaining the original flavor of the path. This model is used principally when creating freeform paths that are not intended to have straight edges. The Reshape tool uses this very manual model. It works in conjunction with the Direct Selection tool.

Free transformation is similar to basic transformation. Many different transformations may be performed on an object without switching tools, but some features of basic transformation are not available using this model. This model is often used to perform skews and perspective distortions that are harder to do using other models. The Free Transform tool uses this model and so does the Selection tool.

Liquify distorts the shape of objects where they fall within a specified area of effect (the brush). The brush may be moved through the document, transforming all the objects it touches or only those selected. This model is principally used to create artistic effects or to make a shape look less computer-generated. The Warp, Twirl, Pucker, Bloat, Scallop, Crystallize, and Wrinkle tools use this model.

3.2

Basic Transformation

The basic transformation tools are fundamental to an understanding of Illustrator. Used in conjunction with the Direct Selection tool, they provide a wide array of transformational possibilities. With the exception of the Twist tool, the basic transformation tools all behave in the same way. The Twist tool only varies slightly and those differences are noted in the Twist tool section, later in this chapter. All basic transformations require making a selection before transforming. Commonly, entire objects are transformed, but any selection, including individual anchor points and line segments may also be affected.

There are two basic ways to transform: numerically and by eye. Numeric transformation performs a specific mathematical change on an object, such as scaling it 75%. Numeric transformations are cumulative. Once scaled 75% an object may be scaled again, but the next scaling is based on its new size. To return the object to its original size you would need to undo the transformation or figure out the math to fix the scaling. In a visual model an object is transformed by an unspecified amount, until you are satisfied with it. Illustrator figures out the exact calculations for you.

Both forms of transformation may be performed about the object's center, or some other location in the document. This point the transformation is referenced from is the *point of transformation*. Since most transformations involve moving an object in some way, setting the point of transformation greatly speeds up the task of positioning objects. By default the point of transformation will be located in the center of the bounding area of the object or objects selected. The point of transformation is indicated with a target crosshair icon that appears when objects are selected and a transform tool is active.

To transform an object numerically about its center, double-click on the transform tool (exception: the Twist tool). A dialog box for the transformation appears, allowing you to specify the amount of transformation to be performed. Preferences for the tools exist here as well, allowing you to control how the transformation takes place.

All the dialog boxes have check boxes allowing you to specify if the transformation should affect the objects, pattern fills of the objects, or both. In the event selected objects do not contain pattern fills, the option will be dimmed. When transforming by click-dragging, you can affect a pattern fill and not the objects by holding down the tilde (~) key as you drag. This technique works when moving, scaling, rotating, reflecting, and shearing, but not twirling.

These dialogs also feature a Copy button. In the event Copy is clicked instead of OK, the specified transformation is performed on a duplicate of the selected objects placed directly atop the current object. Clicking (Option) [Alt] OK or Return also performs the action on a duplicate.

To transform an object numerically about a different point of transformation, position the cursor in the new point of transformation and (Option) [Alt] click. The cursor will switch to a crosshair with an ellipsis next to it when the (Option) [Alt] key is depressed. The tool's dialog box appears allowing you to specify the required transformations. The transformations are applied to the objects about the point of transformation. Although it does not display a point of transformation icon, the Twist tool does support this feature.

To visually transform objects about their centers, click-drag with the Transform tool. A temporary guide will preview the transformation as you drag. Hold down the Shift key as you drag to constrain the transformation to the default constrain angle. Hold down the (Option) [Alt] key as you drag to transform a copy of the object. Be sure to add the modifier keys after you begin to drag and hold them down until you release the mouse.

To visually transform an object about a different point of transformation, click once with the Transform tool to set the point of transformation. The crosshair will position itself in the new point and your cursor will change to the black transformation arrowhead. If you decide to change the point of transformation at this point, click-drag directly on the point to reposition it or double-click in the new location. With the point of transformation established, click-drag to transform. A temporary guide will preview the transformation as you drag. Hold down the (Option) [Alt] key as you drag to transform a copy of the object. Be sure to add the modifier keys after you begin to drag and hold them down until you release the mouse.

Mistakes to Avoid

Not allowing enough room to drag. When you position the cursor before dragging to transform, be sure you leave enough space between the cursor and the point of transformation. If you click-drag close to the point of transformation, it will be harder to control the transformation.

Issues to Consider

Setting a point of transformation is easier than moving an object later. Many users always transform objects about their centers and then reposition the objects as needed. Using the point of transformation correctly often saves the step of repositioning.

The Twist tool doesn't support copying. You cannot twist a copy of the selected object by holding down the (Option) [Alt] key. Work around this by copying the object first and then choosing Edit: **Paste in Front**.

3.3

Rotate Tool
Type "R"

Use the Rotate tool, to turn objects about a single point. *(For more information, see 3.2, Basic Transformation.)*

Rotate Dialog Box

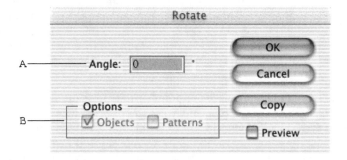

A. **Angle**

Use this field to set the angle of rotation. Rotation is measured about a standard 360 degrees counterclockwise. Positive numbers are counterclockwise, negative degrees are clockwise. Since the degrees go in a circle, it is usually easier to think of things going from 0 to 180° counterclockwise and 0 to –180° clockwise rather than 270°, which is –90°.

B. **Options**

Enable the options to transform objects, pattern fills or both. At least one option must be enabled.

Related Issues

3.4

Reflect Tool   *Type "O"*

Use the Reflect tool to flip objects across an axis, creating a mirror image. *(For more information, see 3.2, Basic Transformation.)*

Reflect Dialog Box

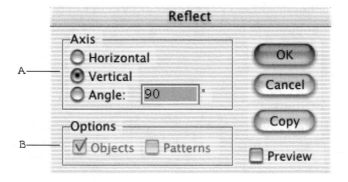

A. **Axis**

Use this to set the axis the objects are reflected across. The axis objects are reflected across may be set to horizontal (0°) or vertical (90°) or a specific numerical value. The value is relative to the point of transformation. When reflecting visually, drag in the direction you want the object to end up.

B. **Options**

Enable the options to transform objects, pattern fills or both. At least one option must be enabled.

Related Topics

3.19 The Free Transform Tool
*9.5   Object: Transform: **Reflect***
*9.8   Object: Transform: **Transform Each***
*13.14 Effect: Distort & Transform: **Transform***
Chapter 35, "The Transform Palette"

3.5

Twist Tool

Use the Twist tool to distort objects in a spiral pattern. The Twist tool can only affect entire objects, does not support (Option) [Alt] copying, and it cannot be double-clicked to numerically transform about an object's center, but behaves the same as other aspects. It also does not utilize the point of transformation cursor that the other Basic Transformation tools do. You can still click to set a point of transformation; you just won't see the crosshair icon.

The Twist tool works best when used in small increments. At larger values, objects become unrecognizable. When visually twisting objects, consider positioning the cursor outside the objects and then dragging in the direction you want to twirl the art. The Twist tool does not work on live type, graphs, or symbol sets.

Issues to Consider

You can twist numerically. Although you cannot double-click the Twist tool to get a dialog box, you can (Option) [Alt]-click to twist to a specific degree.

Related Topics

*12.23 Filter: Distort: **Twist***
*13.15 Effect: Distort & Transform: **Twist***

3.6

Scale Tool   *Type "S"*

Use the Scale tool to resize objects. Objects may or may not be scaled proportionally. *(For more information, see 3.2, Basic Transformation.)*

When scaling visually, the Shift key constrains the transformation differently depending upon the direction you drag. Dragging vertically with the Shift key down, constrains the width of the objects, scaling only the height. Dragging horizontally, constrains the height of the objects, scaling only the width. Dragging diagonally with the Shift key down, scales the object proportionally.

Drag toward the point of transformation to scale down, drag away from it to scale up. For best results, position your cursor away from the objects you are scaling to give yourself plenty of room to see what you are doing.

Scale Dialog Box

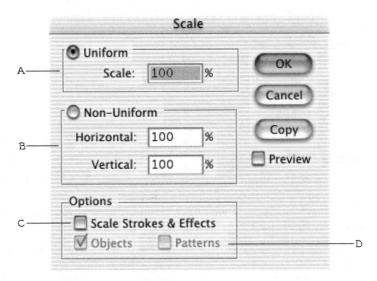

A. **Uniform** (-20000 to 20000%)

Use this option to scale and object both horizontally and vertically by the same amount.

B. **Non-Uniform** (-20000 to 20000%)

Use this option to scale an object disproportionately.

C. **Scale Strokes & Effects**

This option sets the Scale Strokes & Effects preference. Enabling this option means that strokes and effects are scaled with the object instead of retaining their specified values. For example, a 1 point stroke affected by a 150% scale would be set to 1.5 points rather than staying 1 point. An offset path effect with 10 points of distance would become a 15-point offset. This maintains the relative look of the objects. Care should be taken when using this option not to scale strokes too thin for printing. Because Scale Strokes & Effects is a preference, the setting is used as the default for all scaling, whether or not the scaling is done with this tool. *(For more information, see 8.12, Edit: Preferences: **General**.)*

D. **Objects & Patterns**

Enable the options to transform objects, pattern fills or both. At least one option must be enabled.

Related Topics

1.2   The Selection tool
3.19   The Free Transform Tool
9.6   Object: Transform: **Scale**
9.8   Object: Transform: **Transform Each**
13.14 Effect: Distort & Transform: **Transform**
Chapter 35, "The Transform Palette"

3.7

Shear Tool

Use the Shear tool to slant objects. Shearing tilts two parallel sides of an object at a specific angle while leaving the other pair of sides alone. The result is an object that tilts. Shear is vital for techniques such as isometric scaling. *(For more information, see 3.2, Basic Transformation.)*

When visually shearing an object, the movement of the cursor affects both the angle and the axis. The direction you drag sets the axis and the distance sets the angle. The farther you drag the greater the angle of the shear will be. For this reason, many users add the Shift key as they shear to constrain the axis to horizontal or vertical, simplifying the process.

Shear Options

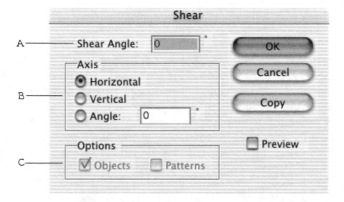

A. **Shear Angle**

This field describes the tilt that is applied to the sides that are not held static.

B. **Axis**

In the Shear dialog box, the Axis buttons refer to the sides that are held static. Set to the commonly used horizontal or vertical axis or enter a custom value.

C. **Options**

Enable the options to transform objects, pattern fills or both. At least one option must be enabled.

Related Topics

3.8

Reshaping

Reshaping is a way to edit the positions of specific anchor points while retaining the look and feel of the curve. This is commonly done to apply a tweak to customized paths. Editing anchor points requires the use of the Direct Selection or Direct Select Lasso tools. When selected anchor points are moved, their direction points are moved as well. Since the curvature of path is created by positioning direction points, editing the position of anchor points often means going back and editing direction points as well. Often, paths may curve in on themselves or take unexpected angles.

Reshaping addresses this by allowing you to set points which remain constant and then reshaping the edited path by adjusting the direction points on the remaining points. Reshaping also allows users to distort paths by adding anchor points on-the-fly.

3.9

Reshape Tool

Use the Reshape tool to add anchor points, establish control points, and change the position of anchor points.

To begin using the Reshape tool, first select the anchor points to be edited. The Direct Selection or Direct Select Lasso tools are commonly used for this. Next, use the Reshape tool to establish control points. The direction points of these control anchor points are not edited during repositioning. They will retain their original look and feel. To establish control points, either click directly on an anchor point with the Reshape tool or click-drag with it to marquee select a series of points. Shift select points to toggle them. Control points display a guide box around them. Once control points are established, click-drag a control point to reposition the selected anchor points. The control points will be moved freely, while the remaining selected points are repositioned slightly to retain the overall look of the path. Unselected points do not move at all.

To add anchor points with the Reshape tool, click directly on a selected path. When the cursor is atop the path, it will display a box with a dot in it to the lower right. The added point will become a control point. This is commonly done to reshape a line segment. Select the segment with the Direct Selection or Direct Select Lasso tools. Next click-drag on the selected segment. A new anchor is created and the path is reshaped as you drag. This is superior to click-dragging on a segment with the Direct Selection tool, which often causes the path to cross itself.

The Reshape tool only works on paths. It does not work on meshes, envelopes, or bounding areas for text.

3.10

Liquify Tools

The Liquify tools enable the user to "paint" with distortion effects. This allows you to visually distort part or all of an object. The effects may be applied to paths, raster images, and meshes, but not live type, symbol sets, or graphs. The results can vary an object dramatically or merely tweak its edges. All the tools in the suite share a common footprint shape or "global brush." Setting the global brush for one tool will set it for all the tools in the suite.

Brush dimensions may be set numerically or visually. To set the size and shape numerically, double-click on any tool in the suite. Use the Global Brush Dimensions fields to establish the shape of the brush.

To set the dimensions of the global brush visually, hold down the (Option) [Alt] key when using the tool and click-drag. As you drag, the brush shape is resized. Drag away from the brush to increase its size, drag toward the brush to decrease its size. Add the Shift key as you drag to create a perfectly circular brush. Enable the Show Brush Size checkbox in any liquify tool's preference dialog box to see a preview the footprint when using the tool. Otherwise the cursor will display as a crosshair, making the results surprising.

If a selection is active, the transformation will only affect those selected objects. This includes selections that contain only line segments and anchor points. If nothing is selected, all of the objects that fall under the footprint of the brush when it is first clicked will be affected. Objects affected will be highlighted while the tool is in use. Commonly, a selection is made to isolate the effects of the tools.

To use a liquify tool, click-drag the tool over objects in the document. A temporary guide appears, displaying the effects of the transformation when the mouse is released. The longer you hold the cursor in one area, the greater the effect will be. The distortion has a cumulative effect. Once an area begins to be distorted, dragging through there again will distort the distorted shapes further. The effects can become dramatic very quickly. The center of the brush will create a greater impact than the edges. Hold down the Shift key as you drag to constrain the cursor's movements to the default constrain angles.

Global Brush Dimensions Dialog Box

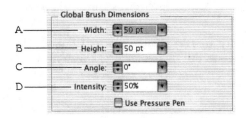

A. **Width & Height** (1 to 1000 pts)

Use these options to set the base size of the brush. If either dimension is different, the brush will be elliptical instead of circular.

B. **Angle** (0° to 360°)

Set the angle to determine the attitude of the brush. The size and angle of the brush both play a role in how the brush will affect objects. Values set outside of the allowed range are converted to their in-range equivalents.

C. **Intensity** (1 to 100)

The intensity field determines how strongly the brush applies the effect, with 1 being almost no effect, and 100 being a strong impact.

D. **Use Pressure Pen**

A pressure sensitive tablet can be used to control the intensity of these tools, creating an effect that is stronger the harder you press down on the stylus.

3.11

Warp Tool

Use the Warp tool to distort objects by adding dips, bumps, and twists to it. Dragging from the inside to the outside of the shape will cause the path to bulge. Dragging from the outside of the path to the inside causes the path to bend in. At high intensity settings, these bends and bulges can become lengthy, tapering arms. At low intensity settings, they are mild dips in the path.

Double-click the Warp tool to change the tool options. In addition to the global brush dimensions, this dialog features the Warp Options.

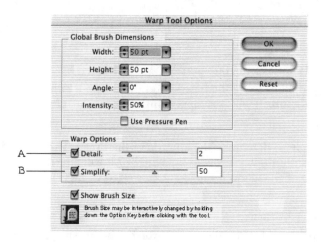

Warp Tool Options Dialog Box

A. **Detail** (1 to 10)

The Detail setting controls the closeness with which the warp follows the cursor. It may be set from 1 (does not follow closely) to 10 (more accurate, less smooth). Detail is activated by default. Unchecked, the Warp tool cannot add anchor points to the path. This results in a tool that can move anchor points and adjust direction points but not add points to the path.

B. **Simplify** (.2 to 100)

Simplify is similar to the smoothness settings of the Paintbrush and Pencil tools and the menu command Object: Path: **Simplify**. It acts upon the created path to reduce the number of anchor points needed to describe the curve. Simplify may be set in values from .2 to 100 in hundredths of a point increments. The greater the number, the fewer anchor points will be used. By default, simplify is activated. Disabling the feature will cause Illustrator to draw paths with hundreds of points.

3.12

Twirl Tool

Use the Twirl tool to distort affected areas in a spiral pattern. The effect is similar to the effects created by the Twist tool. It can also be used to create ripple effects.

Double-click the Twirl tool to change the tool options. In addition to the global brush dimensions, this dialog features the Twirl Options.

Twirl Tool Options Dialog Box

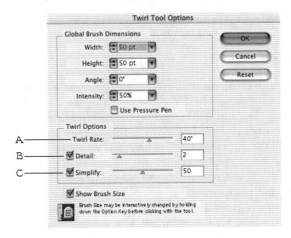

A. **Twirl Rate**

Twirl rate sets the amount of distortion applied. Positive numbers spin the distortion counterclockwise, negative numbers go clockwise. At lower intensities, the distortion will twirl less rapidly. The longer the mouse is held down, the tighter the twirl. Dragging with this tool, even at low intensity settings, may result in a chaotic line. Commonly, users click and hold down in one place to add the distortion and then drag to adjust it. Another option to consider is to use a flatter brush.

B. **Detail**

This option is the same as the Warp tool's. *(For more information, see 3.11, Warp Tool.)*

C. **Simplify**

This option is the same as the Warp tool's. *(For more information, see 3.11 Warp Tool.)*

3.13

Pucker Tool

Use this tool to pinch paths in sharply and to pull up short spikes. The effects produced are like locally applied Pucker versions of the Pucker & Bloat Filters and Effects. The tool adds and drags anchor points with independent direction handles that stretch away from the anchor points. The result is a curved upward spike if you drag from the inside of the object out and a pinch if you drag from the outside of the object in. The Pucker tool's only options are the Detail and Simplify fields, which are the same as the Warp tool's. *(For more information, see 3.11, Warp Tool.)*

3.14

Bloat Tool

Use the Bloat tool to create smooth curves into and out of a path. The effects produced are like locally applied Bloat versions of the Punk & Bloat Filters and Effects. If you click and hold down on the inside of a path, anchor points are added to the path and pushed away from the path towards the outside of the brush until the path matches the brush. If you click and hold down on the outside of a path, anchor points are added to the path and pushed into the path towards the outside of the brush until the curve matches the brush. The direction points on the added points will all be smooth. The Bloat tool's only options are the Detail and Simplify fields, which are the same as those of the Warp tool's. *(For more information, see 3.11, Warp Tool.)*

3.15

Scallop Tool

Use the Scallop tool to create many concave or convex curve segments along the edge of a path. This is often used to create detail that would be time-consuming using manual methods. Drag on the interior of a path to create a series of sharp, close curves similar to those made with the Pucker tool pointing to the exterior of the shape. Drag on the exterior to create the same sort of spikes pointing to the interior of the shape. Whether a tool is on the interior or exterior of a path is determined by the location of the tool's center point crosshair.

The tool functions by adding anchor points to the path with curve handles at acute angles to each other. This produces m-shaped scalloping in the path.

Double-click the Scallop tool to modify its options.

Scallop Options

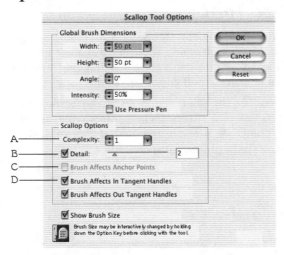

A. **Complexity** (0 to 15)

Use this option to set how closely the scallops the brush creates are to each other on the path.

B. **Detail** (1 to 10)

This option allows the Scallop tool to add anchor points to the object. Deactivated, the tool can only modify existing direction and anchor points. The higher the detail value, the more anchor points and curves will be added to the path. The Detail checkbox is activated by default.

C. **Brush Affects Anchor Points**

When this option is activated, the tool draws anchor points toward it rather than leaving in their original position. The Scallop tool is set to affect direction points (or Tangent Handles) by default. The Scallop tool may have up to two of these three boxes checked at a time. When this option is checked, the tool can reposition points along the original path. Unchecked, anchor points are added, but not repositioned. This produces a path that more closely follows the original shape.

D. **Brush Affects In/Out Tangent Handles**

Paths have a clockwise or counterclockwise flow. A direction handle that is before its anchor point on a curve is an "in" point. One that follows the anchor point on the path is an "out" point. The Brush Affects In Tangent Handles and Brush Affects Out Tangent Handles boxes enable the Scallop tool to pull direction points near it no matter where they fall on the curve. Both direction points being pulled gives the edges the scalloped look. Unchecking either of these boxes will mean that the tool only pulls on one direction point, leaving the other point following the original shape of the path. The resulting distortion is more of a linear wave than a scallop.

3.16

Crystallize Tool

The Crystallize tool is essentially the Scallop tool with a slightly different operational interface. Click-dragging with the Crystallize tool on the outside of a shape pushes curves into the path. Click-dragging with the Crystallize tool on the inside of a shape pull curves out of the path.

The Crystallize tool has the same option set as the Scallop tool. By default, though, the Crystallize tool affects anchor points whereas the Scallop tool affects direction points. As a result, this tool changes the edge contour of shapes more dramatically, producing spines and spikes.

3.17

Wrinkle Tool

Use this tool to create an irregular edge on an object. The effect is similar to a locally applied Roughen filter or effect. The Wrinkle tool adds and randomly offsets points to a path, double-click the Wrinkle tool to set its options.

Wrinkle Tool Options

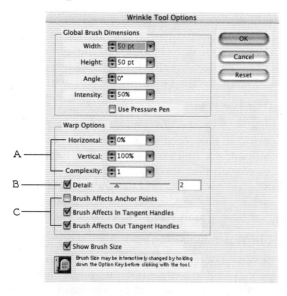

A. **Horizontal & Vertical** (0% to 100%)

The Horizontal and Vertical fields control the amount the added anchor points are offset from the original path. At 0% settings for both horizontal and vertical, the Wrinkle tool simply adds anchor points to the path. Setting a larger amount creates a more dramatic affect by pushing the points farther off the path.

B. **Detail**

This option functions the same as the Scallop tool's. *(For more information, see 3.15, Scallop Tool.)*

C. **Brush Affects**

This option functions the same as the Scallop tool, except that the Wrinkle tool can affect all three types of points.

3.18

Free Transformation

Free Transformation uses a bounding box model. The Selection Tool somewhat and the Free Transform tool completely utilize this model. In free transform, a bounding frame appears around selected objects and is then modified, causing the selected objects to be changed. Objects are transformed around the opposite point on the bounding box that is dragged. It differs from basic transformation in a number of ways:

- It is entirely visual. There is no way to make a precise numeric adjustment other than the default constrain angles.

- The point of transformation must be the center or one of the eight points on bounding box.

- Objects cannot be duplicated as they are transformed.

- It is quicker than other models of transformation

- It allows for series of different transformations to be applied without switching tools.

- It features Skew and Perspective transformations, which are not available elsewhere.

3.19

Free Transform Tool

Type "E"

Use the Free Transform tool to visually transform selected objects.

To use the tool, a selection must be made. The selection may be anchor points and segments, but usually entire objects are transformed in this way. To temporarily switch to the last selection arrow used, hold down the (Command) [Ctrl] key. When the Free Transform tool is chosen, selected objects display a bounding box. The bounding box is a rectangular guide with eight handles encompassing all of the selected objects. The four handles on the corners are referred to here as "corner handles." The handles in the middle of sides are "side handles." Use the following guidelines:

- **Moving.** To move an object with the Free Transform tool, click-drag from the inside of the frame area to the location you want the objects to be. When the cursor passes inside the bounding box, it will become the transformation arrowhead, indicating you may reposition the object.

- **Scaling.** To scale an object, click-drag on a handle. Click-drag a corner handle to scale both width and height. Click-drag a horizontal side handle to scale height. Click-drag a vertical side handle to scale width. By default, an object will be scaled in the direction opposite the handle being dragged. Hold down the (Option) [Alt] key as you drag to scale about the center. Hold down the Shift key when scaling from a corner handle to constrain the proportions of an object.

- **Rotating.** To rotate an object, position the cursor on the outside of the bounding box. The cursor will become a curved double-headed arrow, indicating you may rotate the objects. Click-drag to rotate the objects about the center of the bounding box. Hold down the Shift key as you drag to restrict the rotation to the default constraint angles.

- **Reflecting.** To reflect an object, click-drag from one corner handle completely across the object and release on the other side. Reflecting in this way cannot be constrained with the Shift key. For this reason it is not commonly performed with the Free Transform tool.

- **Reshaping freely.** To freely reshape the bounding box, click-drag on any handle. After you have begun to drag, hold down the (Command) [Ctrl] key. If you drag on a corner handle, the box is distended, creating a skew effect on the objects. If you drag from a side handle, the bounding box becomes a parallelogram as the side you drag is repositioned. The effect is similar to a constrained shear.

- **Mirroring a transformation.** If you add the (Option) [Alt] key as you (Command) [Ctrl] drag a handle, the handle opposite the one dragged is transformed an equal and opposite amount. If you drag a corner down and left, the opposite corner is dragged up and right. The effect is much like a traditional shear.

- **Adding perspective.** If you add the Shift key as you (Option-Command) [Alt-Ctrl] drag a corner handle, you create a perspective effect. The handle opposite the dragged handle is held fixed. The Shift key constrains the cursor to dragging 0° or 90°. As you drag in one direction, the opposing handle is dragged in to meet the approaching handle. The other two corner handles remain in their original positions. If you (Option-Shift-Command) [Alt-Shift-Ctrl]-drag a side handle, you shear about a constrained angle.

Issues to Consider

The Free Transform and Selection tools are sometimes confused, since they both use the bounding box and behave similarly. Be sure you have the Free Transform tool selected in the toolbox.

As you transform objects, the bounding box will also be transformed. To reset the bounding box to its original orientation, choose Object: Transform: **Reset Bounding Box**. Resetting the bounding box makes it easier to see how the dragging will reshape an object.

Special Tools

Symbolism Tools

Symbols are used to reduce file size, to create custom effects with repeating objects, and to integrate objects for export as SWF and SVG files. Symbols also enable greater object management by enabling objects to be modified and styled while retaining the ability to easily replace the original graphics.

Symbols are objects that are saved in the Symbols palette. Almost all objects may be made into symbols, including text, gradient meshes, transparent objects, objects with opacity masks, and raster art. Graphs and enveloped objects cannot become symbols but objects using envelope effects may. Symbols used in a document are *instances* of the symbol. Instances of the symbol are linked to the symbol in much the way styles are linked to objects. Multiple instances of a single symbol are smaller in file size than multiple copies of the same objects.

Instances may be transformed, styled, brushed, and given transparency and still retain their connection to the source symbol. If the symbol itself is modified, the instance will reflect the changes. Instances may be reconnected to different symbols and still retain their modifications. When selected, instances display only their bounding rectangle. The items shapes are displayed in Outline mode, when they are being transformed and as you use the symbolism tools on instances. Instances must be bounded by a rectangle. You cannot direct select and modify parts of this rectangle and you cannot skew or perspective-distort the rectangle.

The Symbol Sprayer tool creates bounded sets of instances. These symbol sets are groups of instances bounded by a rectangle. A symbol set may contain instances of different symbols. Like individual instances, symbol sets only display as bounding boxes in outline mode. Using the symbolism tools, you can edit individual instances within the set. As with instances, symbol sets may be edited using the common transformation tools, except for direct selecting points and segments, skewing and perspective.

Symbol sets and instances may be converted to a group of instances by choosing Object: **Expand**. The result will be a group object that could be further ungrouped as needed. This is true even if the set contains but a single instance or path.

Symbol tools share a common set of options. To set the options for any tool, double-click it. Setting options for any of the following settings affects all of the symbolism tools.

Symbolism Tool Options Dialog Box

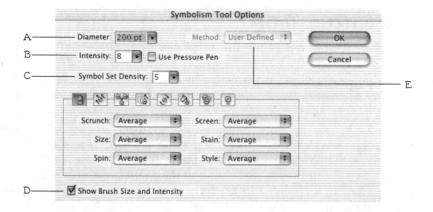

A. **Diameter** (1 to 999 pts)

Use this option to set the footprint of the tool, or its brush size. To increase the brush size on-the-fly, click the] key. Decrease it by clicking the [key

B. **Intensity** (1 to 10)

Use this option to set the tool's degree of effect. Greater numbers produce a larger effect. For example, when using the Symbol Sprayer tool, lower numbers produce fewer symbols; higher numbers place more.

C. **Symbol Set Density**

Use this option to control the instances' attraction to each other as you create a set. A higher number will result in instances being drawn closer to each other, creating a tighter pack in the set. Check the Use Pressure Pen check box to control density using a pressure sensitive tablet, such as a Wacom.

D. **Show Brush Size and Intensity**

Use this option to preview the area affected by the tools. The brush size is indicated by the size of the circle. The intensity is the color of the circle.

E. **Method**

Use this setting to affect the model tools used when editing instances. The Symbol Sprayer uses a more complex set of options and the Symbol Shifter does not use these options. All other symbolism tools use these options.

Average

Average gradually smooths out the density of the instances the longer you hold down the cursor.

Random

Random pushes or pulls a random amount.

User Defined

This option pushes or pulls as long as you have your cursor down.

Related Topics

34.1 Symbols Palette Overview

4.2

Symbol Sprayer Tool   *Shift-S*

Use the Symbol Sprayer tool to create instances and symbol sets and to add instances to symbol sets.

The Symbol Sprayer tool uses a set of options that is common to all of the Symbolism tools. To access these preferences, double-click on any symbolism tool. *(For more information, see 4.1, Symbolism Tools.)*

To use the Symbol Sprayer to create an instance, select a symbol from the Symbols palette and click with the tool. An instance is created. To create a symbol set, click-drag with the tool. As you drag, temporary guides populate the page under your cursor, indicating where instances will be placed when the mouse is released. When the mouse is released, the set is created.

To add instance to a set, first select a symbol set and then click or click-drag to add instances to the set. Instances in a set do not need to be of all the same symbol. (Option) [Alt]-click on instances to remove them from the set.

Issues to Consider

Use the Symbol Sprayer options to control the way that instances are distributed into a set. These six options are analogous to the aspects of symbols sets controlled by the other symbolism tools. The options for the Sprayer affect how sets are created. Each setting has a choice of Average (which eventually makes everything the same), or User Defined (which changes things based upon input from you). Average is most noticeable when adding symbols to an existing set, when the symbols are set to sizing and values based upon the symbols already in the set.

Symbol Sprayer Options

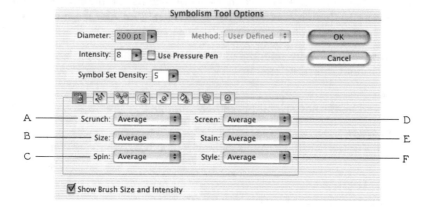

A. Scrunch

User Defined sets the density to the original symbol size. Average bases density on symbols already in the set.

B. Size

User Defined sets the symbols at the size they were created. Average bases sizing on symbols already in the set. The scaling of symbols already in the set are averaged to produce an aggregate value for newly added symbols.

C. Spin

Set to User Defined to rotate instances in the direction of the cursors as you spray symbols. Set to Average to spray instances without orientation.

D. Screen

User Defined sets to 100% opacity. Average bases opacity on symbols already in the set.

E. Stain

Set to User Defined to spray instances tinted with the current fill color. Set to Average to spray without changing colors.

F. **Style**

Set to User Defined to spray instances that use the current appearance saved in the Style palette. Set to Average to spray without styling objects.

4.3

Symbol Shifter Tool

Use this tool to change the stacking order of instances within a set and to manually control the position of objects.

To reposition objects, click-drag with the tool on a selected symbol set. Instances are dragged in the direction of the cursor's movement. The tool needs to be atop an instance for it to move. Moving instances within a set is not as fluid as moving objects about a document. If fact, it is nearly impossible to position specific objects exactly. If your design requires specific placement, consider placing independent instances rather than adding them to a set.

Shift-click on an instance to bring it to the front of the set, (Option) [Alt]-shift click to send symbols to the back. Using smaller diameter brushes makes it easier to change the order of specific instances.

4.4

Symbol Scruncher Tool

Use this tool to draw instances closer to the cursor or to push them away from the cursor.

To attract instances to the cursor, position the cursor atop a selected symbol set and click. Instances are drawn to the position. To repulse instances, hold down the (Option) [Alt] key as you click. The manner in which instances are attracted or repulsed is determined by the Method preference for the tool.

4.5

Symbol Sizer Tool

Use the Symbol Sizer tool to scale instances. It is commonly used to scale instances within a set. Individual symbols and sets can be scaled as a unit with any of the scaling tools.

To increase the size of an instance, click-drag on the instance. Instances in the tools footprint are scaled up. To decrease the size of an instance, (Option) [Alt] click on it. Scaling occurs from the center of the instance. Shift-click to remove instances from the set. (Option Shift) [Alt Shift] to scale down objects while preserving the density. Commonly, this adds many small instances.

The Method setting for the Symbol Sizer tool determines how objects are scaled. User Defined scaling scales as long as the cursor is down. Random applies a random amount of scaling (up or down). Average Scaling gradually scales all of the instances within the area to the same size.

Symbol Sizer Options

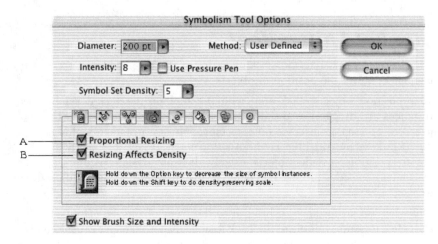

A. **Proportional Resizing**

Use this option to preserve the width-height ratio of the instance when scaling. Uncheck to scale instances irregularly.

B. **Resizing Affects Density**

Use this option to retain the relative spacing of instances as they are scaled. Unchecked, instances are not repositioned as they are scaled.

4.6

Symbol Spinner Tool

Use the Symbol Spinner tool to rotate instances.

To rotate an instance, click and hold down on an instance with the tool. A temporary arrow guide appears, indicating the direction of the instances the cursor is over.

The Method setting for the Symbol Spinner tool determines how objects are rotated. Average slowly brings the orientation of objects to the same value, the longer you hold down the mouse. Random rotates the instance a random amount. If you hold down the mouse, different random rotations will be applied until you let up the mouse. User Defined rotation rotates the instances in the direction the cursor is dragged.

As with other symbolism tools, the intensity setting affects the Symbol Spinner tool. The higher the setting, the more each instance will rotate when hit by the cursor.

4.7

Symbol Stainer Tool

Use the Symbol Stainer tool to tint, or recolor instances. The effect is similar to using the Tints & Shades option available to brushes. Very light and dark colors are not dramatically changed, white and black areas are not affected at all.

To tint an instance, click and hold down on an instance with the tool. Instances below the cursor are tinted.

The Method setting for the Symbol Stainer tool determines how objects are tinted. User Defined tints the instances based upon the current fill color in the Color palette. The longer the mouse is down, the greater the tint applied. Average gradually adjust the tint values of instances to become the same, the longer you hold the mouse down. This has no affect unless instances have different tints. Random applies a random hue tint to the instances.

Hold down the (Option) [Alt] key to decrease the amount of tinting, Hold down the Shift key to keep the amount of change applied to an instance constant. This is used when a color has already been applied to an instance and you are applying a new color. The amount of change stays the same as the color shifts to the new value.

Issues to Consider

Staining increases file size. Applying stain to instances increases the file size of the document. This increase is passed along when exporting SWF and SVG files. Care should be exercised when using this command.

4.8

Symbol Screener Tool

Use the Symbol Screener tool to adjust the opacity of instances.

To adjust the opacity of an instance, click and hold down on an instance with the tool. Instances below the cursor are made less opaque. To increase the opacity of instances, (Option) [Alt] click on them.

The Method setting for the Symbol Screener tool determines how objects are adjusted. User Defined continues to increase or decrease opacity as long as the cursor is down. Random applies a random opacity value to the instance. Average gradually adjust the opacity values of instances to become the same, the longer you hold the mouse down.

4.9

Symbol Styler Tool

Use the Symbol Styler tool to apply styles to instances. Styles are applied to the objects that comprise the instance. Unlike styles applied to paths, styled symbols may have an amount of the style applied to them, causing the effect to be gradually applied. The effect is similar to symbol staining except that styles are adjusted.

To apply a style of an instance, select an item from the style palette and click and hold down on an instance with the tool. Instances below the cursor are styled based on the current style. To decrease the amount of style applied to instances, (Option) [Alt]-click them.

The Method setting for the Symbol Styler tool determines how objects are adjusted. User Defined continues to increase or decrease Style as long as the cursor is down. Random applies a random amount of Style to the instance. Average gradually adjust the style values of instances to become the same, the longer you hold the mouse down.

4.10

Graph Tools

Use the graph tool suite to define and customize graphs, and to enter graph data. Graphs are visual expressions of an underlying core set of data. Data may be entered directly into Illustrator or imported from popular spreadsheet applications. Users can customize the appearance of graphs, alter data on-the-fly, and even change the graphs dynamically using variables.

Illustrator features nine kinds of graphs and has a tool for each graph. You may switch freely between graph types, though, so it is not required to start with the correct graph tool. As objects are modified, it is possible to combine multiple graph types in the same graph.

Graphs in Illustrator are actually a special arrangement of grouped objects. As long as the objects are all grouped, they remain a graph and may be edited by changing the underlying graph data. This prohibits the objects use in other ways. For example, graphs cannot be used as a mask or become symbols. Graphs are most commonly not a group of objects but a group of groups. That is, in a column graph they may be a group of numbers (the value axis) grouped to a group of open paths (the dividers) grouped to the rest of the graph. This complex grouping provides a utility when selecting and manually modifying graphs. Ungrouping a graph results in it losing its connection to the editable graph data. The graph will still look and print the same, but it will not be available to be updated as data changes, or to switch between graph types and add automatic graph features.

Graphs will have a default grayscale styling regardless of the current fill, stroke, and appearance.

Issues to Consider

Although respectable, the functionality of Illustrator's graphing tools can be frustratingly limited. Many users find their needs quickly outpacing the tools abilities. Basic utility, such as comma formatting of legends is not available. Local formatting is often lost upon a change in graph data. Users who find themselves preparing graphs for print extensively often resort to other products, work-around, or use graphs as comping tools before creating graphs manually.

Graphs may become dynamic objects. Although not a major breakthrough in graphing, the ability to connect graphs to variable data is noteworthy. *(For more information, see Chapter 41, "The Variables Palette.")*

4.11

Creating Graphs

The basic process for creating a graph is to first define a bounding area for the data using any of the graphing tools. Next enter or import the data for the graph. This is done using the Graph Data dialog box. This dialog box is available throughout the life of the graph, making it possible to change the graph at any time. Next the graph is modified and options are altered as needed. Individual parts of the graph may be selected and changed. Items such as legends and dividing marks may be added at any time. Even the basic kind of graph may be changed freely.

Part of the customization process may involve establishing graph designs. Designs are custom saved objects used to style graph columns or markers. Designs are a preferred model for styling graphs as opposed to selecting and styling the objects in the graph manually. This is because manual formatting may be disregarded in the common event that the graph data is altered.

Graphs may be created visually or numerically. To create a graph numerically, click with any graph tool in the document. The Graph dialog box appears, enabling you to establish the bounding area for the data. The entire graph, including legends and value axis will commonly be larger than this. The number entered here represents the area the graph data will occupy.

To create a graph visually, click-drag with any graph tool in the document. A temporary guide follows the cursor, indicating the area the graph data will occupy. Hold down the Shift key as you drag to set the width and height to the same value. Hold down the (Option) [Alt] key as you drag to drag the graph from its center, rather than a corner.

Upon initially establishing the size of the graph, the graph data dialog box opens. It will be available to be recalled and changed unless the graph is ungrouped. The graph dialog box looks like a basic spreadsheet application. There is an entry field and buttons across the top and an array of cells, which contain the graph data. A vertical sequence of cells is a column; a horizontal sequence is a row. The graph data dialog box is unlike spreadsheets in that it does not support equations. Only the first row and column, which are used for the values and categories, may contain alphanumeric data. Alphanumeric data in different rows and columns does not appear in the graph. To use a number, like a year, as value or category, put it in quotation marks.

A black box indicates the active cell. Navigate through the cells by clicking directly on a cell with the mouse or by using keys on the keyboard. The arrow keys accept the data in the current cell and move one cell in the direction pushed. The Return key accepts data in the cell and moves one cell down in the column. The Enter key accepts the data in the cell. The Tab key accepts the data and moves you one cell to the right in the row. Shift Tab adds the next unselected cell to the right to the cell selection. You can select all the cells between the active cell and another cell by Shift-clicking on the cell. Select multiple cells to copy and paste graph data. Since Edit: **Clear** only removes the contents of the current cell, Edit: **Cut** is the fastest way to remove the contents of many cells at once.

The Graph Data Options

A. Value Bar

This displays contents of current cell. Illustrator can handle numbers up to 10,000,000,000. Very large numbers will be displayed in the Value Bar using a scientific notation.

B. Import Data button

Click to import tab or comma delimited text. These are commonly available to be exported from most spreadsheet and database applications.

C. **Transpose Row/Column Button**

This flips all the rows and columns. This can be useful in the event that a graph is going backward. This cannot be performed on a selection, but must be done to the entire graph.

D. **Switch x/y:**

This button changes the x and y coordinates or data on a scatter graph. It is not available for any other graph type.

E. **Cell style**

Click to establish the number of decimal places numbers should be rounded to and the default Column Width in digits. Column Width does not restrict the data that may go into a column, and it does not preclude manually resetting specific dividers (see "Column Dividers," below).

F. **Revert**

Click to return the graph data to the state it was in the before the last time the data was applied or saved.

G. **Apply**

This updates the graph, redrawing it based on the current data. If you close the graph data dialog box without applying the data, you will prompted to save your changes. Saving the data applies the changes.

H. **Column Dividers**

Click-drag a divider to resize the column. Columns are usually resized to accommodate the data used,

---

4.12

Rectangle-Based Graphs

The Column Graph, Stacked Column Graph, Bar Graph, and Stacked Bar Graph tools have the same interface. They all produce graphs that express data as bars. The larger a value is, the greater the size of the bar that represents it.

In a graph design workflow, rectangle-based graphs utilize the Object: Graph: **Column** command. *(For more information, see 9.82, Object: Graph: **Column**.)*

Issues to Consider

Use the Rectangle Graph options to set graph types and options that affect the overall graph. To set the preferences for a graphing tool, double-click on the tool. This will set the options for the next graph you create. To edit the options of an existing graph, select the graph and choose Object: Graph: **Type**. Alternatively, select the graph, press (Control) [Right]-click and choose Type.

Rectangle Graph Options

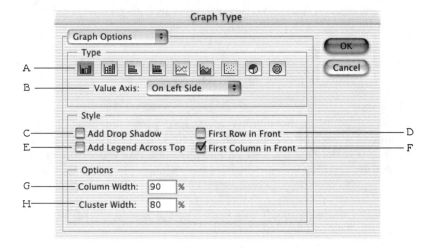

A. Type

Use the buttons to switch the basic kind of graph. You may switch graph types at any time. The bounding area for data will remain the same. Different graph types have different options available to them.

B. Value Axis

Use this option to select where you want the reference numbers to be constructed. The value is the amount of the thing being graphed. In Column and Stacked Column, the values may be displayed on the left, right, or on both sides of the graph. In Bar and Stacked Bar, they can go on the top, bottom or both. Graphs with two value axes may set options for each differently. *(For more information, see 4.13, Value Axis.)*

C. Add Drop Shadow

Use this option to add a 100% black drop shadow to the data bars offset to the upper right. Many users eschew this option in favor of building a graph design that features a drop shadow. This accords them the option to set the offset distance, determine the color of the shadow, and apply transparency and effects to the drop shadow.

D. First Row in Front

Use this option to layer the first row in front of the last row instead of the other way around. This option is only noticeable when graphs have a Cluster Width greater than 100%.

E. Add Legend Across Top

This option switches the location from the side and vertical to the top and horizontal. In practice this option often overlaps objects.

F. First Column in Front

This option sets the stacking order such that the first column appears on top of the remaining ones. This is noticeable in graphs with a Bar or Column width greater than 100%.

G. **Bar Width/Column Width** (1 to 1000%)

Use this option to set the width of a bar or column relative to the bounding area allotted it in a graph. Bars and columns are allotted a specific portion of the graph area based on the data and space available. Use this field to establish the amount of that space the bars occupy. Values over 100% will cause the bars and columns to encroach on each other.

H. **Cluster Width** (1 to 1000%)

Use this option to set the width of a data series relative to the bounding area allotted it in a graph. Categories are allotted a specific portion of the graph area based on the data and space available. Use this field to establish the amount of that space the bars occupy. Values over 100% will cause the categories to encroach on each other.

4.13

Value Axis

Use these options to set establish value ranges, to set the length of separating tick marks and to create labels for values. The values are the units of measure of the graph; categories are the things being measured. Depending on the type of graph, the value axis may be in different locations. Graphs that use the Both Sides option in Graph Options will have a separate menu for each of the axis. Some options, such as the Override Calculated Values section, cannot be set differently for different axis.

Value Axis Options

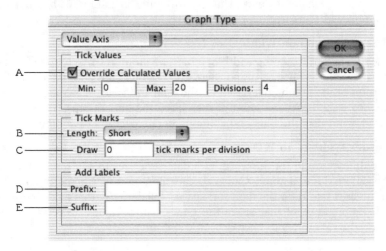

A. **Override Calculated Values**

Use this option to replace the default values with a custom range. Use the Min and Max fields to set the smallest and largest values used, respectively. The range set here will broken by the number of dividing Tick Marks set in the Divisions field. You are not restricted in any way when setting the min and max numbers. If the maximum value is smaller than the largest data value in the graph, the data bars will extend out of the data bounding area, popping themselves out of the graph. The default number of divisions is a tool preference established by the last defined number.

B. **Length**

Use this option to set the size of the dividing open paths. Set to None to leave the marks out completely. Full length Tick Marks extend to the opposite edge of the graph. Short Tick Marks are about 2% of the total width of the graph.

C. **Draw**

Use this option to set the number of tick marks in each division. Tick marks are small open paths used to make it easier to see distance in an axis. The number of divisions may be set using the Override Calculated Values field.

D. **Prefix**

Data in this field will be added prior to the value in the graph. Commonly this is used to add things like currency symbols.

E. **Suffix**

Data in this field will be added prior to the value in the graph.

4.14

Category Axis

Use these options to add tick marks to the category axis of a graph. Categories are the things being measured by a graph. The category axis will usually have a legend added automatically. The definitions of the fields are the same as they are for the Value Axis.

4.15

Column Graph Tool

Use the Column Graph tool to create graphs with vertical rectangles aligned along a horizontal axis. This is a highly utilized graph type. It is often used to express a change in data over time, such as yearly sales figures. Column graphs often utilize a series model. A series model compares different things over the same measures, such as two salesperson's figures each month over a year.

Set up a series model by organizing data in the graph data dialog box. Leave the upper-left corner cell empty. Enter labels for the series in the next cells to the right. In the earlier example, these series' might be the names of the salespeople. Enter the categories in the far-left column (remember to omit the first cell). These might be the months you are comparing sales performances. Enter the values in the corresponding cells and refresh the graph. The category labels (y axis in the graph) will be generated for you. Adjust the value axis options for the graph as needed.

4.16

Stacked Column Graph Tool

Use the Stacked Column Graph tool to create graphs with stacked vertical rectangles aligned along a horizontal axis. Since each series appears in a single stack, this style of graph is commonly used to show aggregate results by category, not change over time, such as total sales per month.

To switch between a column chart showing results over time and a stacked column showing total results open the graph data dialog box and click the transpose x/y data. This will make the series labels the categories. In the earlier examples, the salespersons become the categories and their sales are stacked on top of each other. This shows the aggregate results of the work and compares them to each other.

4.17

Bar Graph Tool

Use the Bar Graph tool to create graphs with horizontal rectangles aligned along a vertical axis, essentially a column graph on its side. The category axis is set along the side and values run along the bottom. The first category in the graph data dialog box will appear at the top of the graph.

4.18

Stacked Bar Graph Tool

Use the Stacked Bar Graph tool to create graphs with stacked horizontal rectangles aligned along a vertical axis. The category axis is set along the side and values run along the bottom. The first category in the graph data dialog box will appear at the top of the graph. As with stacked column graphs, these graphs are commonly used to express totals rather than to make a direct comparison.

4.19

Line Graph Tool

Use the Line Graph tool to create graphs with small squares marking data values. Commonly, straight paths connect the data points, creating a line that charts the progress of a value over categories. Line charts are commonly used to chart a value over time and to compare data series. Data is typically arranged in the graph data dialog box the same way that it is in column graphs. Take care to be clear with line graphs. Lines that overlap each other repeatedly or try to display too much data are often unclear.

In a graph design workflow, line graphs utilize the Object: Graph: **Marker** command. *(For more information, see 9.82, Object: Graph: Marker.)*

Issues to Consider

Use the Line Graph options to set graph types and options that affect the overall graph. To set the preferences for a graphing tool, double-click on the tool. This will set the options for the next graph you create. To edit the options of an existing graph select the graph and choose Object: Graph: **Type**.

Line graphs have the same Value and Category options as rectangle-based graphs. The Type and Style sections of the Graph Options dialog is also the same as in rectangle graphs. Note that while rectangle graphs default to a Min value of zero, line graphs do not, defaulting instead to a value at or near the lowest value in the data.

Line Graph Options

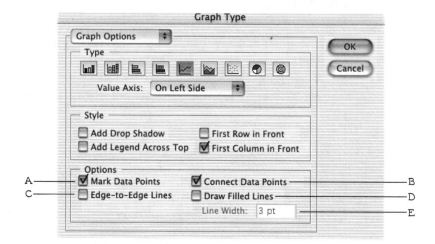

A. Mark Data Points

Use this option to indicate the position of data in the graph using rectangular data points. If neither this option nor connect data points are enabled, the graph will be blank. By default, the data points will be marked with rectangles.

B. Connect Data Points

Use this option to set a series of straight, open paths between the data points. These paths are located behind data points and are grouped together.

C. Edge-to-Edge Lines

Use this option to set the data points and lines to the edges of the graph instead of inset. This creates a more dramatic graph, but may make it less clear. This option affects data points as well as lines and does not require lines to be used.

D. Draw Filled Line

Use this option to join data points with closed rectangular paths instead of open paths. This is useful for creating connectors that have both a fill and stroke.

E. Line Width

Use this option in conjunction with Draw Filled Lines to set the width of connecting rectangles.

4.20

Area Graph Tool

Use the Area Graph tool to create a stacked line graph. The Area Graph tool creates filled polygons whose tops are a line that charts the values in the graph. Area graphs are commonly used to show aggregate values.

The Area Graph tool has no unique graph options. Its value axis, category axis, and graph options settings are the same as those for rectangular graphs.

Mistakes to Avoid

Not using the First Row and First Column in Front options. Due to the nature of the way data is displayed, the First Row and First Column in Front options are crucial here. If you don't use these options, the large, rear data will obscure all the other information.

4.21

Scatter Graph Tool

Use the Scatter Graph tool to create line graphs that compare two sets of variables for a series. Scatter graphs are unique in that they are used to track two independent variables for a series. For example, a graph might chart the linear distance a rocket traveled against the height it achieved. Or the sales figures against the number of cold calls made. Scatter graphs look and feel much like a line graph, but each data point contains two data values (distance traveled and height for example). This makes scatter graphs easy to generate from existing data without interpreting it. It also means that scatter graphs may not follow an easily understood path, as the series is all values and no categories.

To set up the graph data dialog box for a scatter graph, each series needs two columns of data. Set a series title as needed in the first cell of the graph data dialog box. The vertical axis data will go in the first column under the title. Horizontal data will go in the cell to the right of the vertical data. Many users include two cells with subtitles for the data columns in the second row. Alphanumeric data outside of the first row will not appear in the graph. So, in the previous example the first cell in the upper left might be "rocket 1" the two cells in the row below that could be "height" and "distance." The cell below that would be the first height recorded, with distance in the cell to the right of that. Labels for these axes would need to be created manually.

The Scatter Graph tool has the same options as the Line Graph tool except for Edge-to-Edge Lines. Scatter Graphs chart data edge to edge by default. *(For more information, see 4.19, Line Graph Options.)*

4.22

Pie Graph Tool

Use the Pie Graph tool to create elliptical graphs divided into wedges to show relative amounts. Pie graphs total all the values in a graph row and express each field as a percentage of that sum. It is not necessary for you to calculate percentages before creating a pie graph.

Issues to Consider

Use the Pie Graph options to set graph types and options that affect the graph overall. To set the preferences for a graphing tool, double-click on the tool. This will set the options for the next graph you create. To edit the options of an existing graph select the graph and choose Object: Graph: **Type**.

Pie graphs have no Value or Category Axis. The Style options are the same as for rectangular graphs.

When creating pie graphs, each row of data will generate a separate pie. Each data series should occupy its own row. Labels for the rows and columns are added as in other graphs. Pie graphs cannot accept graph designs and must be styled manually.

Pie Graph Options Dialog Box

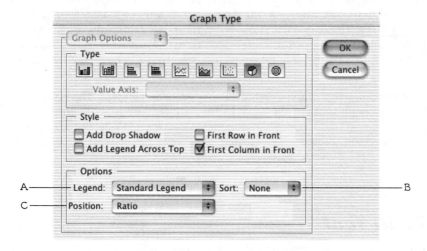

A. Legend

Use this option to set the type of legend created. Set to standard, this creates the corresponding color squares and text associated with other graphs. Set to Legends in Wedges to omit the boxes and place the legend text directly on the graph wedge it represents. Text set this way will generally need to be manually edited for size and placement. Set to None to omit legends.

B. **Sort**

Use this option to position the wedges in the pie based upon values. Set to None the wedges will orient themselves clockwise from the top around the graph based on the order they are in the graph data dialog box. Set to First, the largest value will appear in the first position around the graph (starting from the top center and moving clockwise) and the other values will appear in the order they were entered. Set to All to sort all graph values from largest to smallest. This option cannot be set differently for different series within the same graph.

C. **Position**

Use this option to control the relative size of each pie in a multiple series graph. Set to Even, the pies will be sized the same. Set to ratio, the pies will be larger the greater the sum of the series is. Set to Stacked, the pies will use a ratio sizing and center align themselves one atop the other.

4.23

Radar Graph Tool

Use the Radar Graph tool to create graphs that represent data as points about a circle. The Radar Graph tool is similar to a line graph except that instead of running in a linear direction, the data series travel around 360° to create a closed shape. The data starts at the 90° vertical axis and moves clockwise. For each data point in the series, a reference axis extends as a radius line segment. The vertical axis is the only value axis, though. Area graphs do not have a category axis.

When creating area graphs, each data series runs in columns. The options for the Area Graph tool are the same as they are for line graphs, although the Edge-to-Edge lines option is redundant here. When using full length tick marks, concentric circles are created. *(For more information, see 4.19, Line Graph Tool)*

4.24

Mesh Tool

Use the Mesh tool to convert paths to gradient mesh objects, to add anchor points to a mesh, and to edit the position of mesh anchor points. The mesh tool may be used to affect gradient meshes as well as the envelopes created when using the commands under Object: **Envelop Distort**.

Issues to Consider

Mesh points are actual points. Mesh and envelope points may be edited for position using standard tools, like the Direct Selection and Convert Anchor Point Tools, as well as the Mesh tool.

Gradient and pattern fills do not translate well. Converting a path with a gradient or pattern fill to a gradient mesh will result in an object with all black-filled points. To retain the gradient's appearance in a mesh, you must choose Object: Expand: **Expand to Gradient Mesh**.

Converting a path to a gradient mesh. To convert a path to a gradient mesh, position the Mesh tool atop a path. The path need not be selected. If the Use Area Select Preference is activated and the path has a fill, you can also click on the interior area of a path. The mesh cursor will display a "plus" symbol when you are in a viable location to place a mesh point. Click the mouse and the path is converted to a mesh. An anchor point is added in the location that you click. If you clicked directly on a path, a single mesh segment will run from the point clicked to the opposite side of the path. Direction points will be added as needed to emulate the shape of the object. If you clicked on the interior of an object, four mesh segments will be created.

Adding points. To add points to mesh or envelop, click anywhere on or in the interior of a mesh or envelope. When the cursor is over a position where it can add a point, a plus (+) sign is displayed next to the cursor. Clicking on a mesh segment will create an anchor point and two new mesh segments.

Removing points. To remove an anchor point from an envelope or mesh, (Option) [Alt] click directly on the point with the mesh tool. A minus sign is displayed next to the cursor when you are about to remove a point this way.

Repositioning points. To edit the location of mesh point, click-drag on it with the Mesh tool. The point is moved freely. Hold down the Shift key as you drag to constrain the movement of the point to one of the two mesh lines. To edit the position of a direction point, click-drag on the direction point with the Mesh tool. If you drag toward the anchor point that controls it, the direction point moves by itself. If you rotate the direction point, the direction point and the direction point opposite it are rotated together. Add the Shift key as you drag to affect the direction point and all the other direction points on the point in unison.

4.25

Gradient Tool   *Type "G"*

Use the Gradient tool to position the 0% and 100% locations of a gradient fill. When a gradient is defined, colors are established for the 0% (beginning) and 100% (ending) locations of the gradient. Other colors may be established in-between, but there is a minimum of these two colors in a gradient.

To set these positions geographically in an object that contains a gradient fill, first select the object that contains a gradient fill. Next click-drag with the gradient tool. A temporary guide follows the cursor, indicating the direction and distance of the gradient when you release the mouse. The position you initially clicked on will be the 0% location in the gradient. The position you release the mouse will be the 100% location of the gradient. The distance and direction between the points will be the distance and direction of the gradient. Hold down the shift key to constrain the cursor to the default angles.

Double-click the Gradient tool to open or bring forward the Gradient palette.

Issues to Consider

In objects with multiple gradient fills, either the cardinal or the topmost gradient is affected. If an object contains more than one gradient fill, make sure the fill you want to adjust is cardinal (highlighted in the Appearance palette) or, in the event that a non-gradient fill is cardinal, at the top of the Appearance palette. After being edited for gradient position, the fill becomes cardinal automatically.

The distance and colors of a gradient plays a role in its printability. Gradients with colors that are too similar or are too far apart geographically may not print as expected. The changes in the gradient may be visually apparent, creating a posterized look called "banding." *(For more information, see 23.1, Gradient Palette.)*

4.26

Eyedropper Tool   *Type "I"*

Use the Eyedropper tool to set the current default appearance of paths and type to match objects in the document and to reset the appearance of objects and type to be the same as other objects. Styles and character attributes may be set as well as typical object attributes. The current default attribute is the one that will be applied to the next object created. The Eyedropper tool has preferences that control its behavior and is often used in conjunction with the Paint Bucket tool. *(For more information, see 4.30, Paint Bucket Tool.)*

Issues to Consider

Matching the appearance to another object. To reset the appearance of paths and type to match objects in the document, first select the object to be changed. Next, click the Eyedropper tool on an object. The appearance of the selected object will be changed to match the existing object. If the object is type, the eyedropper cursor will add a "T" character.

Resetting the default appearance. To reset the default appearance and type settings for a document, click on an object with the Eyedropper tool when nothing selected.

Double-click the Eyedropper tool to modify its options. The Eyedropper options are in the same dialog box as the Paint Bucket options. Uncheck any of the characteristics in the nested list to omit the attribute from being recorded by the Eyedropper tool. For example, you may wish to reset the font of an object to match another, but leave the point size alone. Uncheck the Size check box to omit that setting from being sampled. Uncheck a category to omit that entire attribute from being sampled.

Accessing the Paint Bucket tool. Temporarily switch to the Paint Bucket tool by holding down the (Option) [Alt] key.

4.27

Paint Bucket Tool *Type "K"*

Use the Paint Bucket tool to apply the current default appearance of paths and type to any objects in the document. To apply the current default settings for objects or type to an object, click on it with the Paint Bucket tool. The object need not be selected to have its attributes changed.

Double-click the Paint Bucket tool to modify its options. The Paint Bucket options are in the same dialog box as the Eyedropper options. Uncheck any of the characteristics in the nested list to omit the attribute from being applied by the Eyedropper tool. For example, you may wish to apply the font of an object to match another, but leave the point size alone. Uncheck the Size check box to omit that setting from being applied. Uncheck a category to omit that entire attribute from being sampled.

Temporarily switch to the Eyedropper tool while using the Paint Bucket tool by holding down the (Option) [Alt] key.

4.28

Measure Tool

Use the Measure tool to record the distance and direction between two points, to set the defaults for the Move command and to open the Info palette. Click with the Measure tool anywhere in a document to open or bring forward the Info palette. While the Measure tool is selected, the Info palette displays a Distance (D:) and Angle field below the X/Y and Width/Height fields, respectively. Click-drag from one point in a document to another. As you drag, a temporary guide is displayed, showing the distance and direction that the cursor has been dragged from the initial position clicked. As you drag the distance and angle fields display values on-the-fly. Shift drag to constrain the cursor movements to the default angles.

The distance and direction recorded by the Measure tool inform the default settings for the Move Command (Object: Transform: **Move** or double-click the Select or Direct Selection tool). Often, users will use the measure tool to measure a distance and then apply the Move command.

Double-click the Measure tool to open the Guides & Grid preference dialog box. *(For more information, see 8.15, Edit: Preferences: **Guides & Grid**.)*

4.29

Blend Tool
Type "W"

Use the Blend tool to convert paths into blend objects and to add objects to blends by establishing blend reference points. The Blend tool is similar in function to the command Object: Blend: **Make**. Both convert at least two selected paths to a blend object. The Blend tool is different in that it enables users to establish the anchor points as reference points for the blend. The blend is based upon those anchor points and the objects created in the blend are adjusted to make the blend correct. This often results in sizing effects that cannot be accomplished using the Make Blend command. Manually blending in this way is often done to correct incomprehensible blends created from complex objects.

To convert two objects to a blend, click the tool directly on a path and then click directly on another path. The paths needs not be selected. If the Area Select Preference is enabled, you may click anywhere on a filled path. When preparing to start a blend, the blend tool cursor will display an "x" in the lower right. A "+" will be displayed when the tool is atop a viable second shape for the blend.

To add an object to an existing blend, the process is the same as creating a blend except that one of the objects clicked must belong to a blend.

To establish blend reference points, click directly on the anchor point of the objects to be blended. Intermediate objects will be blended as though they were moving from one point to the other.

Double-click the Blend tool to open the Blend Options dialog box. Use the options in this dialog box to set the preferences for the next blend created or to modify a selected blend.

Related Topics
    9.52   Object: **Blend**

4.30

Auto Trace Tool

Use the Auto Trace tool to create paths based upon areas of solid color in bitmap files. The bitmaps traced may be in any color mode and may be embedded or linked. This tool is affected by the Type & Auto Tracing preferences. *(For more information, see 8.13, Edit: Preferences:* **Type & Auto Tracing***.)*

The Auto Trace tool is functional for rudimental traces but should not be used for complex jobs. The ability of the tool to create shapes is also beholden to the quality of the original. Even the better auto traces usually need adjustment. For repeated, complex tracing, many users often consider dedicated tracing applications such as Adobe Streamline.

To create a path from an area of solid color in a bitmap object, click with the tool directly on the area to be traced. The cursor must be at least six pixels away from the area to be traced.

To trace only part of an object, click-drag in the object to be traced from the point you want to start tracing to where you want to stop. To add to a live trace, click-drag from the point where the paths should connect.

4.31

Web Slicing Tools

Use the Web Slicing tools to define and select areas for the cells and tables created when using Illustrator's Save for Web command. Commonly, HTML pages use a table to define graphic space. Each graphic in a cell is saved as a different image. This allows for a greater control of graphic space and allows different parts of a complete image to be optimized in different ways.

Slices may be created manually or created from an object. Slices created from objects are logically connected to the object. As the object is repositioned or transformed, the slice is modified as well. This provides great flexibility. Illustrator can create several different kinds of slice in this way. *(For more information, see Chapter 9, "The Object Menu.")*

Slices created by the Slices tool are called user slices. User slices are a fixed size and are a class of object. They do not print and must be rectangular, but they appear in the Layers palette, and can be selected and transformed in most of the ways other objects can. If a slice is modified, in a way that makes it nonrectangular, its slice area becomes rectangular again based upon its bounding box, but the underlying vector shape is retained.

Related Topics
*9.33   Object: **Slice***

4.32

Slice Tool

Use the Slice tool to create User Slices. Click-drag to create a slice. A temporary guide follows the cursor, indicating where the slice will be created when the mouse is released. Hold down the Shift key as you drag to create a sliced with the same height and width. Hold down the (Option) [Alt] key as you drag to create a slice from its center. To reposition a slice as you are creating it, hold down the spacebar.

4.33

Slice Select Tool

Use the Slice Select tool to select and modify slices. Since the Slice Select tool can only select slices and not other objects, using it is the same as locking all of the non-slice objects in the document. To select a slice with the tool, click on a slice. Position the cursor directly atop a slice point and click-drag to resize a slice horizontally or vertically.

4.34

Scissors Tool

Use the Scissors tool to break a path at a specific point. This is often done to customize a path or to create new paths. To cut a path, click on it with the scissors tool, You may click on an anchor point or the path. The path need not be selected to use the scissors tool, but it is common practice to do so to see the anchor points on the path. Two anchor points are created in the position you clicked, one on each side of the break.

When used on closed paths, an open path is created, when used on an open path it creates two open paths. After the tool is used on a path, one anchor point and the segment connected to it are selected. This anchor point will always be at the ending side of the original path. The beginning and ends of paths are easier to picture on open paths. If you click and drag from left to right with the Line tool, the left anchor point is the beginning of the path and the right anchor point is the end. If you use the Scissors on this path, the segment on the right will be selected after the line is cut.

4.35

Knife Tool

Use the Knife tool to create closed paths based on the intersection of existing paths and lines drawn by the Knife tool. This is commonly done to create custom shapes from simpler paths.

To use the Knife tool, click-drag with the tool. A freeform guide follows the movement of the cursor, indicating where objects will be cut when the cursor is released. All objects the Knife touches will be affected unless a selection is active at the time the tool is used. In that case, only the selected objects will be affected.

Hold down the (Option) [Alt] key before pressing the mouse when using the Knife tool and the cursor will be constrained to a straight line. Add the Shift key to constrain the movement of the cursor to the default angles.

The Knife tool does not work on open paths without fills. Open paths with fills will be treated as if they were closed.

4.36

Hand Tool

Use the Hand tool to reset the view location of a document. To use the Hand tool, click-drag in the document. The location the cursor is initially clicked will be reset to the position the cursor ends up when you release. The effect is similar to pushing the page to a new location. Temporarily access the Hand tool while using any other tool by holding down the Shift key.

Double-click the Hand tool to reset the view depth to fit in window.

4.37

Page Tool

Use this tool to reset the imageable area when printing from Illustrator. This is commonly used when manually tiling large images or to reset the location on the page objects print without moving the objects. Illustrator documents display the imageable area for the currently selected printer as a dotted line rectangle. This area is called the page tiling. It can be shown or hidden by choosing View: **Show Page Tiling**. The dimensions of the tiling area are determined by choosing File: **Print Setup** and setting a paper size and orientation.

To reset the page tiling area, click with the tool. The position clicked becomes the lower-left inside margin of the page tiling. Click-drag to drag the page tiling bounds into a new position. Double-click the page tool to position the lower-left corner of the page tiling.

Issues to Consider

Small artboards may clip the page tiling. If the artboard is smaller than the page tiling, only part of the page tiling will display. This is usually an issue only if you are trying to tile pages or are printing directly from Illustrator. In these cases, make sure your artboard is larger than your page tiling.

Many graphics from other applications are in the lower left of the page tiling. For example, exported paths from Photoshop are placed in the lower-left corner of the page, even though they are in the center of the artboard. Use the Page tool to reposition the page tiling.

4.38

Zoom Tool   *Type "Z"*

Use the Zoom tool to reset the view depth of a document. View Depth is the percentage of the object's actual size that is being displayed onscreen. 100% view depth would mean that the object is appearing onscreen at the size that it will print. This is slightly inaccurate, and also assumes a 72 dpi monitor resolution. The Zoom tool can enlarge a specific portion of a document, or pan in or out incrementally.

Illustrator has 23 preset view depths from 3.13% to 6400%. Click with the Zoom tool to step to the next largest preset view depth. The location clicked will also be centered in the window. Hold down the (Option) [Alt] key and click to reset the view depth to the next smallest preset value. By default, the Zoom tool displays a plus (+) sign in its cursor. When the (Option) [Alt] key is down, it displays a minus (-) sign. If the center of the Zoom tool is blank, it means you are at 6400% view depth and cannot pan in further.

To use the Zoom tool to enlarge a specific portion of a document, click-drag with the tool. A rectangular marquee follows the cursor, displaying the area that will be enlarged to fit the screen upon release of the mouse. Double-click the Zoom tool to reset the view depth to 100%. To change the location of the marquee as you drag, hold down the spacebar. To drag a marquee from the center, (Control) [Right-click] after you have started dragging. To retain the current view depth after you have started dragging, drag back to the position from which you started.

Color Controls

Color Control Overview

The controls at the base of the toolbox enable you to set the fill and stroke of objects and to open commonly used palettes.

5.2

Fill   *Type "X"*

Use the Fill swatch to set the default fill color, to access the Color Picker, and to change an object's (cardinal) fill.

Fill is the graphic attribute of the interior of a path. Paths describe an area; the fill describes how to treat the area. Both open and closed paths support fills. Fill areas connect the ends of an open path with a straight line. Fills may be transparent space, flat colors, gradients, or patterns. Raster images do not have fills.

Objects may have more than one fill. The last fill selected is said to be the cardinal fill. In objects with more than one fill, the cardinal fill is displayed in the fill swatch. The cardinal fill of a selection is indicated in the Appearance palette by a square around the swatch. Fills may be styled with transparency and effects. *(For more information, see Chapter 17, "The Appearance Palette.")*

The fill swatch displays the cardinal fill of selected objects. If objects with different fills are selected a question mark is displayed. The contents of the fill swatch are applied to the next object created. Some objects have default fills that supercede this:

- Type objects receive a 100% black fill. Regardless of the current fill option, type is filled black.

- Graph components default to grayscale fills separated by 12.5% black ink. Common fills are 12.5%, 25%, 37.5%, 50%, 62.5%, 75%, 87.5%, and 100% black.

- Mesh points on a gradient mesh when more than one point is selected are styled with the color that is already in that location, regardless of the current fill.

To reset the default fill or to change the fill of a selected object, the fill swatch must be forward of the stroke icon. When the fill swatch covers the upper left corner of the stroke icon, the fill attribute is editable. Click the swatch to bring it forward. Once the fill is forward, change it by doing one of the following:

- Double-click the swatch to access the color picker. *(For more information, see 20.5, Color Picker.)*

- Use the Eyedropper tool to sample a fill from another object.

- Manipulate the sliders in the color palette

- Click a predefined item from the Swatches palette or an open swatch library.

- Click a predefined item from the Style palette.

To apply the current fill to objects in the document, drag the fill swatch directly onto the object. To set the stroke to the same color as the fill, drag the fill swatch onto the stroke swatch.

To save the current fill as a swatch, drag the fill swatch directly into the Swatches palette. (Option) [Alt] drag the swatch onto an existing swatch in the Swatches palette to replace the existing swatch. *(For more information, see 33.1, Swatches Palette Overview.)*

Issues to Consider

The fill icon is used to describe the colors attached to anchor points in a gradient mesh. Meshes themselves will display a question mark fill when selected unless all the mesh points have the same color value.

The fill icon is used when defining steps in a gradient. These steps are not the fill of the object, but rather components of its fill. *(For more information, see 23.1, Gradient Palette Overview.)*

Envelopes have their own fills independent of the objects they affect. To adjust the fill of an enveloped object, you must choose Object: Envelope Distort: **Edit Contents**. *(For more information, see 9.61, Object: Envelope Distort.)*

Some path techniques that alter an object's fill restore the changed fill if the effect is reversed; some do not. For example, converting an object to a mask changes its fill and stroke to none. Releasing the mask does not return the fill and stroke attributes. Conversely, making objects into a Compound Shape changes the fill and stroke to those of the top object in the shape. Releasing the compound shapes returns the objects original fill and stroke values. These techniques are noted as they appear in later chapters.

Fills actually exist behind an applied stroke. This is why strokes are half inside the fill area. In some instances, such as small text with a stroke, this intrudes on the clarity of objects. Fill can be put in front of stroke. *(For more information, see 17.1, Appearance Overview.)*

The fill swatch in the toolbox is the same as the one in the Color palette. They both display the same value and as one is brought forward, so is the other.

5.3

Stroke   *Type "X"*

Use the stroke swatch to set the default stroke color, to access the Color Picker, and to change an object's (cardinal) stroke.

Strokes are attributes that describe what runs along a path. Strokes straddle paths, half on the interior and half on the exterior. They may be solid colors, patterns, or brush strokes. The appearance of strokes is further affected by the options in the Stroke palette and the Appearance palette. *(For more information, see 30.1, The Stroke Palette.)*

5.4

Swap Fill and Stroke   *Shift-X*

Click this icon to swap the fill and stroke values. Click it again to swap them back.

5.5

Default Fill and Stroke   *Type "D"*

Click this icon to set the fill to white and the stroke to black with a weight of 1 point. More specifically, this icon sets selected objects or the default values to the default style in the Style palette. This is the first style in the palette. You will recognize it because it contains the same icon as Default Fill and Stroke in the toolbox.

Issues to Consider

The default style may be changed in the Styles palette. (Option) [Alt] drag a style swatch onto the default swatch in the Styles palette. The Appearance summary may also be (Option) [Alt] dragged onto the default swatch icon.

To set an object to either black or white fill or stroke, many users find it convenient to start with the default swatch. For example, to set a black fill and no stroke, you could set the object to the default fill and stroke, swap the fill and stroke and then set the stroke to none.

5.6

Color
Type "<"

Click this button to open or bring forward the Color palette. If objects are selected, the last used solid fill will be applied to them. This is only an issue if the object has a gradient, pattern, or none fill. Otherwise, the object's fill is already in the Color palette. If an object has multiple fills, the cardinal fill will be displayed. *(For more information, see 20.1, Color Palette.)*

5.7

Gradient
Type ">"

Click this button to open or bring forward the Gradient palette. If non-gradient objects are selected when you click, the current gradient will be applied to the object.

5.8

None
Type "/"

Click this button to set the current fill or stroke attribute to a value of none. None is the same as transparent. An object with a fill and stroke of none is invisible.

Issues to Consider

No weight is the same as a None color. Setting a stroke weight of 0 sets the stroke color to None.

Some tools set can set the fill to none automatically. The Brush, Line, Arc, Rectangular Grid, and Polar Grid have tool options which automatically set the Fill to None.

View Controls

View Controls Overview

The view control buttons at the bottom of the toolbar set the display of the document to one of three viewing modes. Different open documents may be set to different view modes. These buttons do not affect objects in any way.

The following shortcuts apply to all three viewing modes.

- **Change Views.** Use the F key to cycle through the View Modes. Press it repeatedly to move to the next mode.

- **Hide all palettes.** Press the Tab key to hide all open palettes, including the toolbar. Press the Tab key again to reveal the palettes. When the palettes are hidden you may still view individual palettes by choosing them from the Window menu.

- **Hide all palettes except toolbar.** Press Shift-Tab to hide all the palettes. Press Shift-Tab again to reveal the palettes.

6.2

Standard Screen Mode

This is the default view for every new document. It displays the image window, allowing access to the scrollbars, title bar, magnification box, and status bar.

Issues to Consider

This is the only view mode that lets you see underlying information and other windows. This includes other open file, different windows of the same document, and other applications.

6.3

Full Screen Mode with Menu Bar

This view hides the edges of the image window, including the scrollbars, title bar, magnification box, and status bar. The document area fills the screen, obscuring other windows.

Issues to Consider

The menu bar and commands remain visible. Use this mode to reduce clutter and maintain access to tools and commands.

This mode is a window-size trick. Illustrator has resized the document window to be just larger than your current monitor. If you have a multi-synching monitor and increase your monitor resolution, you'll see the edges of your document.

This mode hides the information in the title and status bars. You will not be able to see the view depth, document mode, document title, color profile, or view options in this mode.

6.4

Full Screen Mode

This view hides the menu bar and the edges of the document. The document area fills the screen, obscuring other windows.

Issues to Consider

Shortcuts still work in this mode. Although the menu is not visible, keyboard commands and shortcuts still function in this mode.

This mode is primarily used for display. It's oppressively hard to get work done in this mode. It is usually reserved for displaying finished work, especially with the palettes hidden.

The File Menu

File: New
(Command) [Ctrl]–N

Use this command to create a new document. New documents are commonly created to start a new project and to create a temporary workspace for pasting image information while working on another project.

Mistakes to Avoid

Failing to set artboard size appropriately. Although vector art can be scaled up and down freely, there are some good reasons to set the artboard to the size of the image you intend to create. The artboard size is the area that fills the window when you choose View: **Fit in Window**. Setting it to the size of the art you want to make will make navigating the document easier.

The artboard is the page size when files are saved in the PDF format. Things outside the artboard are cropped and not visible in a PDF. Setting it to close to the size of the art will save you and your PDF audience time zooming and out.

Finally, setting the artboard to size helps you visualize the final artwork relative to the size at which it will be used.

Confusing artboard size with Page Size. Although they have similar fields and are often the same areas, artboard and page size are not the same thing. Page size must be chosen from the list of sizes supported by your printer, artboards can be sized freely.

Issues to Consider

New documents have limited impact on memory. Unlike pixel based applications, Illustrator documents take up little available memory. Many users utilize additional documents to isolate objects, store ideas, and to paste back and forth without incurring a performance hit.

The settings in the New Document dialog box may be edited after the document is created. The artboard settings are available by choosing File: **Document Setup** and the color mode may be changed by choosing File: **Document Color Mode**.

The New Document Dialog Box

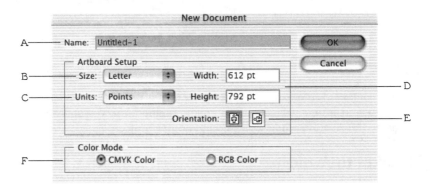

A. Name

Use this field to set the default document name field when saving a document for the first time. New documents are not saved and assigning one name in this field only saves you the step when the file is actually saved.

B. Size

Use this field to automatically set the artboard to one of the preset sizes. Choosing one of these sizes populates the Width and Height fields. If you enter your own values in the Width or Height fields this field will read Custom.

C. **Units**

Use this field to set the unit of measure in the Width and Height fields. The units chosen here become the General measuring preference (Edit: Preferences: **Units & Undo**).

D. **Width/Height** (1 to 16383 points)

Use these fields to set the size of the artboard.

E. **Orientation**

Click the unselected icon to switch the values in the Width and Height fields. This field is not related to the orientation field in the Page Setup dialog box.

F. **Color Mode**

Click a radio button to set the color mode of the document to CMYK or RGB. Any work done for printing should be in the CMYK mode. Any work done for onscreen should be in RGB.

Document Features

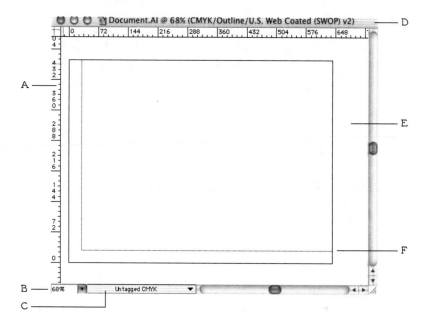

A. **Rulers**

Rulers are used for reference and to create guides. Rulers are optional and may be shown or hidden. *(For more information, see 14.21, Show Rulers and 14.24, View: **Guides**.)*

B. **View Depth**

This field shows the current view depth percentage of the document. Set the amount by typing directly into this field and pressing Enter or Return or by choosing one of the preset amounts from pop-up menu to the right of the field.

C. **Status Bar**

Use the Status Bar to display information about the current document. (Option) [Alt] click the Status Bar to reveal amusing hidden options. The hidden option *Ted's Home Number* is the phone number for Adobe Customer Support.

Current Tool

Use this option to display the currently selected tool. This can be useful for inexperienced users and when using the Precise Cursors preference.

Date & Time

This option displays the current date and time, based on your computer's clock.

Free Memory

This displays the amount of available memory Illustrator has. This is shown as a percentage of the total available and the raw RAM. This option can be useful to track performance as documents become complicated.

Number of Undos

This option shows the number of undos and redos available. The numbers are based on your actions, not on available memory. Redos will only appear after you have undone something.

Document Profile

This option displays the current color profile attached to the document. If no profile is being used, this will display as Untagged RGB or CMYK. *(For more information, see 8.10, Edit: **Color Settings**.)*

D. **Title Bar**

The title bar displays information about the file and how it is being viewed. From the left to right, the first item is the file format icon. Each file format that Illustrator can save has its own file icon. This icon displays the format the file is saved in. If the file is new and unsaved, it will display the Illustrator native format by default. If the document has been changed from its saved state, the icon will be dimmed. In this way you can see if the document's current condition has been saved. Next the name of the current file and the current View Depth percentage are listed. Following the view depth in parentheses is the document's color model and information about the document's display. The view mode is listed next. It will show Outline or Preview. Previewing options, such as

Pixel Preview or Overprint Preview are also listed. When the Proof Colors option is activated, the document's color profile will be displayed. When editing Opacity Masks the name of the mask is displayed followed by "/Opacity Mask."

E. **Artboard**

This solid line indicates the location of the document's artboard. *(For more information, see 7.43, File: Document Setup: **Artboard**.)*

F. **Page Tiling**

This dotted line indicates the document's page tiling. The page tiling shows the relative positions objects will appear when printing directly from Illustrator. This is often the same area as the artboard but need not be. *(For more information, see 7.43, File: Document Setup: **Artboard**.)*

7.2
_____

File: *Open* *(Command) [Ctrl]-O*

Use this command to open any of the file formats Illustrator supports. Commonly this will be Illustrator native files (AI), Encapsulated PostScript (EPS), and Portable Document format (PDF) files. Illustrator can open a wide variety of formats, both vector and pixel based. A list of understood formats is available in the Show field of the Open dialog box.

Issues to Consider

Illustrator is well-integrated with Photoshop. Illustrator can open native Photoshop files with a high degree of flexibility. Photoshop layers can be flattened or imported as a series of independent objects. Slicing and image mapping may be imported as well. These options will be available in the dialog that results when opening a native Photoshop file. Photoshop 6's shape layers are opened as masking paths atop raster art. Other features, like type and transparency are not opened as live features.

Opened pixel files are marginally editable. Although Illustrator can open many pixel file formats, it still has limited pixel-editing capabilities. Consider whether a file should be opened or placed.

Some features must be reinterpreted. Features in other applications may not translate perfectly when opening in Illustrator. For example, FreeHand's Paste Inside command is reinterpreted as a clipping mask. Illustrator will usually warn you when this is happening.

Multiple page files not supported. Illustrator doesn't support more than one page in a document. When opening multiple page documents Illustrator supports, such as a PDF, Illustrator will offer a dialog box, allowing you to choose which page to open.

Drag and drop to open files. File icons may be dragged directly onto the Illustrator application icon (or an alias or shortcut to the application) to open them.

Illustrator can read formats it can't write. The following file formats can be opened by Illustrator but Illustrator cannot write to them: CorelDraw (CDR), Filmstrip (FLM), FreeHand (FH4 to FH9), Kodak PhotoCD (PCD), Microsoft RTF (RTF), and Microsoft Word (DOC). This means you will be able to open one of these files, but will need to save it in a different format.

The Open Dialog Box

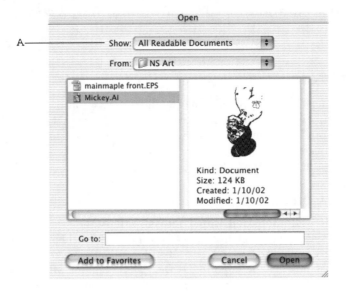

A. **Show**

This pop-up menu enables you to isolate the types of files listed in the window. For example, if you set it to Illustrator (AI), only Illustrator native files will be displayed in the window. If you set it to All Documents, the window lists every file in the directory, whether or not Illustrator can open it. By default, the menu is set to Readable Documents, which displays all the documents Illustrator can open.

7.3

File: Open Recent Files

This submenu displays a list of recently opened files. This way, you can open a file by choosing its name from the submenu, rather than the using the Open command. Only saved files are included in the menu. A new document that was closed without saving will not appear.

7.4

File: Revert

Use this command to reload the document from its saved state. This discards all the changes made and returns the document to the condition it was in the last time you saved. Any dialog boxes associated with opening the file will also be displayed as a document is reverted. This command is not available to new documents that have not been saved.

Issues to Consider

Revert is less common than undo. Often, revert is used because a document is so snarled a user would prefer to start over. Since it is easy to undo many steps in Illustrator, many users prefer to undo repeatedly rather than to revert.

7.5

File: Close   *(Command) [Ctrl]–W*

Choose this command to close the active window. If any changes have been made, you will be prompted with a dialog box giving you options to Save, Don't Save, or Cancel the closing.

7.6

File: Save   *(Command) [Ctrl]–S*

Use this command to write the file into nonvolatile memory. When a file is saved it is written from RAM to a hard drive or some other storage media.

This process is important. Saving a file preserves it in case of system crash and it allows you to place the file into a specific location or directory. The saving process also structures the data so that it may be handled by different applications.

You should save a file early and often. The first time a file is saved, the Save dialog box will open. Take care that the file is saved in the location that you want and given the correct name and format for your purpose. After the initial time a file has been saved, the Save command will update the document without a dialog box.

Mistakes to Avoid

Saving a file in the wrong file format. Illustrator has five file formats it can create from this dialog box. Each format has a specific function. Be certain the format you are writing is the one you intend.

Saving instead of exporting. Illustrator can write fifteen file formats from the File: **Export** command. Each format has a specific function.

Incorrect file saving options. Each of the file formats Illustrator can save has a set of options attached to it. Some Save options, such as earlier version of the file formats, will alter the file data in ways that cannot be recovered later.

Using lazy or disorganized filenames. Doing so makes it hard to locate the appropriate image down the road. Many designers fall into the habit of creating multiple versions of an image, adding the numbers "2," "3," or "4" after each variation. Then they tag the word "final" at the end of their preferred file. If they make a series of last-minute edits, they wind up with file names containing "final 2," or "use this one," which easily leads to the wrong graphic getting imported and used. File names should be as clear and simple as possible. Often, this means using a numerical job-tracking system, but some users name them after the focus or purpose of the image itself.

Failing to include the proper extension in the filename. A dot and the abbreviation for the file format you have selected should be included at the end of the file's name. These extensions are optional for some files on the Mac but required on the PC. Even in Mac-only shops, the convention is required for Internet delivery of files. Further, the habit makes it easier to identify file types without inspection.

By default, Illustrator will not add the extension itself, but it does offer you a check box in the Save dialog box called Append File Extension. Change this option to always add the extension by going to Edit: Preferences: **Files & Clipboard** and choosing Append Extension: **Always**.

Issues to Consider

You can't undo a Save command. You can still undo after having saved a file, though. If you accidentally save a file, you would need to undo or redo to the state you wanted the file and then save again.

Macintosh is the only platform that recognizes four-letter image codes. Windows, Unix, and other platforms require the same three-letter codes. For Mac users, this only becomes an issue when images are being prepared for distribution across platforms.

Avoid adding file extensions manually. Although you can easily type in an extension on your own, try not to, unless you're absolutely sure. There are literally hundreds of different viable extensions. If you add the incorrect extension to a file on a Mac, you may not be able to read it on a PC.

Don't delete the extension when naming the file. Illustrator may automatically add the file extension, but it doesn't prevent you from accidentally removing it. When you first access the Save As dialog box, only the filename (and not the extension itself) is highlighted, which enables you to quickly enter a new name. However, if you highlight part of the current name to modify it, it's easy to include the extension as well, and replace it with whatever text you add.

7.7

File: Save As *(Command-Shift) [Ctrl-Shift]-S*

Use the Save As command to save an additional copy of your image or to change the file format of a file. The command is similar to the first time you save a file. From the same dialog box, you have options to name the file, choose a file format, and place the file into a directory. If the file is given a new name or a new location, a new file is created. The original file will not reflect any of the changes you have made after the last save. The active document will then become the new document.

If the file is given the same name and location, the original file is overwritten by the new one. You will be prompted with a dialog box asking if you are sure you want to do this. This is commonly done to rewrite the file's saving options. For example, if a file were saved without embedded fonts you could use Save As to write over the file, this time embedding the fonts, without creating a second file.

File: **Save As** uses the same dialog box that appears when you initially save a document. The name of the file is automatically inserted into the Name field.

Mistakes to Avoid

Creating unnecessary copies of an image. Unnecessary copies lead to confusion and extra file management.

Accidentally overwriting the original image. If you intend to create a separate file, you must change the name. Leaving the name unchanged and saving it to the same location as the original image overwrites the original with the new copy, just as if you'd chosen File: **Save**.

Saving a new copy to the wrong place. If you assume that Illustrator automatically places the new copy in the right place, it may wind up in the application folder, on the Desktop, a previous job folder, or any other location on your hard drive.

Issues to Consider

Duplicate files from the system, not the application. To copy a file to a new location, such as a Zip disk, save the finished file to your hard drive and move it to the media manually instead of saving it directly from Illustrator. This prevents late edits from being lost on the hard drive version. Save As should be used for creating different versions, not copying identical copies.

7.8

File: Save a Copy   *(Option-Command) [Alt-Control]-S*

Use Save a Copy to write a new version of a file to disc while keeping the current version active. This command is often used to create a series of related files or to record a particular point in the progress of a file.

The command uses the same dialog box as Save As. Illustrator will add the word "copy" to the name of the document.

Issues to Consider

Save a Copy is unaffected by Undo. This makes it easy to apply a technique, Save a Copy of the file and then Undo the command. For example, type could be converted to outlines, saved as a file, and then turned back into live type by undoing the original command.

Save a Copy is well-suited for sequential work. Processes where a series of slightly different files are required are a good fit for the command.

Save a Copy is often used for backsaving. Some workflows require the files be saved to earlier versions of the Illustrator or EPS format. Since saving to earlier versions disables advanced features when the file is read back in, creating a second file is a good way to preserve the original file. Save a Copy enables you to write an earlier version without affecting the current file.

7.9

File: Save As: File Formats

The file formats described in the sections below may be written using the Save As command.

7.10

File: Save As: Adobe Illustrator Document (AI)

The native Illustrator file format is essentially a PDF file. The native version retains all formatting and features and can be used as a brush, swatch, style, or symbol library. Adobe Acrobat can open Illustrator files directly. InDesign and PageMaker 7 can also both place a native Illustrator file.

With each release of Illustrator, new features are added and the native file format is modified. Previous versions of the software cannot handle the new features and cannot open the newer files. To provide the ability to hand a file to someone with an earlier version of the software, you can write to an earlier version of the format. Writing to an earlier version, or "backsaving" will typically cause the file to lose some functionality, even when opened in Illustrator 10.

Mistakes to Avoid

Saving for incompatible applications. Many popular applications, such as QuarkXPress, cannot accept the native Illustrator format. Do not save the file in the native format for use in this workflow. Consider saving as an EPS file instead.

Saving to earlier formats disables features. Saving to an earlier version of the format may change objects. This change will not be apparent until the file is closed and opened or reverted. Backsaving will cause the following (cumulative) changes to your document:

  – **Illustrator 9.** Envelopes and symbol sets are expanded and only editable as objects.
  – **Illustrator 8.** Appearances, transparency, and effects are expanded. This will commonly result in raster art.
  – **Illustrator 7.** Blends, gradient meshes, and brushstrokes are expanded.
  – **Illustrator 6.** Templates are handled differently.
  – **Illustrator 5/5.5.** Imported images are discarded.
  – **Illustrator 4, 3.2, 3.** Gradients are expanded and layers are flattened.

Illustrator Native Format Options Dialog Box

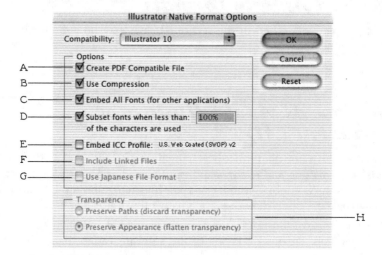

A. **Create PDF Compatible File**

Use this option to write a file that can be opened correctly in Adobe Acrobat. Files saved with this option can be opened directly in Acrobat and are more compatible with other Adobe applications. Without this option, the file opens in Acrobat but only displays text explaining that the document was saved without this option and cannot be displayed.

This option increases the file size of documents, especially those with symbols. Consider the uses of the file when saving.

B. **Use Compression**

This option applies the PDF compression to the document. It reduces the size of the PDF component of the file, but increases the time required to save the file.

C. **Embed All Fonts** (for other applications)

Use this option to include fonts in the document. Including fonts increases the file's size but produces a file that can be printed from another application without the presence of fonts. This is a highly useful option, since it streamlines the hand-off process of files. Embedding fonts does not mean that the text in the document is editable on its own. The document still requires fonts be active and available on a system to set or edit type. This only means that the file can be placed into another application and printed without the fonts it uses being turned on in the system.

D. Subset fonts when less than

Use this option to limit the character outlines that are embedded in the file when using the Embed All Fonts option. Embedding fonts increases file size. This option reduces the characters included in the file to only those actually used, thereby reducing file size. Unchecked, the entire typeface will be embedded.

The value field sets a limit. If more than this percent of the total typeface is used in the document, the entire typeface is embedded. If less than this amount is used, only characters actually used in the document are embedded. Subsetting fonts is a good idea, but it has its downside in some workflows. It makes the type less editable if the file is opened in other applications and the amount of file size savings is not that great. If other applications, such as Acrobat, are apt to edit this file, consider not subsetting.

E. Embed ICC Profile

Check this box to embed the color profile for the current working space into the document. The working space and profile will be either RGB or CMYK depending on the document's color mode. If the color settings for the document are set to Emulate Illustrator 6, this option will not be available.

F. Include Linked Files

Check this option to embed external links upon saving. Linking files creates flexibility in a workflow, but can cause problems when files that contain links are then linked to other files. This option embeds the linked files into the Illustrator file, increasing its file size, but making it more complete for handoff and printing.

G. Use Japanese File Format

This option makes files saved in Illustrator 6 or earlier formats compatible with Japanese systems.

H. Transparency

Use this option to control how unsupported features are translated when saving files to earlier formats. The native file format did not support transparency until Illustrator 9. Saving to 8 or earlier will require that something happen to objects that use transparency.

Preserve Paths (Discard Transparency)

This keeps the core vector shapes and discards the transparency attributes.

Preserve Appearance (Flatten Transparency)

This renders the objects based on the settings in Document Setup. This may result in pixels or vectors or both, depending upon the art used.

7.11

File: Save As: *Adobe PDF (PDF)*

PDF is the Portable Document Format. PDF files are cross platform. Users on Macs, PCs and on Unix systems can read the format. The format is popular because it can embed font and graphics information, creating a self-contained and highly compressed file.

Commonly, the format is read using the free Acrobat Reader application. PDFs are also read in Web browsers equipped with the widespread PDF plug-in. Many documents on the Internet are saved in the PDF format because of its ability to preserve a document's overall appearance and the ease of creating PDFs. PDF files are also a common transmittal method for files between designers, clients, and service bureaus. Adobe's for-cost Acrobat application provides greater functionality for PDF files for proofing and printing.

Mistakes to Avoid

PDF files open in Acrobat. Once saved as a PDF, documents open by default in Acrobat or the Acrobat Reader and not Illustrator. To edit a PDF in Illustrator, you must open the file from within Illustrator. Alternatively, on the PC change the associations for the file. On the Mac in OS X, select the file in the Finder and choose File: **Show Info**. Select the Open with Application option and choose Adobe Illustrator.

Assuming Illustrator can edit all PDF files. PDF files created by saving from Illustrator are easy to open and edit in Illustrator. PDF files created in other ways may not be as easy to edit, and in fact, may not open correctly.

Removing editing abilities incorrectly. When saving a PDF, you will have the option to reduce the document's file size by giving up some of its editing options. In workflows where the PDF is the only file produced, this is usually a poor trade. In a workflow where the PDF is a duplicate file intended for the Internet, it makes more sense.

Issues to Consider

The artboard sets the page size. The PDF file you create will be clipped by the artboard when it is opened in Acrobat. Be sure your artboard is the size you want. Parts of objects outside the artboard will be cropped off. The objects are retained, however and may be edited with Acrobat's Object TouchUp Tool or by opening the document in Illustrator.

Subsetting fonts in a PDF will make the font difficult to edit inside of Acrobat. If your work is being submitted to a service bureau and you'd like them to be able to fix a last minute typo, consider not subsetting.

Acrobat may be a better place to generate thumbnails for a PDF.
Thumbnails generated in Illustrator are based on the bounding box of
the objects, not the artboard size. The thumbnail of the page generated
may not be the same size as the PDF.

Adobe PDF Format Options

PDF options are grouped by function into two sets. One set is designed for
general PDF use, and one for on screen viewing only. Users may set their own
options to create a custom set.

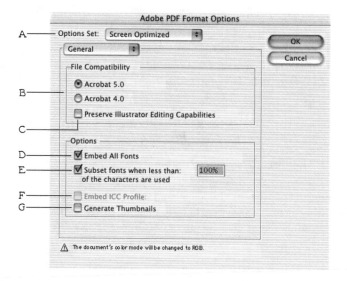

A. Options Set

Choose from the list of options to define a likely group of options for the
file. The Web options set the document to RGB color, reduce the resolution of graphics to monitor resolution (72 dpi for color & gray, 300 dpi
for line art) and reduce the file's size by omitting thumbnails and some
of Illustrator's editing abilities.

B. File Compatibility

Set the level of PDF you wish to create. Acrobat 4.0 is based on the PDF
1.3 format, which does not understand transparency. Transparent
objects saved into the 4.0 format will be expanded and may not print as
anticipated. If there are objects in the document that would be affected
in this way, Illustrator displays a warning in the lower-left corner of the
dialog box.

C. **Preserve Illustrator Editing Capabilities**

Use this option to create a file that is larger in size, but has more editing capabilities. When this function is turned off, Illustrator discards elements other than those required to print the file. The Brushes, Swatches, Styles, and Symbol palettes are all emptied. Effects, Brushes, Blends, Compound Shapes, Symbols, and Envelopes are all expanded. The file is still valid and editable, but the "live" nature of these features is destroyed.

D. **Embed All Fonts**

This option is the same as for a native Illustrator file. *(For more information, see 7.10, File: Save As: **Adobe Illustrator**.)*

E. **Subset fonts when less than _% of the characters are used**

This option is the same as for a native Illustrator file. *(For more information, see 7.10, File: Save As: **Adobe Illustrator**.)*

F. **Embed ICC profile**

This option is the same as for a native Illustrator file. *(For more information, see 7.10, File: Save As: **Adobe Illustrator**.)*

G. **Generate Thumbnails**

Use this option to build thumbnails into the PDF file. A thumbnail is a low-resolution picture of the page's contents. Thumbnails increase file size slightly. Acrobat users use them to make it easier to navigate through a file. Thumbnails may also be generated in Acrobat.

Compression Settings

Use the compression settings to control the handling of pixel images in the document. Raster art may be both compressed and downsampled. Downsampling reduces the number of pixels in an image to fit a set standard. Compression changes the way the pixel data is recorded, potentially by changing the value of the pixels.

Compression and downsampling may be set differently for color, grayscale, and line art images.

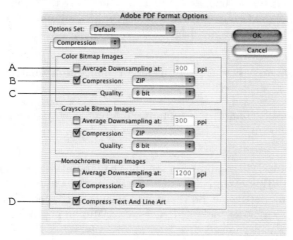

A. Average Downsampling at x ppi

Check these boxes and then use these fields to set the effective resolution of raster art in the file. Effective resolution is the pixels in an inch at the size the object is, regardless of scaling. Downsampling will discard extra pixels to create a file of the resolution called for in the fields. Pixels are never added in this process. For printing, common resolutions for color and grayscale art are 1.5 to 2 times the line screen used to print the work, 800–1200 ppi for line art. For onscreen display, common resolutions are 72 dpi for color and grayscale images, 300 ppi for line art.

B. Compression

Use this menu to set the kind of compression applied to images. Uncheck the box to leave raster art uncompressed. The following choices are available:

Automatic

Illustrator will use the compression scheme it decides is best suited to your art.

JPG

Choose this item to use JPG compression; a lossy method best suited to continuous tone images. JPG is available for Color and Grayscale bitmap images.

Zip

Choose this item to use ZIP compression; a lossless method best suited to images that contain areas of solid color. ZIP is available for all image types.

CCITT

Choose this option to use the kind of compression used in fax machines. The Consultative Committee on International Telegraphy and Telephony developed this lossless model, which is well suited for monochrome images. Most fax machines use the Group 3 option, although the Group 4 is better suited for general use. CCITT is available for monochrome images.

Run Length

This is a lossless scheme available for monochrome images.

C. Quality

Each model of compression supports different quality options. Choose from the following:

JPG

Part of the JPG compression scheme changes pixels' values to reduce file size. This essentially trades file size for quality. Use the Quality menu to determine how strongly images are affected. Maximum results in a better-looking, larger image. Minimum produces a lower-quality smaller image. *(For more information, see 7.24, Export: JPG.)*

Zip

Use this menu to choose the method of ZIP compression used, 8-bit or 4-bit. You should use a method that corresponds to the kind of images that are in the document. If you do, the compression will be lossless, otherwise image quality may suffer. If you are using 4-bit images, you should use 4-bit compression. In all other cases, 8-bit is used. These images are more common and using 8-bit ensures that the compression will be lossless.

D. Compress Text and line art

Use this option to use run length compression on the data that stores text and line art information. In this instance line art refers to vector lines and not monochrome raster art.

7.12

File: Save As: *Illustrator EPS (EPS)*

Use the EPS file format when your workflow involves placing or opening your document into an application that does not support the Illustrator native format. QuarkXPress is a prominent example. EPS, which stands for Encapsulated PostScript is a popular format in the industry and is widely generated and understood. Illustrator can also be read an EPS file as a brush, swatch, style, or symbol library.

Issues to Consider

EPS files cannot contain ICC profiles. You cannot embed a profile for color management inside an EPS file. Additionally, some color management software cannot affect EPS files. These are factors to consider when considering color management workflows.

EPS files preview poorly. When placed into another application, such as QuarkXPress or InDesign, the preview that you see on the page is typically a poor representation of the final art. This is doubly true if the EPS is scaled up. Do not confuse the preview with the printed results.

Previews print to non-postscript printers. Some non-PostScript printers can't handle Illustrator art. When attempting to print Illustrator art, the preview will be printed instead of the vectors. This results in poor quality printing.

EPS Format Options Dialog Box

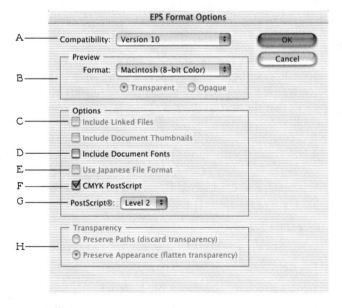

A. **Compatibility**

Set the version of the EPS you wish to create. The feature set for EPS files is analogous to the set for native files. As you save to earlier formats, some features may be altered. See the native Illustrator format section or a list. Saving to an earlier format has no affect on another application's ability to place a file, only to open it. QuarkXPress can place any level of EPS, but Illustrator 8 can only open an Illustrator 8 or earlier EPS.

B. Preview

Use this option to control the screen preview Illustrator builds into the file. This is the preview used when the file is placed into another application, not the preview you see in the Open dialog box. Including a preview increases the file's size, but is important if the file is to printed in any other application.

There are two preview formats, Macintosh and TIFF, each with two color depths, and an option to omit the preview. Most Macintosh applications can read either type of preview. Choose 8-bit to include a full color preview, Black and White to make a line art preview. Both Macintosh formats treat negative space as transparent in the preview. Files on the PC, or going to the PC should be saved with a TIFF preview. TIFF previews may be full color or line art. TIFF format previews may be set to treat negative space as transparent or opaque.

C. Include Linked Files

Check this option to embed external links upon saving. Linking files creates flexibility in a workflow, but can cause problems when files that contain links are then linked to other files. This option adds the linked files to the Illustrator file, increasing its file size, but making it more complete for handoff and printing.

D. Include Document Fonts

Use this option to include fonts in the document. Including fonts increases the file's size but produces a file that can be printed from another application without the presence of fonts. This is a highly useful option, since it streamlines the hand-off process of files. Including fonts does not mean that the text in the document is editable on its own. The document still requires fonts be active and available on a system to set or edit type. This only means that the file can be placed into another application and printed without the fonts it uses being turned on in the system.

This option is similar to the Embed Fonts options available in the native and PDF file formats except that fonts cannot be subset in this model.

E. Use Japanese File Format

This option is associated with the Illustrator 5.5 and earlier file formats.

F. CMYK PostScript

Use this option to include alternate CMYK definitions for RGB objects. Some printers cannot handle RGB data. This option provides a way to print the data without changing the RGB nature of the art.

G. PostScript

Use this option to set the level of PostScript used in the document. This should be set to the level of the printers in your workflow. The PostScript printers used in your workflow will be attached to a specific level of PostScript. Most printers are PostScript level 2. Newer machines may be

Level 3, capable of a much wider dynamic range for gradients and the ability to render gradient meshes as vectors. If you have are going to print to any level 2 devices, set the PostScript Level to 2.

Some old machines only understand PostScript Level 1. To save to the 1 level, you must set the compatibility of the document to Version 8.0.

H. Transparency

When saving an EPS with 8.0 or earlier compatibility, use these radio buttons to discard or maintain transparency. Illustrator may include both raster and vector versions of transparent art. This increases file size, but provides greater flexibility when printing and proofing. Versions 8.0 and earlier did not support transparency.

Preserve Paths

Check to discard transparent effects and maintain the core vector shapes.

Preserve Appearance

Check to expand the appearance of the transparent art based on the settings found in File: **Document Setup**. Depending on how the transparent objects are styled, this expanding will result in either masked raster art, new vector shapes to describe the areas of transparency, or both. In either case the art will not be as editable as it was before.

7.13

File: Save As: SVG (SVG)

SVG stands for Scalable Vector Graphics. It is an XML-based alternative to pixel graphics that are viewable in a Web browser. The browser must be equipped with an SVG viewer plug-in.

In many ways, SVG can be compared to SWF, the other online option for vector graphics. Both offer interaction, sophisticated scripting and animation. SVG has some color and text handling advantages over SWF. Also, SVG is an open format and can be used by anybody without needing to pay royalties to MacroMedia. It is also a refinement of the HTML language, and browsers will soon be written to accommodate it without requiring plug-ins. Currently, though, it is not widely adopted.

There are two file formats associated with scalable vector graphics; SVG and Compressed SVG (SVGZ). The compressed version can be up to 80% smaller than the regular version, but it cannot be edited by a text editor. Both formats use the same dialog boxes when saving.

Issues to Consider

Some objects are rasterized. Gradient meshes are rasterized. Images without Alpha channels are converted to JPGs, images with Alpha Channels become PNGs.

SVG effects need to be at the bottom of the Appearance palette list. If an object uses an SVG filter effect, it must be the last item in the Appearance palette (just before transparency) to function correctly.

SVG Options Dialog Box

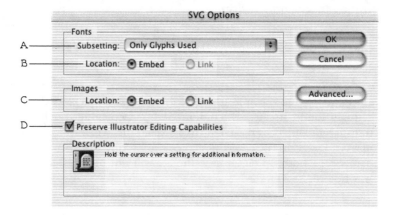

A. Subsetting

Use these options to determine which set of characters are linked to or embedded in the SVG file. The Only Glyphs Used option embeds only characters utilized in the document. The remaining options are typically used when text must be dynamic, such as type a user would enter, or type that came from a server.

B. Location

Use this option to embed or link the character sets. Embedding increases file size, but the characters are always available for the file to use. Choose Link to reduce the file size of the document by linking the SVG file to an exported CEF (Compact Embedded Font) file.

C. Images

Use this option to link or embed raster images into the SVG. As with type, embedding raster art increases file size but ensures the art will be available as needed.

D. Preserve Illustrator Editing Capabilities

Use this option to open and edit the SVG file later in Illustrator. This increases file size, but makes the document more flexible.

Advanced SVG Options

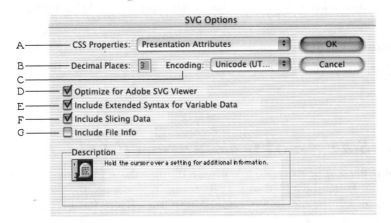

A. **CSS Properties**

These settings determine how style attributes are recorded in the saved file:

Presentation Attributes

This is the default option. It saves the attributes in a manner that allows for the most flexibility for certain edits and transformations.

Style Attributes

This option trades larger file size for the highest degree of flexibility in transformations.

Style Attributes (Entity References)

This model gives quick delivery times and smaller file size.

Style Elements

This model trades slower rendering speed for the ability to move style elements to HTML files.

B. **Decimal Places** (1 to 7)

This option is similar to flatness, only numerically reversed. Higher values result in larger files but better image quality.

C. **Encoding**

This option determines how data is written into the file. UTF 8, the default, is understood by all XML processors. ISO 8859-1 and UTF 16 do not support file metadata.

D. **Optimize for Adobe SVG Viewer**

This option increases rendering time for SVG Filter Effects.

E. **Include Extended Syntax for Variable Data**

This option includes data needed for variable substitution.

F. **Include Slicing Data**

This option maintains information on slice locations and the optimization settings.

G. **Include File Info**

This option includes the file metadata when the UTF-8 encoding model is selected.

7.14

File: Save As: SVG Compressed (SVGZ)

Use this file format to create a smaller SVG file. These files transmit faster online but cannot be edited with a text editor. Typically two files are created, an SVG for editing and an SVGZ for posting. The options for this format are the same as for SVG.

7.15

File: Save for Web *(Option-Command-Shift) [Alt-Control-Shift]-S*

Use this command to create Web optimized pixel graphics and accompanying HTML files. When creating an image for the Web, this command enables you to preview the effect of multiple compression settings and file format options. This way, you can determine the appropriate combination of image quality and file size. For the best results, choose this command for a document in RGB color mode.

Issues to Consider

Don't confuse this command with Exporting. Illustrator can create HTML, JPG and SWF files using the File: **Export** command. Save for Web is a better tool for all pixel-based Web output. It offers a preview, multiple options, transfer times, and slice controls.

Editing slices. The Save for Web command enables you to save an image based on multiple slices (as produced by the Slice tool or Object: Slice commands). When you export the image, it splits into a series of smaller files. The HTML code required to reassemble the image in a Web browser is saved with the components.

Don't be intimidated by the glut of features. The Save for Web command is practically a standalone application. Its interface is complex for the user who simply wants to generate smaller Web graphics. However, the Save for Web command is more efficient than saving an image directly into the desired file format. Once you determine the settings that work best for your particular images, they can be saved and reused easily. Also, the dialog is the same in Photoshop, ImageReady, and GoLive.

The bounding box for type is different than for objects. Art saved for the Web is turned to pixels based on its bounding area. Type objects include the white space for capital letters and leading in their bounding boxes. This will add white space around text you may not want. Consider converting text to outlines before saving for the Web. You can then just Undo the change to get live type back.

The keywords in File Info are not added to any HTML output as metatags. Although they have the same name and general usage, the two technologies are not connected. Keyword metatags need to be added manually to any HTML output.

Only 4.0 level browsers understand CSS Layers. By default, Illustrator translates layers into Cascading Style Sheets layers using the widely understood DIV tag. 3.0-level browsers will not understand this tag. If you want to create HTML with the widest possible audience, consider disabling this feature.

Transparency Grid turned on in the Save for Web dialog box. The displays in this dialog box all show transparency as a checkerboard. Users unfamiliar with this feature should refer to the Document SetUp portion of this chapter.

Save for Web has its own preference file. If the Save for Web feature is behaving poorly, consider deleting its preference file. It will be in the same directory as Illustrator's preferences.

Make your final choices at 100% view depth. In the course of optimizing, you may change the view depth. Be sure to view your settings at 100% to get a clear look at the work before saving.

Save for Web is a dialog box. You can't choose Edit: **Undo** in a dialog box. If you enter a setting or value incorrectly, you will have to reset it manually.

Reset & Remember settings. Hold down the (Option) [Alt] key to change the Cancel and Done buttons to Reset and Remember, respectively. Reset returns the settings in the dialog box to the previously saved or remembered settings. Remember stores the current settings with the file, allowing you to Reset them later. Done differs from Cancel in that it dismisses the dialog box after it remembers the current settings.

The Save for Web Dialog Box

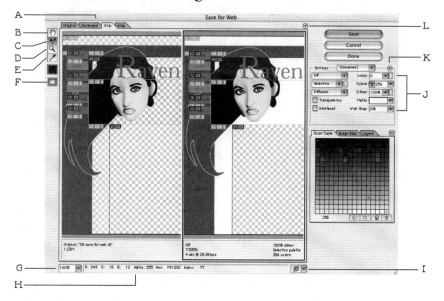

A. View Tabs

These tabs control the preview images that display in the Save for Web dialog box:

Original

Choose this option to display only the original image, with no applied compression.

Optimized

This option displays a single compressed version of the image, based on the current settings of the dialog box.

2-Up

This option displays the original image, plus an optimized version (based on the current settings in the dialog box). As you manipulate the settings, the optimized version changes to reflect the new values. This way, you can compare the compressed image to the original.

4-Up

This option displays the original image, plus three compressed versions. One is based on the current settings, and the other two are automatically given settings that further reduce the quality and file size. This way, you can pinpoint the settings that give you the best balance between size and quality, and still compare them to the original.

Click a preview to specify the settings you want to apply when you click OK. A black border indicates the current preview.

B. **Hand Tool**

Use this tool to scroll the images within the preview frames. When you drag one preview, any others move as well. This way, you can continue to compare the same image areas.

C. **Slice Select Tool**

When the current image contains multiple slices, this tool enables you to select one or more of them by clicking or Shift-clicking. You can't change the size or position of the slices, but you're able to apply different compression settings to each one. Remember that a sliced image ultimately exists as a series of different files; therefore, each one can receive different settings, and can even exist in a different file format. For example, you can draw a slice around an important image area, and then apply settings to it that retain the most detail. You can set the remaining slices to a much lower compression setting, producing an image that takes less time to display on screen.

Double-click a slice to access the Slice options dialog box.

D. **Zoom Tool**

Use this tool to enlarge or reduce the images in the preview frames. It works the same as Zoom tool in the toolbox. When you click one preview with the Zoom tool, the others respond in kind. This enables you to continue comparing the same image areas.

E. **Eyedropper Tool**

Use this tool to sample color values from the image preview. The targeted value appears in the color swatch, located directly beneath the Eyedropper tool. Eyedropper colors are highlighted in the Color Table and are available as a Matte color. Colors sampled with the Eyedropper can be added to the Color Table by clicking the New Color icon in the table.

F. **Toggle Slices Visibility**

When an image contains multiple slices, click this button to display or hide them in the preview frames.

G. **Zoom Level**

This option enables you to choose a predefined zoom percentage from the available pop-up. To zoom to a particular percentage, manually enter the desired value in the field.

H. **Color Readouts**

These items display the current rgb, hexadecimal, Alpha and Index values of the preview color currently underneath the cursor. The Alpha value displays the opacity level of the pixel on a scale from 0 to 255. 0 is transparent and 255 is completely opaque. Only the Original image and PNG 24 images will display an Alpha other than 0 or 255. Index is used for optimizing GIF and PNG 24 files. The index number indicates the colors position in the Color Table.

I. **Preview In**

This option enables you to preview the current image in the Web browser of your choice. When you click this button, your operating system launches the designated browser and opens the image in a new window. The image will open in a temporary HTML page containing the optimized output, the settings used to generate it, and the HTML connected to it.

To set a different browser, choose an item in the Select Browser menu, to the button's immediate right. To add a new browser to the list, choose Other from the menu, then direct Illustrator to the desired program.

J. **Settings**

This pop-up menu displays a list of 14 predefined settings for creating GIF, JPG, or PNG images. You're not committed to using these settings; however, many people use them as a starting point by choosing an option then fine-tuning the values. It's also possible to add your own settings to list.

K. **Optimize Menu**

This menu contains the following items:

Save Settings

Choose this command to save the current settings into a separate file, stored in Illustrator's Optimized folder (Adobe Illustrator 10/Presets/Save for Web Settings/Optimize). The settings are then available as an item in the Settings pop-up menu.

Delete Settings

Choose this command to delete the item currently established in the Settings pop-up menu.

Optimize to File Size

Choose this command to access the Optimize to File Size dialog box, which enables you to compress a Web graphic to a specific file size. From there, you can fine-tune the level of quality by tweaking the remaining settings.

In the dialog box, you can tell the command to use the current Save for Web settings, or you can let it choose GIF or JPG on-the-fly, based on which option produces the best results. Also, if the image contains multiple slices, you can tell the command to apply the size limitation to the currently selected slice, to each image slice, or to the total size of all slices combined.

Repopulate Views

Choose this command to draw new image previews, based on the settings of the currently selected frame. When the dialog box is set to 4-Up, the new previews consist of the following: The original, the preview that was selected when you chose the Repopulate Views command, and two previews that result in smaller file sizes.

Link Slices

> Use this command to connect the optimize settings of at least two selected slices. Linked Slices are optimized using the same settings, so that as you change one slice's optimize settings, the other's changes as well. Linked Slices are indicated with a figure eight "link" icon in the slice. Auto slices are linked automatically.

Unlink Slices

> This command breaks the connection between selected linked slices.

Unlink All Slices

> This command breaks the connection between all linked slices. It has no effect on auto slices.

Edit Output Settings

> Use this command to open the output settings dialog box. The Output Settings dialog box is also available in the Save Optimized As dialog box. Output settings establish conventions for writing HTML. Space prohibits detailing these settings here.

L. **Preview Menu**

The items in this menu enable you to affect the display of the preview images.

Browser Dither

> Choose this option to simulate how a Web graphic will display on an 8-bit color monitor, the type most widely in use around the world. This way, you can anticipate the amount of dithering that will result from the reduced number of colors.

Download Times

> These options determine the download time listed at the bottom of each preview.

GIF Optimization Controls

GIF files are well-suited to images with areas of solid color. GIFs support transparency and, although it cannot be done in Illustrator, animation. The following settings are available when you choose GIF in the Settings pop-up menu.

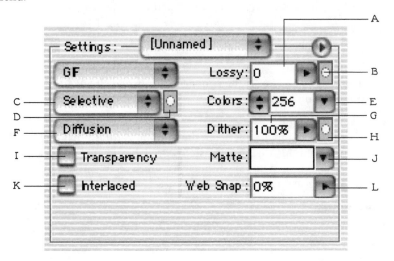

A. **Lossy**

This slider determines how much detail is retained in a GIF image. Low values retain more detail, resulting in higher file sizes; higher values reduce the level of detail, resulting in a lower file size.

B. **Use a Channel to Modify Lossy Setting**

This option enables you to protect part of a GIF from excessive compression. To use this feature, you must select the area and create an Alpha channel before opening the Save for Web dialog box. *(For more information, see 23.5 Save Selection as Channel.)*

Click this button to access the Modify Lossiness Setting dialog box. In the Channel pop-up, set the desired alpha channel. By manipulating the Min and Max sliders, you're able to independently control the amount of compression applied to the masked and unmasked areas.

The starting position of the sliders is based on the current Lossy setting. For example, if the Lossy slider is set to 30, the Min and Max sliders default to 30 and 100, respectively. This means that the area protected by the alpha channel receives the least amount of compression (30), and the unprotected area receives the most (100). If you move the Max slider down to 60, you limit the amount of compression applied to the unmasked areas. If you move the Min slider, you change the current Lossy setting, which in turn increases or decreases the amount of compression applied to the masked area.

For the most intuitive results, set the desired Lossy setting, then manipulate the Max slider to produce the desired balance.

C. Color Reduction Algorithm

The options in this pop-up menu determine the method used to create a GIF image's color table. Choose from the following categories:

Dynamic Options

The Perceptual, Selective, and Adaptive options use an algorithm to create a table based on the relationship between the image colors and the value entered in the Colors field. The table's values are regenerated any time you edit or re-optimize the image.

Fixed Options

The Web, Mac OS, Windows, Black & White, and Grayscale options are fixed, or use a predefined palette of colors. The set of available colors is always constant, but the actual table depends on the colors available in each particular image.

The Custom Option

This option refers to a custom-designed or pre-existing color table. For example, if you modify a color table or optimize an existing GIF, the table is considered Custom.

D. Use a Channel to Influence Color Reduction

This option is essentially the same as "Use a Channel to Modify Lossy Setting," described earlier. Here, the dialog box determines that any colors masked by an alpha channel are reproduced more accurately during the conversion process. (Unlike the other command, this option does not offer sliders for Minimum or Maximum values.)

E. Colors

The Color setting establishes the maximum number of colors available to a new color table. The Auto setting picks a number of colors based on the contents of the image. The number of colors in a table is indicated in the lower left of the color table.

F. Dithering Algorithm

Dithering distributes pixels to create the illusion of more colors. It is especially useful when using a Web palette. Dithering typically increases a file's size. The dithering method determines how the indexed colors are distributed throughout the image. Dithering should be done with caution. Many browsers dither already, and dithering the image as well may degrade it. Be sure to turn on the Browser Dither Preview and view at the size it will be used before adding a dither.

None

With no dithering selected, Illustrator changes each image pixel to its closest equivalent in the color table. In images with more continuous tones, this usually results in harsher color transitions and visible banding. This option does result in smaller GIFs.

Pattern

> This uses a predefined pattern to redistribute the colors, attempting to compensate for the lost tones. It does a poor job, and should not be used.

Diffusion

> This method randomizes the colored pixels, creating the illusion of additional colors.

Noise

> This method is similar to Diffusion, but it randomizes pixels more evenly throughout the image.

G. **Dither Amount**

Available only when you set Diffusion in the Dither pop-up, this field determines the degree of smoothness between color transitions. Higher values result in smoother transitions, but larger file size; lower values result in harsher transitions, but smaller file size.

H. **Use a Channel to Modify Dither Setting**

This option is essentially the same as "Use a Channel to Modify Lossy Setting," described, earlier. Here, the dialog box determines that any colors masked by an alpha channel are reproduced more accurately by the dithering process.

I. **Transparency**

This box enables you to retain a transparent area in the converted image. GIFs support transparency only on Alpha 0 areas. Pixels in a GIF are either transparent or opaque. Partially transparent pixels will be flattened against the Matte color.

J. **Matte**

This option enables you to anti-alias edges against a specific color when including transparency. By default, the edges of a transparent section are not anti-aliased. This causes a jagged appearance. Use this option to matte the edges against the background color of the HTML file the GIF will be placed in, making the edge appear smooth. It is also the color used to fill negative space when transparency is turned off. This option works in conjunction with the Transparency feature in two ways. Both methods require that you know the background color of the Web page that will display the graphic.

First, when the Transparency box is checked, it encircles any soft-edges in the image with the value established in the Matte pop-up menu. This way, when a browser loads the graphic, the edges appear to fade into the background. It doesn't fill the entire image with the matte color—it only fills to the outer perimeter of the edge detail, adding transparency beyond that point. This way, you retain a little flexibility when placing the graphic.

When the Transparency box is unchecked, it fills all transparent and semi-transparent areas in the current with the established Matte color. This way, you retain the appearance of a transparent GIF, without actually building transparency into the file.

K. Interlaced

Check this box to produce an interlaced GIF, or one that gradually refreshes onscreen in multiple passes. When unchecked, the GIF loads all at once.

L. Web Snap

This option enables you to gradually convert each image color to its closest equivalent in the browser-safe palette. At low values, only the colors that differ slightly from their closest equivalent are affected; at higher values, more colors are converted.

In the dialog box's color table, any color converted to its closest browser-safe equivalent is tagged with a small white diamond.

JPG Optimization Controls

JPG files are well suited for images with a lot of continuous tones, The following settings are available when you choose JPG in the Settings pop-up menu. Many of the options also appear in the JPG Options dialog box.

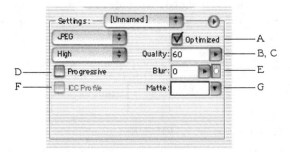

A. Optimized

Presumably, this option "optimizes" the compression method applied to a JPG image. It produces a slightly different type of JPG, called an Optimized or Enhanced JPG. This check box has little if any impact on the overall file size, and it produces an image that is not understood by all browsers.

B. Compression Quality

The items in this pop-up menu enter preset values in the Quality field (15, 30, 60 and 80). These choices do not override the slider, which may still be adjusted.

C. **Quality**

How small you make a file depends on the amount of image quality you want to retain. This slider allows you to set a Quality value from 0 (lowest quality, smallest size) to 100 (highest quality, largest size). Many users decide upon one preferred value for all of their images—a value of 40 or 50 avoids most of the visible artifacting while producing a satisfactory file size.

D. **Progressive**

Progressive images appear in a series of passes, giving the viewer a rough-and-ready idea of how a graphic appears before it's fully refreshed. When this box is unchecked, the image is saved as a baseline JPG, which appear in your browser one line at a time, from top to bottom.

E. **Blur**

This option hinges on the fact that JPG compression reduces the size of soft transitions more successfully than hard color breaks. In theory, it stands to reason that blurring the image would enable you to reduce the file size without raising the compression setting. In practice, however, raising the blur setting above zero produces little more than a blurry image. Ignore this option and lower the Quality slider, if necessary.

F. **ICC Profile**

When this box is checked, the image's color profile is included in the JPG file. However, the average browser cannot recognize embedded profiles. Leave this option unchecked and save the addition 3–4K in file size.

G. **Matte**

When you choose a color from the pop-up menu, it replaces the image's transparent areas. (Choose the Other item to define your own value.) When you save the file, the image is flattened.

PNG-8 Optimization Controls

The options that appear when PNG-8 is set in the Settings pop-up menu are also available when optimizing a GIF. (For full descriptions of their purpose, see "GIF Optimization Controls," earlier this section.)

PNG-8 files can contain up to 256 separate colors. Like GIF, it is appropriate for areas of solid color, and sharp details such as line art or type. A PNG-8 file uses a more advanced compression scheme than GIF, and therefore tends to be 10–30% smaller than a GIF of comparable dimensions. However, browser support for this format is limited.

PNG-24 Optimization Controls

The options that appear when PNG-24 is set in the Settings pop-up menu are also available when optimizing a GIF. (For full descriptions of their purpose, see "GIF Optimization Controls," earlier this section.)

PNG-24 files support 24-bit color. Like JPG, they are appropriate for preserving the fine details of a continuous-tone image. Like GIF and PNG-8, it is able to preserve crisp detail, such as line art, logos, or type. PNG-24 also supports multilevel transparency, which preserves up to 256 levels of transparency to smoothly blend the edges of an image with the background color. A PNG-24 file uses the same lossless compression method as PNG-8, and therefore tends to be larger than a JPG of comparable dimensions. Browser support for this format is limited.

SWF Optimization Controls

The options for optimizing SWF files with this interface are the same as the File: Export: **SWF** options except that the Save for Web version has no control over raster art. Using Save for Web enables you to create HTML files that integrate Flash and other file formats by slicing. For more information on SWF options, see the Export section later in this chapter.

SVG Optimization Controls

The options for optimizing svg files with this interface are the same as the File: **Save** options. Using Save for Web enables you to create HTML files that integrate Scalable Vector Graphics and other file formats by slicing. For more information on SVG options, see the Save section earlier in this chapter.

Color Table Controls

Use the Color Table to control the specific pixel colors used in a file. Only GIF and PNG images contain a color table.

To edit a color in the table, double-click on it. The transparency color swatch (indicated by a checkerboard) cannot be edited. Colors may be selected by clicking on them. Shift-click to select a sequence of contiguous colors in the table. (Command) [Ctrl] click to select noncontiguous swatches. Colors are highlighted when pixels of that color are clicked with the eyedropper.

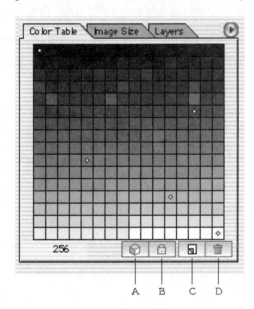

A. **Web Snap**

This shifts selected swatches to the nearest equivalent Web safe colors. Web safe colors are indicated in the table with a white diamond.

B. **Lock Color**

This prevents colors from being snapped to Web safe or being omitted if the color number is reduced. Locked colors. Click again to unlock colors. Locked colors are indicated with a square tab in the lower right.

C. **New Color**

Click to add the Eyedropper Color to the Color Table as a locked swatch.

D. **Delete Color**

Click to delete selected swatches from the color table.

Color Table Menu

The commands in the color table's submenu enable you to sort, select, and otherwise interact with the different values.

Image Size Controls

Use the Image Size tab to set the geographic size of the pixel image produced. This does not affect the size of the vector graphics at all. The original size is listed for reference.

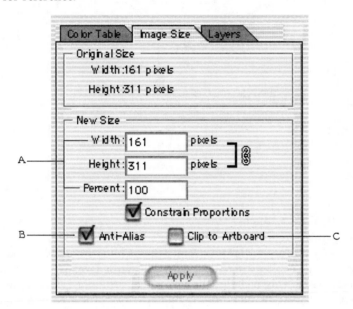

A. **Size Fields**

Set the width and height of the output using the pixel dimensions or the percent field. The Constrain Proportions check box locks the width and heights together, so that they scale proportionally.

B. **Anti-Alias**

Check to produce pixels with anti-aliased edges. Anti-aliasing produces smoother edges by changing the colors of edge pixels.

C. **Clip to Artboard**

Check to set the size of the artwork to the artboard size, rather than the bounding areas of the objects. Objects outside the artboard will be cropped.

Layers Controls

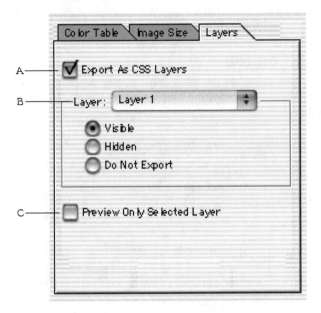

A. **Export As CSS Layers**

Check this box to convert Illustrator's layers to Cascading Style Sheet Layers. Layers are a DHTML feature that is understood by 4.0 or higher level browsers. The content of each Illustrator layer is written into an HTML layer. This includes the tables that are used to assemble sliced graphics. Slices are often used in interactivity. For this reason, layers can be shown and hidden on export.

B. **Layer**

Each layer in the Illustrator file is listed in this menu. Select the Layer to be controlled from the list. Choose from the radio buttons to make each layer Visible, Hidden, or not exported. Hidden layers are included in the file, but are not shown by default. Commonly, a script or link will be used to show the layer on some event.

C. **Preview Only Selected Layer**

Click to hide the other layers from the preview window.

7.16

File: *Place*

Use the Place command to incorporate other files into an Illustrator document and to create template layers for tracing. Illustrator can place all of the formats it can open. Once chosen from the Place dialog box, art centers itself in the current window.

Placed files can be linked or embedded. Linked files are indicated by two intersecting diagonal lines in the bounding box. Embedded files are completely copied into the Illustrator file. Linked files are referenced, but not completely copied into the Illustrator document. As the referenced file changes, the data in the Illustrator document can change as well. Embedded art cannot be updated automatically in this manner. Links are managed in the Links palette. *(For more information, see 26.1, Links Palette Overview.)*

Placing as a template creates a new layer at the bottom of the layer stack with the template option activated. The new layer will be named "template x" with x being the placed file's name. *(For more information, see 25.6, Template Layers.)*

Issues to Consider

Embedded art is editable. The effect is the same as pasting the art into the document. Linked art is editable, but some features do not work on linked art. For example, you may set the opacity of linked raster art, but not apply many of the filters to it.

Illustrator Native and Illustrator EPS files do not appear in the Place dialog by default. You may still place these formats by choosing All Documents in the Show field.

Linked files are independent. Linked files must be present and in the correct directory for the file to be printed correctly.

Linked art can be embedded upon saving. When saving as an Illustrator native or EPS file, linked art can be embedded using the Include Links option. PDF, and SVG graphics embed all linked art. Once embedded, the connection to the external file is severed.

Text file formats cannot be linked. Text documents, like RTF and TXT cannot be linked but must be embedded instead.

Placed art may contain conflicting color definitions. Documents placed may contain swatches with the same names as existing swatches. The colors may also be defined differently, causing a change to existing objects. Illustrator will warn you when this is about to happen and allow you to keep the current definition or accept the imported one.

Place Dialog Box Options

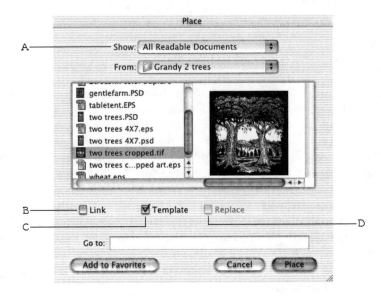

A. Show

Use this list to isolate a particular file format you are looking for, to view all the files in a directory, or to show all readable formats.

B. Link

Click to link the external file rather than embedding it.

C. Template

Click to add the art to the document as a template

D. Replace

Use this option to swap a selected link with a new one. To use this option, a linked file must be selected before choosing Place. The replacement file will be aligned about the center of the old file.

7.17

File: Export

Use this command to create a new file based on the current document. This command is commonly used to generate file formats not available through Save or Save for Web. Typically, this is needed when the file is to be processed in a different application or by a user that does not have a copy of Illustrator. This command does not alter the current file or the saved version of the file in any way. Export is not affected by Undo.

Issues to Consider

Illustrator and Photoshop can swap files easily. Although you can export a Photoshop file, you can also copy and paste and drag and drop Illustrator objects directly into Photoshop.

Exporting flattens many Illustrator features. None of Illustrator's live effects like brushes or envelopes will remain editable upon reopening the exported file in Illustrator. This seems obvious for raster formats, but it is also true for vector formats like the metafiles.

7.18

File: Exportable File Formats

The file formats described in the following sections may be exported from Illustrator 10.

7.19

File: Export: AutoCAD Drawing (DWG) & Interchange File (DXF)

Both of these file formats are standards in the Computer Aided Drafting (CAD) industry of engineers and architects. The Drawing format is the standard file produced by CAD applications and the Interchange format is the tagged data file version. Commonly, AutoCAD users prefer the DWG file. Both formats have the same set of file options.

DXF/DWG Options Dialog Box

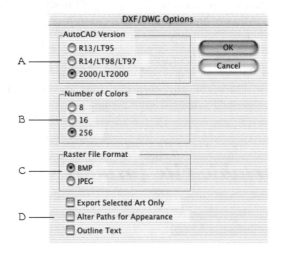

A. **AutoCAD Version**

Use this option to set the file compatibility for the level of the user who receives the file.

B. **Number of Colors**

AutoCAD files are converted to RGB color and can contain only a limited number of colors. Use this option to set the number available in the file.

C. **Raster File Format**

Use this option to encode pixel data in the image as BMP or JPEG format. This option only affects how the raster art is handled. The exported file has its own format.

D. **Options**

Use these options to affect how the objects are handled. Export Selected Art Only discards all but selected objects in the document. Alter Paths for Appearance re-creates vectors based upon any envelopes, compound shapes or Styles that may effect the objects shape. Outline Text converts type into outlines.

7.20

File: Export: BMP

BMP is a raster file native to some PC applications. It supports high resolution but not separation color. BMP files are generally not the first choice for file format among graphic arts professionals.

The BMP file options start with a portion of the rasterize dialog box. Set the resolution of the art to one of the common presets or a custom value. Set the Color Mode of the art to RGB, Grayscale, or bitmap. Art can also be anti-aliased to create smoother edges. Next, in the BMP Options dialog box, set the File For Windows or OS/2. If you selected grayscale in the rasterize dialog, you may choose from 4- or 8-bit depth. 8-bit color is 256 grays, 4-bit is 16 grays. Grayscale Windows BMPs can also be compressed using run length encoding.

7.21

File: Export: Computer Graphics Metafiles (CGM)

Metafiles are a class of files commonly used on the PC to transfer vector data. CGM is a vector-based file format typically used in architectural drawings. Like all metafiles, it is easily changeable between applications that support it. CGM files convert color to RGB and break some Illustrator objects into simpler segments. They do not completely support all Illustrator features and will convert objects to pixels or expand them to maintain their appearance. There are no user definable options for this format. Files export into the same directory as the Illustrator file with the same base name.

7.22

File: Export: Enhanced Metafile (EMF)

Enhanced Metafiles are vector metafiles that support 32 bit color. This means they support CMYK. They do not completely support all Illustrator features and will convert objects to pixels or expand them to maintain their appearance. There are no user definable options for this format. Files export into the same directory as the Illustrator file with the same base name.

File: Export: JPEG (JPG)

JPEG stands for the Joint Photographic Experts Group, which devised the format. Use the JPG format for images intended for the Web and as a compressed alternate to TIFF or PSD. JPGs may also be created using the Save for Web command. A key difference in the two methods is the ability to define high-resolution and CMYK output using export. JPG is commonly used for archiving images and in clip art photo CDs. Because of the compression model they use, JPGS are ill-suited for images with areas of flat color.

JPEG Options Dialog Box

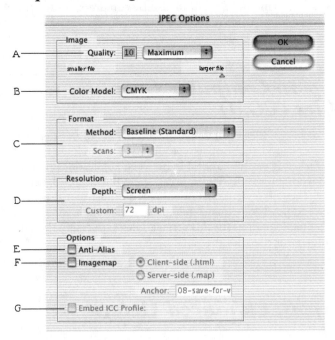

A. Quality

Use this option to control the level of compression applied to the image. JPG compression may change pixel data to reduce file size. This can result in artifacts and color shifts. The more compression is applied, the more the image is damaged.

Quality is measured on a scale from 0 to 10, with 10 being the least compression and damage. Use the slider or quality field to set the value or choose a preset amount from the Quality pop-up menu. Unlike Save for Web, this dialog offers no preview to project the effects of the compression. Many users find a value of 5 or 6 produces a good balance of quality and compression.

B. **Color Model**

Use this menu to set the color model of the pixels created to CMYK, RGB or grayscale. Web browsers cannot display images in the CMYK mode.

C. **Format**

Use this menu to determine the way a JPG loads in a Web browser. Baseline (Standard) loads one line at a time from the top down. Baseline Optimized files load the same way but are structured differently to be more compressed. They are not as universally accepted as Baseline (Standard). Progressive JPGs load in passes, or scans, of increasing detail. This affords the viewer a sense of the graphic without having to wait. Set the number of scans from the pop-up menu. The more scans there are, the faster it will refresh but the longer it will take to load over-all.

D. **Resolution**

Use this to set the number of pixels created in the resulting file. Screen produces 72 dpi, Medium 150 dpi and High makes 300 dpi images. Choose Custom to activate the Custom field, enabling you to define your own value.

E. **Anti-Alias**

Check to generate pixels with anti-aliased edges. This produces the appearance of smoother curves.

F. **Imagemap**

Check to generate an .HTML or .MAP file as well as a JPG when used in conjunction with the imagemap feature in the Attributes palette. Imagemaps designate areas within Web pages as links to other pages. Users click an object to go to another page. Imagemaps may be built into the HTML page viewers load (Client-side) or resident on the server that pushes the HTML files (Server-side). The Anchor field designates the name for the map in the code.

G. **Embed ICC Profile**

Check this box to embed the color profile for the current working space into the document. The working space and profile will be either RGB or CMYK depending on the document's color mode. If the color settings for the document are set to Emulate Illustrator 6 this option will not be available.

7.24

File: Export: Macintosh PICT (PCT)

The Picture (or PICT) format is a Macintosh file format intended for display. The format is not widely support on Windows. PICTs support vector shapes, but convert type to outlines and render many objects with rasters. PICTs do not support CMYK color. Occasionally, PICTs are used because of their compatibility with lower-end applications. Unlike Photoshop, Illustrator does not offer any user definable options for the PICT. Files export into the same directory as the Illustrator file with the same base name.

7.25

File: Export: Macromedia Flash (SWF)

Use this command to generate files to be viewed in Web browsers, the Flash Player, and for import into Flash. Flash is Macromedia's SWF authoring program. Adobe LiveMotion and Swift3D also produce SWF files. SWF files are the most widespread vector format on the Web today. They may contain pixels, but are famous for their animation and interactivity features. SWF files can be printed at high resolution, but are not typically part of a print workflow. SWF files use RGB color.

Illustrator can write its layers to SWF as one static image file, as a series of static image files, or as a sequenced animation. Because there are almost no timing controls available, only simple loop animations are typically generated directly out of Illustrator.

Issues to Consider

Exporting bypasses slices. When you export to SWF, the entire document is exported as a whole, rather than a series of slices. This means you can't set up different portions to different formats.

Imagemaps are resident in HTML, not in SWF. If you're using the imagemap feature in the Attributes palette to create links, the map is created in the HTML file you export, not in the SWF. This is important if you intend to use the SWF by itself or in a different HTML document.

Not all Illustrator features translate to SWF. Some objects are flattened and colors may shift. In most cases the art retains its appearance, if not its editability or original format.

Illustrator symbols and symbol sets become graphic symbols and instances in Flash. Symbols used in an Illustrator document are passed directly to SWF and become Flash graphic symbols. The objects on the page become instances of the symbol. Changes made by the symbolism tools, such as staining, are translated as Effects. Other Illustrator objects are brought in as Groups. This direct recognition of symbols is handy and reduces file size.

SWFs require a plug-in to read. Although the vast majority of Web browsers are capable or reading an SWF file, it does require a plug-in. Some viewers may not be capable of seeing an SWF without downloading and installing a free plug-in first.

Macromedia Flash (SWF) Format Options

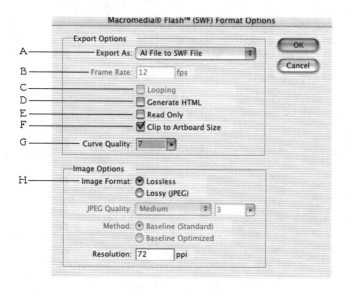

A. Export As

Use this pop-up menu to control the conversion of Illustrator's Layers to SWF.

AI File to SWF File

Choose this option to generate a single, static SWF file. This is commonly done when using the image as a graphic on a Web page or when preparing a file that will imported into Flash for animating. Layers are not translated into Flash Layers.

AI Layers to SWF Frames

Choose this option to generate a single SWF file with the contents of each layer populating a frame. The layers are written to frames from bottom to top, with the lowest layer being the first frame. This is commonly done to produce an animated sequence.

AI Layers to SWF Files

Choose this option to write each layer to its own SWF file. Each new file is named sequentially for the layer it came from. The Layer on the bottom of the stack is named "file_L1.SWF" with "file" being the name of the original Illustrator file. Each subsequent layer is named using the same convention. This is commonly done in preparation of editing the files in Flash.

B. Frame Rate

Use this option to set the speed at which frames are displayed in the SWF file. This is only available when exporting to frames. The default frame rate is 12 frames per second, which is also the default in Flash. The rate of 12 frames per second is enough to show smooth movement and transfer quickly.

C. Looping

Use this option to instruct the SWF to play again upon completing the sequence of frames. This is common for techniques such as making animated banner ads. This is only available when exporting to frames.

D. Generate HTML

Use this option to generate an HTML document to control your SWF file. SWF files can be viewed directly in a Web browser without being inside of an HTML page. When viewed directly, SWF files resize themselves to fit the browser window and are viewed using browser default parameters. An HTML file instructs the browser to display the art at the size it was created and sets parameters for its viewing.

E. Read Only

Use this option to generate a file that can only be read. This protects the file from being imported into another application, including Flash. This is usually done to keep other people from picking up your work and reusing it. Do not choose this option if you intend to import or edit the SWF later.

F. Clip to Artboard size

This option sets the bounding area for the SWF based on the artboard size and not the bounding area of the images.

G. Curve Quality

Use this slider to reduce curve integrity and file size. Setting this option to low amounts distorts curves, creating angles, and lumps. Setting to higher amounts preserves the integrity of the path, but results in a larger file. Many users leave this option set to the default 7, which produces no noticeable curve degradation.

H. Image Format

Use these options to control the resolution and compression of pixels in the SWF. Pixels are passed to the SWF from images in the document and in the translation of some Illustrator objects that SWF does not support. *(For more information, see A.5, Preparing a file for SWF.)*

Image Format

Set this to Lossless or Lossy (JPG) to compress the data. The terms Lossy and Lossless refer to the fact that some compression schemes change pixel values to reduce their file size (lossy) and some do not (lossless). The lossy model used is JPG. Choose lossy or lossless based on the kinds of pixel data you are exporting. Photographs and images with a lot of gradients are better served with JPG compression. *(For more information, see 7.15, File: Save for Web.)*

Resolution

Use this option to set the resolution of the pixel objects created. This affects the print quality of the objects, not the geographic size of them. If the SWF is intended only for online viewing a 72 ppi resolution is appropriate. If you intend to print the SWF as well, a print ready resolution should be considered. Increased resolution also increases file size and transfer time.

7.26

File: Export: PCX (PCX)

PCX is the PC Paintbrush native format. PC Paintbrush is an older application, but it is still in use today. The format is pure pixels, supports high resolution and full RGB color. Use the options to set the resolution of the art to one of the common presets or a custom value. Set the Color Mode of the art to RGB, Grayscale, or bitmap. Art can also be anti-aliased to create smoother edges.

7.27

File: Export: Photoshop (PSD)

Use this command to generate a Photoshop native file. This is commonly done in preparation for editing work in Photoshop or ImageReady. Typically, this is done to produce an effect or perform a task that cannot be done easily in Illustrator. Although it renders most objects as pixels, this format retains more editing features than any other pixel format.

Issues to Consider

Illustrator objects may also be pasted or dragged directly into a Photoshop document. Text that is pasted or dragged does not remain live type. Exporting should be used to translate a complete document into the Photoshop format. Use Copy & Paste to convert individual objects on demand.

Some Illustrator features are not fully supported by versions of Photoshop prior to version 6. Illustrator's Compound Shapes, for example, are correctly interpreted as Shape Layers in Photoshop 6. Shapes Layers are a Photoshop 6 feature that is not supported by earlier versions.

Template layers are not included when exporting. Convert template layers to regular layers before exporting if you want to include them in the PSD file.

Hidden objects are not exported. However, hidden layers are included when determining the overall space the file occupies, and may add white space to the PSD file.

Photoshop Options Dialog Box

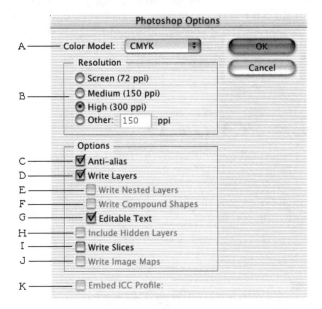

A. Color Model

Use this pop-up menu to choose the color mode of the document produced. By default, this will be the same color mode as the Illustrator document. Choose from RGB, CMYK, and Grayscale.

B. Resolution

Use this option to set a document resolution appropriate for the document's purpose. Choose from one of the common settings or choose Other to create a custom setting. Set resolution for work to be printed based upon the line screen of the best device it will be printed on. Remember that line screen is not the same as printer resolution. A common standard for file resolution is 1.5 to 2 times the line screen. High-end commercial printing is often done at a 150 line screen. Multiply by 2, and you get the 300 ppi resolution in the High setting. A laser printer may only be able to print to 75 lines per inch, requiring a 150 ppi file.

C. Anti-Alias

Anti-aliasing provides a one-pixel transition along the edges of objects. The transitional pixels blend colors together and objects to transparent space as needed. The effect is slight but substantial. The thin blend disguises the jagged stair-stepping of pixels, creating a much smoother line to the eye. This is an important check box to activate. Unless you have a specific reason for turning it off, it should always be used.

D. Write Layers

Use this option to generate Photoshop layers to match the Illustrator layers in the document. This maintains the ability to organize and access objects. It is also an excellent way to maintain the shapes of overlapping objects and a key to creating live text layers in Photoshop. Unchecked, the generated PSD will contain a single, merged layer, discarding the contents of any hidden layers. It is worth noting that even with Write Layers unchecked, the PSD created will contain a Layer and not a Background Layer.

Activating the Write Layers option enables further options related to writing layers.

E. Write Nested Layers

Use this option to translated Illustrator's nested layers into Photoshop Layer sets. This retains the organizational structure implied by nesting layers. This option is only available in documents that contain nested layers and when the Write Layers option is selected.

F. Write Compound Shapes

Use this command to convert Illustrator compound shapes into masked Photoshop shape layers. Photoshop retains the live relationship of the compound shapes, allowing you to further modify the paths in Photoshop. Do not confuse compound shapes with compound paths. Compound shapes are only created using the Pathfinder palette. Objects created using the similar Effect: **Pathfinder** are also not translated to shape layers using this command. This option is only available in documents which contain compound shapes and when the Write Layers option is selected.

G. Editable Text

Use this option to convert text into Photoshop text layers. This maintains the editable nature of the text, and allows it to be included in the Photoshop document as actual type. To retain the stacking order, Illustrator writes all the objects in the layer with the text as separate Photoshop layers. The layers are grouped together as a Photoshop layer set, named for the Illustrator layer. This option is only available in documents which contain text objects and when the Write Layers option is selected.

H. **Include Hidden Layers**

Use this option to retain hidden layers in the exported PSD. Without this option, Illustrator discards any layers that are not visible. This option is only available in documents that contain hidden layers and when the Write Layers option is selected.

I. **Write Slices**

Use this option to include Illustrator slices in the generated PSD.

J. **Write Image Maps**

Use this option to include image maps created using the Attributes palette in the generated PSD file. This option is only available in RGB documents and only ImageReady can read image maps.

K. **Embed ICC Profile**

Check this box to embed the color profile for the current working space into the document. The working space and profile will be either RGB or CMYK depending on the document's color mode. If the color settings for the document are set to Emulate Illustrator 6 this option will not be available.

7.28

File: Export: *Pixar (PXR)*

Check this box to export a rasterized version of the file in the PXR format. Pixar is a company that produces high-end 3D animation, including the famous *Toy Story*. The PXR format is associated with individual frames of that animation. The PXR options are rasterize options: RGB or Grayscale model, resolution, and anti-aliasing.

7.29

File: Export: *Targa (TGA)*

Use this command to export a rasterized version of the file in the Targa format. Images are saved in the Targa format to be imported and combined with digital video sequences driven by video boards from TrueVision, Media 100, and Radius. Exporting will start with the common rasterize dialog box, offering options for RGB or Grayscale color, resolution, and anti-aliasing. When saving RGB, the Targa Options dialog box offers bit depth choices for 16, 24, or 32 bits/pixel. At 32 bits per pixel, the exported file will contain an Alpha Channel marking the transparent areas. This is useful in compositing when replacing areas with video, as in a chroma-key.

7.30

File: Export: Text Format (TXT)

Use this option to export text to the .TXT format. TXT is a widely accepted format for transferring text between documents. Almost any application capable of importing text can understand TXT. The format does not retain any text styling or font information and only the text is exported. Graphics are not included.

If a text selection is made, only the selected text will be exported. With no text selected, all the type in the document is exported. Text may be selected for export using the Type tool or a selection tool. Most basic forms of type are available for export, including path, area, and point type. Type in a graph is not exportable, nor is type used as a scatter brush or in symbols. In the event that you have selected only nonexportable type or that the document does not contain type, Illustrator generates a TXT file that says "no text in the document." Be sure to inspect your TXT file upon export to ensure correctness.

7.31

File: Export: Windows MetaFile (WMF)

The Windows MetaFile is an RGB vector format commonly used for clip art in Microsoft Office for Windows. The format does a clumsy job handling curved paths, adding many points to the path, and making them harder to edit. They do not completely support all Illustrator features and will convert objects to pixels or expand them to maintain their appearance. There are no user definable options for this format. Files export into the same directory as the Illustrator file with the same base name.

7.32

File: Manage Workgroup

The Manage Workflow commands make possible a collaborative online imaging environment, in which multiple users are able to download, edit, and upload the same images without the risk of accidentally overwriting or losing the files. This workflow is based on Web Distributed Authoring and Versioning (WebDAV) server technology, which is also supported by Photoshop 6 and ImageReady 3.

When files (or assets) are managed by a WebDAV server, the user experience is as follows:

- Multiple users can download copies of the same asset.

- One user at a time can check out an asset, or lock the original file on the server while editing a copy of it in a remote location.

- After making changes to an asset, the user can then upload the changes to the server. This way, other users are able to download the new information, but not make changes to it.

- When finished with an asset, the user checks it in, or makes the new version available for downloading and editing.

You must be able to connect to an existing WebDAV server before using this feature. *(For additional information, visit www.webdav.org.)*

7.33

File: Manage Workgroup: Open

This command is only available after you've checked out an asset from a WebDAV server, and the file is open in Illustrator. Choose it to upload your changes to the server and release your lock on the file.

7.34

File: Manage Workgroup: Checkout

Use this command to check out a file that you already have open from a workgroup server.

7.35

File: Manage Workgroup: Cancel Check Out

This command enables you to check in an asset without updating changes to the server. The original file is untouched, as if it were never checked out. Use this option when you don't want to save any changes you've made.

7.36

File: Manage Workgroup: Save

Use this command to save a checked out file from a workgroup server.

7.37

File: Manage Workgroup: *Save As*

Use this command to save a checked out file from a workgroup server using the Save As dialog box.

7.38

File: Manage Workgroup: *Place*

Use this command to place a file you have checked out and opened.

7.39

File: Manage Workgroup: *Logoff All Servers*

Use this command to log out of all active workgroup servers.

7.40

File: Manage Workgroup: *Workgroup Servers*

Use this command to upload a local copy of a file to a managed server.

Issues to Consider

Downloading changes only. To download any changes to an asset from its managed file on the server, open the local file and choose File: Manage Workflow: **Download from Server**.

Setting download options. To access the download option preferences, choose Edit: Preferences: **Workgroup**. Set one of the following items in the Download from Server pop-up menu:

• **Always.** When you set this item, Illustrator automatically downloads any changes to the asset when you open the local file.

• **Ask.** Here, when you open the local file, a dialog box will appear if any changes have been made to the original asset.

• **Never.** Here, no dialog box appears when changes have been made to the original asset. You must update the local file manually, by choosing File: Manage Workgroup: **Open**.

7.41

File: Scripts

Use this command to execute a script. Scripts are a way to automate behavior in Illustrator. Scripts are similar to Actions, but more powerful. An Action can instruct Illustrator to perform a series of commands, but a script can instruct your computer to perform a series of commands. This could involve other applications as well as a series of steps or Actions in Illustrator. Scripts for Illustrator may be written in JavaScript, AppleScript, or Visual Basic.

Illustrator's predefined scripts are contained in the directory Adobe Illustrator/Presets/Scripts. Positioning a script in this directory and re-launching Illustrator will add it to the pop-up list of scripts Illustrator offers.

7.42

File: Document Setup *(Option-Command) [Alt-Ctrl]-P*

Use the Document Setup dialog box to set document options related to the artboard, transparency, and printing. Document Setup controls both printing from Illustrator and the way objects are treated when printing from other applications.

The dialog box is broken into three portions: Artboard, Printing & Export, and Transparency.

7.43

File: Document Setup: Artboard

Use these options to set the size of the artboard, the handling of raster images in outline mode, and the way the pages tile when printed from Illustrator. The artboard sets the page size when saving to PDF, but it is not the same as Page Setup.

Artboard Options

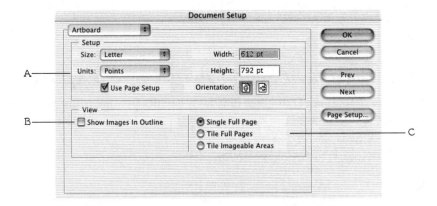

A. Setup

Use these settings to control the size of the pasteboard. This is often done to adjust settings set in the New Document dialog box. Choosing a common dimension from the Size pop up menu populates the width and height fields with the measure listed in the Units menu. The Units field also sets the Ruler units for the document. Ruler units default to the General setting in the Units and Undo preference, but may be set independently. As with all fields in Illustrator palettes and dialogs, any unit of measure entered directly in the fields will be translated to the default units.

Check Use Page Setup to set the width and height to match the Page Setup dimensions. You may still adjust the width and height settings, but if you do, Use Page Setup will become unchecked.

B. Show Images in Outline

Check this box to display previews of raster images rather than bounding boxes when in outline mode. Raster images preview in outline mode by default when on Template layers whether this box is active or not.

C. Page Tiling

Use these radio buttons to control the way documents print from Illustrator. The printable area from Illustrator is called the Page Tiling. The Page Tiling size is set by the Page Setup size. By default, the Page Tiling is set to single Full Page. Only one page prints from Illustrator. Choosing Tile Full Pages places as many full page tiling areas as can completely fit on the artboard. This option is commonly used to design spreads and crossovers. The artboard must be large enough to completely contain multiple pages for this option to have any effect. Choose Tile Imageable Areas to completely fill the artboard with page tiling areas. The entire artboard will be printed, regardless of the number of pages it takes or if the page tilings fit completely into the artboard. To manually reposition page tilings, the Page tool is used. *(For more information, see 4.40, Page Tool.)*

7.44

File: Document Setup: *Printing & Export*

Use these settings to control how Illustrator handles printing paths, gradients, and gradient meshes.

Printing & Export Options

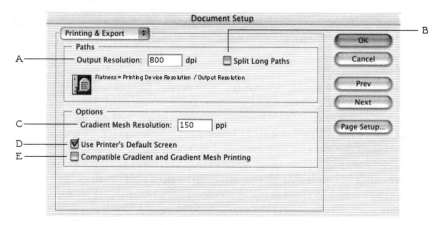

A. Output Resolution

This option is used to determine the accuracy of curved paths when printing by setting the default output resolution of objects. Since printers print short, straight lines and not curves, curved lines are expressed as many side polygons for printing. Output resolution is used to determine how accurately the paths are expressed. Flatness is a measure of the accuracy of paths upon printing. A higher flatness value results in a less accurate, but easier to process curve. Flatness can be calculated by dividing the printers resolution by the Output Resolution of the document. For example, printing a document with the default 800 dpi output setting to a 2400 dpi imagesetter results in a flatness of 3. This is an accurately low flatness. A flatness of 3 is fine for laser printers. Imagesetters may print up to a flatness of 8.

Output resolution is commonly used when files are printing slowly or not at all. Output resolution is lowered to increase flatness.

B. **Split Long Paths**

This option breaks a path Illustrator considers long into a series of shorter paths in an attempt to resolve printing problems. This may irrevocably alter the appearance of paths. For this reason, Split Long Paths is typically only enabled when a document fails to output correctly, and should only be enabled on a copy of a file. The principle behind split long paths is that a series of open filed paths, if positioned correctly, will print the same as a single long complex path and is easier to process. This doesn't always happen and, after splitting, the path is less editable.

C. **Gradient Mesh Resolution**

This setting controls the resolution used for gradient mesh objects when printing to a non-PostScript Level 3 printer. Only Level 3 PostScript printers can output Gradient Meshes as vector shapes. When printing to other devices, Illustrator temporarily substitutes a raster version of the objects. The vector shapes are retained in the document and only printed as rasters.

D. **Use Printer's Default Screen**

By default, gradient objects print using the screening built into the printer. The output of some low-resolution printers (600 dpi or less) can be improved by turning off the default screening and using Adobe screens.

E. **Compatible Gradient and Gradient Mesh Printing**

This option substitutes JPGs for gradients and gradient meshes. This is done to compensate for some printers having a problem with these objects. Use this option only if you know that your printer has these problems.

7.45

File: Document Setup: Transparency

Use these settings to control whether transparent objects are printed as pixels or vectors, the manner in which transparency is displayed, and printed.

Transparency Options

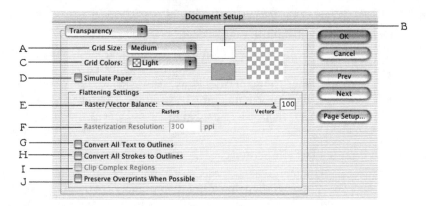

A. Grid Size

Use this menu to set the size of the transparency grid. Do not confuse this with the Grid, which is unaffected by this command.

B. Pasteboard Color

Click this swatch to set the color between the gray swatches in the transparency grid and the color of the entire pasteboard when using the Simulate Colored Paper option.

C. Grid Colors

Click this swatch to set the color of the checkerboard squares.

D. Simulate Paper

This option is used to forecast color when printing on colored paper. The pasteboard color is shown instead of white. Objects colored white are painted with the pasteboard color and colors are adjusted onscreen to simulate the blending with the pasteboard color.

E. Raster/Vector Balance (0 to 100)

Raster/Vector balance is set on a scale of 0 to 100. The higher the number, the more vectors are retained in the conversion process. At a setting of 0 all the selected objects are rasterized and become embedded images.

At settings around 25 Illustrator will retain simple vector shapes but rasterize more complex ones. This often leads to color mismatching where raster meets vector and should only be considered for low-memory systems.

At settings around 50, Illustrator preserves most vectors and only rasterizes complex art. As the settings move up the art must be more and more complex for Illustrator to rasterize it. At 100 Illustrator will preserve as many vectors as it can. As noted earlier, this does not necessarily mean the art will remain vectors.

F. **Rasterization Resolution**

Use this field to set the pixel resolution of any raster art that is created in the flattening process.

G. **Convert All Text to Outlines**

Use this option to preserve the shapes of letters during flattening by converting them to paths.

H. **Convert All Strokes to Outlines**

Check this box to force all strokes to be converted to filled compound paths. Unchecked, Illustrator will retain live strokes on some objects. Typically, this happens when the fill but not the stroke of a path is transparent.

I. **Clip Complex Regions**

This option reduces the visual difference between vector and raster artwork by putting the boundaries between raster and vector art along object paths. This may result in increased file complexity and slower print times.

J. **Preserve Overprinting When Possible**

This option attempts to retain the overprinting status of objects not affected by transparency when printing separations.

7.46

File: Document Color Mode

This command sets the color mode for the document. Illustrator's document color model sets the color space for all the objects in the document. There are two models to choose from, RGB and CMYK. RGB is commonly used for Web or onscreen graphics, and composite printing. CMYK is commonly used for separation printing. Color separation is a key component of high-end commercial printing.

Issues to Consider

Spot color is usually defined in the CMYK space. Both models support spot color, but only CMYK makes sense for most color jobs. Spot colors are usually printed with a black plate. Defining a spot black in RGB would be possible, but potentially logistically problematic. Since there is not a great advantage to working in the RGB space for spot color, most users simply stick with CMYK.

Alternate color definitions are not alternate color spaces. You can use RGB color sliders to define a color in a CMYK document, but you are not defining an RGB color, you are defining CMYK color with RGB numbers. The only way to convert color spaces is through the Document Color Mode command.

Links are converted to the color mode of the document. Linked or embedded art of a different color space is converted to the document's color space for printing.

7.47

File: *File Info*

This feature enables you to annotate your images with information about the file and its creator. The information is called "metadata" and it is used in XML workflows. Users search the data, giving them information about the file before they open it.

Mistakes to Avoid

Adding information not used by the end-receiver. If you aren't utilizing a workflow that employs metadata, you shouldn't bother to include this information.

Assuming that the data will be shared in all versions of the file. No exported versions of the file, even PSD files retain the File Info data. Versions of the native file before 9 do support the feature. Even Saved EPS versions of the file dismiss the data. Only native AI, PDF, and SVG files retain the data.

General Settings

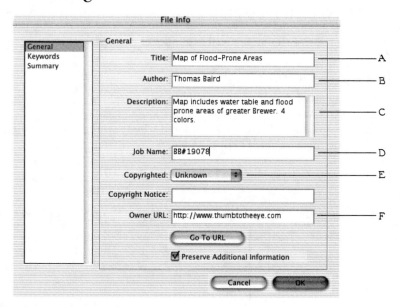

A. **Title**

Use this field to indicate the title of the piece. This may be different from the filename, especially in shops using automated page composition, where it is not uncommon for file names to be assigned nondescriptive names by databases.

B. **Author**

Enter the file creator's name. This may or may not be the same as the copyright holder.

C. **Description**

Enter a blurb about the file to describe its contents.

D. **Job Name**

This is commonly used to enter the name or number of the project the file is associated with. In some workflows, it may also be used to indicate the first appearance of the file.

E. **Copyrighted**

Use this menu to indicate the copyright status of the file. If you are copyrighting a file, be sure to include the copyright notice information in the field below this one. Copyrighting work is a legal process. Be aware that simply indicating that a file is copyrighted does not give it full legal protection from use.

F. **Owner URL**

You can list a website address that applies to the image, such as one containing additional work by the same artist. Anyone clicking on the Go To URL button will automatically connect to the listed address.

Keywords Settings

Enter keywords that can be used when searching for the document. Commonly, this list is comprehensive, including many keywords for the document. These keywords are not considered when saving for the web. They do not become metatags in HTML documents saved from the file.

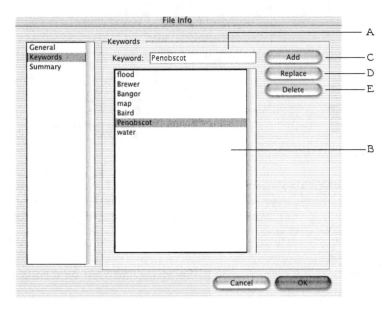

A. **Keyword**

Use this field to type in the keyword you want to add. Highlight one of the Current Keywords by clicking on it to populate this field. Once the word is in this field, you can Add, Replace, or Delete it.

B. **Current Keywords**

This pane displays all of the keywords that have been entered into the file. To edit or remove a keyword, click on it to highlight it. The field will populate the Keyword field and become available for change or removal.

C. **Add**

Click this button to create a new keyword from the contents of the keyword field.

D. **Replace**

Click this button to substitute the contents of the keyword field for the selected keyword in the Current Keyword pane. This is typically used to correct typos. Select a keyword from the pane, adjust its spelling in the editable Keyword field and then click this button to complete the process.

E. **Delete**

Click this button to remove the currently selected keyword.

Summary

This section lists the metadata in the document and the checkout status if the document is used in workgroup server model. Summary data cannot be edited.

7.48

File: Separation Setup

The Separation Setup dialog box is a necessary first step in the unusual process of printing separations from Adobe Illustrator. The dialog box options are used to control the colors, size, style, and marks printed when separations are called for from the Print dialog box. A button in the Print dialog box will also open this dialog box.

Issues to Consider

Separations from Illustrator are unusual. Commonly, page layout applications are used to make separations. They have an easier interface and a more robust set of options. Professional users commonly place files into Quark, InDesign, or PageMaker for separation.

Not all printers can make separations. Typically, PostScript printers are used to make separations. Non-PostScript inkjet printers cannot be used in conjunction with this feature.

Know your PPD. The first step in setting any options in this dialog box is to choose a PostScript Printer Description (PPD) file. Choosing the correct PPD is important in this process. The incorrect PPD may result in poor spot shape and incorrect printing results.

The Separation Setup Dialog Box

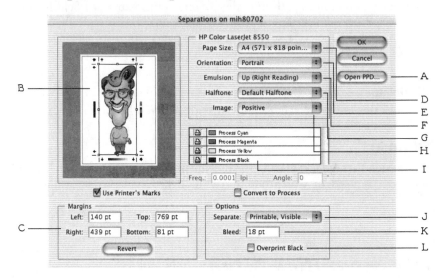

A. **Open PPD**

Click this button to select a PostScript Printer Description file to begin the process of separation. Since many of the choices in Separation Setup are derived from the choice of PPD, this is an important first step. Once a PPD is chosen, it becomes the default setting until another PPD is chosen.

PPD files are stored on the Macintosh in the System folder, in the Extensions folder, in the Printer Descriptions folder.

B. **Print Preview Area**

The Print Preview area displays a proxy of the page to be printed based on the current options. A thumbnail of the art is surrounded by a bounding area and, if selected, printer's marks. The bounding area sets the location of crop marks. If the command Object: Crop Marks: **Make** command has been used, the bounding area will be based upon that size. Click-drag a corner handle of the bounding area to reset the separation area. Click-drag the crop bounding area to reposition the printing area on the page. Repositioning or resetting the crop area does not affect the location of objects or crop marks in the document.

C. **Margins**

The Margin fields indicate the crop area's position relative to the lower-left corner of the page. Reposition the crop by entering new values. To return the crop position to its default value, click the Revert button.

D. **Page Size**

Use this pop-up menu to set the size of the page the separations are printed on. The choices in this field are determined by the PPD chosen. The PPDs for Adobe Acrobat and most imagesetters allow custom page sizes.

E. **Orientation**

Set the direction of the page to Portrait (vertical) or Landscape (horizontal). This is commonly done when printing to film to minimize costs.

F. **Emulsion**

Emulsion refers to the silver halide that coats one side of lithographic film. When printing to film, jobs are specified as to which side the emulsion will be on depending on the specifics of the process used. Options here are described by which side the emulsion is on when you are looking at the film so that you can read text correctly. Up (right reading) means that the emulsion is facing you when you can read the text correctly. Down (right reading) describes the opposite side.

G. **Halftone**

Traditional halftone printing represents tones in an image as a sequence of tiny spots of varying sizes. Images are converted to these spots upon printing. The size of the grid the spots are printed in is called its "screening." Screening describes the number of halftone spots that could fit in a linear inch. For this reason, it is commonly expressed as "lines per inch." In a printing job, the highest line per inch value that can be effectively reproduced is used. This limit is set by the combination of paper and printing press used.

Printer resolution describes the smallest dot the device can produce. A 600 dot per inch (DPI) printer makes dots 1/600th of an inch. Better printers can produce smaller dots. Dots are printed in clusters to produce halftone spots.

This setting controls the line screen and resolution for the job. The PPD used will determine the resolutions available. This setting should be based upon the paper/press combination used in the job.

H. **Image**

This setting is used to print the image as positive or negative. In most high-end printing environments, this is set to negative.

I. **Inks**

This field lists all the process and spot inks used in the document. The left column contains a printer icon indicating that the ink will be printed. Click the icon to exclude the ink from printing. Click the name of each ink to display the line screen (pulled from the Halftone field above) and screen angle. Click the Convert to process check box to separate spot colors as process inks.

J. **Separate**

Use this pop-up menu to override the printing status of layers. By default, only visible layers set to print will be separated. Set to Visible Layers to override the Print setting for visible layers. Set to All Layers to override the visibility and printing options of all layers and separate everything. It is uncommon to separate layers hidden or non-printing layers.

K. **Bleed**

This field expands the printable area beyond the document's crop marks. Bleeds are important for documents where art runs to the edge of the page or are to be trimmed.

L. **Overprint Black**

Check this box to override attribute settings and force black to overprint.

7.49

File: Page Setup *(Command-Shift) [Control-Shift]-P*

Illustrator has no unique Page Setup options. The Page Setup dialog box is the same in Illustrator as it is in other applications. The settings for Page Setup depend upon the type of output device and print driver installed on your operating system. Options typically include paper size, orientation, printer specific options, and so forth.

Page Setup is available through File: **Document Setup** as well. Page size from this dialog box may also be used in Document Setup to control the size of the artboard. Page Setup values are also used to control the Page Tiling.

7.50

File: Print *(Command) [Control]-P*

Use this command to send the document to a printer or to a file. This is usually done for proofing. Illustrator is not designed as a print engine and does not have the printing features of a page layout application.

The features of the print dialog box will vary depending upon the printer you have and the print driver you are using. The Illustrator specific features are listed below.

The Print Dialog Box

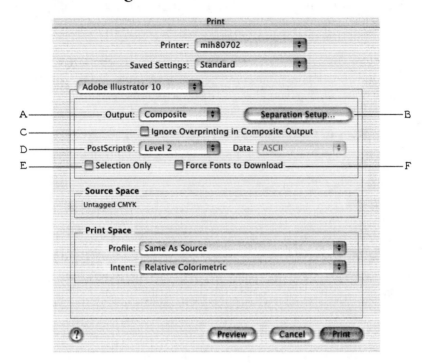

A. Output

Choose Composite or Separate from the pop-up menu. Composite prints a picture of the file on a single page. Most of your printing from Illustrator will be in this model. Separate is only available if a Separation Setup and PPD are defined for the document and your printer supports separation printing. This model of printing prints a different piece of paper for each color component used. It is typically used on final film output or to check the viability of a file for film output.

B. Separation Setup

Click this button to open the separation Setup dialog box. *(For more information, see 7.48, File: **Separation Setup**.)*

C. Ignore Overprinting in Composite Output

Check this option to instruct Illustrator to disregard the overprinting status of objects when printing composite. Overprinting is typically only used with separation printing. It may cause unnecessary color darkening when used with composite output.

D. PostScript

Use this menu to set the level of PostScript used when printing. Most PostScript printers today are Level 2. If you are certain you have a level-3 machine, use that option. Otherwise, set the option to 2.

E. Selection Only

Check this option to print only selected items in the document. This is often done when attempting to isolate a printing problem or to save printing time by omitting unnecessary elements.

F. Force Fonts to Download

Use this option to force the printer to process the fonts in the document. Without this option, the printer may substitute its own fonts, potentially causing print differences or type reflow.

7.51

File: Quit/Exit   *(Command) [Control]-Q*

Use this command to exit the application. If documents are unsaved, you will be prompted to save each unsaved file individually before quitting may be executed.

The Edit Menu

Edit: Undo *(Command) [Ctrl]-Z*

Undo works the same as it does in other programs: selecting it reverses or "undoes" the last applied command. Illustrator supports successive use of the Undo command. This means that upon undoing one command, you may Undo the one before that, and so on. Redo reverses the process, recalling the change you undid.

Illustrator does this by temporarily saving a new version of the document into RAM each time a command is executed. When you use the Undo command, Illustrator recalls the earlier version of the document from RAM. Not every change you make is recorded in this process. Commands that affect Illustrator in general rather than a specific document cannot be reversed with this command. For example, you cannot undo any change made to Illustrator's Preferences or any command from the Window menu, which open and close palettes. Also, commands that affect how a document is viewed, like the Zoom and Hand tools, and commands which are essentially document preferences, such as View: **Snap to Point** are not reversible with this command.

Since the undo/redo process is a function of memory, the available RAM limits it. If RAM is not available, undo/redo will fail. Although you cannot determine the exact number of undos you will get, you can keep track of Illustrator's memory use. Set the Status Bar in the lower left of the document to Free Memory. As the percent free dips lower, you may expect performance slow downs and eventually undo will fail. This typically only happens in very complex documents. *(For more information, see 8.14, Edit: Preferences:* **Units and Undo***.)*

Issues to Consider

Redoing a command. Choose (Command-Shift) [Ctrl-Shift]-Z to reverse an undone command or action. Or, choose Edit: **Redo**.

Not all commands are reversible. Some commands that do not change existing objects but establish preferences for future objects are reversible and some are not. For example, with nothing selected, changes in the Type palette may be undone, but changes in the Paragraph palette may not.

Undo also recalls the selection state of the document at the time of the edit. That is, items affected by Undo will be selected once the command is executed. This is commonly used to recall an unsaved complex selection.

Undo is document-specific. Each document has its own undo/redo chain. The more documents open, the greater the RAM requirements upon the system.

Undo is a linear process. If you undo a command and then execute another command, you may undo and redo the last command, but you will not able to undo or redo the one before that. The original thread of undo is overwritten and cannot be recalled.

Each keystroke is not reversible. Undo does not reverse individual typed characters.

8.2

Edit: Cut   *(Command) [Ctrl]-X*

The Cut command clears the selected items while copying them to the Clipboard. You can reintroduce the cut objects by choosing one of the Paste commands. This command is only available when an object is selected or when text in a field is highlighted.

8.3
Edit: Copy

Copy saves any selected objects to the Clipboard. The Clipboard is a section of RAM reserved for transferring information about or between documents. You can think of the Clipboard as a temporary "holding area" for information. Use one of the Paste commands to introduce copied objects to the document.

Issues to Consider

Copy only refers to the act of writing information to the Clipboard. In some dialog boxes, Illustrator uses the term copy to indicate that a command will be applied to a duplicate of a selected object, rather than the object itself.

How you copy is controlled by a preference. When you copy you are writing data to the Clipboard in a specific format. Although this doesn't affect your ability to paste in Illustrator, it may affect what happens when you paste into other applications, particularly if you're pasting transparent objects. *(For more information, see 8.19, Edit: Preferences: **Files & Clipboard**.)*

8.4
Edit: Paste

Pasting places the contents of the Clipboard into the document. Objects pasted will be centered in the current window.

Issues to Consider

Objects will be pasted into the currently targeted layer. *(For more information, see 25.32, Paste Remembers Layers.)*

Many of Illustrator's tools allow for the automatic duplication of shapes. Using many tools, adding the (Option) [Alt] key as you move or transform an item duplicates it. This obviates the need to copy and paste. *(For more information, see 1.2, Selection Tool; 1.3, Direct Selection Tool; and 3.2, Basic Transformation.)*

Text copied from another program retains no formatting when pasted into Illustrator. An exception to this is Adobe PageMaker. Text blocks copied in PageMaker (using the Selection tool) retain formatting information when pasted into Illustrator. The translation is imperfect, however, as Illustrator breaks paragraphs into single lines of type.

Some applications that create vector shapes do so in a proprietary way. This prohibits objects created in those applications from being pasted into Illustrator. Vector shapes created in QuarkXPress and Macromedia FreeHand may not be pasted into Illustrator. Paths pasted from Flash often have many anchor points and are unruly. Photoshop paths may be pasted freely.

8.5

Edit: *Paste in Front/Back*

(Command) [Ctrl]-F, (Command) [Ctrl]-B

These commands place the contents of the Clipboard into the document in the exact position it was copied or cut from rather than the center of the current window. Pasted objects will be directly in front of or behind selected objects in the stacking order. This is useful for rectifying complex stacking arrangements without using Send to Front/Back. If nothing is selected, the pasted shapes will be positioned at the top or the back of the stack.

Issues to Consider

These commands work when pasting between documents. When making complicated edits in crowded documents, consider cutting the objects to be modified. Create a new document and choose Paste in Front. After making the changes required, the edited objects can be returned to the correct positions by copying them and choosing Paste in Front again in the original document.

Other options may interfere. If the Paste Remembers Layers option is activated, it may be impossible to paste objects directly in front of or behind selected objects. *(For more information, see 25.32, Paste Remembers Layers)*

These commands are based on ruler origins set at the time the objects are written to the clipboard. If the ruler origins have been reset or are different between documents, these commands may produce unexpected results.

These commands don't work when typing. When an insertion point is active in a line of type these commands will not be available.

8.6

Edit: *Clear*

Choosing Edit: **Clear** is the same as pressing the Delete (or Backspace) key.

8.7

Edit: *Define Pattern*

This command defines a new pattern swatch based upon the currently selected objects. Pattern swatches may be applied to fills and strokes and are used in defining pattern brushes. Pattern swatches are bound by rectangles. The bounding rectangle and the objects within it are repeated horizontally and vertically to create a tiled wallpaper effect in the fill or stroke of the object. For this reason, pattern swatches are often called pattern "tiles."

The box that bounds the tile must have a fill and stroke of none and be behind the other objects in the pattern. If you do not define the pattern with this shape, Illustrator will create the bounding box for you. The bounding box Illustrator creates will completely enclose all of the selected objects exactly.

Pattern swatches may also be defined by dragging selected objects directly into the Swatches palette. Conversely, dragging pattern swatches out of the Swatches palette pastes the swatch objects and bounding box into the document. This is often used to create alternate versions of pattern swatches.

Mistakes to Avoid

Attempting to use the New Swatch command to create a pattern swatch. The New Swatch command and button in the Swatches palette create new color swatches.

Trying to create a pattern from a selection that contains illegal objects. Patterns, gradients, masks, meshes, blends, graphs, placed files, rasters and objects with effects that create rasters or symbol instances are not allowed in patterns. Selecting the objects and choosing Object: **Expand** before creating a pattern works around some of these problems.

Confusing the swatch in the palette with the actual pattern. Pattern swatches bounded by oblong rectangles preview inaccurately in the Swatches palette. The swatch preview in the swatches palette is a square, based upon the area the bounding box sweeps out when rotated 90°. This created an inaccurate preview when the bounding box is not square.

Attempting to edit type in a pattern swatch. Live type may be used in a pattern swatch, but once used, is no longer editable as type. Commands such as check spelling and create outlines will not affect a pattern swatch. To edit in this way, the object must be expanded or a new pattern must be established.

Issues to Consider

Live effects don't remain live. Compound shapes, brushes, and effects are allowable in patterns but do not remain live within the pattern. For example, a calligraphic brush stroke may be used in a pattern, but the pattern will not be updated as the brush is edited.

The bounding box of the pattern swatch need not entirely encompass the shapes in the pattern. This is often used to create continuous patterns and in pattern brushes. *(For more information, see B.25, Creating Seamless Patterns.)*

8.8

Edit: *Edit Original*

Edit Original opens linked placed files in the applications that authored them. Saved changes to the linked documents will be updated upon returning to Illustrator. It is the same as the command of the same name in the Links palette menu. *(For more information, see 26.9, Edit Original.)*

8.9

Edit: *Assign Profile*

Use this command to attach or remove a color profile to a document. This option is only available when Illustrator is using Color Management. This command is commonly used to assign a color profile that differs from the application's default working space or to not manage a document. *(For more information, see 8.10, Edit: **Color Settings**.)*

Assign Profile Options Dialog Box

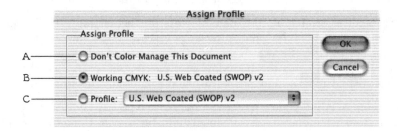

A. Don't Color Manage This Document

Use this option to disregard color management for this particular document. This option enables you to turn color management off for just the current document. This is useful because you do not need to change your color settings to temporarily turn off color management.

B. Working Space

This option assigns the default profile for the document's working space. The profile is established using the Color Settings dialog box. *(For more information, see 8.10, Edit: **Color Settings**.)*

C. Profile

Use this option to assign a profile other than the default chosen in Edit: **Color Settings**. *(For more information, see 8.10, Edit: **Color Settings**.)*

8.10

Edit: *Color Settings*

Use the Color Settings to establish color spaces for RGB and CMYK color modes, to establish color space conversion policies and to set options related to color conversion.

It may seem redundant to establish a color space for a color mode. Color mode, establishes the way color is described; color space defines the specific set of colors used. The intention of establishing a specific color space is to improve the ability to forecast color on the monitor and to establish a profile for color management. Color spaces are defined as profiles. Color profiles are said to be device independent color. This means the values attached to an image may be altered to accommodate the vagaries of different monitors and output devices.

Although many devices traffic in the same color spaces, inconsistencies in their mechanics make them interpret the same color information differently. The same image may look different on different monitors. Making color match on devices that use different color spaces is even more challenging. Why should an image printed to a toner-based (CMYK) laser printer look the same as it does on an RGB monitor? Or the same as when printed on an ink-jet printer?

Profiling devices is the process of measuring and evaluating these inconsistencies against known constants. The result of this process is the profile, which is a digital file that is used to track color and convert it between spaces. Customized profiles are typically created by professionals using expensive equipment. Illustrator provides many common profiles that, although not specific to your devices, may be used in lieu of investing in a specially created one.

Illustrator utilizes two kinds of color profiles, RGB, and CMYK. The RGB profile describes the color space of monitors. The CMYK profile describes the color space of your output device. When using color management to forecast color onscreen, both profiles are considered to arrive at the color that is sent to the monitor.

Mistakes to Avoid

Assuming turning on color settings changes color onscreen. Illustrator does not alter the color information sent to the monitor unless you enable View: **Proof Colors**.

Using managed color in an unmanaged environment. Illustrator files with embedded color profiles placed in applications that are not using color management, that use different color management, may result in color mismatches onscreen and in composite proofs. Be certain that all of the software and hardware along your production chain are compatible.

Issues to Consider

Not every user will require these settings. In some workflows it can even be detrimental. Commonly, profiles are used by professionals working in an established color-management workflow. Usually these workflows also involve printing to a limited number of specific devices.

Determine your working spaces. Determine the most appropriate color profiles for your work. If you are working for onscreen display, consider using the established sRGB color space, rather than your monitor profile. That working space, though limited in colors, is broad in its ability to reach many viewers successfully.

Illustrator native and PDF files can embed profiles, EPS cannot. When saving a file in the native or PDF file formats you may embed a color profile. The profile embedded will be determined by the color mode of the document; RGB profiles in RGB files, CMYK documents in CMYK files.

Color Settings Dialog Box

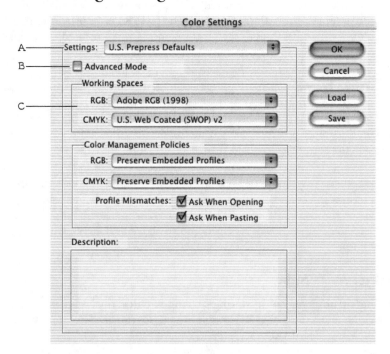

A. Settings

When you first choose the Color Settings command, this pop-up menu offers a list of factory-installed setups. Choosing one resets the values as necessary throughout the dialog box. The proper context for some of these options is obvious—for example, Color Management Off and

Emulate Illustrator 6 are geared for environments that avoid the use of profiles altogether. The remaining settings sound useful, but it can be difficult to predict if they dovetail with your specific requirements.

For the best results, establish your own settings and save them as a separate file. Illustrator automatically places the file in the Application Support/Adobe/Color/Settings directory on your system. The filename subsequently appears in the Settings pop-up.

B. Advanced Mode

Check this box to enable the Conversion Options settings and to expand the profile options in the menus.

C. Working Spaces: RGB

Use this command to establish the working RGB space. The RGB pop-up menu lists the following items when the advanced box is unchecked:

Monitor RGB

This option results in Illustrator simply using the current color space of the monitor. If desired, profile your monitor using the Adobe Gamma utility to modify the display.

Adobe RGB (1998)

The recommended choice for print work, this option displays a much wider color range than sRGB, Apple RGB, or ColorMatch RGB. Adobe intends this color space to be a viable option for prepress professionals requiring the largest gamut possible. Interestingly, its gamut includes many values that cannot even display, let alone print. When this occurs, some colors are clipped, which means that two or more similar color values are averaged together into one. However, this phenomenon is rarely noticeable in print, and in fact it allows for a little more flexibility when adjusting color.

Apple RGB

Based on the range of an Apple 13-inch Trinitron monitor, this option is the color space used by many other design applications.

ColorMatch RGB

This option represents the range of a Radius PressView monitor.

sRGB

Short for standard RGB, this option represents the color space of HDTV, and is promoted primarily by Hewlett-Packard and Microsoft. If you're not part of a workflow using this space, there is little need for this option. Some users convert Web graphics to sRGB, because this space displays the same characteristics of most PC monitors. However, its range is small—and when you consider that many CMYK values fall outside the sRGB gamut, you can see that it's a poor choice for print professionals.

When the Advanced button is checked in the Color Settings dialog box, the RGB pop-up is expanded. It displays all RGB color profiles currently available to your system, and you're also able to save and load RGB profiles that haven't been installed into your operating system.

D. **Working Spaces: CMYK**

Use this setting to establish the working CMYK space. If you are working with a specific profile or with hardware that ships with a standardized profile, you will want to select it. Show all the profiles by clicking the Advanced box.

Mistakes to Avoid

Using sRGB in a print environment. While this standard is well suited for previewing smaller-gamut images such as Web graphics, it's a poor choice for the print professional.

Assuming that these settings result in a "calibrated" monitor. Choosing an RGB working space is sometimes referred to as monitor calibration, but that's only true in a sense. True calibration requires that additional tools, such as a calibration cup, be used every day to ensure that your monitor displays those colors as consistently as possible.

Issues to Consider

Space prohibits a full discussion of the intricacies of profiling. However, the Adobe Gamma utility—available at *www.adobe.com*—offers a basic method of profiling the displayable range of your monitor.

Color Management Policies

Profiles can cause as many problems as they try to resolve. One of the most common issues is images that already contain an embedded profile. Here, you must determine whether the profile will be retained, replaced, or discarded outright. Also, when you open Illustrator 6 images (which couldn't use profiles) or images that were intentionally created without profiles, you must determine whether or not to convert them to your current working space.

This is important, because profiles were never intended to be swapped around with wanton abandon. If you mistakenly convert an image tagged with one profile to another, you can literally change its color content, which in turn produces unexpected on-press color shifts. Fortunately, the Color Management Policies act as a series of roadblocks that alert you whenever a potential conflict arises. From there, you can make any necessary changes. (Recommended settings appear after each item, in italic.)

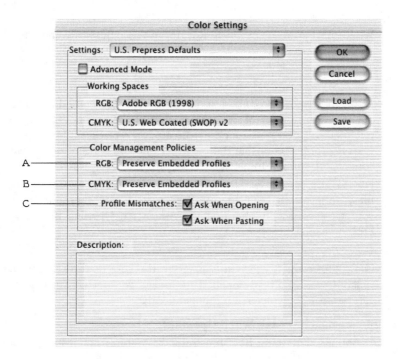

A. RGB (Convert to Working RGB)

These options determine how Illustrator will process an RGB document with a mismatched or missing profile.

Off

When this option is set, Illustrator doesn't recognize any embedded profiles, nor does it convert to the working space. The color appearance is not affected. Color management is essentially off for the document.

Preserve Embedded Profiles

Use this option to instruct Illustrator to recognize and retain a profile embedded in an image.

Convert to Working Space

Here, Illustrator converts the image to the current RGB working space. Most of the time, this option is the best choice—it enables you to convert an image into a color space optimized for your viewing conditions. (Give yourself a choice by checking the Ask When Opening box under Profile Mismatches, below.)

B. CMYK (Preserve Embedded Profiles)

These options determine how Illustrator will process a CMYK image with a mismatched or missing profile.

Off

When this option is set, Illustrator doesn't recognize any embedded profiles, nor does it convert to the working space. The color appearance is not affected.

Preserve Embedded Profiles

Here, Illustrator recognizes and retains a profile embedded in an image. Because the CMYK working space is based on a target output method, don't be quick to discard or replace any embedded CMYK profiles—choosing the incorrect one could result in a flawed conversion, ruining the image.

For the best results, lean toward keeping any embedded CMYK profiles, until you have a specific reason to set another one. (Give yourself a choice by checking the Ask When Opening box under Profile Mismatches, below.)

Convert to Working Space

Here, Illustrator converts the image to the current CMYK working space. If you've already opened the image without converting, you can perform the conversion independently.

C. **Profile Mismatches (Ask When Opening)**

These options determine how Illustrator responds when you open an image that conflicts with the established working space.

Ask When Opening

When this option is checked, Illustrator displays a Profile Mismatch dialog box, enabling you to accept, change, or refuse the current color management policy. When unchecked, the current policy is automatically followed.

Ask When Pasting

This option is an issue if you routinely copy information from one image and paste it into another. When this option is checked, Illustrator displays a Profile Mismatch dialog box, enabling you to accept, change, or refuse the current color management policy. When unchecked, the current policy is automatically followed.

Conversion Options

The following options determine the properties in effect when you convert an RGB image to CMYK. These options are only available in Advanced Mode.

- **Engine.** In this pop-up, choose the desired color management module. It defaults to Adobe (ACE), Illustrator's internal, the best choice when working primarily in this application. Depending on your workflow, you may require choosing a different CMM, such as Kodak's Digital Science Color Management System or Apple's ColorSync.

- **Intent (Perceptual).** Set the desired rendering intent in this pop-up, or the method used to convert color spaces. Choose from the following options:

  - **Perceptual (Images).** Here, the relative color values of the original image are maintained as they are converted to the target color space. While the overall color may change, the visual relationship between them is preserved.

  - **Saturation (Graphics).** Here, the relative saturation values of the original image are maintained as they are converted to the target color space. Any values outside the intended gamut retain their original saturation values, but are moved just inside the gamut.

  - **Relative Colorimetric.** Here, color values falling outside the target gamut have the same lightness value, but are positioned just inside the gamut.

  - **Absolute Colorimetric.** This option ignores white point matching during conversion. This typically results in the poorest translation, and should be avoided.

- **Use Black Point Compensation.** This option determines how the darkest image information will be handled during conversion. In almost every instance, you'll want to leave it checked. This way, the darkest neutral color of the original color space is mapped to the darkest neutral color of the new color space. Otherwise, the darkest neutral color is simply mapped to black, which may push the overall colors out of balance.

8.11

Edit: Preferences

Program settings that affect Illustrator's default behavior are called Preferences. These settings can be altered on-the-fly whenever Illustrator is open. Individual tools and commands also have preference settings. Collectively, these settings are stored in a file. On the Mac OS, the file is called Adobe Illustrator 10 Preferences and it is located in the Preferences folder in the System folder. On Mac OS X, the file is located in the Preferences folder in the Library folder for the current User. In Windows, the file is called AIPrefs and it is located in the Windows/Application Data/Adobe/Adobe Illustrator 10 folder. In Mac OS X, preferences are set by choosing Illustrator: **Preferences**.

There are eight Preferences panels (where we specifically prefer a setting, we've included it after the title of the preference).

8.12

Edit: Preferences: *General*   *(Command) [Ctrl]- K*

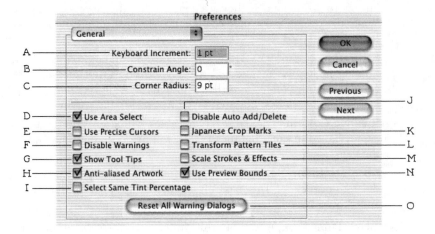

A. Keyboard Increment (.5 point)

The position of selected items may be altered by using the arrow keys on the keyboard. This setting controls the distance an item is moved with each keystroke.

B. Constrain Angle (0°)

The Constrain Angle determines the default orientation for a document. This is used to set the angle of objects created with the Type, Rectangle, and Rounded Rectangle tools and to set the angle other tools will snap to when holding down the Shift key. By default, this preference is set to 0°, which means rectangle tops will be flat and the other tools will snap to 45°, 90°, 135° and 180°. If this preference is changed, Illustrator rotates the snap to values by the amount specified. It also rotates the Grid to make this plain.

In instances where isometric scaling is required, the constrain angle can be quite useful. For an example of this, see the techniques section. In other cases, the preference should be left at the default.

C. Corner Radius

This setting determines the size of the curve created by default when using the Rounded Rectangle tool. The value may be set in this dialog box, or when using the Rounded Rectangle tool. The preference will be updated to reflect the last radius used. Since it is easy to set the curve of a rectangle directly in the document by clicking with the Rounded Rectangle tool this preference is uncommonly used. For more information on using the Rounded Rectangle tool, see the Tools section.

D. **Use Area Select** (On)

Use Area Select makes it easier to select entire paths using the Direct Selection tool in preview mode. When activated, clicking in the interior of a path that contains a painted (non-None) Fill with the Direct Selection tool in Preview mode will cause all the points and segments along the path to become selected. When this preference is turned off, the Direct Selection tool behaves the same in Preview mode as it does in Outline mode.

Most users leave this preference activated as it makes it easier to select objects. However when using it, selecting line segments in Illustrator can sometimes be difficult since an imprecise click will select an entire path. Some users prefer to turn the preference off, allowing them to quickly drag-select line segments. When it is necessary to select entire paths with the Direct Selection tool, these users simply hold down the (Option) [Alt] key to switch to the Group Select tool.

E. **Use Precise Cursors**

Illustrator has two sets of tool cursors: a set that looks like the tool (the standard set) and a set based upon crosshairs (the precise set). Clicking the Caps Lock key toggles the sets. This preference changes the default set from standard to precise.

F. **Disable Warnings**

This preference instructs Illustrator to play an alert sound instead of displaying a warning in the event that you attempt to use a tool in a way that produces no results. Commonly, these errors are caused by imprecise cursor placement or objects that do not support the feature you are trying to use.

In practice, you should leave the warnings on until you are quite comfortable with the tools, after which you will find there is a productivity benefit to turning them off.

G. **Show Tool Tips** (On)

This option displays the name and keyboard shortcut for a tool or palette when the cursor is over the item. This includes named items, such as styles and brushes and custom shortcuts you create using Edit: **Keyboard Shortcuts**.

H. **Anti-Aliased Artwork** (On)

This option adjusts the onscreen display of objects to make curves appear smoother. It has no effect on the way files print or rasterize and is only used to compensate for the inability of monitors to show smooth edges correctly. This option affects screen redraw time and may slightly hinder very complex documents. It should be left on until a noticeable slow down occurs.

I. **Select Same Tint Percentage**

This option makes the Select: Same: **Fill/Stroke** commands select only objects with the exact same tint percentage rather than simply the same color. Tints are only available to objects styled using Global swatches such as spot colors.

By default, Select: Same **Fill/Stroke** will select all objects with the same color definition. In a document where all the objects are different tints of the same spot color, this command would select everything. Enabling this option restricts the selection to only those colors with the same tint percentage. *(For more information, see 11.9, Select: **Same Fill/Stroke**.)*

J. **Disable Auto Add/Delete** (Off)

This option disables the ability of the Pen tool to temporarily switch to the Add a Point and Subtract a Point tools. By default, the Pen tool will switch to the Add Anchor Point tool when atop a selected line segment and to the Delete Anchor Point tool when atop a selected anchor point. This behavior makes it easier to edit paths without switching tools. This option disables that ability.

K. **Japanese Crop Marks** (Off)

This option changes the style of the crop marks Illustrator makes from Western to Japanese. Japanese crop marks differ from Western by having intersecting right angles for corners and crosses for sides. This preference affects crop marks made when executing the Object: Crop Marks: **Make** command and the marks Illustrator makes when printing. Changing this preference does not change existing crop marks in the document and is unrelated to the Filter: Create: **Trim Marks** command.

L. **Transform Pattern Tiles**

This option determines whether transformation tools and commands will affect patterns by default. All the transformation tools, commands, and palettes have the option of affecting objects, pattern tiles, or both. This option sets the default behavior to include patterns in the transformation. This preference may also be set in any transformation dialog box and in the Transform palette menu.

M. **Scale Strokes & Effects**

This option determines whether or not scaling tools and commands will affect strokes and effects as well as objects. This preference may also be changed in the Scale dialog box and in the Transform palette menu.

N. **Use Preview Bounds** (On)

This option instructs the Info and Transform palettes to include strokes and effects when measuring an object. Since strokes extend outside the vector shape, the actual area a stroked object occupies is larger than the vector shape that defines it. Use this option to measure and transform the actual size. This preference has no affect on commands that create shapes.

O. Reset All Warning Dialogs

This option clears the Don't Show Again option that may be attached to some warning dialog boxes. Upon clicking this button all applicable warning dialog boxes will be shown. This preference does not override the Disable Warnings preference.

8.13

Edit: Preferences: *Type & Auto Tracing*

A. Size/Leading

This option sets the increments attached to keyboard shortcuts for type size (the size of the characters) and leading (the line height of type).

B. Tracking

This option sets the increments attached to keyboard shortcuts for tracking (the space between characters and words) and kerning (the space between two characters). To track, select at least two characters. To kern click an insertion point between two characters.

C. Baseline Shift

This option sets the increments attached to keyboard shortcuts for baseline shift (the distance up or down a character sits from its default position).

D. Greeking

This option determines the type size at or below which text greeks. Greeking is the onscreen substitution of illegibly small type with gray bars. Greeking does not affect the way a document prints or rasterizes. This measure is relative and based upon a 100% view depth. Using a

6-point greeking limit, 6-point type would greek when viewed at 100%. but not at 101% (since it would appear larger than 6 points). Likewise, 12-point type viewed at 50% would appear to be 6 points and greek.

E. Type Area Select

This option increases the clickable area needed for selecting a type object from only its baseline to the entire space the type sweeps out. This makes selecting type easier but can be cumbersome in complex documents. Unlike the Area Select option, Type Area Select affects the clickable area in Outline mode and whether or not the type is painted.

F. Show Font Names in English

This option displays the names of non-English language fonts in English in the type and font menus. This is important since the names of double-bit fonts don't translate correctly into Roman characters and are indecipherable.

G. Auto Trace Tolerance

This option determines the accuracy of paths created by using the Auto Trace tool. The number represents the distance from the raster edge, in pixels, the created path may be. Values may be set from 1 to 10 in 1/100th increments. The lower the setting, the more closely the created paths will follow the edge of the shape being traced. Lower settings result in paths that are closer matches, but have more anchor points. Higher settings use fewer points, but may be less accurate.

H. Tracing Gap

This option specifies the amount of space the auto trace tool may omit when calculating where an edge ends. These settings allow the Auto Trace tool to skip naturally occurring gaps and divots in a scan and stick to a truer edge. The value is measured in pixels and may range from 0 to 2 in 1/100th increments. A setting of 0 turns this function off. A setting of 2 instructs the Auto Trace tool to disregard gaps of up to 2 pixels when creating an edge.

8.14

Edit: Preferences: *Units & Undo*

Illustrator supports seven different units of measure; points, picas, inches, millimeters, centimeters, pixels, and Q. Points and picas are traditional typographers units. 12 points is equal to 1 pica and 6 picas are in an inch. Q is a unit of type equal to a quarter centimeter. It is only available as a type unit.

Dialog boxes support the use of measures other than the default. Type the abbreviations for the measuring unit into a field after the required unit. Illustrator will convert the measure to the default. For example, if the default unit for a document is points, and you type "2 in" into a dialog box, the result will be 144 points.

The abbreviations for units of measurement are as follows: Points (pt), Pica (p), Millimeter (mm), Centimeter (cm), Pixel (px), Inch (in, or open-quote), Q (q).

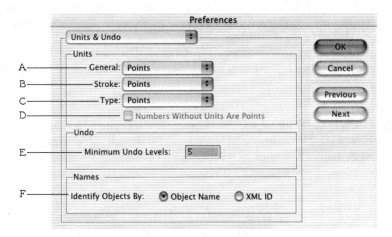

A. **General**

This option sets the default measuring units used for filters, effects, rulers, objects, transformations, and any place measuring is required (except as noted below).

The ruler units of a document may be set independently of the Units: General preference. (Control) [Right]-click directly on the rulers and choose the desired measure from the contextual menu. Changing ruler units in this way does not affect the preference setting.

B. **Stroke**

This option sets the default measuring units used for strokes. The default unit for strokes is points. Setting the preference to a different value does not alter the Stroke Size pull down menu in the Stroke palette that displays points.

C. **Type**

This option sets the default measuring units used for type. The default unit for type is points. Setting the preference to a different value does not alter the Font Size pull down menu in the Character palette that displays points.

D. **Numbers Without Units Are Points**

This option is used when the General units are set to picas. When the option is enabled, units typed in a dialog box without adding a "P" to specify picas are considered to be points instead of picas. This makes it easier to key in sizes. For example, without this option, 8 points would be keyed in "0p8" instead of just "8."

E. Undo: Minimum Undo Levels

This option establishes the minimum number of Undo steps that will be available per document. To reverse commands, Illustrator reserves an amount of RAM to keep track of the progress of a document. Illustrator will commonly be able to undo more steps than the specified amount. But its ability to do so is based upon the complexity of the documents, the number of documents open, and the tasks that must be undone. This setting establishes a minimum, rather than a maximum as in other applications.

F. Names

This option determines whether objects are identified by the object's name or XML ID in the Variables palette. By default, objects are named by their object class, such as <path>. Objects may be assigned different names in the Layers palette.

8.15

Edit: Preferences: *Guides & Grid*

These options control the appearance of Guides and the document Grid. It does not affect the transparency grid.

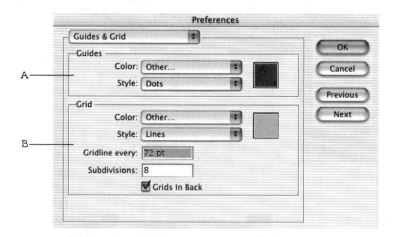

A. Guides

Establish the color of guides by selecting a color from the pop-up list, or clicking on the swatch to use the color picker. Choose whether guides will be solid or dotted lines in the Style menu.

B. Grid

Establish the color of the grid by selecting a color from the pop-up list, or clicking on the swatch to use the color picker. Gridlines are the thicker lines than the subdivision lines which separate them. Establish the frequency of gridlines and subdivisions in these fields. The default settings divide the document into inches and eighths of inches. The grid may appear behind or in front on objects.

8.16

Edit: Preferences: *Smart Guides & Slices*

These options determine what is displayed when using the Smart Guides feature and the display of Slices.

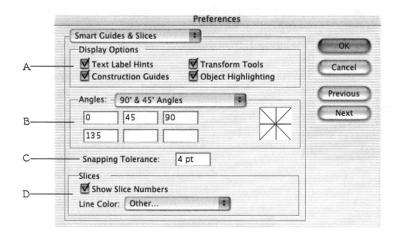

A. Display Options

Text Label Hints appear as words indicating when the cursor is atop anchor points or paths. Points of object intersection are also indicated. Guides are temporary guides intended to help align objects. Transform Tools displays smart guides when using the transform tools. Object Highlighting highlights objects when a selection arrow is over it.

B. Angles

This option determines the angles at which an object must be dragged or transformed to display Smart Guide lines. Presets for common angle combinations may be chosen or manually entered into the fields provided.

C. Snapping Tolerance

This option determines the distance from an object a selection arrow may be and still select it when using Smart Guides. Objects within that distance are treated as though the cursor were directly over them. This is useful when positioning objects since selection arrows will be drawn to other objects, making exact alignment easier. The distance allowed may be from 0 to 10 points. The measure is relative to view depth percentage.

D. **Slices**

Use these options to establish the color of slice lines and if their numbers are displayed. For more information, see Object: **Slice.**

Edit: Preferences: *Hyphenation*

Use these options to determine which default language Illustrator uses to hyphenate and which words Illustrator will not hyphenate at all. Words such as proper nouns can be added to the Exceptions list manually to prevent their being broken. These exceptions are not related to the Learned Words list.

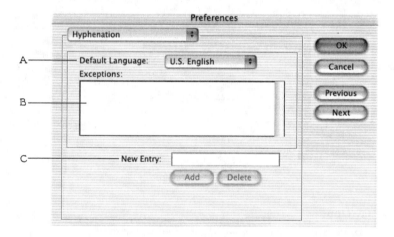

A. **Default Language**

Use this menu to select the default dictionary used for hyphenation.

B. **Exceptions**

This pane lists words Illustrator will not hyphenate. Click an item from the list to select it in preparation for deleting it.

C. **New Entry**

Type exception candidates into this field. Click the Add button to move them into the Exceptions pane. Click Delete to remove an exception from the pane.

8.18

Edit: Preferences: *Plug-ins & Scratch Disk*

These preferences control where Illustrator loads its plug-ins from and which drives are used for temporary memory.

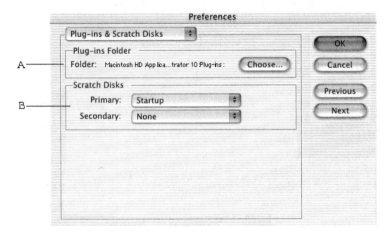

A. **Plug-ins Folder**

Use the plug-ins button to indicate the location of the plug-ins folder Illustrator should read at start-up. In most workflows this remains set at the default, which is the plug-ins folder located inside the Illustrator folder. In some workflows, multiple plug-in folders are established and switched between. This is done to isolate tools used or to set up different Startup documents with different default brushes, swatches, styles, and symbols.

B. **Scratch Disks**

Use the Scratch Disks settings to determine the volumes Illustrator will use as scratch disks. When Illustrator runs low on RAM, it temporarily uses available disk storage space as RAM. The volume it uses is called a scratch disk. This process is less efficient than real RAM and will run more slowly. Some users partition disk space or purchase additional drives strictly for this purpose.

8.19

Edit: Preferences: *Files & Clipboard*

These preferences handle data in and out of Illustrator. The Clipboard is used to store data temporarily that has been copied or cut. It is a principle model of shuttling small amounts of data between applications.

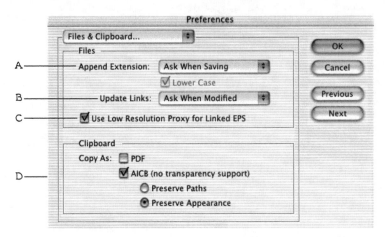

A. **Append Extension**

Use this option to determine how the file suffix extension is handled when saving files. Ask When Saving includes a check box in the Save dialog box to add the file format extension. Always adds the extension by default and None does nothing at all.

B. **Update Links**

Use this option to determine how linked external files should be treated in the event that they are edited in another application. Manually takes no action. Automatic refreshes the link without warning and Ask When Modified displays a prompt.

C. **Use Low Resolution Proxy for Linked EPS**

Use this option to display the EPS preview of a link. This choice increases redraw time and improves productivity at the cost of worsened onscreen display.

D. **Clipboard**

Use this option to determine what format copied data is recorded in. The PDF format supports transparency whereas the AICB (Adobe Illustrator Clip Board) format must either render transparency as pixels or discard transparent effects. Note that you may Copy to both formats simultaneously. The format you choose may affect the results when pasting into other applications. Some applications can support PDF pasting, some do not. Further, some support PDF pasting but do not accept the transparency. For example, Photoshop 6 does not recognize Compound Shapes when pasted from a PDF Clipboard. It correctly sees vector shapes, but does not recognize the Compound Shape and fails to give you the option to create a Shape Layer.

8.20

Edit: Preferences: Workgroup

Use these options to determine how Illustrator behaves when interfacing with a workgroup server. A workgroup server manages files using the WebDAV model. WebDAV stands for Web Distributed Authoring and Versioning. It is essentially a file-transfer system that has business features, such as permissions and check out. These systems are intended to prevent multiple users from altering the same file in different ways. When a file is "checked out" a user is working on the file and it is unavailable to others. Files are checked back in after they are altered. These preferences are only useful for users that are connected to this sort of system.

Workgroup Preference Options Dialog Box

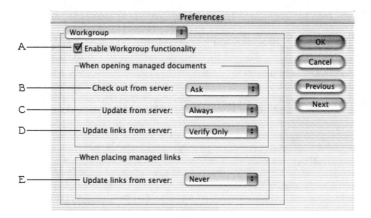

A. Enable Workgroup Functionality

Check this option to enable Illustrator to recognize workgroup servers. Unchecked, files cannot be checked in or out using this system.

B. Check Out from Server

Use this option to establish whether or not Illustrator will warn you when you open files on the workgroup server. Set to Ask, you will be prompted to formally check the file out every time you open a managed file. Set to Never and the station will not check out files by default, but will open a local copy on your station. Set to Always to check files out without prompting.

C. **Update from Server**

This option determines what happens when there is a newer version of a managed file you are editing on the server. Always updates the file without prompting. Never retains the local copy on your station without prompting. Ask displays an option to update the file.

D. **Update Links from Servers**

This option determines what will happen when files linked to the managed file are updated on the server. Always updates the link without prompting. Never retains the local version on your station without prompting. Ask displays an option to update the link. Verify Only checks the links but doesn't update them.

E. **Update Links from Server**

This option determines what will happen when you place a file on the server that contains links. Always updates the link without prompting. Never ignores the links. Ask displays an option to update the link.

8.21

Edit: **Keyboard Shortcuts**

(Option- Shift-Command) [Alt-Shift-Ctrl]-K

Many of Illustrator's tools and commands can be accessed or executed using keyboard shortcuts. Use this option to manage the shortcuts Illustrator assigns to tools and commands.

Keyboard Shortcuts Options Dialog Box

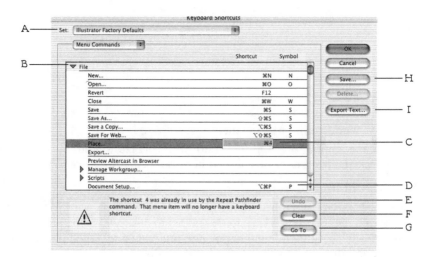

A. **Set**

Collectively, a group of shortcuts are considered a set. Illustrator ships with two shortcut sets, the Illustrator Factory Defaults and Adobe Illustrator 6. The Factory Defaults are the current default settings, while the Adobe Illustrator 6 settings are based on the version of Illustrator before Adobe standardized the interfaces of their products.

You cannot modify these sets. Once you begin to, the set renames itself Custom.

B. **Twirl Down**

Click these triangles to toggle the display of the contents of a menu.

C. **Shortcut**

Click the shortcut field to assign a shortcut to a tool or command. Click the field and then click the key combination you wish to assign. Changes are highlighted in red. If the combination is illegal or is in use, an alert dialog box will appear.

D. **Symbol**

Items with shortcuts may also have a symbol. The symbol is the character that will appear in parentheses in the tool tips when the cursor rests over a tool for a moment.

E. **Undo**

Click this button to return a changed keyboard shortcut to its default.

F. **Clear**

Click this button to remove a selected keyboard shortcut.

G. **Go To**

Click this button to navigate in the palette to a command or tool whose shortcut you have appropriated. When you assign a keyboard shortcut that is already in use you will be warned that you have done this. Click this button to select the command whose shortcut you have used so that you can assign it a new one.

H. **Save**

Click this button to create a new named set of shortcuts. Once saved, the shortcut set will appear in the Set menu. This enables you to switch between sets based on your needs. Saved sets are stored as files with the extension ".kys."

I. **Export Text**

Click this button to save the shortcuts as a text (.txt) file. Saved in this format you can print or search the shortcuts for your reference.

The Object Menu

Object: Transform

Use the commands in the Transform menu to alter selected objects. The Rotate, Reflect, Scale, and Shear commands available here are also available by double-clicking on the tools of those names. They function the same as their tool counterparts except that the center of transformation is always the center of the items selected. To execute any of these commands a selection must be made first.

9.2

Object: Transform: Transform Again

(Command) [Ctrl]-D

Use the Transform Again command to repeat the last executed transformation on the current selection. Transformations include moving, scaling, reflecting, scaling, shearing, skewing, and perspective. It does not work on the Liquify tools or Twirl commands.

Issues to Consider

The transformation may include duplication. This makes Transform Again well-suited for quickly creating sequences of objects. Most transformation commands and tools include a Copy option. This executes the transformation on a duplicate of the selected object. If the last executed transformation included Copy, Transform Again will duplicate as well.

The repeated transformation is executed about the same point of transformation as the original. This may cause the second transformation to produce different result than the first. For example, a Perspective Transform created with the Free Transform tool, has a specific point the perspective is heading toward. If you apply transform again to another object, it will not be transformed the same as the first, but rather toward the same point. Commonly, this affect is desirable and creates continuity. If the desired affect is an exact reproduction of the first command, consider creating an Action or a Style with a transform Effect.

9.3

Object: Transform: Move   (Command-Shift) [Ctrl-Shift]-M

Use the Move command to reposition selected items a set distance and direction.

Issues to Consider

Move remembers last move. The default values in the fields of the Move dialog box are the distance and direction of the last object moved in the document. This includes objects moved by dragging, but not movement that occurred incidentally as part of another transformation, such as Scale. If the last move included Copying, the Move dialog preview will include the duplication as part of the preview.

Move is connected to Measure. When you use the Measure tool, the distance and direction measured become the defaults for Move. This is often used to populate the fields in the Move dialog box.

The Move dialog box can be opened by typing Return when Selection or Direct Selection tools are active or by double-clicking on the Select or Direct Selection tools to open the dialog box.

Move Dialog Box

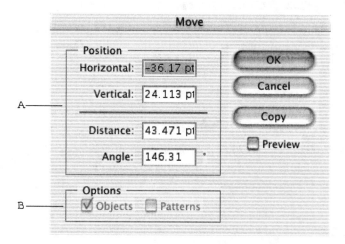

A. **Position**

Use these fields to set the distance and direction objects are moved. Values may be set by the horizontal and vertical distance or distance and angle. Positive distances are up and to the right, negative values are down and to the left. The four fields are dynamically connected, as you type values into one field, the other fields update as well. So, for example, if you enter the same, positive amount horizontally and vertically, the Angle field will read 45° and the distance will be calculated.

B. **Options**

Check to transform objects, pattern fills in objects, or both.

9.4

Object: Transform: *Rotate*

Use this command to rotate selected objects about their centers by a specified amount. The dialog box for this command is the same as double-clicking on the Rotate tool. *(For more information, see 3.3, Rotate.)*

9.5

Object: Transform: *Reflect*

Use this command to reflect selected objects about their centers by a specified amount. The dialog box for this command is the same as double-clicking on the Reflect tool. *(For more information, see 3.4, Reflect.)*

9.6

Object: Transform: Scale

Use this command to scale selected objects about their centers by a specified amount. The dialog box for this command is the same as double-clicking on the scale tool. *(For more information, see 3.6, Scale.)*

9.7

Object: Transform: Shear

Use this command to shear selected objects about their centers by a specified amount. The dialog box for this command is the same as double-clicking on the Shear tool. *(For more information, see 3.7, Shear.)*

9.8

Object: Transform: Transform Each

(Command-Option-Shift) [Ctrl-Alt-Shift]-D

Use Transform Each to Scale, Move, Rotate, and or Reflect objects numerically or by a random amount. Transform Each transforms selected objects relative to themselves, rather than the center point of the bounding box for all the selected objects. Because of this, the command is often used to introduce variance to a series of objects, or to apply the same transformation to multiple objects without repositioning them.

Issues to Consider

Transform Each may be applied as a Transform Effect. Transform Each may also be applied as an Effect by choosing Effect: Distort & Transform: **Transform**. The only difference in the dialog boxes is that the Effect version allows multiple duplicate copies.

Random transformations are calculated each time Random is checked. When applying a random Transform Each, the random effect may not be to your liking. The random amount can be reset and reapplied by disabling the Random check box and then turning it on again.

Transform Each uses the reference point interface from the Transform palette. The changes applied by the command are applied from one of nine points about the bounding box of each item. These points are based on the bounding box of the items selected, and not necessarily on the items themselves.

Transform Each Dialog Box

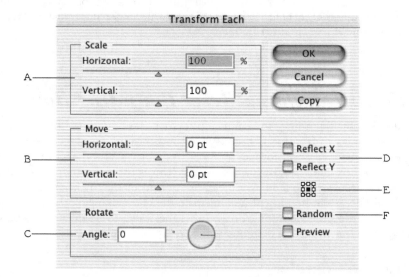

A. **Scale**

Use these fields or sliders to scale selected items horizontally and vertically. Objects may be scaled between –4,000% and 4,000%. By default, though, the sliders only go up and down between 0% and 200%. Enter amounts larger than that directly into the fields.

B. **Move**

Use these fields and sliders to reposition selected objects. Positive values move objects up and to the right, negative values move things down and to the left. Values between -4000 and 4000 pts may be entered. Values larger than 100 must be typed into the fields.

C. **Rotate**

Use these fields to rotate selected objects about the chosen reference point on their bounding boxes. Values may be entered directly or by dragging the radius arm.

D. **Reflect**

Use these check boxes to reflect selected objects about the X or Y axis.

E. **Point of Transformation Proxy**

Use this grid to establish the point of transformation for any changes made to selected objects using Transform Each. The proxy point represents locations on the bounding box of each selected object. This enables transformation to take place about a corner or side, rather than the center.

F. Random

Enabling this option sets the transformation to a random amount. The values entered in fields become the upper limits for the transformation. Random does not affect Reflect.

Object: Transform: *Reset Bounding Box*

Use the Reset Bounding Box command to snap the bounding box transformation guides to 0°. This is useful when transforming an object using the Selection or Free Transformation tools. As objects are transformed, the bounding box guide is transformed as well. This is true no matter which tool is used to transform to item. As objects are transformed away from their original attitude, it can be difficult to anticipate the effect dragging a corner may have. Resetting the Bounding Box returns the frame to its default position, making it clear the effect dragging will have upon an item.

Issues to Consider

Reset Bounding Box does not use the document's default angle. The command always sets the bottom of the bounding box on a 0° angle, even if the documents defaults are set differently.

Hiding the Bounding box does not impact this command. Reset Bounding Box works even if the Bounding Box is hidden.

Object: *Arrange*

The Arrange submenu resets the position in the stacking order an object has on its layer. Every object is in front or behind every other object. This relationship is called the Stacking Order. By default, objects are stacked in the order they are created. The newest object is on top, the oldest object is in the back. This rule is followed for all objects; the letter at the end of a word is in front of the letter in the beginning. Each Layer has its own stacking order. Objects at the bottom of a layer may still be above objects on lower layers.

The Arrange commands enables selected objects to be repositioned in the stack on their layer.

Mistakes to Avoid

Trying to move a grouped item to the top or back of the stack. Groups require objects to be next to each other in the stacking order. Attempting to move a single item in a group to the top of the stacking order will only move it in front of the other objects in the group. Some techniques, such as Clipping Masks, create Groups automatically.

Issues to Consider

Other commands allow more exacting control of the stacking order. In complex documents, the Arrange commands may not supply enough control over the exact positioning of objects. To position an object precisely, consider manually repositioning items using the Layers palette or Cutting the Object and Pasting in Front or Back of the required object.

9.11

Object: Arrange: Bring to Front

(Command-Shift) [Ctrl-Shift]-]

Use this command to set the selected objects to the top of the stacking order of the layer. If multiple items are selected, the objects are repositioned with their relative stacking order intact.

9.12

Object: Arrange: Bring Forward

(Command) [Ctrl]-]

Use this command to move the selected objects one step forward in the stacking order of the layer. This command is often repeated until the objects are in the correct position. If multiple items are selected, the objects are repositioned with their relative stacking order intact.

9.13

Object: Arrange: Send To Back

(Command-Shift) [Ctrl-Shift]-[

Use this command to set the selected objects to the back of the stacking order of the layer. If multiple items are selected, the objects are repositioned with their relative stacking order intact.

9.14

Object: Arrange: Send Backward

(Command) [Ctrl]-[

Use this command to move the selected objects one step backward in the stacking order of the layer. This command is often repeated until the objects are in the correct position. If multiple items are selected, the objects are repositioned with their relative stacking order intact.

9.15

Object: Arrange: *Send to Current Layer*

Use this command to position the selected items in the back of the stack of the currently selected layer. Objects grouped to selected objects are repositioned as well. To use the command, select the objects to be repositioned and then click on the name of the destination layer. Choose the command to reposition the objects. This command is often manually executed by dragging the selection icon from one layer to another.

9.16

Object: *Group* *(Command) [Ctrl]-G*

Use the Group command to create a Group object from the selected items. Commonly, groups are created to organize related objects or to when using techniques that require groups, such as Clipping Masks. Group objects are selected with a single click from the Selection arrow. This makes it easier to select and move them and retain their relative positions of the objects to each other. Objects that are members of a group may still be selected and modified independently using the Direct Selection tool.

Group objects are treated as a single unit for many commands. Commands like Blend behave differently when applied to a group than to path objects. Groups may also be styled as a single object and are required for some Effects and techniques to work.

Items in a group are positioned next to each other in the stacking order. When a group is made, all the objects are repositioned underneath the topmost object in the group. This may include objects changing layers. The group object is indicated in the Layers palette with its component objects available under a drop-down menu. The group is then all the objects between the top and bottom objects in the group. If objects are positioned between those objects by Paste in Front/Back or dragging an object in the Layers palette, the object is added to the group. Likewise, objects dragged out of that position in the Layers palette or pasted into a new location are removed from the group. Repositioning all of the members of a group is the same as Ungrouping them.

Group objects may be grouped to other objects or other groups. This can create a hierarchy of grouping. The Group Selection tool is designed to make selecting through this tree easier.

Mistakes to Avoid

Making Groups unintentionally. Some techniques result in Groups. For example, Object: Clipping Mask: **Make** creates groups automatically. Pathfinder commands that result in multiple shapes create a group automatically. Expanding a blend results in a group. There are many instances where groups are generated without you choosing the group command. There is nothing wrong with this, but it can lead to confusion as you begin to edit shapes.

Destroying Layer organization and Styles with Groups. Objects organized or styled by layer may be repositioned as they are grouped. A commonly example is a clipping mask applied to all the objects in a complex, multi-layered document. Clipping masks create a group, pulling all of the objects out of their layers into the layer the mask is on. The organization and layer-level styling of the objects is destroyed.

Selecting objects when groups are required. Some techniques, such as opacity mask, create group effects by default, selecting objects will not give you access to the new group's opacity mask.

Issues to Consider

Grouping is essential to the Pathfinder Effects. The Effect: **Pathfinder** commands do not work on single objects. You must Group objects before applying Pathfinder Effects. This only applies to the pathfinder commands found under the Effects menu. You may make Compound Shapes using the Pathfinder palette without Grouping.

9.17

Object: Ungroup　　　　*(Command-Shift) [Ctrl-Shift]-G*

Ungrouping releases the Group relationship on objects. They are no longer part of a Group object and may be selected with the selection tool independently.

Issues to Consider

Ungrouping objects doesn't return them to their original position in the stacking order. Grouping objects repositions them so that they are next to each other in the stacking order. Ungrouping does not reverse this. It leaves the objects in the positions they were in before ungrouping.

Ungroup is sequential. Ungroup releases objects that are grouped together. If one of the Grouped objects was a group itself, it would be released from the first group, but retains its group relationship with the other objects. Continue choosing Ungroup to release additional groups.

9.18

Object: Lock

(Command)(Ctrl)-2

Use the Lock commands to temporarily prohibit items from being selected. Locked items preview and print, but do not respond to the selection tools. This makes the objects harder to modify. Locking is commonly done to affix an object in a specific position or to facilitate the selection of other objects.

Objects, groups and layers may also be locked using the layers palette.

Mistakes to Avoid

Assuming locked objects cannot be deleted. Locked objects can be deleted using the delete command in the Layers palette.

Assuming that locked objects cannot be modified. Locked objects can be styled by applying Effects to the Layer or Group they are in.

Confusing Hide Edges with Lock. The Hide Edges feature stops selection highlighting, making it look as though the Selection tools are having no effect, and the objects are Locked.

Locking layers instead of objects. Layers may be locked using the Layers palette. Unlocking is done in the same way. Locked Layers do not respond to the Object: **Unlock** command. Locking Layers is commonly done to isolate object series that is in the right location. The Object: **Lock** command is best used for locking objects quickly to select objects around it or for less complicated documents.

9.19

Object: Lock: Selection

(Command) [Ctrl]-2

Use Lock Selection to Lock the selected objects. This is the same as clicking the lock icon for the items in the Layers palette.

9.20

Object: Lock: All Artwork Above

Use Lock All Artwork Above to lock all objects in front of the selected objects. Objects must overlap the selected object and be higher in the stacking order than the selected object to be locked. This is commonly used to make it easier to select objects that are obscured by other objects. This command does not work on objects grouped to the selected object. No visual cue indicates the command has been executed, except that Lock icons appear next to affected items in the Layers palette.

9.21
Object: Lock: ***Other Layers***

Lock Other Layers locks all of the layers in the document except the ones the current selections are on. Objects are not locked using this command, Layers are.

9.22
Object: ***Unlock All***   *(Command-option) [Ctrl-Alt]*–2

Unlock All releases all locked objects, enabling them to be selected. The command has no affect on locked layers, only objects.

Issues to Consider

Unlock All can unlock unwanted items. This command unlocks all of the locked objects. This can lead to extra work as objects that should remain locked will need to be selected and locked again. When many items are locked, consider manually unlocking specific objects using the Layers palette.

9.23
Object: ***Hide***

Hide objects to temporarily make them invisible. Hidden objects cannot be selected and do not print. Hiding is commonly done to temporarily remove an object that obscures another, that is slow to preview, or is cumbersome in some way.

Mistakes to Avoid

Hidden objects affect the bounding box in EPS files. The area occupied by hidden objects is included when determining the geography an EPS file occupies when placed into another application. This can lead to confusion and inefficiency. This is not the case in Illustrator native files.

Hiding objects that should be deleted or saved in another file. Hidden objects increase file space and processing time. Hiding should be temporary. If objects are not vital to the document, they should be deleted or saved into another file for reference later.

Issues to Consider

Layers offer more control. When hiding and showing objects frequently, consider isolating the objects on layers. Layers can be hidden, making it easier to manage many objects.

9.24

Object: Hide: Selection *(Command) [Ctrl]-3*

Use Hide Selection to hide the selected objects.

9.25

Object: Hide: All Artwork Above

Use Hide All Artwork Above to hide all objects in front of the selected objects. Objects must overlap the selected object and be higher in the stacking order than the selected object to be hidden. This is commonly used to make it easier to select objects that are obscured by other objects. This command does not work on objects grouped to the selected object.

9.26

Object: Hide: Other Layers

Hide Other Layers Hides all the layers in the document except the ones the current selections are on. Objects are not hidden using this command, layers are.

9.27

Object: Show All *(Command-option) [Ctrl-Alt]-3*

Show All reveals all hidden objects, enabling them to be selected and printed. The command has no affect on hidden layers, only objects.

Issues to Consider

Show All may show too many items. This command releases all the hidden objects. This can lead to extra work as objects that should remain hidden will need to be selected and hidden again. When many items are hidden, consider manually unlocking specific objects using the Layers palette.

9.28

Object: Expand

Use the Expand command to change a selected object or an object's attributes into a Group comprised of new objects while maintaining the object's look and feel. Editable objects and attributes like strokes, gradient fills, pattern fills, envelopes, blends, and symbol sets may be expressed as objects rather than flexible attributes. This removes the freely editable nature of the attribute, but is required for some techniques and workflows. For example, a user may want to edit one object inside a pattern fill. Expanding gives you access to the objects inside the pattern by changing the fill to objects. Objects are also often expanded to simplify them for printing.

The effect of Expand depends upon the type of object and attribute it is applied to. Strokes are translated to compound paths. Gradients are expanded to either a gradient mesh or a masked series of lines or ovals. Patterns are expanded to masked pattern tiles. Symbol sets are expanded to individual symbols. Envelopes are expanded to component shapes. Blends are expanded to individual objects.

Mistakes to Avoid

Attempting to expand objects that cannot be expanded with this command. Objects that have live effects such as brushes and styles must be expanded using Expand Appearance. Typically, the objects that result from expanding appearance may then be expanded. Compound Shapes must be expanded using the expand button in the Pathfinder palette.

Attempting to expand objects that cannot be expanded at all. Gradient meshes, unlike gradients, cannot be expanded to vector shapes. They must be rasterized to simplify them. Graphs are ungrouped, rather than expanded.

Attempting to expand transparency. Transparency is not removed with the Expand command. Simplifying transparency effects is done using Object: **Flatten Transparency**.

Expanding gradients to the incorrect number of objects. When expanding a gradient that will be printed, specifying too many objects can slow down processing time. In most printing environments, only one object is needed per point of distance of the gradient. The distance of the gradient is the distance of the color change. Calculate this with the Measure tool by clicking from the start to the end of the gradient. Don't check the size of the object that has the gradient, check the distance the gradient occupies in the object. Some printing facilities cut this number in half, using only one object per two points of distance in the blend. This may look jagged onscreen, but usually prints smoothly.

Issues to Consider

Dashed lines do not expand correctly. Dashed lines become solid lines upon expansion. Many users work around this by creating pattern brushes to make dashed lines. Pattern brush strokes may be expanded correctly using Expand Appearance. Another option is to apply transparency to the dashed line and then choose Flatten Transparency. When flattening for this purpose, set the Raster/Vector balance at 100. Afterward, reset the transparency.

Expand is the best method for converting gradients to gradient meshes.
Expand is an easy way to convert an object with a gradient fill to a gradient mesh. The appearance of the gradient is maintained, and the object may be modified as a mesh. The alternate method, clicking on the gradient object with the Mesh tool, converts all the mesh points to black, destroying the gradient effect. This can be rebuilt, but it is needlessly time consuming.

Expand is necessary for some printing workflows. Some high-end printing workflows that convert colors and supply in-rip trapping cannot correctly process some Illustrator objects. Brushes, symbols, and other complex objects may require expanding for color definitions to be processed correctly. If you are working in, or sending work to, this sort of environment you will typically be informed of this up-front. Users in this environment commonly favor a two-file workflow. Preparing a native Illustrator file with features intact, and then saving another expanded file (commonly an EPS) for placement into a layout file.

Expand Dialog Box

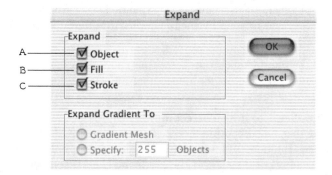

A. Object

Check the object option to expand type, envelopes, symbols, symbol sets, and blends. Expanding type objects is the same as creating outlines. Expanded envelopes appear the same but are no longer freely editable as envelopes. They become concrete vector shapes instead. Symbol sets expand to individual symbols. Symbols may themselves be expanded to produce selectable objects. Blends expand to the shapes described by the blend.

B. Fill

Check this box to create component object groups from gradients and pattern fills. Both types of fills expand to masked objects groups. This means the path of the object becomes a clipping mask for the objects that describe the contents of the path. Pattern fills are described as a series of pattern tiles laid out below the mask. This enables customization of individual elements in the fill.

Gradients may be expanded to a specified number of objects or to a gradient mesh. In the case of objects, each color change in the gradient is converted to a path. Linear gradients are comprised of filled rectangles. Radial gradients are comprised of filled ovals.

Expanding gradient fills to gradient meshes follows the same model. The original object becomes a mask, this time for a mesh object. Linear gradients are based on a rectangular mesh, radial ones on a circular mesh. Mesh points are added and colored to reproduce the gradient.

C. **Stroke**

Check this box to convert a stroke into a filled path. The stroke color of the original object becomes the fill color of the new object. Overprinting on strokes is transferred to the fills. Strokes on closed paths become compound paths to account for the negative space. Strokes on open paths do not. Expanding a stroke is the same as choosing Object: Path: **Outline Stroke**.

9.29

Object: *Expand Appearance*

Use the Expand Appearance command to convert brushes and objects that contain effects or have more than one fill or stroke into their component shapes. Brushes and effects take up additional memory and can cause difficulty and confusion for service bureaus. Expand Appearance is commonly used to reduce the file to simpler shapes or to edit the shapes in ways that were previously unavailable.

When an object's appearance is expanded, the result is a group. The group will be comprised of the objects that made up the original object. If the object was a brush, the group will be comprised of the original path and objects that describe the space the brush occupies. The shapes created will depend upon the type of brush and the objects used to define the brush initially. Commonly the shapes will themselves be a group.

If the initial object had more than one fill or stroke or used an effect, the result will be a group comprised of the elements listed in the appearance palette. Multiple fills and strokes become separate objects in the group. Effects are rendered or converted to objects. If the effects were attached to a specific fill or stroke and objects were created, that fill and stroke and those objects will also be grouped.

Issues to Consider

Expand Appearance may result in raster image objects. Commonly used effects such as Drop Shadow and Feather create pixel images when expanded. Check the Links palette after executing the command to see if new images were created. Alternatively, consult the Embedded Images section of the Document Info dialog box using the Selection Only option.

9.30

Object: *Flatten Transparency*

Use the Flatten Transparency command to remove transparency from selected objects while maintaining their look and feel. This is commonly done to simplify documents for printing, to work around problems, or to predict whether a transparent object will print as rasters or vectors. Transparent objects are also memory intensive. Flattening may be done to simplify unduly complex art.

Transparent continuous tone images, such as soft-edged drop shadows and feathered edges cannot be printed as vector art. Further, printing extensive transparency as vectors may be prohibitively time consuming. Illustrator substitutes raster images for vector shapes where possible when the document is printed. It does this at a rate determined by the Raster/Vector Balance slider in the Transparency section of File: **Document Setup**.

The Flatten Transparency command substitutes objects for transparency directly in the document using the same interface. This allows you access to the shapes and enables you to predict the effect of a specific Raster/Vector balance setting.

Flattening Transparency expands text and converts spot colors to process.

Mistakes to Avoid

Selecting only the transparent objects. For flatten transparency to work, all the objects affected by transparency must be selected. This includes the objects below the transparent object.

Flattening unnecessarily. Flattening is commonly done to predict print results or to solve a printing problem. If it isn't required that you flatten transparency, don't.

Flattening accidentally. Saving a file to a file format that doesn't support transparency, such as the Illustrator 8 EPS file format, will flatten all the objects. Flatten or backsave to a copy so that you retain editable shapes wherever possible.

Setting resolution too low. Raster art may be created in the flattening process. The presence of these images limits the ability to scale the art in Illustrator or when placed into a layout application. Set the scaling of the art to the size you intend to use it before flattening and pick a resolution appropriate for your output. Alternatively, build enough resolution into the art to allow you to scale it up and maintain a useable effective resolution.

Flatten Transparency Dialog Box

A. Raster/Vector Balance

Raster/Vector balance is set on a scale of 0 to 100. The higher the number, the more vectors are retained in the conversion process. At a setting of 0 all the selected objects are rasterized and become embedded images.

At settings around 25, Illustrator will retain simple vector shapes but rasterize more complex ones. This often leads to color mismatching where raster meets vector and should only be considered for low-memory systems.

At settings around 50, Illustrator preserves most vectors and only rasterizes complex art. As the settings move up the art must be more and more complex for Illustrator to rasterize it. At 100 Illustrator will preserve as many vectors as it can. As noted earlier, this does not necessarily mean the art will remain vectors.

B. Rasterization Resolution

Use this field to set the pixel resolution of any raster art that is created in the flattening process.

C. Convert All Strokes to Outlines

Check this box to force all strokes to be converted to filled compound paths. Unchecked, Illustrator will retain live strokes on some objects. Typically, this happens when the fill but not the stroke of a path is transparent.

D. Clip Complex Regions

This option sets the transitions from rasters to vectors along vector paths. This is intended to reduce the color shifts that may occur when part of an object is transparent and another part isn't.

E. Preserve Overprinting When Possible

This option attempts to retain the overprinting status of objects when printing separations. It is usually able to do this on objects that are not involved in transparency. This tends to increase print performance overall.

9.31

Object: *Rasterize*

The Rasterize command converts selected vector objects into pixels. Every Illustrator object that appears in the Layers palette except guides may be rasterized. This is typically done to enable the use of features that only work on raster art, such as the Photoshop filters. Pixels created using this command become embedded image objects, managed in the Links palette.

Issues to Consider

Rasterize can be applied as an effect. This enables you to apply raster effects (though not filters) to the object as though it were rasters while still maintaining the ability to edit it as vectors. This provides additional flexibility.

Rasterize Dialog Box

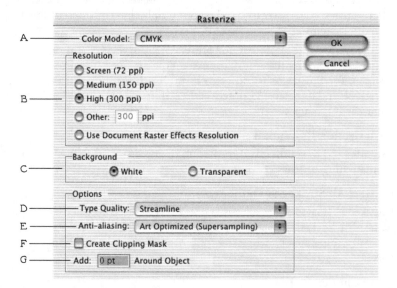

A. **Color Model**

Set the color model of the art created to the document's current color mode (RGB or CMYK), Grayscale, or Bitmap.

B. **Resolution**

Use these radio buttons to set the image's resolution to one of the common values or to a custom setting. Click the Other button to activate the field, allowing you to enter a value specific to your printing circumstances. Set Use Document Raster Effects Resolution to use whatever value is set in Effect: **Document Raster Effects Settings** dialog box.

C. Background

Set this to determine how to fill the area between the raster object and the edges of its bounding box. White creates white opaque white pixels around the objects. Transparent leaves the area as negative space. This edge created using the transparent setting is a pixel edge, not a vector mask.

D. Type Quality

Illustrator has two engines for rasterizing type. Outline creates slightly heavier type than Streamline. Streamlined keeps the type slender and sharper.

E. Anti-aliasing

Use this option to determine how edges are anti-aliased. Set to None to omit anti-aliasing. This works well for line art. Art Optimized creates edges suited for images and Type Optimized works better for images with text. In practice, Type Optimized produces crisper edges than Art Optimized. Some trial and error may be required to find the model that is bet for your image.

F. Create Clipping Mask

Enable this option to generate a vector shape masking the raster art. This provides sharp edges and creates a Group. This can complicate workflow slightly, but has the advantage of vector driven edges. This option over-rides the background setting, creating transparency between the object and its bounding box.

G. Add [space] Around Object

This option increases the bounding box size horizontally and vertically by the amount specified.

9.32

Object: Create Gradient Mesh

This command is used to existing objects to gradient meshes. Both vector and embedded image objects may be converted.

Gradient meshes are part of the mesh class of object, which also includes envelopes. Meshes are comprised of a grid of points connected by segments. Each point on the grid may have up to four segments connected to them. The points and segments may be moved and edited using the standard path editing toolset and techniques.

In the case of the gradient mesh, the points and segments control how color is distributed through the object. Each point has its own fill color. Color blends between the points in a manner described by the segments connecting the points. Since four segments can be attached to each point, color can blend away from a point in four directions toward four different colors.

This makes the gradient mesh a flexible means of describing complex color changes. It is often used to create realistic lighting and textures.

Gradient Meshes require a PostScript level 3 device to be printed as vector shapes. In the event that the file is printed to a different printer, Illustrator substitutes an alternate, raster version of the art temporarily for printing. This is fine, but you should be aware that the art will have the same scaling limitations that all raster art does. The resolution of this art is established in the Printing & Export section of the Document Setup Dialog box.

Gradient Meshes support spot colors, but only if every point in the grid is set to the same spot color. Otherwise, the mesh will separate as process color.

Gradient Meshes can also be created by expanding Gradient fills and by using the Mesh tool. The Create Gradient mesh command is the quickest way to create a mesh with evenly spaced points.

Mistakes to Avoid

Attempting to create Gradient Meshes on objects with gradient or pattern fills. Applying this command to objects with gradient or pattern fills turns them black. The mesh can still be edited but it is time consuming. Gradient fills should be expanded to Gradient meshes, Patterns should be reset to a solid fill color.

Creating a mesh with incorrect resolution. Gradient meshes may print as pixel images. Be sure to set your pixel resolution and avoid scaling the mesh in a page layout program.

Attempting to create photorealistic meshes from imported scans. Detail is only retained with a large mesh grid and even that is blocky. The resulting mesh is also larger in file size.

Issues to Consider

Create Gradient Mesh works on open paths. The path is closed in the process and all but the simplest open paths typically create snarled meshes that are difficult to edit. Nonetheless, the command is available and can be used to create uncommon objects.

Original objects are removed. Upon conversion both image and vector objects are replaced with a mesh object, the original object is cleared. Consider copying the original object prior to conversion if it is needs to be used again.

Converting back to an object from a gradient mesh is cumbersome. Be sure you do not need the shape before converting.

Create Gradient Mesh Dialog Box

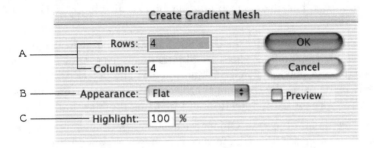

A. Rows & Columns

Use this field to establish the number of horizontal (rows) and vertical (columns) areas created in the mesh. Values may be set from 2 to 50. When converting an image object to a gradient mesh, larger numbers will retain more image detail.

B. Appearance

This field is used to set the base colors of the mesh points created. Set to Flat, the points all stay the same color as the initial object. Set To Center to create a mesh that blends from the objects original color on the sides toward white in the center. The blend is not completely circular in this model. To Edge reverses that, blending from the base color toward white on the outside.

C. Highlight

This field sets the color blended toward when using To Center or To Edge. At 100% the color is white. At lower percents, the color becomes a lighter tint of the original color. At 0% no blending occurs.

9.33

Object: Slice

Use the commands under the Slice menu to create object and user slices, to manage slices and to set slice options. Slices divide a document into parts for assembling as a table in a web page. This enables you to optimize different areas with different settings, and to combine different features such as animations or rollover buttons within the same image. Tables are a common HTML device for controlling graphic space in a web page. Just as a table in a database, HTML tables divide graphic space into cells. The cells may contain images, parts of images, or HTML text. This is done to work around limitations in HTML. Tables are widely accepted by browsers and HTML generating applications.

A slice defines a rectangular area that will become the contents of a cell when HTML is generated by choosing File: **Save for Web**. Slices may be a set geographic area or a based on the bounding box of an object or layer. Each model has its advantages.

Creating a set geographic slice, or User Slice, allows you to plan around a specific space requirement. User Slices are objects themselves. They appear in the layers palette, and may be styled and modified as any object. User Slices are commonly made using the commands Object: Slice: **Create from Guides** and Object: Slice: **Create from Selection** and by using the Slice tool.

Basing a slice on an object, an Object Slice, allows flexibility. As the size and position of the object is altered, the slice is redrawn as well. Object Slices are made using the Object: Slice: **Make** command.

Since a table is rectangular, Illustrator must add additional slices to account for space you have not sliced. These are called Auto Slices. Auto Slices are linked by default. In the Save for Web dialog box, you will be able to set the optimization method for auto slices, but the method will be used for all auto slices.

Slices may contain image or text information. Text information can be converted to rudimentary HTML from Illustrator text or entered manually in the Slice options dialog box. Typically, the text entered is HTML.

Slices may be selected and modified using the Slice Select tool. *(For more information, see 4.34, Web Slicing Tools.)*

9.34

Object: Slice: *Make*

Use this command to create an Object Slice from a selected object, group or layer. The bounding box of the selected items becomes the slice area. If more than one object is selected, slices are defined for each object. If a group is selected or a layer is targeted, the slice fits the bounding area of all the objects in the group or layer. As objects are added and subtracted to the group or layer, the slice changes to fit the new bounding box.

Issues to Consider

Slices made in this way do not appear as objects in the Layers palette. They are modified as the objects they are connected to are modified.

Text may become live HTML text. Selected text objects may be converted directly to HTML using the Slice Options command. Rudimentary characteristics, such as overall size, color, and style are converted to their HTML equivalents.

9.35

Object: Slice: *Release*

Use this command to remove an Object Slice from a selected object or targeted layer and to convert a User Slice into a non-slice object.

Issues to Consider

You don't need to release a User Slice to style it. By default User Slices are styled with a Fill and Stroke of None. You can apply fills and strokes to the User Slice as though it were a standard rectangle. User Slices may be transformed using any of Illustrator's tools. In the event that a User Slice is transformed such that it is no longer a rectangle, the bounding box of the slice is used to define the table cell area.

9.36

Object: Slice: *Create from Guides*

Use this command to create User Slices based on the positioning of the guides in the document. Ruler guides create slices everywhere they intersect the document. Guides created from objects create slices based on the bounding box of the guide. Guides do not have to be unlocked to execute this command and slices are created from all guides, regardless of whether or not they are selected.

Issues to Consider

Use Clip to Artboard in conjunction with ruler guides. Ruler guides extend across the entire pasteboard, creating gigantic slices. Clip to Artboard restricts the placement of slices to within the confines of the Artboard, creating a more manageable document. Many users also set the document setup to a screen resolution size, such as 640 × 480.

9.37

Object: Slice: *Create from Selection*

Use this command to generate a User Slice based on the bounding areas of the currently selected objects. The slice is generated atop the highest object in the stacking order.

9.38

Object: Slice: **Duplicate Slice**

Use this command to copy a selected User Slice or to create a user slice from a selected object slice. Copied slices contain the same Slice Options as the original.

9.39

Object: Slice: **Combine Slices**

This command creates a single slice from all the currently selected slices. The united slice covers the bounding box of all the selected items.

9.40

Object: Slice: **Divide Slices**

Divide Slice creates a series of new, evenly sized slices from the currently selected slices by breaking the slice up horizontally and or vertically. This is commonly done to create a series of identical slices quickly. For example, when creating a vertical navigation bar with a series of stacked buttons, a single slice could be created covering the entire navigation bar and then divided vertically to create slices for each button.

When this command is chosen, the Divide Slice dialog box opens. Slices may be divided horizontally, vertically, or both.

Divide Slices Dialog Box

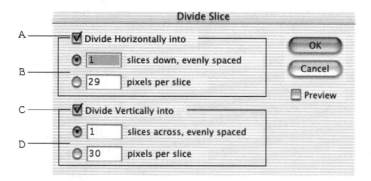

A. **Divide Horizontally into**

Check this option to divide the selected slice into rows horizontally.

B. **Horizontal Divide Method**

Choose a method for dividing slices horizontally. Slices may be divided to create a specific number of evenly spaced slices, or set to a specific pixel size. Slices set to a specific pixel size will repeat until they have filled the original slice. The last slice will fill the remaining space available. It will only be the same size as the others if the pixel size is an integer of the original object size.

C. **Divide Vertically into**

Check this option to divide the selected slice into columns vertically.

D. **Divide Vertically Method**

Use these options to determine how the slice is divided vertically. The options are the same as they are for dividing horizontally (see "Horizontal Divide Method" above).

9.41

Object: Slice: *Delete All*

This command clears all the Users slices in a document and releases all the object slices. It is usually used when it is easier to start the slicing over than to modify existing slices.

9.42

Object: Slice: Slice Options

Choose this command to access the Slice Options dialog box.

Slice Options Dialog Box

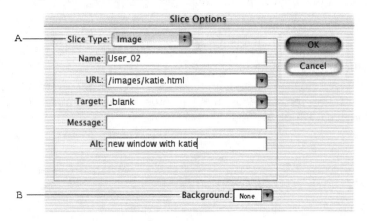

A. Slice Type

The Slice Type menu sets the basic model for the slice to be image or text information.

Image

Image is graphic information. Set a slice to image to generate a web graphic based on the contents of the slice when using File: **Save for Web**. This is the default setting for all slices.

No Image

No Image slices contain text. Graphic information in the slice is not exported when saving for the web.

HTML Text

HTML Text slices write styled HTML into a cell based upon the text in an object slice. This option is only available to type objects that have been made into object slices. HTML Text records the size, color, and styling, such as bold or italic, of the text in the slice, even if the text is styled differently from word to word. As the text in the slices changes, the HTML text is updated to match.

B. Background

Use this option to set the background color of the slice. This will set a background color for the table cell in the HTML generated. Set to one of the colors on the list or choose a custom color from the Color Picker by choosing other. The Eyedropper color is the last color picked in the Save for Web dialog box. This option is available for all slice types.

Image Slice Controls

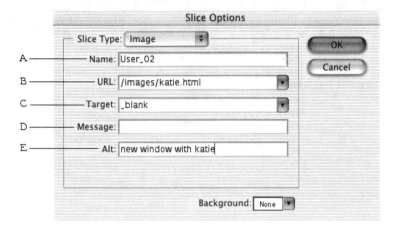

A. Name

Use this to name a slice. Slice names are sometimes used by developers and coders in automated workflows.

B. URL

Enter a web address into this field to generate a link to another web page. The link will be written into the HTML generated when Save for the Web is executed. The cell will act as a button, linking viewers to the address entered in this field. This may be an absolute or relative URL.

C. Target

The target option is used in conjunction with the URL option (above) to set the page the URL link opens in. This is commonly used in an HTML document that contains frames. Frames are given names in an HTML document. Enter the name of a specific frame in the target field or use one of the defaults listed. _blank creates a new web page for the link, leaving the current page open. _self replaces the page with the referenced page in the same frame. This is the default action in most browsers. _parent loads the link into the frame that encases the current frame. _top replaces the entire frameset with the link.

D. Message

Text entered in this field appears in the browser status bar. This is commonly used to provide details about the link, particularly when the URL itself is not descriptive. When this feature is used without using the URL option (above), a null (#) link is generated in the HTML so that the message can be displayed.

E. **Alt**

The Alt tag supplies alternate text to the browsers. The text is displayed while images are loading and on browsers that are set to not display images. Alt tags are important as they are used by the screen reading software used by the visually impaired.

No Image Options

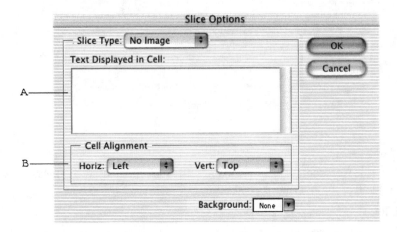

A. **Text Displayed in Cell**

Use the field in the dialog box to enter text that appears in the cell. Typically, HTML is entered into the cell. Non-HTML text that is entered will still appear in the cell in the web page, but will not be styled. Text Object Slices will populate the cell with HTML that describes the size, color and style of the text. This is similar to the HTML Text slice option, except that it is not dynamic and will not updates as text changes. However, unlike HTML text, the text is editable in this field and can be manually adjusted as needed.

B. **Cell Alignment**

Use the Cell Alignment pop-up menus to set the horizontal and vertically alignment of the text within the cell.

HTML Text Options

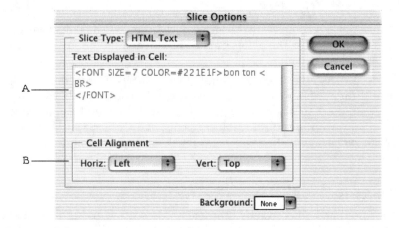

A. Text Displayed in Cell

The information in this field is not modifiable. To change the HTML text, edit the text in the object slice directly on the page. This command does not generate Cascading Style Sheets or record font information. It will not preserve the exact look and feel of the text.

B. Cell Alignment

Use the Cell Alignment pop-up menus to set the horizontal and vertically alignment of the text within the cell.

9.43

Object: Slice: *Clip to Artboard*

This command divides the artboard into auto slices. It also limits slices to the space defined by the artboard. Slices outside the artboard are cropped to fit the space. In the event that the option is deactivated, cropped slices return to their original size. This option is commonly used when planning a web page rather than a graphic.

9.44

Object: *Path*

The Path submenu is used to perform tasks related to path position and structure. It is a vital set of commands for customizing lines and should be understood by serious users.

Object: Path: Join (Command) [Ctrl]-J

The Join command connects two selected anchor points. The points must be the ends of open paths. The points can't be in different groups, be text paths, guides, or part of a graph.

If there is any space between the points, Join connects them with a straight segment. If they are in the exact same location, the two points become one. In this event, the Join dialog box open. The Join options are Smooth, which creates a point with linked direction segments, and Corner, which creates a point with independent direction segments. Use Corner to most accurately retain the look of the paths.

Mistakes to Avoid

Not positioning points exactly atop each other when trying to make a single point. If you didn't see the Join dialog box, a segment was created. The Join dialog box appears whenever two points are about to become a single point, even if the points are without direction segments. If you didn't see the dialog box, a straight line segment was created.

Failing to account for the new Fill. Two filled open segments may appear very differently after they are joined. The fill area will no longer be based on the endpoints of the open paths.

Selecting more than two open points. If you have more than two end points selected, the command will not execute. This commonly happens when entire paths are selected rather than individual points.

Selecting points that are not open. This usually happens with freeform or complicated paths, especially when viewed from afar. Another cause is selecting direction points and not anchor points. This usually happens when switching freely between the Direct Selection and Convert Anchor Point tools. Be certain that you have endpoints selected.

Undo requires reselection. If you join two anchor points and then undo it, both objects involved become selected, rather than the two points you had selected. If you fail to reselect the correct points and join again, you may get an error. This happens as users join two points, then change their mind about the kind of join they wanted. They undo and join again quickly, but they now have a different selection.

Issues to Consider

Average and Join are often used together. Since points must be in exactly the same position to become a single point, Object: Path: **Average** is commonly used to position the points. Using the Average command's Both setting positions points in the same location. Since Average and Join are so connected, there is a keyboard shortcut that performs both functions together. Press (Option-Command-Shift) [Alt-Ctrl-Shift]-J to Average Both and Join two selected points.

Forward direction segments are discarded. The direction segments on open points not connected to existing segments are deleted when the points are joined. To create a curved line joining the points, you will need to manually edit the points.

Snap to point is useful. When attempting to position two anchor points directly atop each other, use the Snap to Point feature (by choosing View: **Snap to Point**). This makes the task easier and gives you a visual cue when items are aligned.

9.46

Object: Path: Average *(Option-Command) [Alt-Ctrl]-J*

Use the Average command to align the positions of selected anchor points. Points can be averaged horizontally, vertically, or both. When averaged, selected points are all repositioned to a position in the middle of the current positions. Alignment takes place about an axis. For example, horizontal alignment moves points so that they are aligned along the horizontal axis. This means the points must move up and down. Averaging both horizontal and vertical moves the objects into the same position. Average is commonly used to straighten out lines and as first step before joining points. To Average and Join paths in one step, choose (Option-Command-Shift) [Alt-Ctrl-Shift]-J

Mistakes to Avoid

Selecting incorrectly. If you select too many, or the wrong anchor points, Average will not achieve the desired results. Be careful to use the Direct Selection tool or the Direct Select Lasso tool when selecting points and be careful about the points you select.

Assuming that averaged points always produce straight lines. Although averaging two anchor points lines them up, the points may have direction segments on them. This will cause the path to curve, even if the points are in line.

Confusing the horizontal and vertical axis. Remember that the align options refer to the axis they will align to, not the direction they will move.

Attempting to average mesh points. Neither envelopes nor gradient mesh points may be averaged.

9.47

Object: Path: **Outline Stroke**

Outline Stroke converts the stroke on a selected object to a closed, filled path that describes the same area as the stroke. The look and feel of the stroke is retained, as the stroke color and overprinting status are transferred to the fill. This is commonly to work around limitations of strokes, to begin a technique that does not function on strokes, or to take advantage of the stroke shape. For example, many users outline Strokes to apply gradient fills to them.

If the original object had a Fill as well as a Stroke, the Fill object remains but has a Stroke of None.

Mistakes to Avoid

Applying Outline Stroke to a brushed path. Outlining a brushstroke removes the brush effect and creates a closed path based on the stroke weight of the path. To create a path based on the appearance of a brushstroke, choose Object: **Expand Appearance**.

Attempting to outline dashed paths. Dashed paths become solid paths when outlined. To outline a dashed path as dashes, apply transparency to the path, choose Object: **Flatten Transparency** and set the Raster/Vector balance at 100.

Issues to Consider

Outline Stroke may also be applied as an Effect. This is usually done as part of a style. When you want to continue to use the objects created, it is better to apply the command directly.

Converting strokes to paths enables you to edit both sides of the stroke. As a filled path, you can alter the width of the shape freely in ways that are unavailable for strokes. Outline strokes also respond differently to some transformation techniques.

End and Join stroke attributes are translated directly when the path is outlined. Rounded end strokes become paths with rounded ends, and so forth.

9.48

Object: Path: Offset Path

Use Offset Path to create a duplicate of the selected object a specified distance from the original. The new path has the same fill and stroke as the original and follows the curves of the path exactly except at the distance specified. This effect appears similar to scaling, but cannot be achieved for objects other than perfect circles and squares by scaling.

If the path is open, the effect is similar to Outline Stroke. The offset distance is applied to both sides of the path and the new object is created behind the original. No distance is added about the ends of an open path.

Offset Path Dialog Box

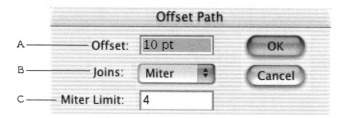

A. Offset

Use this amount to set the distance from the selected path the new path will be. A positive or negative may be specified. A positive number places the new path on the exterior of the original path. A negative amount places the new path on the interior of the original. Paths on the exterior are behind the original object in the stacking order; paths on the interior are in front of the original object.

B. Joins

Use this option to set the way the path will treat corners as it traces about the original object. Set to Miter to make corners sharp, Bevel to make them flat or Round to make them curved. These fields do not set the stroke values for the new path, they control how the new path is drawn. It may be helpful to imagine that Offset Path is placing a stroke of twice the offset distance on the object, outlining the stroke, and then keeping the inside of it for negative offsets or the outside for positive offsets. The Join and Miter limit affect this imaginary stroke.

C. Miter Limit

Use this option to set the way the path will treat corners as it traces about the original object. Miter limit is used in conjunction with Miter joins to determine how far a sharp corner may extend before becoming beveled. This option does not affect the stroke of the newly created path, it determines how the path is drawn relative to the original path.

9.49

Object: Path: Simplify

Use the Simplify command to reduce the number of anchor points of a path. This is commonly done to create a more efficient, more manageable path. Typically, the paths that need simplification are generated by Illustrator's Auto Trace function, poorly created type that has been turned to outlines, AutoCAD files, unprofessional clip art, paths from people who do not know how to make curves with the Pen tool, or paths drawn with the Pencil or Brush tool set at a very low Fidelity.

Issues to Consider

Simplifying will likely change the shape of the path. Unless the path has very few curves, Simplify is apt to change its appearance slightly. Use care when simplifying and be sure to preview the original as you simplify. Be especially cautious about objects that are used for trapping.

Start with a base setting and adjust from there. Many users start with a curve precision of 85-90% and an Angle Threshold of 45°. With Preview and Show Original activated, evaluate the results and adjust as needed.

Preview supplies a readout. The Preview option adds a readout of the number of anchor points before and after simplification to the dialog box.

Simplify Options

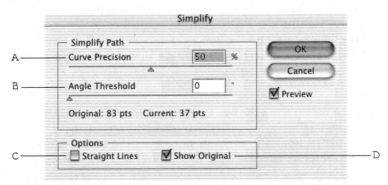

A. Curve Precision

This setting determines how accurately the simplified path should follow the original. The higher the setting, the closer the path will be to the original and the more anchor points will be used. Paradoxically, at very high settings, this can increase the number of anchor points on a curve.

B. Angle Threshold

This setting instructs Simplify not to smooth angles with curves less than the amount specified. This maintains the look of sharper turns.

C. **Straight Lines**

This option generates paths without direction segments. The result is all straight segments. When using this option, a low Angle Threshold is vital to maintain path fidelity. Curve Precision is not available when this option is checked.

D. **Show Original**

This command displays the original path along with the simplified version. The original displays without fill or stroke in the highlight color of the next layer. This option works best with the Preview option activated.

9.50

Object: Path: *Add Anchor Points*

Use this command to add an anchor point to a selected path between every two existing anchor points. The anchor points are added between each point based on the curve of the path and have the correct direction segments to describe that part of the path. This also redraws the direction segments on other points to be accurate with the new points. As the command is reapplied, more and more points are added. This is commonly done in preparation for applying a filter, such as Pucker and Bloat, which works better with more anchor points or to begin manually editing a path.

Issues to Consider

You can also add anchor points with a filter. To add many anchor points to a path at once, apply Filter: Distort: **Roughen** with a size of 0 pt and a Detail setting based on the number of points to be added.

Anchor points can be added one at a time. Use the Add Anchor Point tool to add one anchor point at a time. This is often done when you need to adjust a custom path or are preparing to delete part of a path. *(For more information, see 2.1, Pen Tool Suite.)*

Add anchor points can be used to alleviate extremely long direction segments. Very large direction segments are hard to edit. They can be reduced by adding anchor points to the path. The path retains its appearance, but the direction segments are smaller in size to account for the new points, making them easier to adjust.

9.51

Object: Path: Divide Objects Below

Use this command to perform a variant of the Pathfinder command Divide between the selected object and all the objects it touches. Only one object may be selected for this command to function. The single selected object cannot be a Symbol Set, brushstroke, a raster object, or a mesh.

As with the Pathfinder version of Divide, a new object is created everywhere vector lines overlap each other. The effect is similar to using the selected object as a cookie cutter to stamp shapes out of the all objects it has contact with. Each object is divided where the selected object overlaps it. The original object is deleted after the command is executed.

Issues to Consider

The Pathfinder: Divide command is similar. The pathfinder command creates paths everywhere selected objects overlap. Divide Objects Below creates paths everywhere each unselected path crosses the selected object, rather than all the objects. The effect is similar to a series of repeated pathfinders performed with a single command.

Not all objects are affected. Divide Objects does not affect Symbol Sets, brushstrokes, raster objects, or meshes.

The inclusion of "below" in the name is misleading. This command affects all objects, the selected object touches, regardless of their position in the stacking order.

This command has been renamed to avoid confusion with the Slice feature. Earlier versions of Illustrator called this command Slice. Before that it was known as Apply Knife.

9.52

Object: Path: Clean Up

Use the Clean Up command to delete commonly unwanted objects from a document. These objects are unwanted because they add file size and clutter to the document without benefiting the file. This command does not affect guides, locked or hidden objects, or objects on locked or hidden layers.

Issues to Consider

Clean Up is a fine addition to a file prep Action. Many users build and use Illustrator Actions to prepare a file for handoff to a client or service provider. Such an action typically includes at least removing unused brushes, styles, swatches, and symbols, and running the Clean Up filter. *(For more information, see 15.1, Actions Palette Overview.)*

Clean Up Dialog Box

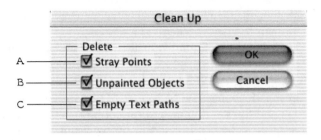

A. Stray Points

Stray Points are single anchor points not connected to anything else. They are commonly created when parts of most, but not all of a path is deleted, such as deleting opposite anchor points of a circle. Another common source of stray points is accidentally clicking with Type tool and then deselecting. Stray points are included with other objects when determining a file's bounding box. This can lead to confusion when importing art into other applications.

B. Unpainted Objects

Unpainted objects are all objects except masks and blend spines with a Fill and Stroke of None. Since these objects are invisible, it may seem intuitive to delete them all. In some cases, invisible boxes representing page or object guides are included to aid in compositing files together in a page layout program. Be certain these guiding boxes are locked before executing Clean Up.

C. Empty Text Paths

Empty text paths are text objects without text. These paths are sometimes created by errant clicking with the Type tool.

9.53

Object: *Blend*

Use the Blend command to create a series of intermediate objects between objects. The intermediate objects create a progressive transition between the position, color, opacity, and shape of objects in the blend. The intermediate objects are held in memory without being actualized onscreen as paths. They are visible in Preview mode, but not in Outline. As objects in the blend are modified, the intermediate shapes are recalculated. This creates design flexibility, since objects may be modified at any time. Blends may not be made from type, raster art, meshes, and symbol sets. Effects and gradients may be blended, but complex styles are typically not translated correctly.

An open path called the "spine" determines the position of the intermediate objects between the blended objects. Together with the spine, the objects in a blend become a single blend object.

Blend objects appear in the Layers palette as a nested group of objects. The objects may be locked and hidden individually. Hiding a single object in a blend does not hide the intermediate objects. Blend objects may also be reordered by changing their position in the Layers palette.

The spine is an open path connecting the centers of two objects in the blend. The spine has a Fill and Stroke of none and cannot be styled. If the spine is repositioned, objects on either end of it will be repositioned as well. The spine is straight and has no direction segments, but may be altered using any of the standard path editing tools. Editing the spine affects the placement of intermediate objects.

Mistakes to Avoid

Using blend objects that contain nonvariable attributes. If objects in a blend have an attribute that cannot be blended, such as a color blend mode or a brush stroke, the intermediate objects will have the attribute but the end object will not. This abrupt change often looks odd and unnatural.

Strokes on smooth color blends. When attempting to create a smooth color transition, strokes typically ruin the effect. In general, strokes make worse blend candidates than fills.

Blending with more objects than needed. When creating smooth color blends, Illustrator builds as many shapes between objects as there is color difference, up to 254 objects. To create smooth color in print, only one object per point of distance in the blend is required (use the Measure tool to determine the distance the blend occupies by dragging from one end of the blend to the other). Reduce the number by setting the blend to Smooth Color and then switching to Specified Steps. The Specified Step default will be the number of steps Illustrator was going to create when using Smooth Color.

Joining open paths used in a blend. Using the command Object: **Join** on an open path that is used in a Blend breaks up the blend. This happens when any path is joined to the blend path, not just other paths in the blend. This commonly happens when trying to extend or add to a path after it is part of blend. To extend an open path in a blend consider using the Pen tool.

Failing to group. Failing to group logically connected objects (such as the objects that comprise a logo) before blending with other objects. Blending multiple objects creates a blend between the objects from the back of the stacking order to the front. Grouped objects are blended as a single unit. This maintains the look and feel of the connected objects and prevents them from blending with each other.

Issues to Consider

Blends may be created and added to with the Blend tool. The Blend tool features the ability to twist blends upon creation.

Objects in a Blend cannot be adjusted using the Align palette. Be sure that objects are positioned as you need before blending them.

9.54

Object: Blend: Make   *(Command-Option) [Ctrl-Alt]-B*

Use this command to convert selected objects to a blend and to add objects to an existing blend. At least two paths must be selected to execute this command, but many may be. Objects in a blend obey stacking order. Intermediate objects will follow this order as well.

9.55

Object: Blend: Release

(Command-Option-Shift) [Ctrl-Alt-Shift] - B

Releasing a blend removes the blend relationship between the objects and clears the intermediate objects. The spine remains and becomes a standard, paintable object. Do not confuse this command with Object: Blend: **Expand**.

9.56

Object: *Blend Options*

Use this command to set the defaults for the Blend command or to change the options for a selected blend. Any part of a blend may be selected to execute this command.

Blend Options Dialog Box

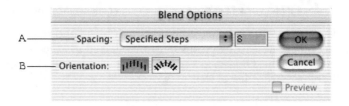

A. Spacing

Use this menu to determine the way the number of intermediate objects are calculated.

Smooth Color

Smooth color creates as many steps between each set of objects as there are differences in color tones. For black to white blends, this number is 254. If colors are closer tonally, fewer steps will be created by default.

Specified Steps

Use this option to create a particular number of intermediate objects between every two objects in the blend. This number can go up to 1,000.

Specified Distance

This sets the number of steps in the blend to the total distance of the blend divided by this number. This value does not necessarily represent the distance between intermediate steps in the blend.

B. Orientation

Use Orientation to rotate the blend and intermediate objects with the curve of the path or leave them square to the page. This option doesn't do anything unless the spine is curved or has more then two points. Set to Align to Page to square the objects to the page. Set to Align to Path to rotate the objects about the path. Be aware that the position of curve handles on a path affects the distribution of intermediate objects. Orientation is available for all blend spacing types.

9.57

Object: Blend: *Expand*

Use this command to make paths out of the intermediate objects. The Blend is replaced with a group made of the new paths and the original blend objects. The spine is deleted. This is often done to customize intermediate shapes or to facilitate a prepress chore. Some users also make blends strictly for the purposes of creating intermediate shapes.

9.58

Object: Blend: *Replace Spine*

This command deletes the spine of a currently selected blend object and replaces it with another path. To execute this command a blend and only one other object may be selected. The replacement spine may be an open or a closed path.

9.59

Object: Blend: *Reverse Spine*

This command switches the positions of the objects in the blend, leaving the spine in the same position. Each object in the blend takes the geographic position of its reverse counterpart in the blend. The center points of each intermediate object as it crosses the spine are used for positioning. The stacking order of the objects is unaffected by this command.

9.60

Object: Blend: *Reverse Front to Back*

Use this command to switch the stacking order of the blend objects without repositioning their location.

9.61

Object: *Envelope Distort*

Use these commands to distort the shape of an object based on another path or a mesh. The effect will be similar to the distort function in the free transform tool except that many points can used to pull and distend and object. Envelope distorts provide flexibility in that the distorted object and the envelope remain independently editable.

Envelope distorts are started by selecting a prebuilt distortion or by using an existing object. Although envelopes can be started a number of ways, once made they are edited and handled in the same manner. Only the envelope or the objects being distorted by the envelope may be edited at a given time. You must choose to edit one on they other. Envelopes are essentially meshes. Gradient mesh points control color, envelope mesh points control distortion. Use the Direct Selection tool to edit mesh points, use the Mesh tool to add and edit points.

Issues to Consider

Envelopes are best suited to curved distortion. By their nature, these distortions lend themselves to organic distortion. Even straight corner mesh points have direction points attached to them. Creating hard corner turns, such as folding a logo over two adjacent sides of a box, will be difficult to produce.

Envelopes must be closed shapes. Deleting mesh points removes them from the envelope, but does not leave an open mesh.

Envelopes themselves do not have fill and stroke but do support other attributes. Enveloped objects support Styles and Transparency. They can become part of compound shapes and may have effects applied to them.

Raster art can be distorted. Linked raster art cannot be distorted with an envelope, but embedded raster art can.

Overlapping areas may be revealed when enveloped. A shape that is cleanly behind another shape may be revealed when distorted by an envelope. To prevent this, consider removing the hidden parts of objects with the Trim Pathfinder before distorting. *(For more information, see 29.8, Trim.)*

9.62

Object: Envelope Distort: Make with Warp/Reset with Warp (Command-Option) [Ctrl-Alt]-W

Use this command to distort selected objects and reset existing envelopes using a prebuilt envelope shape and interface. Once the envelope is applied, it is editable as any envelope.

Issues to Consider

Warped text doesn't export to Photoshop. Although the interface for this feature is identical to Photoshop 6's Text Warp feature, the feature doesn't remain editable when the file is exported to the Photoshop format.

Warp Options Dialog Box

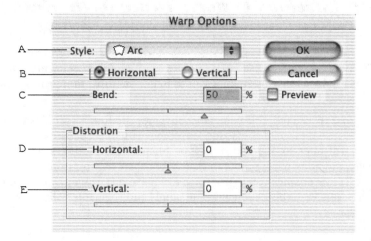

A. **Style**

Choose one of the fifteen basic shapes for the envelope. Each has a small descriptive icon next to its name to illustrate the nature of the distortion. This icon represents the horizontal, 100% version of the warp.

B. **Horizontal/Vertical**

Set to horizontal, the warp's orientation matches the descriptive icon in the Style pop-up menu. Set to Vertical, the warp envelope is rotated 90°, causing the effect to run top to bottom.

C. **Bend** (-100% to 100%)

This slider controls the direction and intensity of the effect. At 0%, an envelope is created but not distorted. Moving the slider to the right creates an effect similar to the Style icon. Moving the slider to the left of center produces the reverse effect. Higher values produce stronger distortions.

D. **Horizontal Distortion** (-100% to 100%)

Use this slider to distend the object side to side. The effect is similar to a perspective distortion. Dragging to the right pinches the left side together. Dragging to the left produces a reverse effect.

E. **Vertical Distortion**

Use this slider to distend the object top to bottom. The effect is similar to a perspective distortion. Dragging to the right pinches the top together. Dragging to the left produces a reverse effect.

9.63

Object: Envelope Distort: *Make with Mesh*

(Command-Option) [Ctrl-Alt]-M

Use this command to establish a rectangle envelope with a grid of mesh points. No particular effect is created upon execution of the command, but an envelope is established. This enables you to begin the distortion process with an evenly spaced sequence of points.

If an envelope is selected, this command becomes the Reset with Mesh command. This will replace the existing envelope with the specified mesh. A check box will offer to Maintain Envelope Shape. This preserves the initial warp shape and adds mesh points to that rather than starting from the original object. This is enables you to use the envelope as a starting point and then add mesh points with this command. The points and segments will follow the envelope shape.

Envelope Mesh Dialog Box

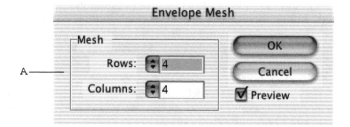

A. **Mesh**

Choose the number of evenly distributed horizontal rows and vertical columns to create in the mesh. This lends itself to creating waves and curves in an object, since a series of mesh points may be easily selected at a pass.

9.64

Object: Envelope Distort: *Make with Top Object*

(Command-Option) [Ctrl-Alt]-C

Use this command to create a distortion based on the interior of the top object of the current selection. All other objects are fit inside the space, distorted by the top object's anchor points. This lends itself for creating textures and grain that follows the contours of a shape.

If the topmost object is an open path, the path is closed upon execution of the command by joining the two open points with a straight line. Envelopes do not support paint styles, so the object loses and printable attributes it may have had.

The top object cannot be complex. It must be a single path or mesh or a symbol that contains a single path or mesh. After the command is executed, the top object becomes a mesh shape. If the envelope is released, the object remains a mesh.

9.65

Object: Envelope Distort: Release

Use this command to remove the distortion caused by the envelope. The original art is returned and the envelope becomes a standard path. If the envelope was created from a warp or mesh the envelope object becomes a gradient mesh.

9.66

Object: Envelope Distort: Envelope Options

This command accesses the Envelope Options dialog box. If an envelope is selected, the options set will apply to it. If an envelope is not selected, the options set the defaults for the next envelope created.

Envelope Options Dialog Box

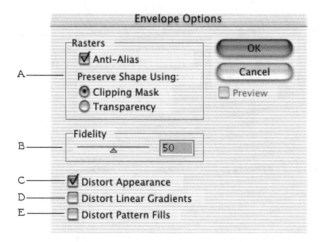

A. **Rasters**

Use this section to determine how pixel images are impacted by an envelope.

Anti-Alias

> Check this box to anti-alias edges of raster art. Anti-aliasing smooths edges and should always be used.

Preserve Shape Using

> Choose a model for preserving negative space, clipping mask vectors or transparent rasters.

B. **Fidelity** (0 to 100)

> Use this slider to establish the closeness the interior art will remain to the envelope. Higher numbers result in a tighter fit to the envelope.

C. **Distort Appearance**

> This option distorts any styles or effects applied to the enveloped objects. In the event that it is not activated, the style is applied to the enveloped shape rather than being distorted by the envelope.

D. **Distort Linear Gradients**

> This option instructs the envelope to distort linear gradient fills in the same manner as the enveloped objects. This will typically result in the gradients that will need to be printed or expanded as gradient meshes.

E. **Distort Pattern Fills**

> This option instructs the envelope to distort pattern fills in the same manner as the enveloped objects.

9.67

Object: Envelope Distort: *Expand*

Use the Expand command to convert selected envelopes into component objects. The effect is the same as choosing Object: **Expand**. If more than one object is created in the expansion the results will be a group.

9.68

Object: Envelope Distort: *Edit Contents/Envelope* (Command-Shift) [Ctrl-Shift]-V

Use this command to make the contents of a selected envelope available for editing. Either an envelope or its contents can be edited at a given time. When the contents of an envelope are being edited, the command becomes Edit Envelope. When this command is chosen, the original objects become available and appear in the Layers palette. The envelope shape appears as a group.

9.69

Object: *Clipping Mask*

Use this command to convert a series of selected objects into a clipping mask group. At least two objects must be selected to execute the command and the topmost object must be a path, compound shape, text object, or a group comprised of those elements. Objects in different groups cannot be part of the same clipping group unless the entire group is selected.

When the command is executed, the topmost object becomes a Clipping Path. The remaining selected objects are only visible in areas where they intersect the clipping path. The objects remain editable but are "clipped" by the boundaries of the clipping path. The clipping path is also called a mask, since it masks, or hides, parts of other objects. The mask and the objects may be repositioned to adjust the visibility of the objects.

Clipping paths produce groups. Like all groups, the clipped group objects are next to each other in the stacking order and housed as a group in the Layers palette. Any object positioned between the clipping path and the bottom member of the group will be in the group and be clipped. This can only happen by dragging objects into that position in the Layers palette or by using paste in front or paste in back. Send Forward and Send Backward treat groups as the single objects they are when moving objects in front or behind them.

The clipping path is given a fill and stroke of None when the command is executed. This can be altered after the mask is created by selecting and styling the mask object. Clipping mask fills only appear in areas where other objects are not. The effect is as if the fill were behind all of the masked objects.

Clipping paths are identified in the Layers palette by an underlined name. Object in a clipping group are separated in the Layers palette by dotted lines.

Mistakes to Avoid

Clipping paths that are too numerous or too complex. Clipping paths increase the complexity of the document. The more clipping paths and the more complex the clipping paths, the greater the likelihood the document will have difficulty printing. Try to keep the use of clipping paths to when you really need them. See the Paths techniques section for cropping techniques.

Confusing Layer Clipping Masks with Clipping Groups. Layers may be clipped using a similar workflow. The command and effect is the same, except the command is housed in the Layers palette menu and affects all of the contents on a layer, rather than only selected objects. *(For more information, see 25.10, Make Clipping Mask.)*

Destroying layer organization with masking. Masking creates Groups. If objects are organized into layers and sublayers, masking them will change their position in the stacking order to the same layer as the top-most path. To retain layer organization, consider Layer clipping paths instead.

Releasing a clipping path accidentally. Creating a Compound Shape with a clipping path releases the clipping group. Joining an open clipping path to another path releases the clipping group.

Issues to Consider

Some techniques create masks automatically. Filter: Pen & Ink: **Hatch Effects** makes masked shapes. The Expand command may convert an object a group of masked objects. Objects that contain a pattern fill, for example, typically become masked objects upon expansion. Objects with gradient fills commonly become masked groups when expanded to either objects or a gradient mesh.

Painting masks sometimes causes problems. Applying a fill and stroke to masks sometimes causes printing issues.

Clipping masks are not retained as editable features upon export to Photoshop. The Photoshop format only retains masks applied to layers.

Open paths may be used to clip. The area clipped includes the area that would be created if the open ends of the path were joined.

The Use Area Select option does not work on Filled Masks. You can select clipping masks quickly using the Select: Object: **Clipping Masks** command.

9.70

Object: Clipping Mask: Make   *(Command) [Ctrl]-7*

Use this command to convert selected objects to a clipping path group.

9.71

Object: Clipping Mask: Release

(Command-Option) [Ctrl-Alt]-7

Use this command to convert a clipping mask group back into standard, ungrouped, unmasked shapes. The Clipping path itself does not regain any fill and stroke attributes that were stripped away when it was converted to a clipping path. Any attributes added later are retained, however. Objects released from a clipping path retain their positions the stacking order.

9.72

Object: *Compound Path*

Compound paths are objects comprised of paths. The areas the paths overlap becomes negative (or transparent) space.

Issues to Consider

Compound paths are created whenever type is converted to outlines. The type characters do not need to have counters for this to happen. Each character in the type becomes a compound path.

In some cases, pathfinder commands create compound paths automatically. This happens when an expanded compound shape is best described with a compound path. For example, a small circle surrounded by a larger one creates a compound path after expanding the Minus Front pathfinder. The effect is not identical in all cases. Expanding the Exclude pathfinder does produce a compound path, but the shapes do not retain their independence as objects correctly unless the objects do not overlap completely.

The objects need not overlap to be a compound path. Some techniques benefit from non-overlapping paths being made into a compound path. For example, the pathfinder commands treat compound paths as a single object. This can be useful to preserve non-overlapping but logically connected objects when using commands such as Minus Back. For more details, see Paths technique section.

Compound paths may fail to create negative space correctly. This commonly happens when many shapes are being made into a compound path, when compound paths are being made into compound paths with other objects, and when receiving outlined type from some older applications. Repairing negative space is a function of the direction of the path. Path direction can be reversed using the attributes palette. *(For more information, see 18.5, Reverse Path Direction.)*

9.73

Object: *Compound Path: Make*

Use this command to convert selected objects into a single compound path object. At least two path objects must be selected to execute this command. The paths cannot be members of different groups. The compound path will assume the position in the stacking order of the highest object and take on the paint style of the lowest object in the stacking order.

9.74

Object: Compound Path: Release

Use this command to undo the effect of the Object: Compound Path: **Make**. The compound path object is replaced with its component paths. Released objects do not return to the paint style or stacking order position they had before becoming part of a compound path.

9.75

Object: Crop Marks

Crop marks indicate the boundaries of the final printed paper size of a job. Press professionals use crop marks to trim a job to size.

Illustrator can provide a single set of crop marks in each document. The marks are not objects and cannot be customized, covered, or edited. Illustrator uses the crop marks to indicate the positioning of printers marks and the cropping area in the Separation Setup dialog box.

Issues to Consider

Illustrator can only produce one set of crop marks per document. If you need more than one set of crop marks in a document, use the command Filter: Create: **Trim Marks**.

This command is rarely used. Since it is uncommon to print directly from Illustrator, this feature is not highly utilized. Crop marks do not need to be created unless you are printing directly from Illustrator and want to cut down the document from the page size.

9.76

Object: Crop Marks: Make

Use this command to generate crop marks and to replace existing crop marks with a new set. Crop marks may be generated from the artboard size, or from a selected rectangle. If a rectangle is selected, the crop marks are generated from its corners and the box is removed from the document. If nothing is selected, the corners of the artboard are used to position the marks. It doesn't matter what tiling options you have selected in the Document Setup dialog box.

9.77

Object: Crop Marks: *Release*

Use this command to remove crop marks from a document. If the marks were created from a rectangle, the rectangle is returned to the document but is set to a fill and stroke of None.

9.78

Object: *Graph*

The graph commands control the appearance and content of graph objects.

9.79

Object: Graph: *Type*

Use this command to set the default options for the graph tools or to edit the options for a selected graph.

9.80

Object: Graph: *Data*

Use this command to open the data dialog box of a selected graph. This is commonly done to add to or change the underlying data in a graph.

Mistakes to Avoid

Selecting only part of the graph. If the entire graph object is not selected, the Graph Data dialog box will open, but not contain any data.

9.81

Object: Graph: **Design**

The Graph Design dialog box manages graph column and markers styles. Columns and markers are custom objects used to represent data in bar and line charts, respectively. Columns and markers update themselves as data changes in the graph. This makes them more efficient than manually editing graphs.

The Design dialog box enables you to create and manage columns and markers. Once created, columns and markers may be applied to entire graphs or a data series.

Issues to Consider

Designs may include special features such as field totals and sliding areas. These features must be established in the document before the design is created.

Designs are available to every open document. Once a design is saved, it may be used by any other open document. The name of the document the design is saved in will appear in parentheses next to the design name in the Design dialog box. Applying a design from another document adds it to the current document. Only applied designs are added. There is no live connection or link between the design and document it was first saved in.

Designs that use brushes are not updated as the brush definition changes. Symbols used as designs are updated if the symbol definition is altered.

Graph Design Dialog Box

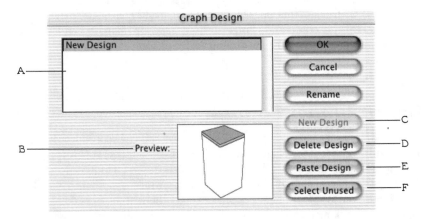

A. Design Names

This pane lists the available designs alphabetically by name. Designs saved in other open documents also list the filename for the design in parentheses. Click on a design's name to select it. Shift-click a second design name to select all of the designs between the two. (Command) [Ctrl]-click to select noncontiguous names on the list. Select more than one design to delete them.

B. Preview

This displays a thumbnail of the currently selected design. If more than one design is selected, the field is blank. Guides are not included in the preview.

C. New Design

Click to create a design based on the current selection in the document. Once clicked, a design is created with a default name ("New Design," "New Design 1," and so on) and a preview of the design appears. Once clicked, the button is unavailable.

D. Delete Design

Click to delete all currently selected designs. Graphs using deleted designs return to their default appearance.

E. Paste Design

This command pastes the currently selected design into the document. This is typically done to edit the design objects before creating a new design. The pasted design objects will appear in the center of the document and be bounded by a rectangle with a fill and stroke of None.

F. Select Unused

This command selects all graph designs that are not applied to any objects in the document. This command usually directly precedes the Delete Design command. Since designs take up memory and file size, deleting designs you do not intend to use is a good idea.

9.82

Object: Graph: *Column*

Use this command to apply a graph design to the selected columns of a graph. If the entire graph is selected, the design will be applied to every column. Commonly, each data series is assigned its own design. The Group selection arrow makes this process quick. Click a column in the graph with the Group Selection arrow to select it, click again to select the rest of the columns in the data series. Click again to select the legend marker. Click again to select the rest of the columns and legend markers. All graph objects are logically grouped to each other in this manner.

Graph Column Options

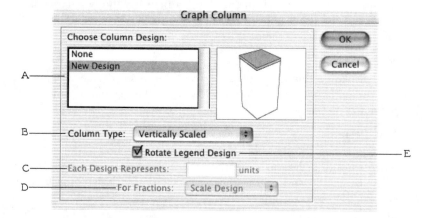

A. Column Design List

Choose a design to apply from the available list. When a design is selected, a preview of it appears at right. Set to None to remove a design from a column.

B. Column Type

Use this menu to choose the way the design is applied to the column.

Vertically Scaled

This option scales the height of the design to fit the space. The width is left alone. This option tends to work better with nonrepresentative designs.

Uniformly Scaled

This option scales the design both horizontally and vertically proportional to the value in the graph. This may cause the designs to overlap each other and the boundaries of the graph.

Repeating

Repeating design use multiple versions of the design rather than a single one. Each version of the design stands for a specified number of units in the graph. The effect is a stack or row of items in the graph rather than a single item.

Sliding

Use the sliding option to vertically scale a specific section of the design and leave the remaining sections unchanged. The area that is vertically scaled, or "slides" is based upon the position of a horizontal guide in the design. If no horizontal guide must be included in the design, the design will slide from the center. Sliding column designs are commonly used to keep one part of a design undistorted while adjusting another part.

C. **Each Design Represents _ Units**

Use this field to specify the number of design elements will be used in the column by tying it to a specific number of units in the graph. For example, if the graph data is 10 and you set this option to 2, 5 designs will be used to represent the column. This option is only available when the Repeating option is chosen.

D. **For Fractions**

Use this option to control the handling of remainders when using the Repeating and Each Design Represents options. Unless the graph data is evenly divisible by the number of units each design represents, some additional fraction will remain. The remainder will either be described by cropping the design proportionally or by scaling the design vertically. The Scale Design options scales the design vertically, the Chop design crops the design proportionally.

E. **Rotate Legend Design**

Check this box to rotate the design in the legend 90°.

9.83

Object: Graph: Marker

Graph markers indicate data positions on line graphs. By default, markers are squares. Use this command to use a design as an indicator instead. By default, designs are scaled to fit the square. The relative size of the design to the square may be indicated by including a square with a fill and stroke of none in the rear of a design. This must be included when the design is created. The invisible square will be set to the size normally occupied by the default marker. The rest of the design will be sized relative to that box.

Mistakes to Avoid

Selecting only part of an existing marker. When substituting one marker for another, be certain that the entire marker is selected. Selecting only part of a marker will not enable you to replace the marker.

Graph Marker Dialog Box

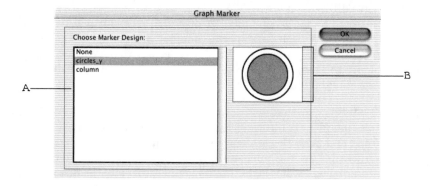

A. Graph Marker List

Use this list of available designs to connect a design to a marker or series of markers. Click the design name to associate it with the selected markers. Choose None to remove existing markers from a graph.

B. Preview

This window displays a thumbnail of the currently selected design.

The Type Menu

Type: *Font*

Use this menu to set the font attribute of selected type and to establish the default font. A font is an application that instructs your computer how to display and print the characters you key into the keyboard. This menu lists all currently available fonts. To set the font for selected type, choose the name of the font from the list. A checkmark appears next to the chosen font in the menu. Only the font attribute is altered using this command.

If a font is chosen when no type is selected, the font becomes the default until another font is chosen or type is added to existing objects. The default font is reset when type objects are selected.

Mistakes to Avoid

Choosing an improperly installed font. Fonts must be properly installed to be used successfully. In workflows without font management software such as Adobe Type Manager or Extensis Suitcase, fonts should reside in the fonts folder in the System folder (Mac), the Library folder (Mac OS X) or the Fonts folder (PC).

Choosing an incomplete font. Fonts include vector information that describes the character shapes to printers. In Type 1 fonts, these are called Printer Fonts and there is a separate printer font file for each type style. TrueType fonts include this information in a single file. All files must be present to use a font successfully.

Issues to Consider

Fonts are usually chosen from the Character palette. Most users prefer to make font selections from the Character palette. The font field in that palette is the same as this command except that it's easier to use and more convenient.

10.2

Type: Size

Use this command to choose a point size for selected type or to set the default size for type. To set the font to one of the default sizes, choose a size from the list. A checkmark appears next to the chosen font in the menu. Only the size attribute is altered using this command.

Chose the Other option from the list and the Character palette is opened or brought forward with the size field highlighted.

Issues to Consider

Type objects or characters may be selected to use this command. Characters are selected using a type tool. Type objects are selected using a selection tool. Either method is fine for setting a font. When a type object is selected, the same font attribute is applied to all the characters. To change the size of individual characters, select them with a type tool.

Font sizes are usually chosen from the Character palette. Most users prefer to make font selections from the Character palette. It has more features and is more convenient.

10.3

Type: **Blocks**

These commands are used to create and release links between area type objects. Text in linked blocks flows dynamically from one box to the next. As text fills one box, it continues on to the next object. Likewise, as text is deleted, or is sized or tracked differently, the text will be adjusted accordingly within the blocks. This enables long strings of text to be managed as a single unit. Commonly, type blocks are used to create the appearance of text columns.

When area text objects are linked, they become a single object. Each bounding area for text remains independent, however, and may be modified and styled without affecting other objects.

Text flows in linked paths from the back of the stacking order to the front. Linked text paths may be reordered in the stack, but text will still flow from back to front.

Issues to Consider

Illustrator is not a layout application. If you have enough type that you are considering linking it, you should consider migrating the work to an application better suited for handling large amounts of type, such as QuarkXPress or InDesign.

Type blocks work well for reusable charts. Linked blocks are commonly used when laying out pages or to facilitate reworking categories and headlines in charts and tables. For example, the dates in a calendar could be created as a series of linked text boxes. Each new month, the first of the month could be set to the right day of the week by adjusting the spaces at the beginning of the block. Subsequent numbers would reflow automatically.

10.4

Type: Blocks: **Link**

Use this command to create linked area type objects. The objects selected for this command may be area type, simple paths, or a combination of the two. For example, you could select two ovals. Linking them would convert them to linked area type objects. If you are linking blocks of existing type, the text will reflow to fit the new area. Path or point type may not be linked.

10.5

Type: Blocks: Unlink

Use this command to release a type block. When this command is executed, text remains in its current container but is no longer connected to other type objects. All the linked type areas in the block must be selected to execute this command.

Issues to Consider

Center aligned text may reflow slightly when unlinked. When unlinked, space characters will be considered when center aligning type. If there are spaces at the ends of lines, the line may adjust itself slightly. If the text is relinked, this will resolve itself. If not, the extra spaces should be deleted to properly align the type.

10.6

Type: Wrap

Use these commands to create and release type wraps. Wrapping is when area type flows around a path object. For example, an object may be used to create a customized margin for text. Text is forced to flow around the path. The path remains editable and may be repositioned to adjust the effect. The effect is similar to features found in popular page layout applications. In QuarkXPress the feature is called Runaround. PageMaker and InDesign call it Text Wrap.

10.7

Type: Wrap: Make

Use this command to create a group from selected area type and simple path objects. Meshes, envelopes and images cannot be used to wrap type; compound paths can. Text will flow into the negative space of compound paths. Multiple paths and multiple type objects may be wrapped at a time. The paths used in the wrap must be in front of the type objects and the type objects must be area type objects.

Once the command is executed, a group is formed containing all the selected objects in the wrap. The group cannot be ungrouped without releasing the wrap.

Issues to Consider

Type may wrap very tightly to the objects. Since the text may abut the wrap objects, many users prefer to make wraps with offset versions of the original object. Use Object: Path: **Offset Path** to create a duplicate, offset version of the wrap object. Set the fill and stroke of the offset path to None. Offset Path can be applied to objects already in a text wrap. The type may not immediately wrap around the new path, however. Nudge the object with the arrow keys on the keyboard to refresh the wrap.

Objects added to the group will also wrap text. Dragging objects into the group in the Layers palette will cause those objects to wrap text as well. The object must be above the text in the stacking order to work correctly.

Objects may be added to the group by repeating the command. To add objects to the wrap, select the objects and the wrap and chose Type: Wrap: **Make Again.**

Stroke weight is not accurately reckoned when making a type wrap. This is especially true if the stroke is a brush stroke. Instead, use closed paths without strokes in wraps.

10.8

Type: Wrap: Release

Use this command to undo a type wrap and convert the group into individual objects. All objects involved in the wrap must be selected to execute this command.

10.9

Type: Fit Headline

Use this command to automatically adjust the tracking and kerning on selected area text to force it to fit within the horizontal width of the text area. Each character will occupy the same width, as though it were from a monospaced typeface, when the command is executed. To do this, Illustrator applies tracking to the entire line and may also adjust the kerning of each letter pair differently. This command is commonly used to quickly adjust type to fit a specified area.

This command works on paragraphs. To execute it, insert the Type tool in a paragraph. If the paragraph wraps to the next line, the paragraph will be pulled onto a single line, if possible.

Mistakes to Avoid

Selecting a paragraph with a soft return. Soft returns confuse this command. Since the width the paragraph occupies is considered in this command, the lines following a soft return are considered as the text is adjusted. This typically results in an incorrectly spaced line before the soft return. This command works best with a short, simple paragraph.

Assuming that edited type will still fit. If you edit or change the type in any way, the type will not be updated to fit the line. You must reapply the command to reset the line.

Failing to change the tracking back for the next line you type. This command sets the tracking default. If you begin to set new type after executing this command, it will be tracked with the same value. Usually, this problem is avoided by setting all the required type and then going back and applying the command.

10.10

Type: Create Outlines   (Command-Shift) [Ctrl-shift]-O

Use this command to replace selected type objects with a group of compound paths based on the vector shapes of the characters. Each letter is replaced with a compound path that represents it. The fill and stroke is retained, along with any appearance settings. The objects are no longer type and may not be edited with type tools.

To execute this command, a type object, rather than type characters must be selected. Use a selection tool to select the type object; you cannot use the Type tool and execute this command. You must convert a complete type object, rather than one or two specific characters. Any kind of type may be converted.

Converting type to outlines makes a greater range of commands available to the object. As paths, individual characters may be manually altered by the selection tools, free transform tools, cut with knife tool, and affected by anything that affects paths.

Issues to Consider

Typos and line breaks are difficult to rectify once type has been converted. Be sure the type is the way you want it before you convert.

This command does not work on bitmap or outline-protected fonts. This command works on unprotected fonts with vector definitions. It works on PostScript Type 1, PostScript Type 3, Open Type, and TrueType fonts.

The vectors produced are only as good as the creators of the typeface. Many Type 3 fonts and Type 1 fonts created in Fontographer that are available online contain poor outlines riddled with excessive anchor points. Be careful when accepting fonts from an unknown foundry.

Converting type to outlines removes the need for font files. Type objects require the presence and activation of fonts to appear and print as intended. Paths do not. Many users convert type to outlines in lieu of submitting fonts when submitting a file to a service bureau. This is commonly done with logos and illustrations that contain a small amount of type. Do not use Illustrator as a page layout program. If you are laying out pages in Illustrator, do not convert all the type to outlines. It will make the file harder to process. *(For more information, see A.10, Preparing a File for Handoff.)*

Type area includes white space; object area does not. When using a command that utilizes the bounding area of an object, like Effect: **Convert to Shape,** you may notice a difference when converting type to outlines. Type characters include white space at the top and bottom of the characters. Type converted to outlines does not include this space and typically has a smaller bounding box.

Some commands convert type to outlines for you. Expanding a compound shape that includes type will convert the type to outlines. Choosing Object: Expand: **Object** converts type to outlines. Flattening transparent type converts it to outlines.

Set the type to the size you want before converting. Built into fonts are details to assist in printing and displaying at different sizes. These are called *hints.* To take advantage of hints, set the type to the size you intend to use before converting it to outlines.

10.11

Type: Find/Change

Use the Find/Change command to search a document for a particular string of characters. Optionally, when found, you may replace the string of characters with another of your choosing. This is commonly used to globally replace one set of words with another. As text is located in the document, it becomes highlighted. This enables you to swap it with the replacement text or to manually edit the text.

After executing a change, be sure to inspect your document to ensure the change has not caused bad type breaks or other problems in the document.

Find/Change Options Dialog Box

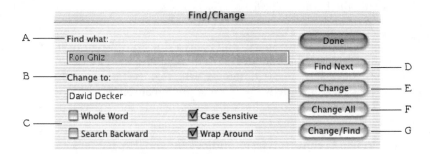

A. Find What

Enter the characters you are searching for in this field. Text may contain any part of the entered text to be found. For example, entering the text "$1" would find exact matches as well as $14" or $100."

This is commonly used to identify a specific phrase, but it may also be used to search for formatting characters. For example, you may wish to find instances in a document where two hard returns are next to each other. Or find where three spaces are used and replace them with a tab. Typically, users copy the type instances they are looking for and paste them into this field.

B. Change to

Use this field to enter the text that will replace the searched for text when the Change buttons are used.

C. Options

Use these check boxes to modify how the search is executed.

Whole Word

This option finds only whole words that match the criterion, rather than parts of words.

Search Backward

This options searches the document in reverse order starting at the insertion point.

Case Sensitive

This option requires that the search match exactly match the upper and lowercase of Find What field.

Wrap Around

This option starts the search at the insertion point, and moves downward through the document. When the end of the document is reached, the search returns to the top of the document and searches downward back to the insertion point. This option provides the most complete search of the document.

D. Find Next

Click this button to search the document for the text string. Use this command to start the search for the string. When an instance of the string is found, it becomes highlighted in the document. Once a string has been found, clicking this button again searches without replacing any text.

E. Change

This command replaces a found instance of the string. Once this command is executed, you will need to Find Next to continue the find and replace process.

F. Change All

This command replaces all instances of the string with the replacement text. No opportunity to omit a match from replacement is given. This command is best used when there is a limited amount of text in the document or in instances where you are sure about the results of the replacement.

G. Change/Find

This command replaces the found instance of the string and searches for the next instance. This command is most commonly used since it offers control over the process and moves it along.

10.12

Type: Find Font

Use this command to find and replace font attributes throughout a document and to create a text file listing the fonts used in the document.

When this command is executed, Illustrator generates a list of fonts used in the document and lists them by font technology. From here the individual fonts may be swapped for others in the document or available in the system. Many users employ this to make global font substitutions in a document.

The font list may be saved as a text file. The text file lists the document name, artboard dimensions, object default resolution, and the fonts used. This list is sometimes used to facilitate communication with a service bureau. In practice, the text file saved from the Document Info palette is more complete and lists more font information.

Find Font Dialog Box

A. Fonts in Document

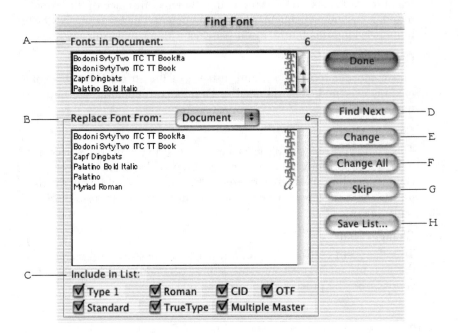

This field lists all of the fonts used in the document. Each different style in a font family (such as bold or oblique) is a different typeface and, hence is listed separately here. The font technology used is indicated with an icon to the right of the fonts name.

Select any of the fonts on the list to begin the process of replacing it with another font.

B. Replace Font From

Use this menu to select whether to substitute fonts from the list of fonts in use in the document or from all of the fonts available on the system. The replacement font choices appear in the large field below this menu. The font technology used is indicated with an icon to the right of the font's name.

Document

This option lists the fonts currently in use in the document. It's easier to choose from this short list, so many users will use the font they intend to use as a replacement somewhere in the document.

System

This option lists all the fonts available in the system. It's the same as choosing from Type: **Font** to set a typeface.

C. **Include in List**

Use these check box to omit some fonts from the Replace Font field. This makes it easier to choose from a shorter list. Typically, it is also used to remove problematic fonts technologies from the list.

Type 1

Type 1 fonts are Adobe's standard PostScript font technology. They are the most reliable and widely accepted fonts for printing in a PostScript environment.

Standard

These are the fonts most commonly installed on most workstations: Chicago, Geneva, Monaco, New York, Courier, Souvenir, Symbol, Hobo, Helvetica, and Times.

Roman

These are the Western Type 1 fonts.

TrueType

TrueType fonts are competitors of the Type 1 fonts. They are widespread in the market, but not universally endorsed by service bureaus. This is because TrueType fonts sometimes cause problems at printing time. Typically, when pages are imposed. The best that can be said for TrueType fonts is that they always print some of the time.

CID

Character Identification fonts are an extension of the Type 1 technology. Their chief benefit is that they support more than the standard 256 characters that can be in a Type 1 font. For this reason they are commonly used in Asian fonts.

Multiple Master

Multiple Master faces are a kind of Type 1 font that includes the ability to customize the look of the face. Illustrator includes a tool for creating customized instances of a Multiple Master face. There are special workflow considerations involved with these fonts. Consult the manual that came with your Multiple Master font for details.

OTF

The Open TypeFace (OTF) technology is a cross-platform font with an extended character set. Although they promise advantages, the fonts are not widely accepted by service bureaus and should be used with caution.

D. **Find Next**

Click this button to search the document for the font. When an instance of the font is found, it becomes highlighted in the document. Once the font has been found, clicking this button again searches without replacing.

E. Change

This command replaces a found font. Once this command is executed, you will need to Find Next to continue the find and replace process.

F. Change All

This command replaces all instances of the font with the replacement font. No opportunity to omit a match from replacement is given. This command is best used when there is a limited amount of text in the document or in instances where you are sure about the results of the replacement.

G. Skip

This command bypasses a particular use of the font from replacement.

H. Save List

This command generates a text file listing details about a widely used command.

10.13

Type: Check Spelling

Use this command to correct spelling errors in the document, to modify the lists Illustrator uses to check spelling and to set the base dictionary Illustrator uses. When the command is executed, you will have an opportunity to review the list of misspellings, correct or skip errors, or add the words to the exception list.

Illustrator has a default dictionary based on the language you specified when Illustrator was installed. This dictionary lists most words but does not include proper names, idioms, or jargon. The User Dictionary provides a place to add and store those words particular to your environment. Both of these lists are used when you spell check a document. You must enter the words into the user dictionary or add them from a document. The User Dictionary is not used when offering alternate spellings for words. The various language dictionaries and AI User Dictionary are stored in the Text Filters folder in the Plug-ins folder in the Adobe Illustrator folder.

This command can be executed without making a selection. Illustrator always checks the entire document, including words that are locked or hidden. Locked or hidden words may be replaced without unlocking or showing them.

Issues to Consider

Spell checking in Illustrator is limited. Compared to the spell checking utilities in most word processing applications, Illustrator's spell check is merely adequate. If you have a substantial amount of text to check, consider checking it in an outside application before pasting into Illustrator.

Spell check is a single action with respect to Undo. All the changes made in the spell check are considered a single step in the Undo chain—that is, you cannot undo some of the changes made in the spell check. All changes will be undone with one Edit: **Undo** command.

Check Spelling Dialog Box

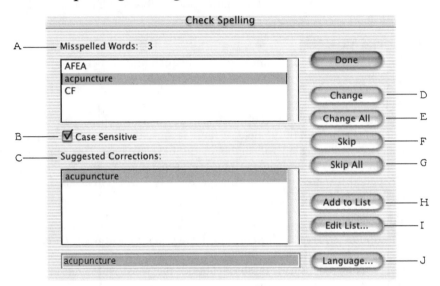

A. Misspelled Words

This field lists all the words that aren't in the current dictionary or in the user dictionary. The number of misspelled words appears at the top of the field. This lists the number of mismatches, not the number of misspellings. Multiple instances of the same misspellings are only counted once.

Highlighting a word on the list will enable you to replace it or add it to the User Dictionary.

B. Case Sensitive

This option lists each instance of a misspelling separately if upper and lowercase are used. This enables you to make a distinction between proper names and common nouns, or proper nouns that are not capitalized.

C. Suggested Corrections

This field lists possible alternatives to the selected item in the Misspelled Words list. These alternates come from the default Dictionary but do not include the items in the User Dictionary. Click a suggestion to populate the replacement field at the bottom of the dialog box.

D. **Change**

Use this option to substitute the misspelled word for the replacement word at the bottom of the field. If there is more than one instance of the same misspelling, Change will fix the currently selected one in the document and then highlight the next instance. This offers you the opportunity to evaluate each instance separately. As long as there is a misspelled instance in the document, the word will remain in the misspelled word field.

E. **Change All**

This option fixes all instances of the misspelling without showing you each one.

F. **Skip**

Use this option to omit the misspelled word from replacement by the word at the bottom of the field. If there is more than one instance of the same misspelling, Skip will highlight the next instance. This offers you the opportunity to evaluate each instance separately. As long as there is a misspelled instance in the document, the word will remain in the misspelled word field.

G. **Skip All**

This option bypasses all instances of the misspelling without showing you each one. If you are using this option, consider adding the word to the User Dictionary instead. In all likelihood, the word will come up again and slow you down again if you don't.

H. **Add to List**

Use this option to add the current word to the User Dictionary file. The word will be added exactly as typed and be removed from the Misspelled words list. All instances of the added word will be skipped.

I. **Edit List**

Use this option to open the Learned Words dialog box. This lists the words currently in the User Dictionary and enables you to edit the list.

J. **Language**

Use this option to change the current dictionary for one of a different language. The various language dictionaries are located in the Text Filters folder in the Plug-ins folder in the Adobe Illustrator folder. This command automatically opens that directory.

Learned Words Options Dialog Box

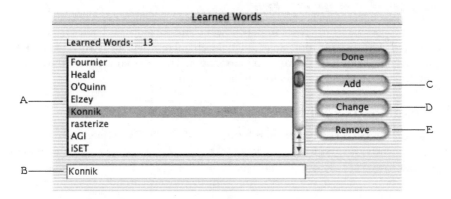

A. **Learned Words**

This field lists the words in the User Dictionary file. Click on a word from the list to begin the process of editing or deleting it.

B. **Text Field**

This field displays the currently selected word from the Learned Words list. If no words are selected, the field is blank. Enter text to add into this field or edit the spelling of existing words.

C. **Add**

Use this option to add the word in the text field to the Learned Words list. If the word already exists in the list, you are prompted with a warning.

D. **Change**

This option replaces the selected word in the Learned Words list with the text in the Text field. Use this to correct errant words.

E. **Remove**

This option clears the selected Learned Word from the list.

10.14

Type: Change Case

Use this command to create upper-, lower-, and mixed-case letters from type selected with a type tool. Selected type characters will be switched to the specified case after the command is executed. This is commonly used to save the time of retyping incorrectly capitalized text.

Mistakes to Avoid

Replacing correctly capitalized letters accidentally. The Mixed Case option converts the first letter of selected words to uppercase and the remaining to lowercase. This will foul words such as "McDonald," "O'Quinn," and "GoLive." Check the words you want to convert carefully.

Failing to anticipate word breaks. Illustrator considers characters separated by white space to be words. Hyphenated words and words separated only by a slash or periods are single words and will not be correctly capitalized by the Mixed Case option.

Attempting to capitalize double byte fonts. This command only works on the Roman, 1-byte fonts. The Chinese, Japanese, and Korean fonts (CJK) use 2 bytes and cannot be capitalized with this command.

Change Case Dialog Box

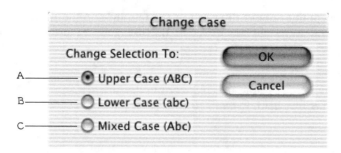

A. **Upper Case**

This option converts all selected text to its capitalized version. It has no effect on numbers or non-text marks.

B. **Lower Case**

This option converts all selected text to its lowercase version. It has no effect on numbers or non-text marks.

C. **Mixed Case**

This option converts the first letter of all selected text to its capitalized version and the remaining letter to the lowercase version. It has no effect on numbers or non-text marks.

10.15

Type: *Smart Punctuation*

Use this command to find and replace specific characters and character combinations with specially designed characters that serve the same purpose but look better.

This command simplifies accessing special characters that are included in typefaces such as ligatures. Ligatures are single characters that represent commonly occurring letter combinations, such as "fl." Using these characters takes advantage of the work of the font foundry and typically results in better looking type. The characters are available, but are often attached to hard-to-recall keyboard combinations.

Smart Punctuation Dialog Box

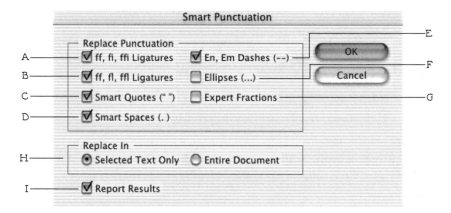

A. **ff, fi, ffi Ligatures**

This command replaces any occurrence of the ff, fi, or ffi letter combinations into ligatures. The appropriate Adobe Expert font containing the ligatures must be installed on your system to make this change.

B. **ff, fl, ffl Ligatures**

This command replaces any occurrence of the ff, fl, or ffl letter combinations into ligatures. The appropriate Adobe Expert font containing the ligatures must be installed on your system to make this change.

C. **Smart Quotes**

This command swaps the inch and foot marks for the appropriate printer's quotation marks. The misuse of quote marks is a common sign of inexperience or poor attention to detail.

D. **Smart Spaces**

This command swaps multiple spaces after a period with a single space.

E. **En, Em Dashes**

This command swaps double and triple keyboard dashes with en and em dashes, respectively.

F. **Ellipses**

This command swaps three periods with ellipsis points. Ellipses points are a single character comprised of three spaced points.

G. **Expert Fractions**

This command swaps hand-made fraction characters such as "1/4" with their single-character equivalents. Fraction characters are usually only built into Expert Set fonts. These must be active on your system to make this substitution.

H. **Replace In**

Use this option to control the behavior of Smart Punctuation.

Selected Text Only

This option inspects only text selected with a type tool. If no type is selected when this option is chosen, Illustrator reports the problem and makes no changes.

Entire Document

This option inspects all the text in the document. Locked and Hidden text is affected by this command.

I. **Report Results**

This option instructs Illustrator to display an alert regarding the actions taken by the command upon execution.

10.16

Type: Rows & Columns

Use this command to convert selected objects to an array of rectangles. If the objects converted are area text objects, the resulting rectangles will be linked area type blocks. The flow of type through the blocks may be specified from four default options. This is the most common use for the command, but path objects can be converted to rectangles using this command. Either paths or area text objects may be selected, but a combination of the two is not allowed. The command does not work on path or point type. The bounding box of the selected objects is used to define the default area the rectangles will occupy.

Rows run horizontally and columns run vertically. Each divides the grid in the opposite axis. Columns run up and down through the space, the width of these columns divides the horizontal length of the array. Rows run horizontally. Their height divides the vertical length of the array. Rows and Columns each have the same sets of options.

Row & Columns Dialog Box

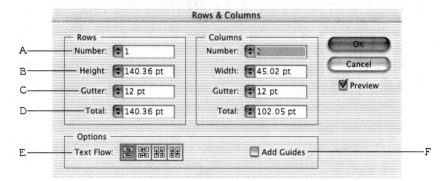

A. Number

Use this option to set the number of horizontal rows and vertical columns that are created. A setting of 1 row, 1 column results in no change in the objects. The fields in this dialog are mathematically connected. Changing the number of rows or columns also changes the height of the rows or columns.

B. Height

Use this option to set the height of each rectangle. Changing the height also changes the gutter.

C. Gutter

This option defines the distance between the rectangles. Changing the gutter also changes the height.

D. Total

This option sets the total size of the width (columns) or height (rows) of the bounding box of the rectangles. It is the sum of (Height × Number) and (Gutter × Number −1). Changing the total also changes the height.

E. Text Flow

Use this option to set the order of text flow through the created type blocks. This option only works if the original objects were area type blocks. The options from left to right are By Rows, Left to Right; By Rows Right to Left; By Columns, Left to Right; By Columns Right to Left.

G. Add Guides

Use this option to frame each rectangle created with a set of guides.

10.17

Type: *Show Hidden Characters*

Use this command to display the nonprinting formatting characters used in type. Formatting characters indicate things like where to break a line. These are keystrokes, like the Return key, which are embedded as characters into type. This command displays those characters to make the formatting apparent. This is typically done to assist in problem solving and editing. The characters are displayed in the default color of the layer.

Common hidden characters include the following:

- **Hard Returns.** Made by the Return or Enter key, these characters force a line break and separate paragraphs. They are indicated by the typographer's paragraph mark.

- **Soft Returns.** Made by Shift-(Return) [Enter], these characters break a line without breaking a paragraph. They are indicated by a left arrow bent 90°.

- **Tabs.** Made by the Tab key, these characters instruct the line of type to continue in a new location, possibly with a new orientation. They are indicated by a horizontal right arrow.

- **Spaces.** Made by the spacebar, they position the line of type one step further along and separate words. They are indicated by a small square.

- **Nonbreaking Space.** Made by (Option) [Alt]-Spacebar, these characters move the line of type over one unit. Words between nonbreaking spaces cannot be separated by a line break as type flows through an area. This keeps words that should stay together connected. Nonbreaking spaces are indicated with a small circle.

- **Discretionary Hyphens.** Made by (Command-Shift) [Ctrl-Shift]-hyphen, these characters indicate where a word should be hyphenated should the need arise. They are indicated by a short hyphen.

- **End of text.** Occurring at the end of the line of type, this is indicated by an infinity symbol.

10.18

Type: Type Orientation

Use this command to set the orientation of the type to horizontal or vertical. A complete type object must be selected to execute this command; individual characters within the type cannot be converted. If type is linked into blocks, all the blocks must be selected. Area, point and path type can all be converted with this command.

10.19

Type: Type Orientation: Horizontal

Use this command to convert all selected type to a horizontal orientation. Horizontal type lines break downward so that type reads top to bottom. This command has no effect on type that is already horizontally oriented.

10.20

Type: Type Orientation: Vertical

Use this command to convert all selected type to a vertical orientation. Vertical type lines break left so that type reads right to left. This command has no effect on type that is already vertically oriented.

10.21

Type: Glyph Options

Use this command to substitute alternates for one or two selected characters when using Kanji fonts that contain such substitutes. This command works only on the Mac and only when using Type 1 CID fonts.

To execute the command, select a character, or Option-click to select a second character. Only two characters may be replaced at a time. Choose one of the alternate sets built into the font from the Glyph Options dialog box. Choose from JIS 78, Expert, and Traditional.

Issues to Consider

Alternate glyphs aren't retained on import. Glyphs return to their defaults when imported into Photoshop, Premier, and After Effects from a native Illustrator file. Save the files as an EPS and then import to retain the alternates.

The correct fonts must be installed to print. As with other alternate characters, like fractions in Expert Sets, the corresponding CID font must be present and active to print alternate glyphs.

The Select Menu

Select: All

Use this command to select all objects available for selecting. Available objects are those that are not enveloped, locked or hidden, or are part of a group or on a layer that is locked or hidden. When an insertion point is active in text, this command selects all the characters, including those in linked blocks or ones that aren't visible, but no other objects.

Issues to Consider

This command often speeds up selection process. In cases where many objects are to be selected, consider using this command, then deselecting unwanted objects.

This command is commonly used to style hidden type. When there is too much type to fit into an area type block, part of the text must be hidden. Select All affects even the hidden type so that it can be styled, set to a smaller size or copied.

Related Topics

2.7   Type Tool
1.1   Selection Tools

11.2

Select: *Deselect*

Use this command to release all current selections. This command is essentially the opposite of Select All; it results in nothing being selected. This command affects objects, but not individual characters. That is, if characters in a block of text are selected, this command deselects them and the type block they are in, rather than deselecting them and leaving an insertion point.

You can also deselect by clicking with a selection tool in an area in the document with no objects.

11.3

Select: *Reselect*

Use this command to repeat the last selection command used. Select All; Select Inverse and all of the Select: Same commands may be repeated by choosing this command. Commonly this is used to expedite making a series of criterion-based selections. For example having selected all of the blue objects in a document using Select: Same: **Fill Color**, you may wish to select all of the ones with red fills. This command provides a keyboard shortcut for that.

If nothing is selected, Illustrator executes the last Select command based on the last object that was selected. So if, have used Select: Same: **Fill Color** and you then select and deselect a single red object, all of the objects with red fills will be selected when you execute this command.

Mistakes to Avoid

Confusing Reselect with Photoshop's reselect command. Photoshop's reselect command recalls the last selection made. This command re-executes the last selection command.

Trying to repeat selection tool selections. Only selections made from the Select menu may be repeated with this command. To recall selections made in other ways, consider saving the selection. *(For more information, see 11.23, Select: **Save Selection**.)*

11.4

Select: *Inverse*

This selection reverses the selection state of all available objects in the document. All selected objects become deselected, all deselected objects become selected. Hidden and locked objects, groups and layers are not affected.

Issues to Consider

This command works on objects. Neither character, nor point selections are considered. If text is active and selected, this command deselects the entire text object and selects everything else in the document. It does not invert the character selection. Likewise, if individual anchor points, mesh points, or segments are selected, the entire object they are is deselected.

This command does support individual object selection within groups. Grouped objects are reversed as any other object in the document.

11.5

Select: *Next Object Above*   *(Command-Option) [Ctrl-Alt]-]*

Use this command to deselect the currently selected object and select the next available object atop it in the stacking order. If the current selection is part of a group, other group members in front of it are bypassed by this command in favor of the next object above the group,

If more than one object is selected, the single object above the topmost object is selected. If there are no objects above the selection, the selection does not change. This command is not available when individual characters are selected.

Issues to Consider

This command is different from the contextual menu command. The Contextual menu for the selection tools offers a command of the same name. This contextual command requires objects to be geographically atop each other as well as in front in the stacking order to function. Select: **Next Object Above** does not. Get the contextual menu when using a selection tool by (Control) [Right]-clicking in the document.

11.6

Select: *Next Object Below*   *(Command-Option) [Ctrl-Alt]-[*

This command is identical to Select: **Next Object Above**, except that it selects objects below the current selection in the stacking order.

11.7

Select: *Same*

This series of commands adds to the current selection by selecting other objects that match the selection's attributes in some way. This is commonly used to facilitate editing a series of objects quickly. Typically, the attributes you will be editing are the same ones you will use as search criteria.

More than one object may be selected to execute this command, but if the attributes of the selection are not the same, the command will have no affect. To be added to the selection, objects must not be locked, hidden, or a locked or hidden group or layer. If no object is selected when one of these commands is executed, Illustrator reactivates the last selected object and performs the command on that object.

Issues to Consider

Attributes of layers and groups are not considered. Objects in groups or on layers set to a matching attribute are not selected by this command unless the objects themselves have that attribute. For example, if you give a layer 50% opacity, the items on the layer appear 50% opaque but actually have 100% opacity by default. If you try to select based on another object that has 50% opacity, objects on the layer will not be selected.

Only cardinal fills and strokes are considered. If an object has more than one fill or stroke, only the fill or stroke attribute highlighted in the Appearance palette is considered when using these commands. The cardinal fill is the last one selected in the Appearance palette. This can be confusing, especially if the cardinal fill is not visible, or is part of a complex style. *(For more information, see 17.6, Attribute Appearance.)*

Envelopes have their own attributes. Objects distorted as part of an envelope are not available for selection by these commands. The envelopes are. To select the original objects, make them available by selecting the envelope and choosing Object: Envelope Distort: **Edit Contents**.

The Magic Wand tool is more flexible. The Magic Wand tool behaves the same way as these commands, selecting objects based on similarity. It differs in that it can select items that are somewhat similar rather than completely exact. This can be useful for selecting a range, such as items with thin strokes. *(For more information, see 1.7, Magic Wand Tool and 27.1, Magic Wand Palette.)*

Related Topics

11.8

Select: Same: *Blending Mode*

Use this command to select all available objects in the document with the same blending mode as the current selection.

Issues to Consider

By default, all objects have the same blending mode. Objects default to a blending mode of Normal. Unless you have changed objects or used techniques that apply blending modes automatically, all objects will be set to the same mode. To locate objects that are set to a different mode, use this command to select all of the objects with a normal blending mode and then choose Select: **Inverse**.

Related Topics

36.2   Blend Mode

11.9

Select: Same: *Fill & Stroke*

Use this command to select all available objects in the document that have the same fill and stroke color and the same stroke weight as the original selection. This is the most exacting criterion available with this series of commands.

11.10

Select: Same: *Fill Color*

Use this command to select all objects in the document that have the same fill attribute as the originally selected object. This compares the specified cardinal fill value, not the onscreen color. Due to styles, effects, transparency, blending modes, and opacity masks, the onscreen color may be different than the value specified in the Appearance palette. Despite the "color" in the name of the command, gradient and pattern fills are affected by this command as well.

11.11

Select: Same: *Opacity*

Use this command to select all available objects with the same opacity value as the originally selected object.

Issues to Consider

By default, all objects have the same opacity. Objects default to 100% opacity. Unless you have changed objects or used techniques to change opacity automatically, all objects will be set the same. To locate transparent objects, use this command to select all of the objects with 100% opacity and then choose Select: **Inverse**.

11.12

Select: Same: *Stroke Color*

Use this command to select all available objects with the same stroke color as the originally selected object. Other stroke attributes such as dashed line, caps and joins are not considered.

11.13

Select: Same: *Stroke Weight*

Use this command to select all available objects with the same stroke weight as the originally selected object. Other stroke attributes such as dashed line, caps, and joins are not considered.

11.14

Select: Same: *Style*

Use this command to select all available objects with the same Style as the originally selected object. The Default style is exempt from this, even if it has been modified or replaced with a different style. For this reason, it is not considered when applying this command.

Related Topics

31.1   Styles

11.15

Select: Same: *Symbol Instance*

Use this command to select all other available instances of the selected symbol object. Symbol sets, even those using exclusively the same symbol as the original object, are not selected by this command.

11.16

Select: *Object*

Use these commands to facilitate selecting items. The first two commands, All on Same Layer, and Direction Handles, require a selection to be made first. The remaining commands are used to select common objects.

11.17

Select: Object: *All on Same Layer*

Use this command to select all objects on the same layer as the currently selected object. If the initial object is on a nested layer all of the objects on the parent layer are selected. The effect of this command is the same as (Option) [Alt] clicking on the name of layer the object is on.

11.18

Select: Object: *Direction Handles*

Use this command to select all of the direction points on an object. None of the anchor points will be selected. This is useful for altering the curves of an object without repositioning it. Commonly, this command is used on complex objects such as meshes and envelopes. This command has no effect on objects without curves, point, path or area type objects and is unavailable for symbol sets and instances.

11.19

Select: Object: *Brush Strokes*

Use this command to select all available objects styled with brush strokes. In objects with multiple strokes, the brush need not be applied to the cardinal stroke.

Related Topics

    19.1 Brushes Palette

11.20

Select: Object: *Clipping Masks*

Use this command to select all of the available objects that are designated as clipping masks. Both clipping mask groups and layer clipping masks are selected with this command.

Related Topics

    9.68 Clipping Mask
    25.10 Make Clipping Mask

11.21

Select: Object: *Stray Points*

Use this command to select all available paths in the document with only one anchor point. Single point objects are often created accidentally by errant clicks with the Type tool or by deleting part but not all of an object. This command typically precedes deleting the stray points. Selecting and deleting the points can be done in one step by choosing Object: Path: **Clean Up**. *(For more information, see 9.51, Object: Path: **Clean Up**.)*

11.22

Select: Object: *Text Objects*

Use this command to select all available type objects.

Issues to Consider

This is often used to style type collectively. Users sometimes execute this command to select all type in a document so that they can set an attribute to the same value. You can do the same thing with the Select All command. You can set type attributes even if other items are selected. Select All also has a keyboard shortcut, making it quicker to execute.

11.23

Select: *Save Selection*

Use this command to save a specific selection in the document. This saves the selection state of the document, not the items themselves. This is commonly done to facilitate selecting the same set of items more than once. Any selection may be saved; the selected state of segments, direction points, objects, and mesh points may all be recorded.

Saved Selections appear by name at the bottom of the Select menu. Recall the selection by choosing the name from the menu. Selections are saved with the document and may be recalled in different sessions. Saving selections does not significantly increase file size.

Mistakes to Avoid

Attempting to recall a selection containing locked or hidden items. Recalled selections cannot unlock or show objects. Any objects in the selection that are available will be selected, but those that are not, will not become selected. No warning will accompany this.

Attempting to recall a selection in the wrong mode. A selection made in opacity mask editing mode can only be recalled in opacity mask editing mode for that object.

Attempting to recall selections containing deleted items. Deleted objects cannot be recalled as a selection.

Editing anchor points in saved selection objects. When you recall a selection that includes specific anchor points, be certain you have the correct points selected. If you have added or subtracted anchor points from the object, the selection may be incorrect. Illustrator saves the order of the points in the path and changing the amount of points may cause the selection to be incorrect.

New Selection Dialog Box

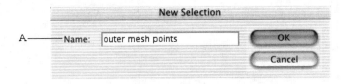

A. Name

This field lists the name of the selection as it will appear in the bottom on the Select menu. Avoid the temptation of accepting the default name and enter a descriptive name for the selection. Selections can have the same name as each other.

11.24

Select: *Edit Selection*

Use this command to delete and modify the names of selections saved in the document.

Edit Selection Options Dialog Box

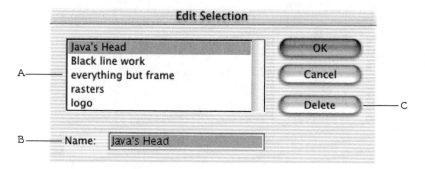

A. Selection Names

This informational window lists all selections saved in the document. Click an item to populate the Name field below. Selected items may be edited or deleted. Multiple selected items may be deleted at once. Shift-click to select contiguous item. (Command) [Ctrl]-click to select noncontiguous items.

B. Name

This field displays the currently selected Selection Name. If more than one name is selected, the first name selected is listed. Retype the name in this field to edit it. Click OK to accept the change or choose another Selection Name from the list to confirm that the edit has been added to the Selection Names.

C. Delete

Use this option to clear all highlighted items in the Selection Names pane.

The Filter Menu

Filters Overview

Filters are automated image editing techniques. Some are intended to produce creative effects; others are designed to facilitate the printing or production process. Some of the filters function only on pixels, some on vectors and some on both.

Effects

Many of the filters in this menu have counterparts in the Effects menu. The difference between filters and effects is that effects remain editable once applied and update themselves dynamically as the object they are applied to changes. For example, arrowheads added to a path using Effect: Stylize: **Add Arrowheads** reposition and re-orient themselves automatically as the path is adjusted. Arrowheads made with the Add Arrowheads filter do not.

The flexible nature of effects make them a good choice for many tasks. Effects come at a price, however. They require more memory than filters to execute and may slow down efficiency on slower machines. Users not familiar with their interface may also find them less intuitive than the straightforward filters.

Filters should be used instead of effects when you intend to use or modify the objects that the filter creates right away or when you intend to use only part of an object. For example, you may be interested in applying Pucker & Bloat to a path and then joining it with a straight path. Using the Pucker & Bloat effect makes a poor choice as it updates itself as the path is changed, changing the straight line you joined. It is possible to expand effects after you've applied them, but this takes more time.

In cases where filters are repeated in effects, they are discussed in the Effects chapter. The interface for filters and effects is the same.

Photoshop Filters

The 10 filter menus in the bottom half of the menu are the same as filters in Photoshop. They function exactly the same as they do in that application. As in Photoshop, these filters function only on pixel images. The same set of filters may also be applied as effects.

Extensive use of Photoshop filters, particularly on imported raster images, recommends a Photoshop workflow. Producing images in Photoshop and then importing them into Illustrator has several advantages over applying the filters directly in Illustrator.

- **Better selection of filters.** Photoshop offers a wider selection of more useful filters than Illustrator.

- **Faster processing.** Photoshop previews and processes pixels faster than Illustrator.

- **Ability to fade filters.** Photoshop enables you to ease the impact of filters you have applied by fading them.

- **Ability to paint with filters and to selectively mask and smooth the impact of filters.** Filters must be applied to an entire object in Illustrator. They can be applied to a selection in Photoshop.

Due to the highly specific nature of the filters and their use and misuse, space prohibits a complete discussion of them here. (However, all of Photoshop's filters are covered in depth in the *Photoshop 6 Shop Manual,* available from New Riders.)

12.2

Filter: Apply Last Filter   *(Command) [Ctrl]-E*

This command applies the last filter used, repeating the settings used. If the last filter command you chose couldn't be executed, it will not appear as a choice here. For example, if you attempt to use Stylize: **Add Arrowheads** on a closed path, you will be warned that the filter couldn't be executed and it will not appear as a choice here. Conversely, if you apply a filter that has no effect, such as attempting Colors: **Adjust Colors** on a gradient, the command will appear here.

12.3

Filter: Filter: Last Filter   *(Command-Option) [Ctrl-Alt]-E*

This command opens the dialog box of the last filter applied with the last settings used. This enables you to make changes to the values used. Filters without dialog boxes are applied directly.

12.4

Filter: Colors

Use the filters in this menu to edit the color values of paths and embedded images.

12.5

Filter: Colors: Adjust Colors

Use this filter to add or subtract color values of paths, meshes, and embedded images using color sliders and to convert color modes of items. This filter does not function on gradients, symbols, or patterns.

Mistakes to Avoid

Creating blacks accidentally. This command adds or subtracts ink percentages, it does not specify new color mixes. Mixing colors here as you would in the Color palette may result in unintentionally dark objects. Keep in mind that the colors are being added or subtracted to the existing color values. It is easy to go too far and maximize colors, creating a rich black.

Judging color onscreen for print. Mixing colors for print based on their onscreen appearance is always a poor idea, even in color-calibrated work environments. Always refer to a print guide for color values when defining color.

Adjust Colors Options Dialog Box

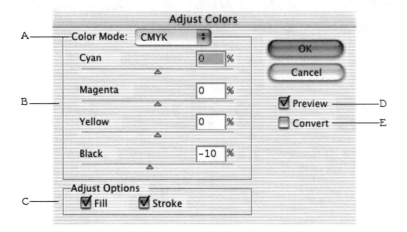

A. Color Mode

Use this menu to set the color mode to be used in adjusting object colors. If the mode of the selected objects does not match the mode chosen, here, the command will not be available. The color mode of selected objects may be converted to the selected mode by choosing the Convert option.

If the selected objects use a spot color or a Global swatch, the Global option will be available. This will adjust colors using a single tint slider The Global option only affects objects that use Global or spot colors. Other selected objects will be unaltered by this command. Colors cannot be converted to Global.

B. Color Sliders (-100 to 100)

Use these sliders to adjust the color values of selected objects. Values are added or subtracted by a specified ink percentage. The amount added or subtracted is absolute, not a percentage of the color value. For example, adding 50% black to an object that is 30% black, results in an 80% black object, not a 45% black.

Setting a negative value pulls out color, a positive value pushes color in. Values set beyond the limit of the color, will result in maximum values. For example, setting 80% cyan for an object that already contains 40% cyan will result in a 100% cyan. For this reason, it is important to assess the color values of the objects before executing this command.

RGB colors are specified using the same percentage scale. This is counterintuitive, since RGB is usually specified using brightness values instead of percents. Multiply the percent by 2.5 to get the rough brightness value.

C. **Adjust Options**

Use these options to control whether to affect the selected objects fill, stroke, or both.

D. **Preview**

This option previews the affect of the change onscreen as you work.

E. **Convert**

This option converts selected objects to the color mode set for the filter. This is commonly used to add colors to grayscale images, or to convert color art to grayscale. Once activated, colors are converted to the specified space and then adjusted based on the color sliders.

12.6

*Filter: Colors: **Blend Front to Back***

Use this command to recolor the fills of objects between two other objects in the stacking order to create a smooth color transition. At least three filled objects must be selected to execute this command. Upon execution, the fills of objects between the front and rear objects are adjusted to create a smooth color transition. The front and rear objects are not affected. In objects with more than one fill, the cardinal fill is used. Patterns, global colors and gradients are not available for adjusting with this command.

Related Topics

12.7 *Filter: **Blend Horizontally***
12.8 *Filter: **Blend Vertically***
9.52 *Object: **Blend***

12.7

*Filter: Colors: **Blend Horizontally***

This command functions similarly to Blend Colors Front to Back. Using this command, objects are blended between the farthest selected objects left and right, regardless of position in the stacking order.

12.8

*Filter: Colors: **Blend Vertically***

This command functions similarly to Blend Colors Front to Back. Using this command, objects are blended between the farthest objects top to bottom, regardless of position in the stacking order.

12.9

Filter: Colors: Convert to CMYK

Use this command in a CMYK color mode document to convert the fills of selected grayscale and bitmap items to the CMYK color mode. This does not work on gradient or pattern fills.

12.10

Filter: Colors: Convert to Grayscale

Use this command to convert the fills of selected items to the Grayscale color mode. This is available for both CMYK and RGB documents. This does not work on gradient or pattern fills.

12.11

Filter: Colors: Convert to RGB

Use this command in an RGB color mode document to convert the fills of selected grayscale and bitmap items to the RGB color mode. This does not work on gradient or pattern fills.

12.12

Filter: Colors: Invert Colors

Use this command to convert the fill and stroke of selected objects to their color opposites. In RGB or Grayscale colors, this can be calculated by inverting the color sliders. For example, a 75% gray would become a 25%. A color of R:0 G:255 B:100 would convert to R:255 G:0 B:155. CMYK colors are not as easy to calculate, but use a similar model. This command does not work on gradients, patterns, or global colors.

Issues to Consider

Invert can be chosen from the Color palette as well. Individual fills and strokes can be converted using the Invert command in the Color palette. This filter converts both fill and stroke at once.

Inverts are similar to complimentary colors. A color's compliment is the color you would need to add to it to make gray. Since the colors are opposite each other on the color wheel, they are sometimes called color opposites. The inverse is close to the compliment, but not quite the same. You can get a color's true compliment from the Color palette menu. Grays do not have compliments.

12.13

Filter: Colors: Overprint Black

Use this command to quickly set the overprinting status of selected objects with black fills and strokes. This command sets all selected objects to overprint if they match a specified percentage of black. *(For more information, see 18.2, Overprint Fill.)*

Overprint Black Options Dialog Box

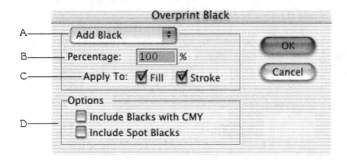

A. Remove/Add Black

Use this menu to apply overprinting (Add Black) or to remove it (Remove Black). This command does not affect the color values of selected objects, only the overprinting status of objects.

B. Percentage

Use this field to set the objects that will be affected by this command. Objects are affected based on the amount of black ink in their fills and or strokes. The object must have a black ink percentage equal to this field to be affected by the filter. The filter only affects items with this exact ink percentage.

C. Apply To

Use this option to set the overprinting status for the fill, stroke, or both. The black content of each attribute is compared to the percentage field.

D. Options

These options include or exclude some black colors based upon their definitions.

Include Blacks with CMY

This option includes blacks that contain CMY colors as well. For example, a color defined C:60 M:0 Y:0 K:100 would normally not be considered for overprinting by this filter because it is a process color. Using this option it would be considered and judged as a 100% black.

Include Spot Blacks
> This option includes spot colors defined with black for consideration in overprinting.

Related Topics

14.3   View: Overprint Preview
18.2   Overprint Fill

12.14

Filter: Colors: *Saturate*

Use this filter to lighten or darken the fills and strokes of selected objects by increasing color intensity. Gradients and patterns are not affected by Saturate, but meshes are.

Issues to Consider

Global or spot colors are adjusted by ink percentages. Applying Saturate to these colors is the same as using Filter: **Adjust Colors** and selecting the Global option. Typically this means that you cannot add color to them, only create lighter tints of the color.

Maxed out color values cannot be saturated. Color values that have reached their maximums cannot be saturated additionally.

Negative values move towards white, not gray. The name saturate implies that this filter will affect the color content of an object and leave the brightness alone. Saturation behaves this way in Photoshop. This filter moves colors closer to white, however.

The Color palette can saturate color definitions. Individual color definitions can be saturated by setting the Color picker to HSB and adjust the S slider. This will not saturate multiple objects at once, but does tint toward gray, rather than white.

Saturate Options Dialog Box

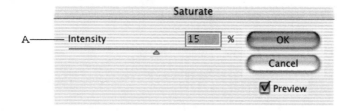

A. **Intensity** (-100 to 100%)

   Use this slider to control the impact of the filter. Set to negative numbers to lighten colors overall, set to positive numbers to increase the intensity of the hue.

12.15

Filter: Create

The filters in the Create menu generate new vector objects based upon a current selection.

12.16

Filter: Create: Object Mosaic

Use this command to generate an array of filled vector rectangles based on the contents of an embedded raster image object. The effect created is similar to a mosaic or to a close up view of a very low-resolution raster file. Detail is typically destroyed in favor of hard transitional edges.

If more than one image object is selected, each object will be converted using the same options. A group will be created by this filter automatically.

Issues to Consider

This command is sometimes used to create a color palette. This command quickly creates a series of color squares based on the contents of an image file. This is a fast way of sampling colors in the image for creating color swatches. The colors can be then used in other objects in the document, creating continuity.

This should not be considered as a way of replacing images. The results of this filter carry little detail and often result in unwieldy files.

Object Mosaic Options Dialog Box

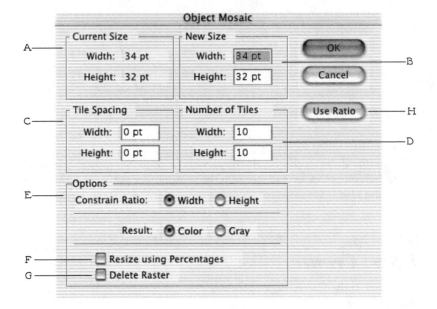

A. **Current Size**

This informational field displays the size of selected image. If more than one object is selected, the field will display N/A rather than the bounding box size for the objects.

B. **New Size**

These fields indicate the size of the bounding box of the rectangle group created. By default, this will be the same size as the Current Size. Set a new size to scale the resulting paths. Each field may be set independently. Having set one field, to create proportional scaling, click the Use Ratio button.

If more than one image is selected, this field will display percents rather than absolute measures.

C. **Tile Spacing**

This field establishes the distance between each of the rectangles in the mosaic.

D. **Number of Tiles**

These fields set the number of tiles created by the filter. Having set one of the fields, to create square rectangles, click the Use Ratio button to set the other field to a value that results in perfect squares.

E. **Options**

Use these fields to modify the rectangle creation process.

Constrain Ratio

These radio buttons set the behavior of the Use Ratio button with respect to the Number of Tiles field. Setting to Width causes the number of height tiles to change when the Use Ratio button is checked, Setting to Height locks the height number, causing width to change when Use Ratio is selected.

Result

Set the color mode of the rectangles created to the document's color mode (Color) or grayscale (Gray).

F. **Resize using Percentages**

This option switches the fields in New Size from absolute sizes, to percent fields. This is set automatically when more than one object is selected.

G. **Delete Raster**

This option clears the selected image object upon execution of the filter.

H. **Use Ratio**

This button reset the New Size or Number of Tiles field to match the proportions of the original object.

12.17

Filter: Create: *Trim Marks*

Use this filter to create a group of eight open paths at right angles to the corners of the bounding box of selected objects. The paths form basic trim marks for cutting out the object. The marks made by this filter differs from the marks created by Object: Crop Marks: **Make** in that they are editable as vector shapes. This also means they can be moved. Care should be taken not to reposition them. Another difference is that more than one set may exist in a document. This is often useful for putting a number of objects up on a page quickly. For example, a series of business cards could be imposed onto a page with these items acting as crop marks.

The paths created are styled with a .3-point stroke set to Registration color. This color prints on all press plates. It should not be confused with black and should not be used for anything except these sort of marks. The paths are also grouped and have no fill.

Related Topics

9.74 Object: **Crop Marks**

12.18

Filter: *Distort*

The filters in this group modify the shapes of path objects. All these commands may also be applied as effects. *(For more information, see 13.9 Effects: Distort & Transform.)*

12.19

Filter: *Distort: Free Distort*

Use the Free Distort command to distend a path using a four-pointed frame as a transformation grid. The effects are similar to those produced using the Free Transform tool. *(For more information, see 3.18, Free Transform.)*

12.20

Filter: *Distort: Pucker & Bloat*

Use Pucker & Bloat to create concave or convex segments on selected paths. *(For more information, see 13.11, Effect: Distort & Transform: Pucker & Bloat.)*

12.21

Filter: *Distort: Roughen*

Use this filter to create a ragged edge. This filter is commonly used to make a path appear more organic by adding imperfections to it. *(For more information, see 13.12 Effect: Distort & Transform: Roughen.)*

12.22

Filter: *Distort: Scribble & Tweak*

This filter randomly distorts objects by modifying the position of anchor points and direction points. *(For more information, see 13.13, Effect: Distort & Transform: Scribble & Tweak.)*

12.23

Filter: *Distort: Twist*

Use the Twist filter to distort objects in a spiral pattern. *(For more information, see 13.15, Effect: Distort & Transform: Twist.)*

12.24
Filter: Distort: Zig Zag

Use the Zig Zag filter to add equidistant anchor points to a path and offset the path's original position. *(For more information, see 13.16, Effect: Distort & Transform: Zig Zag.)*

12.25
Filter: Pen & Ink

The Pen & Ink filters attempt to replicate the traditional art techniques crosshatching. It also produces irregular texture patterns. This is accomplished by placing hundreds of paths of varying size and stroke weight in a pattern and then masking the whole thing. You can define objects to be used in the crosshatching and control the manner the pattern is applied. The Hatch Effect filter creates these groups from vector paths; the Photo Crosshatch filter creates linear crosshatching from embedded raster art.

12.26
Filter: Pen & Ink: Hatch Effects

Use this filter to convert paths into groups consisting of a clipping path and a series of masked paths creating a hatch pattern. The paths used may already be masked or grouped when the filter is applied.

When the command is applied, the selected object becomes a mask for the hatch objects. The hatch object is the design element that is repeated in the effect. As with all masks, the objects are grouped. If the original object uses a style, an effect, or has multiple fills, the appearance may change as a result of this filter.

Issues to Consider

Symbol sets offer more control. Effects similar to those automated by the Pen & Ink filter can be created using symbol sets and then masking them. Symbol sets offer greater control in the process, a wider range of allowable hatches, and produce smaller file sizes.

Brush strokes are often applied to hatches. After applying the hatch filter to an object, many individual hatch objects are created. Many users apply calligraphic brush strokes to the hatches to further the illusion of hand-produced work. Expanded calligraphic brushes are also a common source of new hatches.

Hatch Effects Options Dialog Box

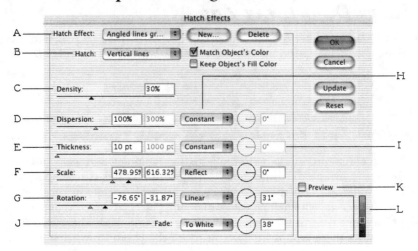

A. Hatch Effect

Use this menu to use a saved series of settings to populate all other fields in this dialog box. Illustrator comes with 25 default settings that utilize default hatches. This is useful, since this sprawling dialog box is often misunderstood.

New

> This button saves the current dialog box settings. You will be prompted to name the hatch. Settings are saved in the file Hatch Sets. This file is saved in the directory Adobe Illustrator 10: Plug-ins: Illustrator Filters: Pen & Ink. Saved Hatch effects are available in the Hatch effects menu in every open file.

Delete

> This option deletes the currently selected settings in the Hatch Effect menu. A warning dialog offers an opportunity to negate the command.

B. Hatch

This option establishes the hatch that is repeated in the masked group. Only saved hatches are available from this list. Object may be saved as a hatch by choosing Filter: Pen & Ink: **New Hatch**. The color of the hatches are set by the following two mutually exclusive options.

Match Object's Color

> This option colors the hatch objects to match the selected path's fill or stroke. The original path's fill is removed. This option should be used when the hatch is intended to take the place of the object's fill.

Keep Object's Fill Color

This option retains the appearance of the object's fill, applying hatch objects atop it. Hatch objects retain their original color attributes. As before, the original object is converted to a mask. To represent the fill, a square of the same size as the object's bounding box is created, filled with the object's fill and sent to the back of the stacking order.

C. **Density** (1% to 100%)

This option sets the amount of hatches used. As density increases, a greater area of the object is filled with hatch objects.

D. **Dispersion** (0 to 300%)

Use this field to control the model used for placement of hatches. The greater the Dispersion value, the more scattered the pattern becomes. At very low settings, the hatches are regimented and proceed in a regulated manner. At higher settings it is difficult to discern a pattern at all.

E. **Thickness** (10 to 1000 pts)

This setting affects the stroke applied to hatch objects. Although it is measured in points, the setting actually refers to percents of the original hatch's stroke weight. For example, a 1-point stroke turned into a hatch and given a 200-point thickness, creates hatches with a 2-point thickness.

F. **Scale** (10% to 1000%)

This setting scales the hatches, based on their original size. It does not scale stroke weight.

G. **Rotation** (-180° to 180°)

This setting turns the hatches about their individual center points within the hatch.

H. **Model**

These fields control how the Dispersion, Thickness, Scale, and Rotation options are applied.

None

This option applies no affect at all.

Constant

This option applies the effect evenly across the shape.

Linear

This option steadily increases the effect across the shape.

Reflect

This option starts the effect at the center and progresses outward.

Symmetric

This option varies the effect evenly and proportionately.

Random

This option applies the effect at random.

I. **Angle**

This option sets the direction of the effect when using the Linear, Reflect, and Symmetric models.

J. **Fade**

This option adjusts the color of hatch objects in a linear fashion. Hatches are changed in color to opaque white or black. These options work in conjunction with the hatch color options.

None

Use this option to omit the fade effect.

To White

This option fades the hatches to opaque white.

To Black

This option fades the hatches to opaque black.

Gradient

This option follows the gradient fill of the object.

Angle

This option sets the direction of the fade.

K. **Preview**

This option provides a useful thumbnail of the results the filter will have. The preview slows down the application slightly.

L. **Density Adjustment Bar**

Click one of the six boxes to fine-tune the Density setting. Darker boxes result in more intense density.

12.27

Filter: Pen & Ink: Photo Crosshatch

Use this filter to redraw embedded raster art as a series of open, crosshatched paths. The intention is to create the appearance that the art was sketched.

When this filter is applied, the tones in the image are evaluated. Light and dark areas in the image are expressed as overlapping open paths. Each tonal range may be set as separate hatches. As more hatches overlap, darker areas are created. The original art is deleted in the process.

Issues to Consider

Copy the art before applying this filter. Many users paste the original art back into the document after applying this filter. This offers the ability to continue to create effects with the image. For example, you can work around the limit of eight hatch layers by reapplying the filter to the pasted art and using different tonal ranges and angles.

This filter is often used on rasterized copies of vector art. You can convert selected art to pixels by choosing Object: **Rasterize.** Some users copy vector art, rasterize it, run this filter, then paste the original vector art behind the crosshatching. This provides texture for the art while keeping everything vectors.

It's usually easier to adjust tones in Photoshop. While it's possible to use the endpoint sliders in the histogram to adjust tonal distribution, it's often more trouble than it's worth. There is no preview to help forecast the effects of the adjustment, or readouts to indicate values. It's easier to adjust tones as desired in Photoshop and apply the filter without using the histogram endpoints.

Photo Crosshatch Options Dialog Box

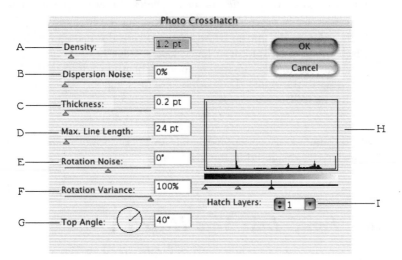

A. **Density** (.5 to 10 pts)
This option sets the distance between paths. The higher the value, the less dense the hatching will be.

B. **Dispersion Noise** (0% to 300%)
This option offset the hatches from each other. It affects density by making the hatches appear more randomly placed and thus more natural. The greater the value, the farther the hatches may be from each other.

C. **Thickness** (.1 to 10 pts)
This set the stroke weight for all paths created by the filter.

D. **Max. Line Length** (5 to 999 pts)

This option sets the size of the longest line that can be created by the filter.

E. **Rotation Noise** (-360° to 360°)

This option sets the additional, random rotation hatches may have from the default.

F. **Rotation Variance** (0 to 100%)

This option determines how much each subsequent hatch layer angle is different from the previous one.

G. **Top Angle** (-360° to 360°)

This option sets the rotation angle for the highest hatch layer.

H. **Histogram**

This displays the distribution of light and dark values in the image as a bar chart. Darker tones are on the left, lighter ones are on the right. The higher the spikes in a range, the more pixels of that particular tone.

Three triangles beneath the histogram indicate the lightest, darkest, and middle value in the image. Hash marks divide the histogram along the bottom by the distribution of hatch layers. Click-drag the middle slider to skew the histogram, including more light tones (drag to the left) or dark (drag to the right). The endpoint sliders may be adjusted by repositioning as well.

I. **Hatch Layers** (1 to 8)

Set the number of overlapping hatch areas. The tones each hatch layer represents are displayed in the histogram.

12.28

Filter: Pen & Ink: New Hatch

Use this command to create new hatches for use in Filter: Pen & Ink: **Hatch Effects**, to delete existing hatches, and to place instances of hatches into the document.

This filter is a management tool for hatches. To create a new hatch, select a basic path before choosing the filter. Multiple paths may be selected, but only path objects may be used. No brush strokes or complex shapes are allowed,

Issues to Consider

Smaller hatches work better than larger ones. Making objects about the size they will be typically used provides greater flexibility and prevents time lost consistently scaling down hatches.

New Hatch Options Dialog Box

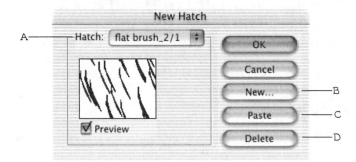

A. **Hatch**

Use this menu to select a hatch from the current set. A thumbnail of the hatch in typical use is displayed. Selected hatches may then be deleted or pasted into the document.

B. **New**

Use this option to create a new hatch shape from the currently selected path. The New Hatch dialog will appear, prompting you to name the hatch. Since you cannot easily edit hatch names, be certain the hatch is named correctly.

C. **Paste**

Use this option to paste the current hatch into the document. This is commonly done to edit the hatch prior to creating a new hatch.

D. **Delete**

Use this option to clear the current hatch and make it no longer available for use.

12.29

Filter: Pen & Ink: Library Open

Use this filter to load a saved Pen & Ink Hatch Sets file. The settings used in the Hatch Effects filter may be saved as a file using the filter Filter: Pen & Ink: **Library Save As**. The default file, Hatch Sets, is stored in the directory Adobe Illustrator 10/Plug-ins/Illustrator Filters/Pen & Ink. This command loads a file from this location to restore settings or from another custom file. Once this filter is executed, you will need to apply the Hatch Effects filter to use the settings.

12.30

Filter: Pen & Ink: *Library Save As*

Use this command to save the settings in the Hatch Effects dialog box as a file. This file may be loaded using Filter: Pen & Ink: **Library Open**.

12.31

Filter: *Stylize*

These filters group selected objects to other objects and adjust paths to create commonly used techniques. They are best applied as Effects.

12.32

Filter: Stylize: *Add Arrowheads*

Use this filter to apply prebuilt objects at the beginning and end of open paths. *(For more information, see 13.24 Effect: Stylize: **Add Arrowheads**.)*

12.33

Filter: Stylize: *Drop Shadow*

Use this filter to create either a pixel or vector-based shadow object behind selected objects. The shadow will only be vector-based if a blur of 0 is used. *(For more information, see 13.25, Effect: Stylize: **Drop Shadow**.)*

12.34

Filter: Stylize: *Round Corners*

Use this filter to adjust paths to create curved corner joins. *(For more information, see 13.29, Effect: Stylize: **Round Corners**.)*

The Effect Menu

Effects Overview

Effects apply commonly used commands and filters to objects on a "live" basis. An effect doesn't permanently alter the definition of an object, it adds information to it. This information is commonly an alternate version of the shape, such as a transformed or distorted version of a path. The alternate version previews and prints, but may be changed or discarded without impacting the original image information. Only the original object appears in Outline view and only the original object may be selected and modified using toolbox tools.

Photoshop Filter Effects

The last 10 groups of effects in this menu (Artistic through Video) are effect versions of Photoshop filters. These effects create alternate raster versions of vector objects. Only Blur, Pixelate, and Sharpen work in CMYK mode files. Applying these filters in Illustrator is cumbersome compared to applying them in Photoshop. They are slow to work, may only be applied to entire images, and cannot be faded. Their use is typically ill-advised. In the event that Photoshop is not available, though, it is better to apply these as effects rather than as filters in Illustrator. As effects, they can be modified or discarded.

Issues to Consider

Effects impact an entire object's shape. You cannot apply an effect to anchor points or segments.

Effects may be applied to fills and strokes rather than objects. This enables complex effects and is essential in understanding the use of effects like Convert to Shape.

Some effects are required for other effects. Some effects, like Rasterize and Outline Object, prepare an object to have another effect applied to it. The uses of these preparatory effects are detailed in the techniques section.

Effects have a cumulative impact on each other. Effects may be applied atop each other. In the case of the some effects, such as the transform, the order effects are applied can greatly impact their outcome.

Effects work on bounding boxes. An effect applied to an object uses the object's bounding box to determine its impact. When effects are applied to layers or groups, the bounding box of all objects on the layer or in the group are used. This is a key difference. Where the effect is applied can greatly impact the results. For example, applying a drop shadow to a series of objects places a drop shadow behind each one of the objects. As the objects overlap each other, their shadows affect each other. Applying a drop shadow to a layer places the shadow behind all of the objects. As the objects cross each other, no shadow is shown.

Layer effects do not translate seamlessly to Photoshop. When you apply an effect to a layer and export the document to Photoshop, you might expect the effect to be translated to a corresponding Photoshop Layer Style. For example, you might expect that the Illustrator effect Stylize: **Drop Shadow** would translate to Photoshop's Drop Shadow Layer Style. This does not happen. The impact of the effect is translated to pixels, the objects appear the same as they did in Illustrator, but the effect does not become a style.

Effects may become a default. After applying an effect to an object, you may notice that the next object you create has the effect as well. This is caused by the option New Art Maintains Appearance found in the Appearance palette. To avoid this, set the option to New Art has Basic Appearance. *(For more information, see 17.7, New Art Has Basic Appearance.)*

Related Topics

13.2

Effect: *Apply Last Effect*   (Command–Shift) [Ctrl–Shift]-E

Use this command to apply to the last used effect to the current selection using the same settings. No dialog box is offered; the last used settings are applied directly.

13.3

Effect: *Last Effect*   (Command–Option-Shift) [Ctrl–Alt-Shift]-E

This command opens the dialog box of the last filter applied with the last settings used. This enables you to make adjustments to the settings used. Effects without dialog boxes are applied directly.

13.4

Document Raster Effects Settings

Use these settings to control the model used when using effects that require vectors be converted to image objects. When some effects are applied to vector objects, such as the Photoshop Filter effects at the bottom of the menu and the SVG Filters, an alternate raster version of the art is created and stored with the document. These raster versions of the art are used when the file is printed. There are opportunities to override these settings in most workflows, and they may be changed at any time. Nonetheless, it is important to inspect and adjust the settings as needed before applying an effect that creates raster alternates.

Issues to Consider

The bitmap mode is rarely used. This mode is not even supported by most of the effects.

Use the color mode of the objects. Don't try to guess the grayscale values you will get when applied to color objects. Define colors in the space you intend to use.

These settings do not affect all rasterization. The settings in this box do not replace the Document Setup rasterization or the objects that are created if you expand a transparent object. Nor do they impact rasters created when you use the Stylize effects. They only affect the raster effects at the bottom of the Effects menu (Artistic through Video).

Document Raster Effects Settings

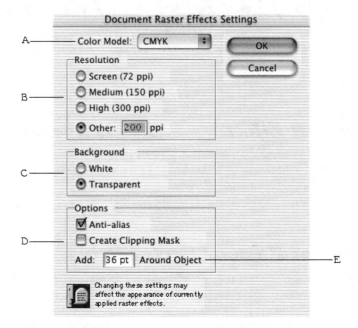

A. **Color Model**

This menu sets the base color space for raster objects. Choose from the document's color mode: grayscale or bitmap.

B. **Resolution**

Use this setting to determine the resolution of the raster art created. Choose from the three popular defaults or set a custom value using the Other option.

C. **Background**

This setting determines how transparent areas will be treated. Set to White to create opaque space, or Transparent.

D. **Options**

Choose from the following items:

Anti-alias

Use this option to smooth the edges of raster art with

Create Clipping Mask

This option adds a vector clipping path to the art to maintain a crisp edge. This option obviates the need for the transparency setting.

E. Add _ Around Object

This option adds a specified offset distance between the art and the clipping path.

13.5

Effect: Convert to Shape

The effects in this menu change the shape of selected objects to an oval, rectangle or rounded rectangle. The created shapes are based on the bounding box of the selected item.

Issues to Consider

These effects are commonly used when objects have more than one fill. One fill will be converted to a shape while the second fill retains the object's original shape. For example, to create text inside a box, the text object may be given a second fill that is converted to a rectangle. The utility of this is that the rectangle is attached to the text. It moves with the text and can automatically expand to fit as the type changes.

Adding a second fill also allows you to apply the effect to objects that do not normally have the ability to support the effect. Gradient meshes and envelopes do not normally accept this effect. Adding a second fill to these objects enables you to apply the effect.

All three of these effects use the same dialog box. These commands open the Shape dialog box. The only difference between the commands is the default shape they use. They can be changed freely. For example, Convert to Rectangle can be used to convert a shape to an ellipse.

Expanding the Appearance converts the effect to vector shapes. Use Object: **Expand Appearance** to convert the effect into a simple vector shape.

13.6

Effect: Convert to Shape: Rectangle

Use this command to convert an object to a rectangle shape.

Shape (Rectangle) Dialog Box

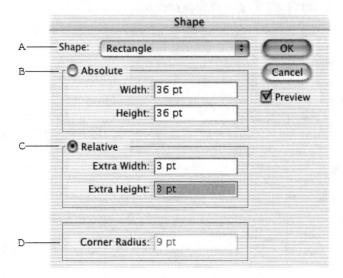

A. Shape

Use this command to set the basic shape the effect creates. Choosing Rounded Rectangle or Ellipse is the same as choosing those effects.

B. Absolute

This option creates an object of a specified size. The size is measured about the center of the selected object's bounding box. This option is commonly used when it is important to set a shape to a specific size.

C. Relative

Use this model to create an object offset a distance from the selected object's bounding box. The number may be positive or negative.

D. Corner Radius

Use this field to set the amount of curve corners have when using the Rounded Rectangle option.

13.7

Effect: Convert to Shape: *Rounded Rectangle*

This command behaves the same as Convert to Shape: **Rectangle** except that it creates rounded rectangles. It opens the Shape dialog box and selects the Rounded Rectangle option from the Shape menu. *(For more information, see 13.6, Convert to Shape: **Rectangle**.)*

13.8

Effect: Convert to Shape: *Ellipse*

This command behaves the same as Convert to Shape: **Rectangle** except that it creates ellipses. It opens the Shape dialog box and selects the Ellipse option from the Shape menu. *(For more information, see 13.6, Effect: Convert to Shape: Rectangle.)*

13.9

Effect: *Distort & Transform*

Use these effects to alter the shape of objects. These effects are often used as to set up a style.

13.10

Effect: *Distort & Transform: Free Distort*

Use the Free Distort command to distend a path using four-pointed frame as a transformation grid. The effects are similar to those produced using the Free Transform tool. The Free Transform tool does not support the high degree of change this effect does, including objects crossing themselves.

Issues to Consider

Free Distort is often used to create live shadows. Applying Free Distort to a second fill on an object creates a second, distorted version of the shape. This lends itself well to creating a perspective cast shadow. The default Style Soft Cast Shadow utilizes this technique.

Free Distort Options

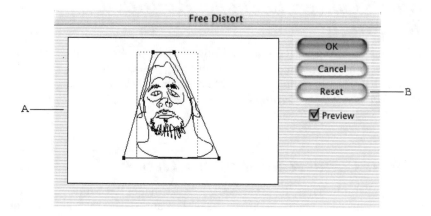

A. Frame Preview

Use this preview to transform selected objects. A solid line previews the object and its bounding box. Use the points at the corner of the bounding box to distort the object. As the object is distorted, a dashed line indicates the original bounding box position.

The points on the bounding box may be dragged outside of the preview window. The shape of the distortion becomes the default for the next use of the filter.

B. Reset

Use this option to reset the transformation bounding box to the bounding box of the object. The effect is to discard any changes to the object and start transforming again.

13.11

Effect: Distort & Transform: Pucker & Bloat

Use Pucker & Bloat to reposition anchor points and adjust curve handles on selected paths. The effect on paths is to create concave or convex segments. Set to negative values, segments become concave, curving into the object and creating spiny corners. This is the "pucker" half of the effect. At positive values, segments become convex, bowing outward and creating rounded corners. This is the "bloat" half of the effect. This effect cannot be applied to anchor points, only entire objects.

Issues to Consider

Anchor points greatly affect the results of this effect. Since this effect operates on anchor points, the number of anchor points on a path greatly affects the results. Commonly, users may add anchor points before applying the effect. Add anchor points manually with the Add Anchor Point Tool or Object: Path: **Add Anchor Points** command.

Tools can apply a similar transformation to parts of a path. The Bloat Tool and the Pucker tool enable you to apply these sorts of effects to parts of a path. Using a tool, of course, creates a permanent change that cannot be adjusted as an effect.

Pucker & Bloat Dialog Box

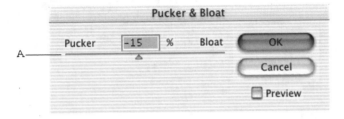

A. **Slider** (-200% to 200%)

Use this to set the effect of the filter. Positive numbers create a Bloat effect; negative numbers create a Pucker effect.

As numbers increase in a positive direction, anchor points on the path move toward the center and anchor points extend outward to the outside of the path. At 100% the anchor points reach the center of the object. Large direction segments pull the curve out in soft curves. After 100%, the anchor points move back outward from the center on the opposite side from where they started. Direction segments at these values are ponderously large and hard to manage.

As numbers move in a negative direction, anchor points extend away from the center. Direction points extend from points on the interior of the path, creating concave segments. At 100% the direction points move to the center of the path. After –100% the direction points begin to cross the center of the shape.

13.12

Effect: Distort & Transform: *Roughen*

Use this effect to create a ragged edge on a path. The effect works by adding anchor points (to the alternate version of the path) and randomly repositioning the points along it. This effect is commonly used to make a path appear more organic by adding imperfections to it.

Roughen Dialog Box

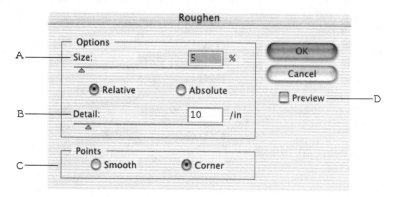

A. Size

This field and slider set the distance the anchor points may be offset from the path's original position. This distance may be measured as relative or absolute.

Relative (0 to 100)

This option sets the slider measure to a percent. The measure is a percent of the size of the original object. When many objects of different sizes are to be Roughened, this setting may contribute to consistency among the objects.

Absolute (0 to 7200)

This option sets the slider to a measured distance. The units used are determined by the setting in Edit: Preferences: Units & Undo: **General**.

B. Detail (0 to 100)

This setting determines the number of anchor points added to the path. The greater the number, the more distorted the path becomes.

C. Points

Use this option to create anchor points either with direction points (Smooth) or without (Corner).

D. **Preview**

This check box previews the filter in the document before it is applied. Uncheck and recheck the option to apply a newly randomized version of the effect.

13.13

Effect: Distort & Transform: *Scribble & Tweak*

This effect randomly distorts objects by modifying the position of anchor points and direction points. The effect is intended to make a path look more organic by adding imperfections to it.

Scribble & Tweak Dialog Box

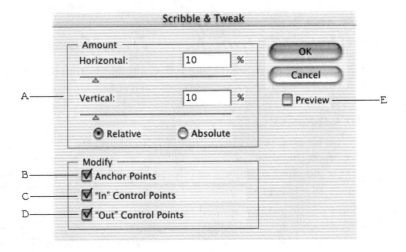

A. **Amount**

These options control the maximum horizontal and vertical distance points may be moved from their original position. This distance may be measured as relative or absolute.

Relative (0 to 100)

This option sets the slider measure to a percent. The measure is a percent of the size of the original object.

Absolute (0 to 7200)

This option sets the slider to a measured distance. The units used are determined by the setting in Edit: Preferences: Units & Undo: **General**.

B. **Anchor Points**

Use this option to affect anchor points with the filter. Unchecked, only the path's curves are affected.

C. **"In" Control Points**

This option causes the filter to affect direction points that lead into an anchor point on a path.

D. **"Out" Control Points**

This option causes the filter to affect direction points that lead out of an anchor point on a path.

E. **Preview**

This checkbox previews the filter in the document before it is applied. Uncheck and recheck the option to apply a newly randomized version of the effect.

13.14

Effect: Distort & Transform: Transform

Use this effect to scale, move, rotate, and reflect an object or multiple copies of an object about a set point of transformation.

Issues to Consider

This effect can be used to create multiple copies of objects. Since this dialog box offers the ability to create multiple copies of an object, many users apply the effect to objects and then expand the appearance to create shapes. These shapes may then be used in a sequential animation.

Object center points are determined by the effect. The center point of an object is determined by the effect's appearance, not the path. Be aware when using the center point to align other objects that it represents the visual center of the bounding box.

Transformed copies are transformed cumulatively. Each copy is behind the one before it and is cumulatively transformed. For example, if you scale two copies of an object 50%, the first object behind the original is scaled 50%; the second is behind the first copy and is scaled 50% of the copy's size.

Transform Effect Dialog Box

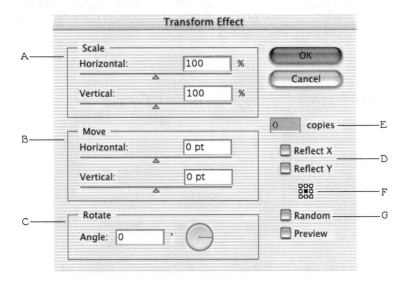

A. **Scale**

Use these fields or sliders to scale selected items horizontally and vertically. Objects may be scaled between −4,000% and 4,000%. By default, though, the sliders only go up and down between 0% and 200%. Enter amounts larger than that directly into the fields.

B. **Move**

Use these fields and sliders to reposition selected objects. Positive values move objects up and to the right; negative values move things down and to the left. Values between −4000 and 4000 pts may be entered. Values larger than 100 must be typed into the fields.

C. **Rotate**

Use these fields to rotate selected objects about the chosen reference point on their bounding boxes. Values may be entered directly or by dragging the radius arm.

D. **Reflect**

Use these checkboxes to reflect selected objects about the X or Y axis.

E. **Copies**

Use this field to apply the transformation to multiple copies of the object.

F. **Point of Transformation proxy**

Use this grid to establish the point of transformation for any changes made to selected objects using Transform each. The proxy point represent locations on the bounding box of each selected object. This enables transformation to take place about a corner or side, rather than the center.

G. **Random**

Enabling this option sets the transformation to a random amount. The values entered in fields become the upper limits for the transformation. Random does not affect Reflect.

13.15

Effect: Distort & Transform: Twist

Use the Twist effect to distort objects in a spiral pattern.

Twist Dialog Box

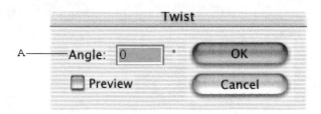

A. **Angle**

Use this field to determine the amount of distortion. Values from -3600°to 3600° may be entered. A positive value twists objects clockwise and a negative value twists counterclockwise. After the upper limits, the limit is subtracted from the entered value. For example a 3601° twist results in a 1° twist.

13.16

Effect: Distort & Transform: Zig Zag

Use the Zig Zag effect to create an evenly jagged line. The effect does this by adding equidistant anchor points to a path and offsetting them from the path's original position. Every other point is offset the same positive amount, the remaining points are offset a negative amount. The corners can be sharp, like a starburst, or rounded, like a sine wave.

Zig Zag Dialog Box

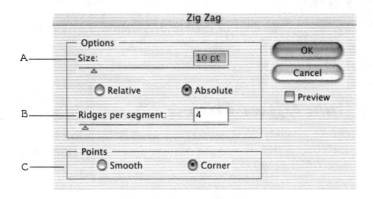

A. Size

This field and slider sets the distance the anchor points may be offset from the path's original position. This distance may be measured as relative or absolute.

Relative (0 to 100)

> This option sets the slider measure to a percent. The measure is a percent of the size of the original object.

Absolute (0 to 7200)

> This option sets the slider to a measured distance. The units used are determined by the setting in Edit: Preferences: Units & Undo: **General**.

B. Ridges per segment

This setting establishes the number of anchor points added per line segment in the object. A setting of 1 ridge per segment adds one anchor point between every two anchor points in the object. Set to higher amounts, this creates tighter zig zags.

C. Points

Use this option to create anchor points with direction points (Smooth) or without (Corner).

13.17

Effect: Path

These effects create live versions of commands found in the Object menu. The effects are typically used to prepare for applying other effects.

13.18

Effect: Path: Offset Path

Use this command to apply the Offset Path command as a live effect. The interface for the effect is the same as the command. *(For more information, see 9.47, Object: Path: Offset Path.)*

13.19

Effect: Path: Outline Object

Use this command to create an alternate, expanded version of an object. In versions of Illustrator prior to 10, this command was commonly used to make text available to have additional effects, such as the pathfinders, applied to it. It is not required in the current version of the application, but remains in the suite so that styles built in earlier versions will function correctly.

13.20

Effect: Path: Outline Stroke

Use this command to create an alternate version of the stroke that is expanded. The non-effect version of this command (Object: Path: **Outline Stroke**) is often used to create a shape from a stroke that will support a fill. This may be done to give the "stroke" a gradient or to apply a technique that requires a fill.

This effect does not enable you to treat strokes on objects like fills. It does, however, make Illustrator think of the inside and the outside of the stroke as separate things. After applying the effect, for example, you could apply the Offset Path effect. If it falls after Outline Stroke in the Appearance palette, the outside of the Stroke will be offset while the inside is unaffected.

13.21

Effect: *Pathfinder*

Use the Pathfinder effects on Type, Groups, and Layers to create effect versions of Compound Shapes. *(For more information, see 29.1, Pathfinder Palette Overview.)*

Issues to Consider

Applying pathfinders as effects enables them to become part of a style. Pathfinder effects are not as powerful as compound shapes since you cannot change an individual item's shape mode. Applying a pathfinder as an effect enables you to save it as part of a style that can be reapplied to other objects. This is really the best reason to use a pathfinder effect.

Pathfinder effects can be used on layers and groups. Applying a pathfinder effect to a layer ensures that all objects on that layer will be impacted. Targeting a layer and creating a compound shape does not impact objects added to that layer later.

13.22

Effect: *Rasterize*

Use this effect to create an alternate raster version for an object. This is commonly done to override the settings in Document Raster Effects Settings. For example, if the document Raster Effects settings called for color images and you needed to create a grayscale version, you could apply this effect to override the defaults for just that object.

13.23

Effect: *Stylize*

Use these commands to create commonly used visual effects. Some of these effects create vector objects, but the bulk of them create effects that will need to print as raster objects. The resolution of the objects created by these effects is controlled by the document setup settings, and not the Document Raster Effects Settings.

Issues to Consider

Heavy mixing of rasters and vectors can lead to complications. Many effects result in pixels masked by a vector at print. This can cause printing to slow down. Mixing can also lead to colors not matching each other correctly.

Soft edges print as raster images. Vectors cannot describe the diffuse edge of a blurred shadow or an inner glow. Rasters must be substituted when printed. Feather, Inner Glow, and Outer Glow all create rasters. Drop Shadow creates rasters if the blur option is used. Rasters are also created in the event the appearance is expanded. Be sure to check the settings in File: **Document Setup** when applying these effects.

13.24

Effect: Stylize: Add Arrowheads

Use this effect to add prebuilt arrowhead designs to the start and end of open paths. The start and ending points of objects may be hard to anticipate with some paths.

In open paths created with tools designed to produce open paths, such as the line segment tool, determining the start and end is easy. The first point you clicked is the start of the path; the point you ended with is the end of the path. In the case of initially closed paths, paths run clockwise. So if you drew a circle and deleted the bottom center point, the start of the path would be on the left and the end would be on the right.

Add Arrowheads Dialog Box

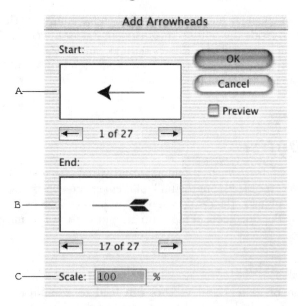

A. **Start**

This field displays the arrowhead design that will be added to the start of the path. Use the forward and backward arrows to navigate to one of the 27 prebuilt choices.

B. **End**

This field displays the arrowhead design that will be added to the end of the path. Use the forward and backward arrows to navigate to one of the 27 prebuilt choices.

C. **Scale**

Use this field to size the arrowhead design relative to the stroke width of the path. The arrowhead designs are scaled to fit on the path as shown in preview. Use this field to scale the design relative to the path.

13.25

Effect: Stylize: Drop Shadow

Use this effect to create an offset drop shadow. The shadow is in the shape of the object that cast it and cannot be distorted independently.

Issues to Consider

The Drop Shadow filter has an additional option. When applying this effect as a filter, an additional option is available: Create Separate Shadows groups the shadow and the object that created it automatically.

Drop Shadow Dialog Box

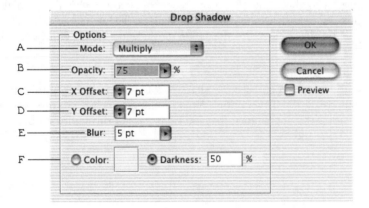

A. **Mode**

Use this setting to determine the blend mode of the shadow object. By default, this is set to Multiply. Multiply darkens the shadow based on the colors below it, creating a realistic shadow. In the event the object's appearance is expanded, the blend mode is carried over to the raster objects that are generated.

B. **Opacity** (100% to 0%)

Use this option to set the transparency of the shadow object. 100% opacity cannot be seen through, 0% is invisible.

C. **X Offset**

Use this field to determine the offset distance the shadow is from the object. Positive numbers move the shadow to the right; negative numbers move the shadow to the left.

D. **Y Offset**

Use this field to determine the offset distance the shadow is from the object. Positive numbers move the shadow down; negative numbers move the shadow up.

E. **Blur**

Use this field to determine how sharp the edge of the shadow is. A setting of 0 creates a hard edge shadow. As the number increases, the edge becomes fuzzy and diffuse. At high values, the shadow's shape becomes indistinct.

F. **Color Options**

The shadow may be colored as a specified color or as a tint of the original objects.

Color

Use this option to choose a color for the shadow yourself. Click the swatch to the right of the option to open the Color Picker dialog box. By default, the shadow will be black. The actual color numbers will be determined by the color mode and Color Settings for the document.

Darkness

Use this option to base the shadow color on the color of the object that created it. This option commonly injects color into the shadow, creating the appearance that light has passed through the object, as in stained glass.

13.26

Effect: Stylize: *Feather*

A feather is a diffuse, soft edge. Objects that are feathered appear to blend into the objects behind them. The blur of a feathered edge progresses in a linear manner from the path to the interior of an object. Use this command to apply a feathered edge to selected items.

Issues to Consider

Feather utilizes an Opacity Mask. To create the feathered edge, Illustrator applies an Opacity Mask to the alternate version of the object. If you expand the appearance of a feathered object, the mask will be attached to the group. To get at the raster image object, you will need to flatten the transparency of the group.

Feather only affects the inside of the object. In Photoshop, a feathered edge spreads in two directions. In Illustrator, the feather only affects the interior of the shape.

Feathers tend to round corners. Since the edge feathers inward, each side affects corners. This tends to turn corners into rounded edges.

Feather is similar to Gaussian Blur. Feather is similar to Effect: Blur: **Gaussian Blur.** Both fade an object to create a diffuse edge. The difference between the two is in how they treat edges. Feather begins at the object edge and progresses to the interior of the object. Gaussian Blur affects both the interior and the exterior of the shape, blurring the same amount on each side of the path.

Feather Options

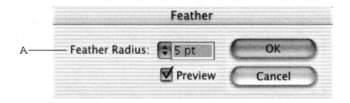

A. Feather Radius
Use this field to establish the distance from the edge of the object the feather affects. Setting to larger amounts increases the blur.

13.27

Effect: Stylize: *Inner Glow*

This command applies a diffuse glow around the inner contour of a shape.

Issues to Consider

Feather utilizes an Opacity Mask. To create the inner glow, Illustrator applies an Opacity Mask to the alternate version of the object. If you expand the appearance of a glow object, the mask will be attached to the group created. To get at the raster image object, you will need to flatten the transparency of the group.

Inner glow requires a fill. Inner glow requires an object to have a fill to have any impact.

Inner Glow Dialog Box

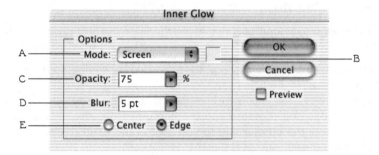

A. Mode

Use this setting to determine the blend mode of the glow. By default, this is set to Screen. Screen lightens the glow based on the colors below it, creating a realistic effect. In the event the object's appearance is expanded, the blend mode is carried over to the raster objects that are generated.

B. Color

Click this swatch to set the color of the glow using the Color Picker dialog box. The color chosen represents the glow at 100% opacity and unblurred.

C. Opacity (100% to 0%)

Use this option to set the transparency of the glow object. 100% opacity cannot be seen through, 0% is invisible.

D. Blur

Use this field to determine the width of the transition between the glow color and the object's color. A setting of 0 fills the object with the glow color. As the number increases, the transition grows larger, increasing the size of the effect.

E. Model

Center

This model starts the glow color in the center of the object. The glow color fills the center, transitioning to the object's color on the edges.

Edge

This model starts the glow color in the edge of the object. The glow transitions into to the object's color in the center.

13.28

Effect: Stylize: Outer Glow

This command applies a diffuse glow around the outer contour of a shape. In all respects it is like an inner glow except that it is applied to the exterior of an object. *(For more information, see 13.27, Inner Glow.)*

13.29

Effect: Stylize: Round Corners

This command creates curved corners of a set radius on selected objects. This effect modifies the vector shapes of objects when it is expanded or applied as a filter.

Round Corners Dialog Box

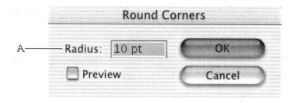

A. Radius

Use this field to set the amount the corners are rounded. In a right angle, the radius can be measured as the distance from the corner to where the curve begins.

13.30

Effect: SVG Filters

Use the SVG filters to create common visual effects when exporting to SVG. SVG filters use XML (a common computer language used on the Internet) to describe the visual effect. The impact of the filters is described as a series of XML properties. Users versed in XML may write their own filters or modify existing ones. Filters imported into the document appear at the bottom of this menu.

Mistakes to Avoid

Applying SVG filters out of order. To function correctly, the SVG filter must be the last item in the Appearance palette, just above Transparency. If you apply other effects after the SVG filters, be sure to re-order them such that SVG appears last in the list.

13.31

Effect: SVG Filters: Apply SVG Filter

Use this command to apply SVG filters, to create new SVG filters, to modify existing filters, and to delete filters from the default list. This command is also accessible by double-clicking on an applied SVG filter in the appearance palette.

Apply SVG Filter Options

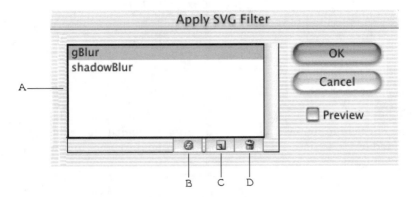

A. SVG Filter List

This panel displays the currently available SVG filters. Select one of the filters on the list to begin the process of editing or deleting it.

B. **Edit SVG Filter**

Use this button to edit a selected SVG Filter. The Edit SVG Filter dialog box opens, displaying the code for the current filter. Edit the code as needed and save. Many users duplicate a filter before editing it. This command can also be executed by double-clicking on a filter in the SVG Filter list pane.

C. **New SVG Filter**

Use this button to create a new SVG filter from scratch, or to duplicate an existing one. Click on the button to create a filter from scratch. The Edit SVG Filter dialog box opens. Only the open and close filter tags are created. To duplicate a filter, drag a filter from the SVG Filter List onto the button.

D. **Delete SVG Filter**

Use this button to delete a selected filter from the list.

13.32

Effect: SVG Filters: Import SVG Filter

Use this command to import SVG Filter definitions from external SVG files. Once executed, an Open dialog box enables you to navigate to the file you wish to import filters from.

13.33

Effect: Warp

This series of commands applies the warp distortions as effects. *(For more information, see 9.61, Object: Envelope Distort: Make with Warp.)*

13.34

Effect: Artistic

These filters distort selected objects by defining areas of similar colors, and then blur them together to form a solid color. The intent is to create the impression the art was created with traditional media.

13.35

Effect: Artistic: Colored Pencil

This filter attempts to make the image appear as if crosshatching were applied to it. Many users apply it to pattern fills. Gradient fills typically do not work well with this command.

13.36

Effect: Artistic: Cutout

This command creates the impression that the image was made from torn construction paper. It does this by reducing the image to a specified number of colors. The impact is similar to posterizing art.

13.37

Effect: Artistic: Dry Brush

This effect tries to simulate the painter's technique of dry brush. When applying traditional dry brush, the paint is not thinned. This produces intense colors, and allows for more marking by individual bristles. This filter defines areas of similar color and fills them with averaged color values. Coarse brush detail is added as well.

13.38

Effect: Artistic: Film Grain

This effect randomly lightens and darkens parts of the image to create the impression of photographic film grain. Film grain is visible emulsion kernels created when using high-speed film, or when photos are greatly enlarged.

13.39

Effect: Artistic: Fresco

This effect groups areas of similar color and outlines them with black or gray strokes. Coarse lines are added throughout.

13.40

Effect: Artistic: Neon Glow

This effect is intended to give the appearance of an object lit by neon lights at night. The image that receives the filter is set to grayscale. White areas become black and a diffuse glow surrounds areas of similar color.

13.41

Effect: Artistic: Paint Daubs

This effect defines areas based on color similarity and then blurs the area. Where colors are substantially different, edges are retained and sharpened.

13.42

Effect: Artistic: Palette Knife

This effect defines area based on color similarity and averages the color in those areas that are roughly the same size and shape. The intent is to emulate the hard, crude marks made when painting with a knife's edge instead of a brush.

13.43

Effect: Artistic: Plastic Wrap

This effect makes selected objects look as though they were wrapped in heat-shrink plastic. Colors tend to desaturate and posterize.

13.44

Effect: Artistic: Poster Edges

This effect posterizes the colors in the image and surrounds each area with black lines.

13.45

Effect: Artistic: Rough Pastels

This effect simulates pastels drawing on paper over a rough surface. Part of the texture of the surface shows in the work. The effect striates the image with saturated color in irregular sizes at a 45° angle. Choose from prebuilt textures or load a Photoshop file as a custom texture.

13.46

Effect: Artistic: Smudge Stick

This effect smears darker areas over lighter ones at a left diagonal.

13.47

Effect: Artistic: Sponge

This effect simulates applying a sponge to a watercolor painting. Detail is lost, and colors are reduced to random, irregular shapes. The contents of the shape areas are blurred, but detail is retained.

13.48

Effect: Artistic: *Underpainting*

This effect simulates the traditional artistic technique of underpainting. Underpainting roughs out areas of color in preparation for painting detail on top. It commonly provides a richer visual appearance. This filter lightens and blurs the image before adding highlight and shadow detail based upon a selected texture. After applying this technique, some users copy the object, Paste it in Front so that it overlaps the underpainting object and then adjust the top object's opacity.

13.49

Effect: Artistic: *Watercolor*

This effect simulates traditional watercolor painting. It does this by defining areas of similar color, averages the color values in those areas, and darkening the edges. The effect also saturates the image and adds dark shadows.

13.50

Effect: Artistic: Blur: *Gaussian Blur*

This effect averages the values of adjacent colors to reduce detail. The effect is faded unevenly over distance to create a more natural blur. The blur may extend outside of the path's shape. This effect is used more commonly applied than other filters and effects.

13.51

Effect: Artistic: Blur: *Radial Blur*

This effect blurs an image outward from a center point. This is commonly used to focus attention on a specific area.

13.52

Effect: Brushstrokes: *Accented Edges*

This effect blurs edges and then lightens or darkens them. The effect is similar to an edge glow or darkened shadows.

13.53

Effect: Brushstrokes: Angled Strokes

This effect finds areas of similar color and blurs those areas, preserving the edge definitions. It also adds streaks of color to the image, lightening or darkening the image in narrow strokes. The strokes run as left or right diagonals.

13.54

Effect: Brushstrokes: Crosshatch

This effect is similar to Angled Strokes. It roughens edges and preserves more detail than Angled Strokes.

13.55

Effect: Brushstrokes: Dark Strokes

This effect blurs areas of similar colors together and then adds dark strokes over the areas at left and right diagonals. The darker the area, the darker the stroke. Very dark areas may paint completely black. The preview window in this filter is not always precise.

13.56

Effect: Brushstrokes: Ink Outlines

This effect blurs areas of similar colors together and then outlines edges with black. Colors are darkened and dulled and light areas are streaked with black.

13.57

Effect: Brushstrokes: Spatter

This effect simulates a clogged airbrush. Color is grouped together in randomly sized clops and then moved slightly, roughening edges.

13.58

Effect: Brushstrokes: Sprayed Strokes

This effect is similar in function to Spatter, but color is moved in more regimented way, creating angled lines.

13.59

Effect: Brushstrokes: *Sumi-e*

This effect is similar to the Dark Strokes effect. The difference is that Sumi-e uses larger, roughly rectangular strokes in its attempt to replicate the Japanese Sumi-e rice-paper painting technique.

13.60

Effect: Distort: *Diffuse Glow*

This effect adds grainy white pixels to the image. The white fades in from the edges, creating a glow effect.

13.61

Effect: Distort: *Glass*

This effect simulates viewing the image through textured glass. Detail is distorted by grouping areas of color and offsetting them based upon a texture. The texture may be one of the four pre-built options or loading from an external Photoshop file.

13.62

Effect: Distort: *Ocean Ripple*

This effect distorts an image to give the impression that it is under water.

13.63

Effect: Pixelate: *Color Halftone*

This effect simulates a close-up view of color halftone spots. Halftone spots are colored cyan, yellow, magenta, and black. They vary in size depending upon tone and are set in grids at angles to each other.

13.64

Effect: Pixelate: *Crystallize*

This effect converts the image to randomly shaped polygons of about the same size. Colors are averaged together to fill the polygons solidly.

13.65

Effect: Pixelate: Mezzotint

This effect breaks the image into small groups of pixels based on a preset shape. Color values are pushed to their extremes. In a grayscale image, this results in solid blacks and whites, in color images, it results in hot color values.

13.66

Effect: Pixelate: Pointillize

This effect simulates the pointillism style of painting by breaking the image into circles of pure color. Each color circle is slightly offset in a random direction to give a more natural appearance.

13.67

Effect: Sharpen: Unsharp Mask

This effect creates the impression of sharper detail by increasing the color differences between pixels. This is a commonly used command that is well recommended for its power and flexibility.

13.68

Effect: Sketch: Bas Relief

This effect reduces images to grayscale and creates a three-dimensional look by applying highlight and shadow detail.

13.69

Effect: Sketch: Chalk & Charcoal

This effect reproduces the image as though it were created with chalk and charcoal on gray paper. The image is reduced to grayscale colors with diagonal strokes representing details.

13.70

Effect: Sketch: Charcoal

This effect is similar to Chalk & Charcoal except that it is on white paper.

13.71

Effect: Sketch: *Chrome*

This effect makes the image look as if it were stamped with a highly reflective metal. The image is blurred, sharpened, and reduced to a grayscale color range.

13.72

Effect: Sketch: *Conté Crayon*

This effect produces a soft-focused grayscale image with hard edges. It can also add texture, as though the conté crayons were drawing atop a rough surface.

13.73

Effect: Sketch: *Graphic Pen*

This effect simulates a Rapidograph-style pen. The image is represented as thin, diagonal black lines through the shadow areas.

13.74

Effect: Sketch: *Halftone Pattern*

This effect simulates an image printed using halftone screens. The image is reduced to grayscale tones.

13.75

Effect: Sketch: *Note Paper*

This effect produces the impression that the image was sketched into highly textured paper. Colors in the image are broken into large areas based on tone and given a texture.

13.76

Effect: Sketch: *Photocopy*

This effect makes the image look as though it were photocopied. Much of the detail is lost as colors are reduced to grayscale tones with harsh transitions.

13.77

Effect: Sketch: *Plaster*

This effect finds the edges in the image, eliminates the detail except for the shadows and adds highlight and shadow detail. The effect simulates a sculpted 3-D image.

13.78

Effect: Sketch: *Reticulation*

This effect represents the image with grainy grayscale blotches. The impression is on India ink on crepe paper.

13.79

Effect: Sketch: *Stamp*

This effect simulates reproducing the image with a detailed rubber stamp. Dark colors are set to black, the remainder of the image is set to white.

13.80

Effect: Sketch: *Torn Edges*

This effect is similar to the Cutout effect. It creates the image as though it were made from torn paper. Only black is used in this effect, however.

13.81

Effect: Sketch: *Water Paper*

This effect blurs the image in the direction of the paper grain and applies brightness and contrast to the image. The impression is similar to the watercolor technique of soaking paper before painting on it to reduce the paper's ability to absorb paint.

13.82

Effect: Stylize: *Glowing Edges*

This effect outlines the edges between similar color areas using lines of saturated color, and then inverts the image. The impression is that the image was made from colored neon lights.

13.83

Effect: Texture: **Craquelure**

This effect simulates an image painted on a cracked, decayed surface. The effect finds edges in the image, blurs them slightly and sharpens the edges. Cracks are adding, giving them shadow and highlight detail, and darken the colors inside the cracks.

13.84

Effect: Texture: **Grain**

This effect provides a variety of ways to add noise to an image.

13.85

Effect: Texture: **Mosaic Tiles**

This effect is almost identical to Craquelure, except that it adds cracks in a regular pattern instead of randomly.

13.86

Effect: Texture: **Patchwork**

This effect breaks the image into a grid of flat colored squares, then adds shadow and highlight detail to make the squares seem three-dimensional. This effect produces a more convincing mosaic than Mosaic Tiles.

13.87

Effect: Texture: **Stained Glass**

This effect defines the image with randomly shapes hexagons. Each hexagon is bordered in black. The effect can also be lit from a gradient behind the object, as if the sun were shining through the glass.

13.88

Effect: Texture: **Texturizer**

This effect creates the impression that the image has been created in a three-dimensional surface. It does this by adding highlight and shadow detail based on a prebuilt image or a custom external Photoshop file.

13.89

Effect: Video: De-interlace

This effect is used to compensate for noise and blurring created when a video image is imported as a photo.

13.90

Effect: Video: NTSC Colors

This effect converts the colors to the palette used most commonly used in television.

The View Menu

14.1

View Menu Overview

Commands in the View menu modify the display of a document. None of the commands alter any objects. Accordingly, almost none of the commands are affected by Edit: **Undo** and Edit: **Redo**.

14.2

View: Outline/Preview   *(Command) [Ctrl]-Y*

Use this command to toggle the document between the Outline and Preview view modes. Preview mode displays items as they will be printed or posted on-line. Artwork mode does not display the painted attributes of items, displaying only the underlying vector framework of the items. Viewing a document in artwork mode often makes selecting and editing shapes easier, while preview mode lets you see what your edits actually result in.

Issues to Consider

Layers can be set to preview or outline independently. Each layer may be set to its own preview or artwork state. This affords even greater viewing control. When an object in a document is very complex and requires a lot of processing power to be displayed, it can be set on its own layer and set to Outline view while the rest of the document is in Preview. *(For more information, see 25.4, Toggle Visibility.)*

Multiple windows may be set to different view modes. Many users open more than one window of the same document by choosing Window: **New Window**. Each window may be set to its own view mode, enabling you to look at a document in both modes at once.

Outline is often used to select items that are obscured by others. Objects that are behind others are easier to select in Outline mode because you can see them. Because the Use Area Select preference *(For information, see 8.12, Edit: Preferences: **General**)* does not work in Outline, you must click on an object's path or center point to select it.

14.3

View: Overprint Preview

(Command-Option-Shift) [Ctrl-Alt-Shift]-Y

Use this command to change the display of the document to forecast the effects of overprint settings. When the command is activated, a checkmark appears next to the command and the title bar of the document adds the words "Overprint Preview" after the document's color mode.

By default, objects are set to knock out. This means that the colors of the objects' colors do not blend with those below them. Overprinting instructs the color of the object to be blended with the objects directly below them. This is commonly done when trapping files. Trapping is a process that accounts for potential mechanical misregistration on printing by blending abutting colors together. Adding colors together darkens them. This preview will show that effect onscreen. *(For more information, see 18.2 Overprint Fill.)*

Issues to Consider

In RGB mode, overprinting only affects spot colors. Non-spot colors set to overprint in a spot color document do not preview differently.

Process white is invisible when overprinting. Overprinting is really an instruction to objects below. White, or paper needs these instructions to become visible. Set to overprint, white objects lack these instructions and disappear. This preview will display that.

Overprint preview does not affect printing or exporting. This option affects the onscreen display of objects only.

Overprint Preview and Pixel Preview are mutually exclusive. You cannot use both preview modes at once.

You can also simulate printing on colored paper. If your project calls are printing on a non-white paper, you can project the effects of this onscreen. Use the Simulate Paper option in the Transparency section of the Document Setup dialog box. *(For more information see 7.45 File: Document Setup: Transparency.)*

14.4

View: **Pixel Preview** *(Command-Option) [Ctrl-Alt]-Y*

Use pixel preview change the document display to forecast exporting the objects as screen-resolution raster art. This option is useful when preparing work that will be saved for web delivery.

When the option is active, objects are displayed with soft, anti-aliased pixel edges rather than hard, crisp vector edges.

Issues to Consider

Pixel previews should be evaluated at 100% view depth. At 100%, you'll be seeing what your online viewer will see. You should judge the image from this depth. At larger view depths, art will be disappointingly pixelated.

Other view options are often used in conjunction with pixel preview. Since pixel preview is commonly used to evaluate web graphics, many users also use the Proof Colors option to simulate monitor gamma. *(For more information, see 14.5, View: Proof Setup.)*

14.5

View: **Proof Setup**

Use this command to prepare to forecast color onscreen using the Proof Colors command. Proof Setup works when Color Management is turned on in the document. *(For more information, see 8.10, Edit: Color Settings.)* The command enables you to attach different color profiles to the document for display. This type of onscreen evaluation of color is called Soft Proofing.

When assigning a profile to a document in RGB color mode, you may choose one of the three default RGB color spaces. To assign another profile, or if you're working in a CMYK document, choose the Custom option from this menu.

Issues to Consider

Soft proofing is prone to failure. Soft proofing relies on the quality of the monitor, the environmental conditions, and the accuracy of the profiles used to succeed. Even at its best, viewing things onscreen is not the same as viewing printed things. Don't consider soft proofing an alternative to traditional press matches.

The color profile assigned to the document is not re-assigned in this command. This command does not change the color profile for the document, it substitutes one for onscreen display only.

Color Management must be turned on. Soft proofing cannot be accomplished if color management is turned off. Make sure that Edit: **Color Settings** is not set to Emulate Illustrator 6.0. Any other setting, even Color Management Off, will enable these settings.

These commands do not interfere with others. You may use pixel preview and overprint preview in conjunction with these Proof Colors.

14.6

View: *Proof Setup: Custom*

Use this command to assign a custom profile for use in displaying documents onscreen. The profile set here does not override the document's color profile.

Proof Setup Options Dialog Box

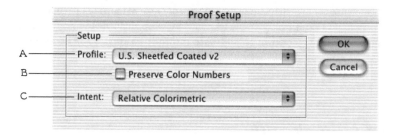

A. Profile

Use this menu to set the profile used for display. The choices are broken into RGB, Grayscale, and CMYK profiles. The grayscale profiles, such as "dot gain 10%" display what color values will look like printed as grays. This also gives an obvious example of the function of this command set. Colors are defined one way (in color), but preview another (in grayscale). The assigned values are still there and may be recalled by turning off the proofing features.

B. Preserve Color Numbers

Deselect this option to forecast what the document would look like if converted to the color space selected. This option is only available when choosing a color profile that is the same color mode as the document.

C. **Intent**

Use this field to specify a model for the math used when changing color spaces. Different models produce different results when handling the transition. The colors of the objects being displayed also lend themselves to different models.

Perceptual

This model attempts to preserve the way colors appear to the eye, even if that means changing the color values.

Saturation

This model sacrifices color accuracy for vividness. It is usually used in business or presentation graphics where color is not critical.

Absolute Colorimetric

This model leaves color definitions unchanged as much as possible. In some cases, this results in the relationships between colors changing as out of gamut colors are pushed into smaller spaces. For example, a bright red and an intensely bright red may appear as the same bright red when converted using this model.

Relative Colorimetric

This model is the same as Absolute Colorimetric except that it provides a more accurate translation, assuming that the image profile is correct. This model is the default for most color management schemes.

14.7

View: Proof Setup: Macintosh RGB

Select this profile for an RGB document to soft proof emulating commonly used Macintosh monitors. This is typically used in conjunction with the Windows RGB model to examine a graphic that is to be used in onscreen display.

14.8

View: Proof Setup: Windows RGB

Select this profile for an RGB document to soft proof emulating commonly used Windows monitor. This is typically used in conjunction with the Macintosh RGB model to examine a graphic that is to be used in onscreen display.

14.9

View: *Proof Setup: Monitor RGB*

Select this profile to soft proof using the color space of your monitor as a proof profile. This is typically used in conjunction with the Macintosh RGB model to examine a graphic that is to be used in onscreen display.

14.10

View: *Proof Colors*

Use this option to activate and deactivate the onscreen proofing option. Whenever a profile is selected, this option is activated automatically. Select the option again to deactivate soft proofing and return the display to defaults.

14.11

View: *Zoom In* *(Command) [Ctrl]-+*

Use this command to increase the view depth one step in the preset amounts. Illustrator has 23 preset view depths from 3.13% to 6400%. This command sets the document to the next highest amount on the list. In the event the view depth is at 6400%, the command will be dimmed and unavailable.

Related Topics

14.12 Zoom Out
4.41   Zoom Tool
29.1   Navigator Palette

14.12

View: *Zoom Out* *(Command) [Ctrl]- Hyphen (-)*

Use this command to decrease the view depth one step in the preset amounts. Illustrator has 23 preset view depths from 3.13% to 6400%. This command sets the document to the next lowest amount on the list. In the event the view depth is at 3.13%, the command will be dimmed and unavailable.

Related Topics

14.11 Zoom In
4.41   Zoom Tool
29.1   Navigator Palette

14.13

View: Fit in Window   *(Command) [Ctrl]-Zero*

Use this command to set the view depth of a document such that the artboard fits in the current window as large as possible. Since artboards and windows vary in size, the depth this command sets the document to will vary. If the window is resized after applying this command, the view depth does not automatically update. This command can also be applied by double-clicking on the Hand tool.

14.14

View: Actual Size   *(Command) [Ctrl]-1*

Use this command to set the view depth to 100%. This command can also be applied by double-clicking on the Zoom tool.

14.15

View: Show/Hide Edges   *(Command) [Ctrl]-H*

Use this command to toggle the preview status of selections. When edges are hidden, selected objects are not highlighted. This is commonly done to examine selected objects without being distracted by the selection highlighting.

Issues to Consider

Hidden edges are inevitably forgotten. Once you are done hiding edges, be sure to show them again. Commonly, the hidden edges are forgotten, leading to frustration when you seem unable to select anything.

Consider saving a selection rather than hiding it. If the purpose of hiding a selection is to preview it without releasing a complex selection, consider saving the selection instead. If you save the selection, you will be able to deselect, view the objects, and reselect them without concern. *(For more information, see 11.23, Select: Save Selection.)*

14.16

View: Show/Hide Artboard

Use this command to toggle the visibility of the artboard. Hiding the artboard makes it temporarily invisible. This is often done to examine a document without contextual distraction. When the artboard is hidden, the command toggles to Show Artboard, enabling you to display the artboard. This command is commonly used in conjunction with Hide Page Tiling to completely remove visual page cues.

14.17

View: Show/Hide Page Tiling

Use this command to toggle the visibility of the page tiling. Hiding the page tiling makes it temporarily invisible. This is often done to examine a document without contextual distraction. When the page tiling is hidden, the command toggles to Show Page Tiling, enabling you to display it. This command is commonly used in conjunction with Hide Artboard to completely remove visual page cues.

14.18

View: Show/Hide Slices

Use this command to toggle the visibility of slices in the document. Hiding the Slices makes them temporarily invisible. This is often done to examine a document without distraction. When slices are hidden, the command toggles to Show Slices, enabling you to display them. *(For more information, see 9.33, Object: Slice.)*

14.19

View: Lock Slices

Use this command to lock User Slices so that they cannot be selected, deleted or modified. When slices are locked, the Slice and Slice Select tool displays a "no" symbol instead of its standard cursor. Existing object slices may still be repositioned and adjusted, but no new object slices may be created.

Issues to Consider

Applying attributes to a user slice converts it to an object slice. Be certain you know which type of slices you have made before assuming they are locked.

Object slices must be locked individually. Select object slices and lock them manually using Object: **Lock** or locking them in the Layers palette.

14.20

View: Show/Hide Template

(Command-Shift) [Ctrl-Shift]-W

Use this command to toggle the visibility of all template layers in the document. Choose Hide Template to temporarily hide any layer that uses the template option. When templates are hidden, choose Show Templates to make them visible again. This is usually done to examine progress while tracing imported art.

Issues to Consider

Use the Layers palette to change template visibility. This command is only really useful if you have multiple templates in a document, and this is unusual. Most users prefer to use the Layers palette to show and hide templates manually.

If you use this command, stick with it. This command does not contextually update with the status of the Layers palette. This means if you use the command to hide template layers, and then manually reset the visibility in the Layers palette, the command will fail to update and still read Show Layers. Use one method or the other.

14.21

View: Show/Hide Rulers   *(Command) [Ctrl]-R*

Use this command to toggle the visibility of the rulers in the document.

Rulers function the same as they do in many other applications. There is a horizontal and vertical ruler, positioned in the top and left sides of the document, respectively. Rulers measure in points, picas, inches, millimeters, centimeters, Q, and pixels. Establish these units in Edit: Preferences: **Units & Undo** or by (Control) [Right]-clicking on a ruler and choosing from the contextual menu. Rulers are commonly used for the following:

- **Determining the position of the cursor.** As the cursor moves, a guide in the rulers tracks its horizontal and vertical progress. This can be useful as you reposition objects.

- **Repositioning the zero origin.** The info and transformation palettes both measure distances from the position the rulers read zero. This point is called the zero origin. This is in the lower-left corner of the artboard by default.

  To reposition the zero origin, click-drag from the crossed guides icon where the rulers meet and to the position you want to reset the ruler to. Double-click the crossed guides icon to return the zero origin to its default.

  To set the zero origin to the upper-right corner of the window, (Option) [Alt] click the crossed guide icon.

- **Creating guides.** Click-drag from a ruler into the document to create a horizontal or vertical nonprinting guide. Guides are useful for aligning objects and laying out documents. *(For more information, see 14.24 View: Guides.)*

14.22

View: *Show/Hide Bounding Box*

(Command–Shift) [Ctrl–Shift]-B

Use this command to toggle the visibility of the bounding box. The bounding box is an option used in conjunction with the Selection tool.

The bounding box displays as a wire frame with eight handles surrounding the selected objects. The box extends to the extreme points in all directions of the selected objects, being just large enough to cover all points on the selected objects. When the Selection tool is active, you can use the bounding box to transform objects by dragging the handles. *(For more information, see 1.2, Selection Tool.)*

While the bounding box enables you to transform objects easily, it can interfere with precise selecting. For example, you may not be able to drag a rectangular object by its anchor points because the bounding box is in the way, causing you to resize the object instead of moving it. Hiding the bounding box makes the selection tool behave like it did in earlier versions of Illustrator.

Issues to Consider

All selections have a bounding box. Illustrator uses the concept of the bounding box when performing many calculations and transformations. You may not see the wire frame, but understanding how a bounding box works will help you to understand techniques like Transform Each and applying effects to layers.

This command has no affect on the Free Transform tool. The Free Transform tool also uses a bounding box model to transform objects. Hiding the bounding box does not impact the behavior of that tool.

14.23

View: *Show/Hide Transparency Grid*

(Command–Shift) [Ctrl–Shift]-D

Use this command to toggle the visibility of the transparency grid.

The transparency grid is a checkerboard that appears behind all objects in the document. It is used to differentiate lighter colors from transparency. Against a white background, it is difficult to distinguish between a light color and a transparent area. The transparency grid provides the contrast needed to differentiate. The transparency grid's squares stay the same size, regardless of view depth. Set the appearance of the transparency grid by choosing File: Document Setup: **Transparency**.

Issues to Consider

The grid serves the same purpose less obtrusively. Many users prefer the grid to the transparency grid. It serves the same function as the transparency grid, but is smaller and less invasive. Users who prefer the transparency grid often do so because they are familiar with the interface from Photoshop. *(For more information, see 14.31, Show/Hide Grid.)*

14.24
View: Guides

Guides are nonprinting vectors used to assist in aligning objects and laying out pages. Guides in Illustrator are similar to guides found in most every digital graphic arts application. Set the appearance of guides using Edit: Preferences: **Guides & Grid**.

Issues to Consider

Guides are commonly created using rulers. Click and drag from either ruler into the document to create a guide.

Any path can become a guide. Any simple path object can be converted into a guide. The Rectangular Grid tool, and Polar Grid tool create objects that are intended to become guides. *(For more information, see 14.27 View: Guides: Make Guides.)*

Guides are locked by default. Unlike other applications, Illustrator's guides are locked by default. Take care when dragging guides from the rulers, as they will need to be unlocked to be repositioned.

Guides are objects on layers. Guides are objects and may be found with all other objects in the Layers palette. Though they are locked and unlocked differently from other objects, they may be shown and hidden as objects in the Layers palette.

Many users prefer to isolate guides on a special layer. Guides are placed onto the active layer when they are created. Creating all the guides on their own layer assists in managing complex documents.

Guides can create slices. Guides can be used to define a layout for a web page. Once guides are positioned correctly, convert them to slices using Object: Slice: **Create from Guides**. Be sure that the Clip to Artboard option is chosen for this technique or the slices will be unusably large. *(For more information, see 9.36, Object: Slice: **Create from Guides**.)*

14.25

View: Guides: Hide Guides *(Command) [Ctrl]-;*

Use this command to toggle the visibility of all the guides the document between hidden and shown. If guides have been manually hidden in the Layers palette, choosing Show Guides will reveal them.

14.26

View: Guides: Lock Guides

(Command-Option) [Ctrl-Alt]-;

Use this command to set the availability of the guides for selection and editing. By default, guides are locked and unavailable for change. When this is the case, a check mark appears next to the command. To toggle the state of the guides to unlocked and back, choose the command again.

Issues to Consider

Unlocked guides may be transformed. Commonly, unlocked guides are repositioned to account for errors or changes in the document, but they are also available to be transformed. A common example is rotating guides to create a perspective grid.

Unlocked guides should be relocked immediately. If you unlock guides to edit them, be certain to lock them once you are done. Unlocked guides are easily selected accidentally and may cause some transformations and pathfinders to fail or act strangely. Unlocked, guides lead to confusion and errors.

14.27

View: Guides: Make Guides

Use this command to convert a selected path into a guide. Be certain that the object is as you intend it and that you do not need it before executing the command.

14.28

View: Guides: Release Guides

Use this command to convert an unlocked, selected guide to a path. If the object was converted to a guide using View: Guide: **Make**, the path is restored with its attributes intact. If the guide was created from the rulers, it will extend the distance of the pasteboard and have no fill or stroke.

14.29

View: Guides: *Clear Guides*

Use this command to delete all guides on unlocked layers. Guides do not need to be unlocked to execute this command. This command is commonly executed to clean up a document that has become untidy with guides.

14.30

View: *Smart Guides*　　　　　*(Command) [Ctrl]-U*

Use this command to toggle the activation of the Smart Guides feature.

Smart Guides are a series of temporary guides intended to make selecting and editing easier by providing contextual visual cues. Many users disregard them since they can be distracting once even basic mastery of the tools is gained. *(For more information, see 8.15, Edit: Preferences: Smart Guides & Slices.)*

Issues to Consider

Smart guides can be useful when you are creating things at specific angles. When creating objects at specific, repeatable angles, smart guides can be more useful than irritating. For example, when using isometric scaling to create technical drawings, you will be using a formula that describes the angles at which objects slant, commonly in 30° increments. Dragging objects in 30° increments is difficult, and repeatedly changing the document default preferences to 30°, 60° and so on is time consuming. But setting the smart guide default angle preferences is easy. There is even a prebuilt 30° option. This way you can tell when you are dragging things at the right angle. *(For more information, see 8.16, Edit: Preferences: Smart Guides & Slices)*

14.31

View: *Show/Hide Grid*　　　　　*(Command) [Ctrl]-"*

Use this command to toggle the visibility of the grid. The grid is a nonprinting grid of lines that appears behind all objects in the document. It has the appearance of graph paper. The grid is useful for aligning objects and differentiating transparent space. Set the grid options by choosing Edit: Preferences: **Guides & Grid**.

Issues to Consider

The grid can be shown and hidden using contextual menus. (Control) [Right]-click with nothing selected to access a contextual menu with this menu command in it.

The grid is set to the document's default angle. The grid is straight because the default document angle is 0°. If you change the document angle, the grid's angle will change with it.

Objects can snap to the grid. This is useful for aligning objects. *(For more information, see 14.32, View: Snap to Grid.)*

Grids are in back of objects be default. If you prefer, switch them to the front by choosing Edit: Preferences: **Guides & Grid** and deselecting Grids in Back.

14.32

View: **Snap to Grid** *(Command-Shift) [Ctrl-Shift]-"*

Use this option to cause objects that are being moved or transformed to snap to the grid. Snapping to the grid means that as an object nears a grid line, it is pulled toward it. This makes it harder to position objects away from grid lines. Objects tend to line up and move along those grid dividers. This can be useful or a headache, depending upon your intentions. This command works whether or not the grid is visible.

14.33

View: **Snap to Point** *(Command-Option) [Ctrl-Alt]-"*

This option causes the cursor to snap to anchor points, guides, the page tiling and artboard edges. This option is great for aligning objects precisely. When the transformation cursor is atop an anchor point using this option, it turns white. When a selection tool is atop an anchor point the cursor displays a white box.

Issues to Consider

Locked objects are not affected. You cannot snap to the point of a locked object.

The cursor is snapping. This means if you want to position two anchor points in the same spot, you must start by dragging from one of the anchor points.

14.34

View: **New View**

Use this command to save a new view into the document. A view records the current view depth, Preview/Outline mode, and location of a document. This includes the status of layers. View options, such as pixel preview and over-print preview are not recorded. Many users utilize several views in a document to make it easy to move between working on a specific section of the document and previewing the whole thing.

Saved views appear at the bottom of the View menu. Select a saved view to return the document to that view.

Issues to Consider

Assign custom shortcuts to views. Custom views can be assigned keyboard shortcuts by choosing Edit: **Keyboard Shortcuts**. This makes getting to saved views even faster.

14.35

View: Edit View

Use this command to delete and rename the custom views saved in a document.

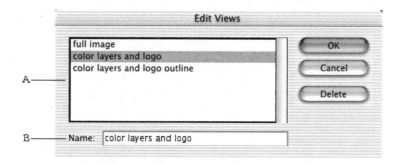

Edit Views Options Dialog Box

A. **View List**

This pane lists all views saved in the document. Select a view to begin the process of editing or renaming it.

B. **Name**

This field displays the name of the View selected in the View list. Retype the name to edit it. Click the Delete button to remove the view from the document.

The Actions Palette

Actions Palette Overview

Actions are a recorded series of commands that you can apply with a single mouse click or keystroke. The result is similar to an extended keyboard short-cut. You can record a complex series of commands or just a single step or two.

Actions are used typically to reduce the repetitive nature of tasks, and to reduce the possibility of errors. For example, upon completing an illustration many users prepare it for hand-off by removing unused brushes, swatches, styles, and deleting any stray points. This can all be done with a single click by preparing an action.

Actions are stored in groups called sets. Sets appear in the Actions palette as folders. Actions are often organized into sets by function. Sets may also be saved and loaded as separate files. This enables you to move actions from one computer to another and to share useful actions with colleagues.

Actions are not the same as scripts. They are similar to scripts produced in AppleScript, JavaScript, or Visual Basic but unlike those scripts, Actions can only execute Illustrator commands. This is an important distinction to make since Illustrator can also execute scripts. In fact, in many workflows, a script may execute an action. *(For information, see 7.41, File: **Scripts**.)*

Actions are commonly used for the following:

- **Setting character and paragraph attributes.** Illustrator does not have style sheets like those used in InDesign and QuarkXPress. To apply many text attributes at once, many users create actions to style type with commonly used values or corporate trade dress.

- **Batch processing.** You can use an action on a series of files without opening them. This is commonly used for tasks such as applying the same color profile to all files in a folder or creating web graphics.

Actions are not as widely used in Illustrator as they are in Photoshop. Part of this is due to the nature of the tasks that are being performed. Photoshop is often more about editing objects instead of creating them. Another reason is that other Illustrator techniques can be used more flexibly to perform a task. For example:

- **Creating commonly used objects is easier as symbols.** Instead of creating an action to create a commonly used shape or logo, it makes more sense to save the objects as symbols and open them as a library.

- **Creating canned special effects is easier as a style.** Instead of creating an action to apply a series of filters, it makes more sense to use effects and save the appearance as a style. This applies the effect and allows you to edit it.

- **Many transformations can now be saved as styles.** Many of the sequential transformations that can be recorded as actions are now available as effects. For example, an action that turned type into outlines and offset the path to create outlined type could be created as a style using effects. This is easier to manage and retains the type.

The controls for recording, duplicating, arranging, and running actions are found in the Actions palette.

15.2

Actions Palette Controls

The Control Buttons are found at the bottom of the Actions palette, when the palette is in List view (as opposed to Button Mode). The first three are labeled with the same symbols for Stop, Record, and Play found on most tape recorders and VCRs. In fact, their function is almost identical.

Action Palette Options

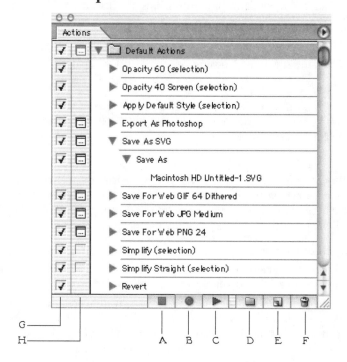

A. Stop Playing/Recording

This button is only available when an action is recording or playing. Click it to stop the current function. The Stop button has the same effect as choosing Stop Recording or Stop Playing from the palette submenu.

B. Begin Recording

Click this button to record additional commands into an existing action. New commands are inserted after the currently selected item. If the action itself is selected, new additions are placed at the end of the current list of commands. The Record button has the same effect as choosing Start Recording from the palette submenu.

C. Play Selection

The effect of this button depends on the selected item. If an action is selected, it executes its sequence of commands. If a single command is selected from within an action, it executes the sequence from that point onward. In both cases, clicking this button is the same as choosing Play from the palette submenu.

To play only the selected command, hold down the (Command) [Ctrl] key while clicking this button. Or, hold down the (Command) [Ctrl] key while double-clicking the command. (Be aware that double-clicking on a command in the Actions palette opens its dialog box. You can enter new settings and click OK to apply the command, but watch out—the new settings are recorded in the action, and the old settings are discarded.)

D. **Create New Set**

Click this button to add a new set to the Actions palette. Doing so produces the same result as choosing New Set from the palette submenu.

E. **Create New Action**

Click this button to access the New Action dialog box, similar to choosing New Action from the palette submenu. (For more information, see "New Action," later this chapter.)

F. **Delete**

Click this button to permanently remove the currently selected item. An alert appears, asking if you want to delete the action or command. Click OK to continue. To bypass the alert, hold down the (Option) [Alt] key while clicking Delete, or drag the item and drop it on the button.

G. **Enable/Disable Checkbox**

When the Actions palette is in List mode, each action (and its component commands) is preceded by either one or two check boxes.

When a check mark is visible in the first box, it indicates that an action is enabled, and can be played at any time. If there is no check mark, the action is disabled—selecting it and clicking the Play button has no effect. By default, this box is checked when an action is created.

To disable an individual command within the action, click the Open triangle next to the action's title and click the appropriate check box. The next time you play the action, Illustrator skips any disabled commands. The primary check mark for the entire action appears red when any of its commands are disabled. Clicking this check mark again enables all disabled commands.

H. **Open Dialog Box Check Box**

This box determines whether or not the dialog box appears while the action is running. By default, Illustrator retains the settings that you applied while recording an action. With Open Dialog Box off, the action simply uses all the recorded settings without opening the dialog box. With Open Dialog Box on, the command's dialog box is opened the next time you play the action. This way, you can enter different settings for a command without the need to record a new action. Click OK to close the dialog box and continue the sequence.

When one command within an action has Open Dialog turned on, a red mark appears in the box next to the action's title. Clicking this mark once turns on all the Open Dialog marks; clicking it again turns them all off.

15.3

Actions Palette Submenu

The following commands enable you to refine the appearance and function of the Actions palette.

15.4

New Action

This command is the equivalent of the New Action control button. Two things happen when you choose this command. It opens the New Action dialog box, where you name the action, assign a keystroke, set, and color to the action. After you close the dialog box, it immediately starts recording an action.

Issues to Consider

F-key assignments are only visible when the Actions palette is in Button mode. To see the keyboard shortcut while in List mode, include the name of the F-key in the title of the action. F-keys are the keys at the top of the keyboard used for keyboard shortcuts with actions.

The New Action Dialog Box

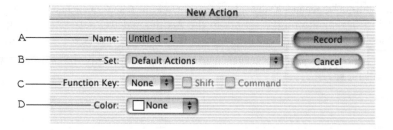

A. **Name**

Name the new action in this field. Be as descriptive as possible, so the action is quickly identifiable. The name can be up to 32 characters long.

B. **Set**

This pop-up menu displays all sets currently available in the Actions palette. If more than one set exists, the one that is currently active appears in the pop-up menu by default. If you want the new action to be placed into a different set, specify that here.

C. **Shortcut Keys**

The only key equivalent you can assign to an action is one of the 15 Function keys of your keyboard. The pop-up menu lists all currently available keys, or the ones that have not been assigned to an action. Even though Illustrator defaults to its own set of F-key shortcuts, they are over-ridden by an action using the same key. In the future, pressing the assigned F-key executes the action, similar to selecting an action from the palette and pressing the Play button.

Shortcuts used by the operating system supercede the ones assigned here. If your computer uses keyboard shortcuts, such as a Powerbook with F-keys assigned to speaker volume, those commands will override your Illustrator settings.

After assigning an F-key, you can add modifier keys to the shortcut by checking the Shift or (Command) [Ctrl] boxes, or both. For example, if you set F5 in the pop-up menu and check the Shift box, pressing Shift-F5 will trigger the action in the future.

Adding modifier keys to the F-key shortcuts increases the possible number of key equivalents to 60.

D. **Color**

This option colors the action when the Actions palette is in Button mode. This is used to color-code actions of similar functions.

15.5

New Set

This command creates a new directory (or set) in the Actions palette. Sets are used to organize multiple scripts in the Actions palette. Sets can store up to 24 scripts. There is no realistic limit on the number of sets you can create.

When actions are saved, a set is saved as a single file. Only the actions in the set will be saved.

15.6

Duplicate

This command makes an exact copy of the current selection. This is often done to begin the process of creating an action that uses many of the same steps as an existing one. You can also duplicate items by dragging them onto the New Action button.

15.7

Delete

This command permanently removes the current selection from the Actions palette, similar to clicking the Delete button in the palette.

Issues to Consider

The Delete command cannot be reversed by choosing Edit: Undo. When an action or command is removed, it can only be restored if it was saved using Save Actions.

15.8

Play

When an action is selected, this command executes its sequence of commands. When a single command within an action is selected, it runs the action from that command onward. This command is the equivalent of pressing the Play button.

15.9

Start Recording

This allows you to add commands to an existing action, similar to pressing the Record button. If the action's title is selected, the new commands are placed at the bottom of the list. If a specific command is selected, the new commands are inserted immediately after it.

Issues to Consider

You cannot record Edit: Undo as part of an action. Not only does it reverse the last command, it erases it from the recording. This allows you to undo erroneous commands and continue recording an action without stopping. If you must add Edit: **Undo** to an action, use the Insert Menu Item command after you've stopped recording.

You cannot record all tools. Paths created by the Pencil tool, the Brush tool, and the Pen tool suite cannot be recorded. You can paste, or insert, these paths as an action step, though. To insert these paths once created, use the Insert Select Path command. *(For more information, see 15.13, Insert Select Path.)*

15.10

Record Again

When a script is selected in the Actions palette, this item allows you to replace all the operations, while leaving its name, F-key, and color untouched. When a single operation is selected, it allows you to replace a single, selected item within an action.

15.11

Insert Menu Item

Certain menu items cannot be included when you record an action. This command allows you to insert them after the action is defined.

When you insert a menu item that uses an editable dialog box, it will always appear when the action is run. Because no Open Dialog checkbox is available for inserted commands, you cannot turn this feature off. When you enter the desired settings in the dialog box and click OK, the action executes the remaining commands. Click the Cancel button in the dialog box to stop the action at its next command.

15.12

Insert Stop

This command pauses an action in progress and displays a dialog box containing a user-defined message. Users may discontinue the action or continue it. Common uses include the following:

- **Manually executing commands.** Certain commands cannot be included in an action, such as selecting a specific object or manipulating a transformation box.

  By inserting a stop, you pause the action long enough to perform the necessary work by hand. When you click the Play button again, the action resumes.

- **Sending a message to the user.** If desired, you can set your own message to appear when the action reaches a Stop. For example, a Stop dialog box inserted at the beginning of an action could describe the action and any special preparations it requires. Messages inserted in the middle of an action usually contain special instructions.

Issues to Consider

Enabling or disabling a Stop dialog box. Like other commands, the dialog box of an inserted Stop is controlled by the Open Dialog checkbox in the Actions palette. To have the dialog box appear, check the box. To ignore the dialog box and only pause the action, uncheck the box. Disable the Stop completely by unchecking the Enable box.

The Record Stop Dialog Box

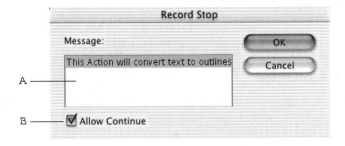

A. Message Box

Here, you can enter a message up to 200 characters long. It should clearly communicate the purpose for stopping. For example, a stop at the beginning of an action could say, "This action expands objects, including type, do you want to continue?"

B. Allow Continue

Checking this box allows the user to choose between continuing and stopping an action from the Stop dialog box. Usually, this option is activated. If this button is left unchecked, the only available option is stopping.

15.13

Insert Select Path

Use this command to paste selected paths into the document as part of the action. Up to 10 paths may be entered a time, but they can only be simple paths. Compound paths, meshes, envelopes, groups, and clipping masks are not allowed.

This command is often used to work around the inability of actions to record pencil, pen, and brush actions. After creating one of these shapes, select the path and choose Insert Select Path to add the shape to the action.

Issues to Consider

An inserted path retains its original position. It will be inserted where it was when the action was created.

Inserted paths do not retain their original attributes. Inserted paths will be styled with the document's current default fill and stroke when the action is run. If the attributes are important, record them as the next steps after insert path.

15.14

Select Object

This command adds a step in an action that selects objects that have a specific word in the notes field of the Attributes palette.

Issues to Consider

Writing a note may be written into an action. For example, one action may create a series of objects and give those objects a note. Later another action can select just those objects.

Set Selection Options Dialog Box

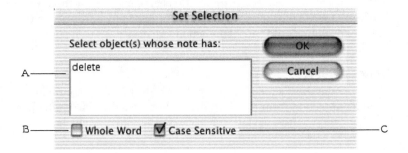

A. **Select object(s) whose note has**

Enter the text to be compared to the note field of the Attributes palette. The entire text must match for the object to be selected.

B. **Whole Word**

Use this option to limit the search to objects that contain the entire phrase. For example, let's say an object has a note of "adobe.com" and the search is based on "adobe." Using the Whole Word option, "adobe.com" would not be selected, because the criterion didn't completely match.

C. **Case Sensitive**

Use this option to only make the search criteria case sensitive.

15.15

Action Options

This command allows you to change the name, F-key, and color of the selected action. The options in this dialog box are identical to the New Action dialog box. *(For more information, see 15.4, New Action.)*

15.16

Playback Options

The items in this dialog box determine the method Illustrator uses to run a script from the Actions palette.

The Playback Options Dialog Box

A. **Accelerated**

When this option is selected, the script plays as fast as Illustrator can apply the commands. This is the preferred setting for everyday work.

B. **Step By Step**

When this option is selected, Illustrator refreshes the screen after each operation in the script.

C. **Pause For** (1–60 seconds)

This option enables you to insert a specific amount of time between each operation. Adding a pause gives users a moment to evaluate the results of the step and stop the action if needed.

15.17

Clear Actions

This permanently removes all current actions from the Actions palette. You cannot undo this command—after the actions are cleared, there is no way to bring them back. The only actions you can recover are the defaults and any actions that you have already saved.

15.18

Reset Actions

This replaces all current actions with the defaults. If you have custom-tailored some of those defaults or do not want to replace your current actions, click Append in the alert. The defaults are added to the end of the palette.

Issues to Consider

You don't have to retain the Default Actions set. Because they were not tailored to your specific work, they're probably of little use. They do illustrate the basic functions of the Actions palette, however, so consider hanging on to them while you become more familiar with the palette. Then delete them to make room for your own actions.

15.19

Load Actions

Use this command to add a pre-existing actions file to the palette. When loaded, the set appears at the end of the current list.

15.20

Replace Actions

Use this command to remove the current list of actions and replace them with a saved set.

15.21

Save Actions

Use this command to save the currently selected set of actions into a separate file. You can only save a set—if you select multiple sets or a single action, this command is not available.

15.22

Button Mode

Although only Button Mode is listed at the bottom of the palette submenu, selecting the command toggles between the two views of the Actions palette.

List View

This option is indicated by the lack of a checkmark next to Button mode in the submenu. Here, the actions are arranged vertically. Each one has a Show arrow. Turn the arrow to display an action's commands; turn the arrow next to a command to display its settings and values.

Actions and commands can only be recorded, rearranged, and edited in List view. It also provides a status report while the action is running–when the commands are shown, each one highlights while it is being applied. If the list is too long to display completely in the Actions palette, it automatically scrolls.

The List view displays the control buttons at the bottom of the Actions palette, giving you quick access to the New, Record, and Play buttons.

Button Mode

This option displays actions as a series of buttons. Actions are arranged sequentially by sets and colored. Keyboard shortcuts for the actions are listed on the face of each button. Actions can be run in this mode with a single-click of the button. No edits to the actions or the sets may be made in this mode. Typically, button mode is used once actions have been established and do not need editing.

The Align Palette

Align Palette Overview

Use the Align palette to reposition objects relative to each other or to the art-board. This is commonly done to square up the position of objects rapidly or to put a set distance between objects.

16.4 Horizontal Align Right

16.3 Horizontal Align Center

16.2 Horizontal Align Left

16.5 Vertical Align Top

16.6 Vertical Align Center

16.7 Vertical Align Bottom

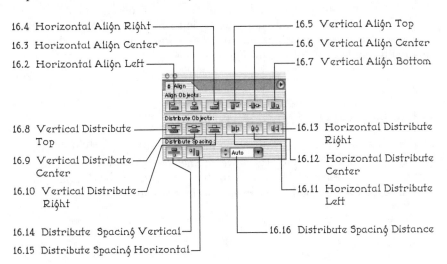

16.8 Vertical Distribute Top

16.9 Vertical Distribute Center

16.10 Vertical Distribute Right

16.13 Horizontal Distribute Right

16.12 Horizontal Distribute Center

16.11 Horizontal Distribute Left

16.14 Distribute Spacing Vertical

16.15 Distribute Spacing Horizontal

16.16 Distribute Spacing Distance

The Align palette can both align and distribute objects. Aligning repositions objects so that they line up. Distribute places an even amount of space between objects.

When aligning objects to each other, you must have at least two objects selected. If you are aligning objects to the artboard, you need only have one selected. *(For more information, see 16.20, Align to Artboard.)*

Issues to Consider

There is no reset button. If you make an error in aligning, you will need to use Undo to fix the mistake. Each click in the palette counts as an Undo.

Align works on objects only. You cannot use this palette to align anchor points on a path. Only objects are affected.

Align respects selections. Although Align works on objects, it does not change the selection state of objects. If anchor points are not selected when objects are aligned, they won't be selected after the objects are aligned. This enables you to align objects as you edit their anchor points without concern that you will need to reselect the correct anchor points.

Align uses bounding boxes. When objects are aligned, their bounding boxes are compared and aligned. This may yield different results than you expect. For example, the center of the bounding box of a star is usually not what we think of as the center of the star. Be sure you visually inspect the position of objects after you align them.

16.2

Horizontal Align Left

Use this command to align objects about the left-most point among the selected objects. Objects only move to the left when using this option. When using the Align to Artboard option from the Actions palette menu, objects are aligned to the left side of the artboard.

16.3

Horizontal Align Center

Use this command to align objects about the center point of the selected objects' bounding box. Objects move to the left or right when using this option. When using the Align to Artboard option from the Actions palette menu, objects are aligned to the center of the artboard.

16.4

Horizontal Align Right

Use this command to align objects about the right-most point among the selected objects. Objects only move to the right when using this option. When using the Align to Artboard option from the Actions palette menu, objects are aligned to the right side of the artboard.

16.5

Vertical Align Top

Use this command to align objects about the top-most point among the selected objects. Objects only move up when using this option. When using the Align to Artboard option from the Actions palette menu, objects are aligned to the top of the artboard.

16.6

Vertical Align Center

Use this command to align objects about the center point of the selected objects' bounding box. Objects only move up or down when using this option. When using the Align to Artboard option from the Actions palette menu, objects are aligned to the center of the artboard.

16.7

Vertical Align Bottom

Use this command to align objects about the bottom-most point among the selected objects. Objects only move down when using this option. When using the Align to Artboard option from the Actions palette menu, objects are aligned to the bottom of the artboard.

16.8

Vertical Distribute Top

Use this command to distribute the objects based on their tops. This places an even amount of space between the top-most points of the selected objects. When using the Align to Artboard option from the Actions palette menu, the highest and lowest objects are aligned with the top and bottom of the artboard and objects are distributed in-between.

16.9

Vertical Distribute Center

Use this command to distribute the objects based on their centers. This places an even amount of space between the center points of the selected objects. Objects move up or down when using this option. When using the Align to Artboard option from the Actions palette menu, the highest and lowest objects are aligned with the top and bottom of the artboard and objects are distributed in-between.

16.10

Vertical Distribute Bottom

Use this command to distribute the objects based on their bottoms. This places an even amount of space between the bottom-most points of the selected objects. When using the Align to Artboard option, the highest and lowest objects are aligned with the top and bottom of the artboard and objects are distributed in-between.

16.11

Horizontal Distribute Left

Use this command to distribute the objects based on their left sides. This places an even amount of space between the left-most points of the selected objects. When using the Align to Artboard option from the Actions palette menu, the left- and right-most objects are aligned with the left and right sides of the artboard and objects are distributed in-between.

16.12

Horizontal Distribute Center

Use this command to distribute the objects based on their centers. This places an even amount of space between the center points of the selected objects. Objects move to the left or right when using this option. When using the Align to Artboard option from the Actions palette menu, the left- and right-most objects are aligned with the left and right sides of the artboard and objects are distributed in-between.

16.13

Horizontal Distribute Right

Use this command to distribute the objects based on their right edges. This places an even amount of space between the right-most points of the selected objects. When using the Align to Artboard option from the Actions palette menu, the left- and right-most objects are aligned with the left and right sides of the artboard and objects are distributed in-between.

16.14
Distribute Spacing Vertical

Use this command to place an even amount of space between selected objects. This is different than the other distribute commands in that the space is placed between the objects themselves, rather than points on an object. So, regardless of the object's size, the same distance will exist between it and the other distributed objects.

This command moves objects up or down so that the same amount of space exists between the top of one object and the bottom of the next. When using the Align to Artboard option, the top and bottom-most objects are aligned with the top and bottom of the artboard and objects are distributed in between.

The amount of distance between the objects is set using the Distribute Spacing distance field *(For more information, see 16.16, Distribute Spacing Distance.)*

16.15
Distribute Spacing Horizontal

This command functions the same as Distribute Spacing Vertical, except that objects are repositioned left to right instead of up and down.

16.16
Distribute Spacing Distance

This option sets the amount of distance placed between objects when using the distribute functions.

By default, this field is set to Auto. This divides the available distance evenly. The objects furthest away from each other don't change positions. If you enter a custom value into the field, you must select a Key Object before executing the distribution. Select a Key Object by clicking on it with a selection tool. The Key Object is the one that will not move. All the other items will be repositioned with the specified distance.

16.17

The Align Palette Menu

The following commands enable you to modify the behavior of the Align palette.

16.18

Show Options

Use this command to expand the palette to show the Distribute Spacing Horizontal, Distribute Spacing Vertical, and Distribute Spacing Distance fields. When these options are visible, this command hides them.

16.19

Use Preview Bounds

This option aligns objects based on their printing area, rather than their actual vector shapes. Due to strokes, styles, and effects, the printing area of objects may extend outside of the vector shape that defines them. This option aligns things based on their print dimensions, rather than their vector shapes.

Issues to Consider

This option is activating a preference that affects other tools. Choosing this activates the Use Preview Bounds preference. This will affect Illustrator's overall behavior, not just the Align palette. You can deactivate the preference here or in preferences. *(For more information, see 8.12, Edit: Preferences: General.)*

16.20

Align to Artboard

Use this command to align and distribute objects about the artboard rather than between each other. The affect this option has on commands is noted in the descriptions. *(For more information, see 7.43, File: Document Setup: Artboard)*

16.21

Cancel Key Object

Use this command to discard the currently selected key object when using the Distribute Spacing Distance option. This is usually used when you change your mind about the key object or make a mistake in choosing it *(For more information, see 16.16, Distribute Spacing Distance.)*

The Appearance Palette

Appearance Palette Overview

The Appearance palette manages the attributes of objects, layers, and groups. It shows you why an object looks the way that it does and it helps you to style objects.

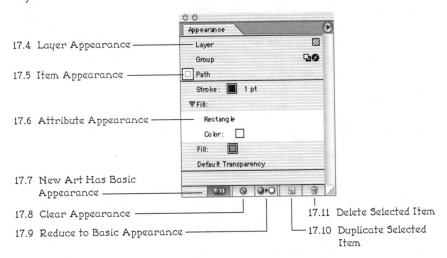

17.4 Layer Appearance

17.5 Item Appearance

17.6 Attribute Appearance

17.7 New Art Has Basic Appearance

17.8 Clear Appearance

17.9 Reduce to Basic Appearance

17.11 Delete Selected Item

17.10 Duplicate Selected Item

While part of the function of Appearance is informational, there are some things you can do with Appearance that you can't do with any other tool or palette:

- **Appearance enables you to create objects with more than one Fill & Stroke.** Using this palette, you can assign additional fills and strokes to objects. This is the only place in the application you can do that. Multiple fills and stokes become useful when creating visual effects.

- **Appearance enables you to put fills in front of strokes.** Strokes are always half inside and half outside a path. They are also in front of the fill of an object. With Appearance, you can reorder them so that the fill is in front. This leaves the stroke only visible on the outside of the object. This is often used in trapping.

- **Appearance enables you to apply effects and transparency to attributes.** Using Appearance, you can set effects and transparency for attributes rather than objects. For example, you can make the fill of an object transparent, but leave the stroke opaque. This ability is the key to a lot of styling techniques.

- **Appearance enables you to clear all attributes of a path at once.** With a single click, you can remove the fill, stroke, effects, and transparency of an object.

17.2

Hierarchical Appearance

Objects can take their attributes from a number of places. Most users know that objects are styled by applying a fill, stroke, and transparency to an object. You can also apply attributes to a Group or to a Layer. They can be given Effects, Transparency, and Styles. Objects that belong to groups or layers that are styled share the attributes of the Layer or Group they belong to. For example, an object on a Layer with 50% opacity appears to have a 50% opacity as well. Objects on layers that are styled still have their own independent attributes. In the previous example of the object on the transparent layer, the object may have a transparency of 100%. This is visually counter-intuitive since the object is 50% transparent. Further, the object may also be set to 50% opacity. This has a cumulative effect. A 50% opaque object on a 50% opaque layer appears to be 25% opaque.

Fills and strokes can also have their own effects and transparency, independent of the object, group or layer that they are in. This, too, has a cumulative effect. A 50% opaque object may have a fill with a 50% opacity, leaving a 25% opaque fill. If this object were also on a 50% opaque layer, the fill would appear 12.5% opaque.

If more than one effect is applied, the order of the effects also plays a role in appearance. Each effect applied changes the things that came before it. For example, if you duplicate an object and then Twist it, the Twist will affect the object and its duplicate. If you reverse the order, you'll be duplicating a twisted object. The first one will twist both objects together; the second will be two independently twisted objects.

17.3

Using the Appearance Palette

The current selection appears in bold in the top section of the Appearance palette, listed by object type. A thumbnail of the object appears next to it. If nothing is selected, that will be indicated as well.

The items that affect a selection are listed from the top down in the Appearance palette. Layers and Groups that affect the item are listed first, then the item. A horizontal line then separates the item from its attributes. In the case of paths, this is the object's stroke, fill, and transparency. In the case of Groups or Layers, this will be any effects or transparency applied.

17.4

Layer Appearance

The presence of items above the current selection means that Layers or Groups affect the object's appearance. The way Layers and Groups affect an item is indicated with an icon. A checkerboard indicates transparency; an "f" in a circle indicates an effect. The default fill and stroke icon indicates that a fill or stroke attribute is applied. Click on a Layer or Group name in the Appearance palette to target that item. All the objects governed by that item are selected and the Appearance palette switches to show the item's attributes.

17.5

Item Appearance

The current selection is indicated in bold with a thumbnail of the item next to it. This is often an object, but it could also be a Layer or Group. If objects of different kinds are selected, the field will read "Mixed Objects." If multiple objects of the same kind are selected, the item will display the name of the kind.

Issues to Consider

Drag and drop the thumbnail to style objects in the document. Click-drag the item's thumbnail from the Appearance palette onto objects in the document to apply the Appearance to the object.

17.6

Attribute Appearance

The attributes of the selection are listed in this section. If the item is a layer or group, any effects or transparency applied to the layer will be listed as will the word "Contents," indicating the items in the layer or group. Double-click effects listed to edit them.

If the selection is an object, fills, strokes, effects and transparency will be listed. If the object is affected by a Style, the name of the style will be listed. Double-click effects to modify them. A swatch indicates the color of each fill and stroke. Stroke weight and dashed status are listed as well. The items listed here are shown from the top down. Reposition items by dragging them up and down in the palette. A guide indicates where the item will reside when the mouse is released. If more than one fill or stroke is used in the object, the last item selected will be indicated with a small box around the item's swatch. This is said to be the cardinal fill or stroke.

If fills or strokes are styled independently, a turndown triangle will reveal the attributes it has. Double click effects anywhere in this palette to edit the values used. Effects can be dragged between attributes. If the effect is dragged onto an attribute, double triangles will highlight the attribute. If the effect is dropped loose in the Attribute section, it will become an object attribute and affect the complete item.

17.7

New Art Has Basic Appearance

Use this command to toggle how the next object created will be treated. Set to New Art Maintains Appearance to retain the exact settings currently in the appearance palette. Set to New Art Has Basic Appearance to discard all effects, including those attached to attributes. Additional fills and strokes are also removed and the object's opacity is set to 100%. This is the "basic appearance": an appearance with only one fill or stroke, and no effects, or transparency.

Mistakes to Avoid

Setting the incorrect cardinal attribute. Be sure you click on the attribute you want to keep. Only the cardinal fill and stroke are retained when art is reduced to basic appearance. Be sure the attribute you wish to keep is cardinal by clicking directly on it in the palette.

Forgetting about this option. Many users new to effects experiment with them and then become frustrated that they every object they create has the last effect they chose.

17.8

Clear Appearance

Click this button to remove all attributes from the selection. The object is left with a single fill and stroke both set to none.

17.9

Reduce to Basic Appearance

Click this button to discard all effects, including those attached to attributes. Additional fills and strokes are also removed. The object's opacity is set to 100% and blend mode to Normal.

Issues to Consider

Opacity Masks are not released. Objects that are part of opacity masks are not released by this command *(For more information, see 36.1, Transparency Palette.)*

Reducing a group to basic appearance only removes group attributes. Group members are not reduced to basic appearance by this command automatically. Any effects that are attached to the objects will remain.

Basic appearances cannot be expanded. Once reduced to a basic appearance, Object: **Expand Appearance** cannot be used on items.

17.10

Duplicate Selected Item

This button duplicates the currently selected fill, stroke, or effect. Any Effect or transparency attached to the item is duplicated as well. The duplicate item is placed atop the original item in the Appearance palette. This is a common way to create multiple fills and strokes for objects.

17.11

Delete Selected Item

This button clears the current fill, stroke, effect, or transparency setting. Objects must have at least one fill and stroke. If you delete the last fill or stroke, it isn't removed, but its value is set to none. Likewise, deleting the object's transparency setting sets it to the default transparency. You may also drag items directly onto this icon to delete them.

17.12

Appearance Palette Menu

Use the options found in Appearance palette menu to modify the appearance of objects and to edit Styles.

17.13

Add New Fill

Use this command when you want to create a new basic fill. The fill will be the same color as the cardinal fill, but will not have any custom effects or transparency settings. The position of the new fill depends on what is selected in the Appearance palette. If an attribute is selected, the new item will be atop it. If nothing is selected, it will be added atop the highest fill. If the name of the object is selected, the Fill will be at the top of the Appearance palette.

17.14

Add New Stroke

Use this command when you want to create a new basic stroke. The stroke will be the same color as the cardinal stroke, but will not have any custom effects or transparency settings. The position of the new stroke is determined the same as a new Fill. *(For more information, see 17.13, Add New Fill.)*

17.15

Duplicate Item

This command is the same as the button of the same name. *(For more information, see 17.10, Duplicate Item.)*

17.16

Remove Item

This command is the same as the button of the same name. *(For more information, see 17.11, Remove Item.)*

17.17

Clear Appearance

This command is the same as the button of the same name. *(For more information, see 17.8, Clear Appearance.)*

17.18

Reduce to Basic Appearance

This command is the same as the button of the same name. *(For more information, see 17.9, Reduce to Basic Appearance.)*

17.19

New Art Has Basic Appearance

This command is the same as the button of the same name. *(For more information, see 17.7, New Art has Basic Appearance.)*

17.20

Hide Thumbnail

Use this command to toggle the visibility of the object thumbnail. Hidden, you cannot drag the thumbnail onto objects to style them.

17.21

Redefine Style

In cases where the current appearance started as a Style but has since been modified, this command saves the changes to the original Style. This is one way to edit a Style. For example, you may start with the default Blue Goo Style and decide to change the drop shadow settings. Before you begin editing, the Style's name appears at the top of the Appearance palette. Once you alter the drop shadow amount the Style name is removed from the palette. This command changes the definition of Blue Goo to whatever you set.

When a Style is redefined, objects that use the Style are updated automatically. This includes Symbols and Envelopes that contain styled objects. Symbol sets and instances styled using the Style Stainer are not updated automatically. To update them, you would need to remove the Style and reapply the new one.

The Attributes Palette

Attributes Overview

The Attributes palette has become a grab bag of unrelated options relating to the handling of objects. It is principally used to set items to overprint. It also has options that control how compound paths behave, whether the centers of objects are visible, HTML links in objects, and an attribute useful in writing actions.

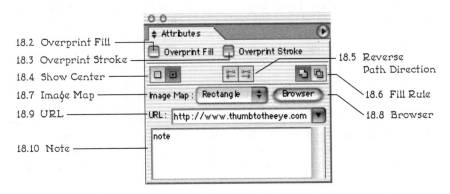

18.2 Overprint Fill

18.3 Overprint Stroke

18.4 Show Center

18.7 Image Map

18.9 URL

18.10 Note

18.5 Reverse Path Direction

18.6 Fill Rule

18.8 Browser

18.2

Overprint Fill

Click this button to set the fill of the current selection to overprint. You should not set anything to overprint unless you know what you are doing as it will affect how the object is handled when colors are separated for high-end printing.

When an object overprints, its colors are added to the colors of any object below. You won't see this when you print to your local deskjet, it only happens when color is separated.

Overprinting is at the heart of a long-standing conventional prepress technique called trapping. Trapping is used to compensate for misregistration on press. The edge of one color is set to slightly overlap the edge of an adjacent color. The thin overlap prevents tiny gaps from appearing between areas of color.

Trapping is an important consideration any time a job is going to be printed. Ask yourself the following questions:

- **Does the job require trapping?** Not every job requires trapping. Single color jobs are never trapped. Many process color jobs also do not require trapping. This is because a commonality of colors used in process printing may create a "bridge" between areas of different colors. If the two abutting colors share at least 20% of one color component, trapping is probably not necessary. The common colors will prevent gaps from showing if misregistration occurs.

  Spot color jobs usually require trapping. Jobs with two or more spot colors or process color jobs with additional spot plates usually require trapping. If different spot colors touch each other, trapping will need to be considered.

- **Who should supply those traps?** If you decide that a job should be trapped, you should next consider who should prepare the traps. Many printing presses and service bureaus have equipment that traps jobs automatically as the file is printed. Other companies prepare the traps manually, often for a fee. Lastly, the designer of the art could prepare the traps as the image is created. This happens less and less frequently as designers push the responsibility for this downstream. Often this is best. If you have a relationship with a printer, let them supply the traps. The money spent will usually work itself out in time and headache saved.

- **How should the traps be built?** If you decide that a job should be trapped and take on the responsibility of trapping files yourself, you will need to know which colors to trap with and how wide to make the traps. You should communicate with your press; they can often provide beneficial suggestions if you are flexible and communicate with them early in the process.

Issues to Consider

Overprinting has no effect on composite printing. Overprinting only impacts the process of making separations.

White should never be set to overprint. Overprinting white is invisible.

Overprinting can be previewed onscreen. *(For more information, see 14.3, View: Overprint Preview.)*

Overprinting can be flattened. Overprinting objects can be broken into component parts by choosing Object: **Flatten Transparency.** This is typically not part of a trapping workflow, but can be useful in some process color techniques.

Related Topics

C.9   *Basic Trapping*
C.10 *Trapping Gradients*
C.11 *Using the Trap Pathfinder*
12.13 *Filter: Colors: **Overprint Black***

18.3

Overprint Stroke

Use this command to set the stroke of the current selection to overprint. Depending on the strategy you use, either the fill or the stroke may be used to supply a trap. *(For more information, see 18.2 ,Overprint Fill.)*

18.4

Show Center

Use this command to display a selected object's center point. The center point is an anchor point that indicates the center of an object's bounding area. In Outline mode, it appears as an "x." By default, only ellipses, rectangles, and rounded rectangles have center points. This command adds center points to other objects.

Issues to Consider

Center points are based on the center of the bounding box. This is not always the same as the visual center of an object. The bounding box is the area swept out by the highest, lowest, and farthest right and left points in an object. The center of this area may not be the same as what you think the center of an object is.

Select objects by their center points. Click the center point of an object to select it. This is a handy way to select an entire object in Outline mode using the Direct Selection tool.

18.5

Reverse Path Direction

Use these buttons to alter the negative (empty) space in a compound path when using the Non-Zero Winding Fill Rule. Compound paths created from more the two objects sometimes fail to produce the correct negative spaces. When this happens, a common area between the paths will not become transparent. Reversing the direction of one of the components of the compound paths may remedy this. *(For more information, see 9.72, Object: **Compound Path** and 18.6, Fill Rule.)*

To use this option, select one of the compound path's component shapes using the Direct Selection tool. Experiment with the two buttons until the negative space is correct. It may take several passes selecting and reversing different objects in the compound path to get the correct combination. Alternatively, consider simply switching to the even-odd rule.

18.6

Fill Rule

Use this command to choose the model used to determine negative space in a selected compound path. There are two options available; the non-zero winding rule and the even-odd rule. The even-odd rule fills every other overlapping space with transparency. No further adjustments are available. The non-zero rule uses the directions paths flow in to determine the transparent areas. The resulting spaces may be modified using the Reverse Path commands. The rules may be changed at any time.

Issues to Consider

Illustrator uses a different default than Photoshop & Freehand. Illustrator defaults to the flexible non-zero rule while the others use the more predictable even-odd rule . You may notice this difference as you exchange compound shapes with Photoshop.

Related Topics

*9.72 Object: **Compound Path***

18.7

Image Map

Use this command to include HTML links based on the selected object. An image map uses a shape as a button to link to a specific web address. The web address you specify using these commands will be written into the HTML generated when you use the Save for Web command.

To use a selected object as an image map, choose either rectangle or polygon from the menu. A polygon will most accurately represent the shape of your path. The rectangle option bases the link on the selection's bounding box. Polygons require slightly larger HTML code to describe than rectangles.

Image maps are different from links in slices in several ways. First, image maps may be exported as a single object, rather than a different object for each link. Secondly, image maps may be polygonal, while slices must be square. If you need to link from a non-square area, consider image maps.

Issues to Consider

Stacking order counts. If two objects with image maps overlap, the image map of the bottom object will be redrawn based on the exposed areas.

This option should not be used in conjunction with slice links. Don't use image maps and slices on the same object. Choose one or the other. Some browsers will fail to recognize the links if you have both. You can certainly include image maps in slices, just don't add slice links as well.

18.8

Browser

Click this button to load the Web address set using the URL command into your system's default browser. This is a quick way to ensure that the link you are attaching is accurate and current. *(For more information, see 18.9, URL.)*

18.9

URL

Use this field to enter the location linked to by an image map. The link may be absolute or relative. An absolute link spells out the exact Internet address to be used, a relative link only includes the file's position relative to the HTML file that provides the link. Typically, relative links are used when you are linking to a web site that you control, absolute links are used when you are linking to someone else's site.

After a link is entered once, Illustrator stores it for use again. By default, the last 30 URLs entered are stored. Recently used addresses are available from the menu on the right of the field.

18.10

Note

Use this field to attach a text note to an object. The field is only visible if Show Note is chosen from the Attributes palette menu. You can enter up to 240 characters. The note can be informational, such as comments to other viewers of the document. It is also used to identify objects so that they can be found quickly in the PostScript text. Prepress professionals trying to find problems in print jobs are usually the ones doing this. Most often, though, the note is used to identify the object for selection by an action.

Illustrator actions can select objects based on the contents of this field. For example, an action might select all objects with notes that said "trash" and delete them. This is often part of a complex action series. It is usually done when steps in the action result in different or complex selections and you need to return to the initial object. For example, a client needed to convert all colors in a legacy color palette to a new color palette. The action written created an object and styled it with the fill and stroke of the color to be removed. Then the action gave the object the note "base." It then selected all the objects with that same fill attribute and converted them all to the new color. Then it deselected, selected the base object and repeated the steps for the stroke. Afterward it deleted the base object. The note made it possible to return to the same object again and again.

18.11

Attributes Palette Menu

Use the options in this menu to change the display of the Attributes palette and to set the number of URLs saved.

18.12

Show Overprint Only

This option collapses the palette so that only the Overprint Fill and Overprint Stroke options are visible. The reverse of this command, Show All, reveals the entire palette.

18.13

Hide Note

This option collapses the palette so that the note field is not visible. Since the Note field takes up a fair amount of monitor space, this is usually a good option to turn on, unless you are currently using that feature.

18.14

Palette Options

This command opens the Palette Options dialog box. The only field in this box enables you to set the number of entries stored in the URL field.

The Brushes Palette

19.1
Brushes Overview

Brushes are a special kind of effect that is only applied to strokes. Brush strokes use saved shapes to alter a path's appearance. Like effects, brushes in outline mode do not display the same shapes that appear in preview mode. As with other effects, brushed objects display a gradient circle next to their names in the Layers palette. Brushes can be changed, modified or discarded at any time.

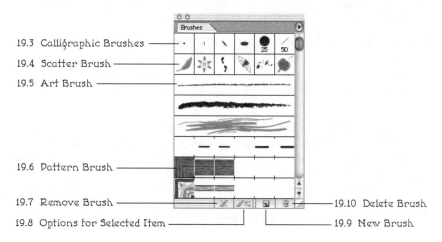

19.3 Calligraphic Brushes

19.4 Scatter Brush

19.5 Art Brush

19.6 Pattern Brush

19.7 Remove Brush

19.8 Options for Selected Item

19.10 Delete Brush

19.9 New Brush

Unlike the other effects, you cannot modify brushes in the Appearance palette. You must apply and modify their impact with the Brushes palette. Apply brushes to any path, but not to meshes, envelopes, symbols, or rasters.

Brushes are a document resource. They are saved in a document. Custom brushes made in one document will not be available in another by default. You should consider brushes in the palette to be objects that are in the document but do not print. Since they take up space in the file, consider removing unused brushes at the end of your working session. Many users do this by building an action to delete unused brushes or by altering Illustrator's default settings.

Issues to Consider

Brushes update their appearance as paths change. As you modify the position and shape of a path, the brush updates itself to match. Many brushes are also affected by stroke color. All brushes are affected by stroke weight. Changing the stroke weight scales the brush effect up or down.

Brushes expand to paths. To replace a brush effect with vector shapes, choose Object: **Expand Appearance**. The component vector shapes replace the brush effect. *(For more information, see 9.28, Object: Expand.)*

Brushes can use pressure sensitive tablets. The appearance of brushes can be altered intuitively using a pressure-sensitive tablet, such as a Wacom. Pressure tablets use a stylus rather than a mouse to control the cursor's movements. The harder the stylus is pressed against the tablet, the more intensely the effect is applied. For example, the thickness of a brush stroke could vary the harder you push. In this respect, the experience is more like traditional drawing techniques.

Brushes are commonly applied with the Paintbrush tool. Although brushes can be on any stroke, they are usually applied with the Paintbrush tool. The paintbrush is useful, because it recognizes pressure sensitive tablets, creates freeform open paths and has a built-in path editing function. *(For more information, see 2.26 Paintbrush Tool.)*

Commands applied to brushed objects reference the path. Commands use the core path, not the brush stroke shape. For example, if you apply Object: Path: **Offset Path** to a brushed object, the command does not consider what the brush stroke looks like. It builds a new shape based on the path without the brush.

To consider the brush shape, the path must be expanded or the command applied as an effect. Expanding a path creates vector shapes from the brush strokes. Illustrator can correctly apply the commands to these new objects. Alternatively, the command may be applied as an effect. In the example above, offset path could be applied as an effect directly to the stroke in the Appearance palette. While this option is more flexible, it is not always possible, since not everything can be done with effects.

Joined paths take the top object's appearance. If you are joining two paths with brushes, the top object's appearance will be used on the new path. Since brush strokes are part of an object's appearance, they may be changed when you join two paths. Make sure the objects with the brush shape you wish to retain is atop the other path. This is true for paths without brushes as well.

Related Topics

2.26   *Paintbrush tool*
42.2   *Brush Libraries*

19.2

Brushes

This pane displays the document's brushes. They can be displayed in two modes: thumbnail view and list view. Thumbnail view lists a small picture of the shapes that define the brush. List view shows the brush's name and an icon to indicate the type of brush that it is. There are four types of brushes. *(For more information, see 19.3, Calligraphic Brushes, 19.4 Scatter Brushes, 19.5 Art Brushes, and 19.6 Pattern Brushes.)*

To apply a brush to a selected object, click the brush in this pane. A square highlights the brush to indicate the one in use. To change the definition of a brush, double click it. The options are the same as when creating a brush from scratch. Multiple brushes can be selected for duplicating or deleting. Shift-click to select contiguous brushes, (Command) [Ctrl] click to select noncontiguous brushes in the palette.

Replace a brush by (Option) [Alt] dragging a brush on top of it in the palette. The brush will be surrounded by a black box to indicate the brush is to be replaced. Reposition a brush in the palette by dragging it into a new position. A black bar indicates the new position it will occupy in the palette.

19.3

Calligraphic Brushes

Calligraphic brushes use a predefined shape, rather than an object. The intention of this effect is to replicate traditional pen and ink marks. This is done by creating a shape that emulates the nib of a traditional pen-and-ink brush. The direction and angle of the paths they are applied to causes the shape of brush-stroke to change. These are the only kind of brush that can be created without first creating objects or patterns,

Calligraphic Brush Options Dialog Box

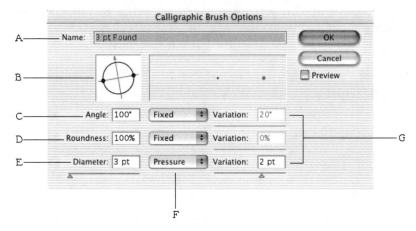

A. Name

Use this field to establish the name of the brush. The name is displayed when the palette is in list view and as a tool tip when in thumbnail view. Many users establish naming conventions for calligraphic brushes. For example "3pt 45° 50% pressure" is much more recognizable in two weeks than the default "Calligraphic Brush 1."

B. Brush Shape Editor

Graphically set the angle and roundness of the brush using this interface. Click to set the angle position, or click-drag the arrowhead to set visually. Click-drag the black balls on the sides to set the roundness.

C. Angle (-180° to 180°)

This field sets the direction, or angle of the brush shape. The brush follows the path it is applied to set at the angle shown here. Picture a horizontal line. A 45° brush will be tilted at that angle at both ends of the line. As the path turns, the brush shape changes with it.

D. Roundness (0 to 100%)

Roundness changes the basic shape of the brush and determines how much the diameter of the brush will change at different angles. The lower the number here, the more dramatic differences will be when the brush is used.

E. Diameter (0 to 1296 pts)

This sets the maximum size of the brush when applied to a 1 pt stroke. The actual size of the brushstroke will be determined by the Angle and Roundness of the brush, and the direction of the path it is applied to.

F. Model

Use these models to determine how the various brush attributes are set.

Fixed

This model uses the value set in the field.

Random

This model uses a random number. The intention is to create a more organic, less computer-generated feel to the art by varying the brush shapes. The range of the randomness is set using the Variance field. Variance may be set in single degree and percent increments for roundness and angle, and in tenth-of-a-point increments for diameter. Random settings are applied to each object that uses the brush, not within the same object.

Pressure

Use this model to set the value based on a pressure sensitive tablet input. As with the random model, a variance amount is given, but the amount of change is based on input from the pressure tablet's stylus. Pushing harder increases the value, pressing lightly decreases the amount. This option is only available on systems with such tablets installed.

G. **Variation**

This field sets the amount of change that can be applied when using the Random model. The variation can be as great as the value set for the attribute. As variation is set for brushes, the long pane next to the Brush Shape Editor changes to display the possible brush shapes. The highest and lowest options for the brush are in bracket; the defined value in is in the center in solid black.

19.4

Scatter Brush Options

Scatter brushes place a set of shapes, or a design around a path. The designs are often placed about the path at random sizes, angles, and distances. This creates an impromptu "scattered" look that gives the brush its name.

Scatter Brush Options Dialog Box

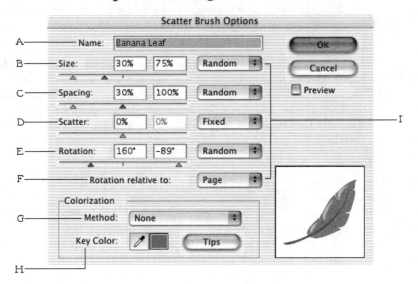

A. **Name**
   Use this field to establish the name of the brush. The name is displayed when the palette is in list view and as a tool tip when in thumbnail view.

B. **Size**
   This field sets the sizing of the design along the path relative to the size it was created. At 100%, it's the same size on the path as the original design was. Consider this as you create objects for scatter brushes. If you are creating full-page art that will be used at a small size, you have less flexibility. Further, as designs are scaled down, stroke weights may also be scaled to unprintably small sizes. Where possible, try to create objects used in scatter brush designs at the size they will be used.

   Another option for scaling is to change the stroke width of the brushed object. Sizing is based on a 1-point stroke. Setting the weight to 2 points is the same as setting the size to 200%. Setting it to .5 points is the same as 50% scaling, and so on.

C. **Spacing**
   This field sets how close to each other the designs are on the path.

Theoretically, at 100%, the bounding box of each design would touch the next. On horizontal and vertical lines they do. On curved lines, the spacing must be adjusted to accommodate the curve and is not quite perfect.

D. Scatter

This field places the designs on either side of the path, rather than directly along it. Positive numbers move the designs up off the path; negative numbers move them down below. The top and bottom of a path are relative to its direction. If you drag with the Brush tool left to right, the path flows clockwise and its top is the same as the top of the artboard. If you drag right to left the path flows counterclockwise and its top is the bottom of the artboard.

E. Rotation

Use this field turns the design the set amount. Rotation takes place about the design's center. The manner that the rotation is carried out is set in the Rotation Relative to field.

F. Rotation Relative to

This field sets the base used when applying the rotation to designs.

Page

This option sets the degrees of rotation relative to the bottom of the artboard. You can think of this as absolute rotation. No matter which way the path turns, the rotation remains the same.

Path

This option places the 0° position in the rotation along the base of the path the design is on. As the path turns, so does the rotation of the design. This is relative rotation; as the path turns the design rotates as well.

G. Colorization

Use this menu to set how stroke color affects the designs.

None

This option disregards the stroke color and retains the colors built into the design.

Tints

This option replaces all the colors in the design with tints of the stroke color. Dark colors in the design are set to the stroke color, lighter colors are set to proportionally lighter versions of the stroke color. The affect is similar to a monotone. Commonly, spot colors are applied to the stroke when using this model.

Tints and Shades

This option retains the black and white colors in an image and distributes the stroke color in-between, based on the tone in the design. Color is typically richer than when using the tints option. Due to the presence of black, you may not be able to print on a single spot plate when using this model.

Hue Shift

This option sets color in the design based upon the key color. Objects of the key color in the design are painted with the stroke color. Other colors are set to similar colors, based upon their similarity to the key color. This option produces the widest array of colors.

H. Key Color

This option sets the part of the design that will be painted with the stroke color when using the Hue Shift option. To set the key color, click the eyedropper on the design thumbnail to the right of key color. The key color is displayed in the swatch next to the eyedropper.

I. Model

These options determine how the size, spacing, scatter, and rotation attributes are applied.

Fixed

This model uses the value set in the field.

Random

This model uses a random number. This option creates a second slider stop and field. Use the two fields to set the upper and lower limits for the attribute. This is often used to create a more organic feel to the art.

Pressure

Use this model to set the value based on a pressure sensitive tablet input. This option is only available on systems with such tablets installed.

19.5

Art Brush Options

The Art Brush drapes a design along a path. The design is distorted and twisted to match the shape of the path.

Art Brush Options Dialog Box

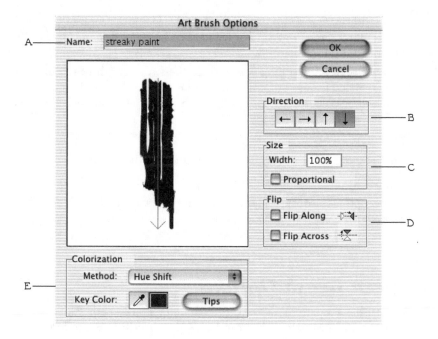

A. **Name**

Use this field to establish the name of the brush. The name is displayed when the palette is in list view and as a tool tip when in thumbnail view

B. **Direction**

These options set the side of the design that is at the end of the stroke. Dragging with the Paintbrush tool, the position your cursor ends in is the end of the path. These options set the part of the design that ends there, setting the overall orientation of the design, Designs that are oriented incorrectly may look odd or distended. Typically, your design should be set in the direction its shape suggests. If your design is tall and thin, it should run top to bottom. If it is wide it might run left to right.

Stroke from right to left

This option set the left side of the design at the end of the path.

Stroke from left to right
> This option set the right side of the design at the end of the path.

Stroke from bottom to top
> This option set the top of the design at the end of the path.

Stroke from top to bottom
> This option set the bottom of the design at the end of the path.

C. Size

This field sets the width of the brushstroke as a proportion of the original design. Check the Proportional field to keep the design closer to the original design's proportions.

Another option for scaling is to change the stroke width of the brushed object. Sizing is based on a 1-point stroke. Setting the weight to 2 points is the same as setting the size to 200%. Setting it to .5 points is the same as 50% scaling, and so on.

D. Flip

These fields reflect the design along and across the path.

E. Colorization

These options are the same as those for the Scatter Brush. *(For more information, see 19.4, Scatter Brush Options.)*

19.6

Pattern Brush Options

Pattern brushes set pattern tiles next to each other along a path. Patterns must be saved as swatches before they can be used in brushes. Six different patterns can be attached to a single brush. Each pattern is used for different parts of a path. This provides a high degree of control, but requires precise work when constructing pattern tiles. Pattern brushes are easy to identify because of their regimented look. For this reason, and because they have special options for rectangles and corners, they are commonly used to provide decorative borders. *(For more information, see 8.7, Edit: **Define Pattern**.)*

Pattern Brush Options Dialog Box

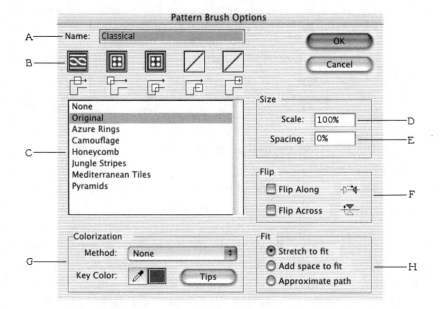

A. Name

Use this field to establish the name of the brush. The name is displayed when the palette is in list view and as a tool tip when in thumbnail view.

B. Tiles

These 5 tiles set the patterns used for different parts of a path. Not every tile needs to be used, but the side tile must be. Brushes built for curves don't need to include inner and outer corner swatches. Brushes intended for closed paths don't need start and end tiles.

To attach a pattern to a tile, click the tile to be set. The tile is highlighted with a thin black box. Next, click on a pattern from the list available.

Side Tile

This tile is required. It is used for all straight sections of the path and corners below 40°.

Outer Corner Tile

This tile is used for outer corners. Inner and outer corners are sometimes hard to anticipate. Picture a path headed straight up. If the path turns to the right more than 40°, the turn is an outer corner. If it turns to the left more than 40°, the turn is an inner corner. Whichever way the path is headed, this is true from the perspective of the end of the path. Take the example of a square. Starting at the lower-left corner of the square, the path moves straight up and then turns 90° to the right. This is an outer corner because it turns to the right more than 40°. The path then continues across the top of the square and turns right again 90° to make the right side of the square. This is also an outer corner because of the direction of the turn relative to the path. If the path turned to the left instead of the right, as if to form an "L" shape, the turn would make an inner corner. As it is, a square has no inner corners, because all its turns are to the right.

Inner Corner Tile

This tile is used for outer corners. (See the previous entry, "Outer Corner Tile," for a description of corner types.)

Start Tile

This tile marks the beginning of the path.

End Tile

This tile marks the end of the path.

C. **Patterns**

All the patterns saved in the current document are listed here. Click a pattern to attach it to the currently selected tile. *(For more information, see 8.7, Edit: Define Pattern.)*

D. **Scale** (1% to 10,0000%)

Use this field to scale the pattern up and down. Alternatively, you can adjust the stroke width to increase the size.

E. **Spacing** (0% to 10,000%)

Use this field to change the distance between the pattern tiles. By default, the bounding box of each pattern in the brush is placed next to each other, creating a continuous effect. Increasing the spacing adds a percentage of the bounding box space between each pattern tile. This is sometimes used to create dashed line patterns.

F. **Flip**

These fields reflect the design along and across the path.

G. **Colorization**

These options are the same as those for the Scatter Brush. *(For more information see 19.4, Scatter Brush Options.)*

H. **Fit**

Use this field to adjust how tiles fit together.

Stretch to fit

This option scales the pattern tiles the amount needed to fit into the space provided. This is commonly used with continuous patterns.

Add Space to fit
> This option leaves pattern tiles as they are and puts empty space between them where they don't fit together. This option is often used for noncontinuous patterns like dashed lines.

Approximate path
> This option is only available for rectangles. It maintains the shape of the pattern tiles by resizing the shape the brush is applied to. When using this option, the tiles will be perfect, but the path may not be.

19.7

Remove Brush Stroke

Click this button to remove the brush effect from a selected path. The path retains its stroke weight, and receives the color and stroke options that it had before the brush was applied.

19.8

Options of Selected Object

Click this button to adjust the settings used to define a brush for an individual object. Most of the settings used to create a brush may be adjusted on an object-by-object basis. The brush itself retains its settings, but the instances of that brush's use may vary wildly. This enables you to tweak the settings to suit a specific need.

All of the brush options are available to be edited except the following:

- Brush instances cannot be renamed

- The direction of an art brush cannot be changed.

- Pattern tiles cannot be substituted.

Issues to Consider

Altering brush definitions can create new brushes. If you adjust the options of a brush that is in use by double-clicking on it in the Brushes palette, you will be given the option to apply the changes to the existing brushes or leave the current brushes alone. If you leave the strokes alone, those objects may become altered instances of the brush. A new brush will be created if you change the direction of an art brush.

19.9

New Brush

Click this button to create a new brush. Only calligraphic brushes can be made without being based upon selected objects or existing patterns. Pattern brushes require only that you have patterns saved in the Swatches palette. This is usually the case unless you have removed the default swatches.

Art and Scatter Brushes require that you make a selection before choosing New Brush. The selection can't be image objects, paths containing effects such as soft drop shadows that contain raster images, or a gradient mesh. Objects that contain effects and symbols are acceptable, as long as the objects can be expanded without creating images.

Issues to Consider

Expanding brushes that were made from live objects does not produce live objects. For example, if you create a brush from a path that has been given an envelope distort, expanding the brush does not produce an envelope distort. *(For more information, see 9.28, Object: Expand.)* Instead the object is expanded the moment you create the brush. This is also true for symbols. A symbol instance can be turned into a brush, but it maintains no connection to the symbol.

Drag a brush onto this icon to duplicate it. To make a copy of an existing brush, drag it onto the New Brush button. The duplicate will have the same options and include the word "copy" in its name. This is often done to create a series of similar brushes.

19.10

Delete Brush

Click this to delete the selected brushes in the palette. You can't delete brushes that are used in styles. The default style "Silver Ribbon" uses the default brush "50 pt Flat," preventing you from deleting all of the default brushes without first at least deleting the Silver Ribbon style. If you delete a brush that has been used on objects, you will be prompted to either expand the brush or remove the brush stroke.

Issues to Consider

It's easy to recall the default brushes. Feel free to delete brushes. The defaults can be recalled as a library. *(For more information, see 42.2, Brush Libraries.)*

19.11

Brush Palette Menu

The options in the Brush palette menu replicate buttons in the palette and provide some brush management commands.

19.12

New Brush

This command functions the same as the button of the same name. *(For more information, see 19.9, New Brush.)*

19.13

Duplicate Brush

This command copies selected brushes in the brushes palette. It is the same as dragging a brush onto the New Brush icon. *(For more information, see 19.9, New Brush.)*

19.14

Delete Brush

This command functions the same as the button. *(For more information, see 19.10, Delete Brush.)*

19.15

Remove Brush Stroke

This command functions the same as the button. *(For more information, see 19.7, Remove Brush Stroke.)*

19.16

Select All Unused

This command selects all of the brushes in the palette that have not been applied to objects or are in used in styles. This is usually done to round up all the unneeded brushes so that they can be deleted.

Issues to Consider

A default style uses brushes. If you are cleaning up unused elements, start with Styles. This way, you delete the reference to the brush. Then Select All Unused will select it as well so that you can easily delete it.

Hidden brushes cannot be selected. To protect a type of brush from being selected as unused and deleted, hide the brush type. Brushes that are not visible are not recognized by this command.

19.17

Show Calligraphic Brushes

This option toggles the visibility in the palette of all calligraphic brushes. If the brushes are visible, a check appears next to the menu command. This is commonly done to reduce the visual clutter that can accumulate. Hiding the brushes also protects that series from being selected when the Select All Unused command is chosen from the Brushes palette menu. For example you may want to delete all of the unused brushes except for the Calligraphic Brushes. To do this, you could uncheck Show Calligraphic Brushes, choose Select All Unused, and delete them. Afterwards, choose Show Calligraphic Brushes again to recall the series.

19.18

Show Scatter Brushes

This option toggles the visibility in the palette of all scatter brushes.

19.19

Show Art Brushes

This option toggles the visibility in the palette of all art brushes.

19.20

Show Pattern Brushes

This option toggles the visibility in the palette of all pattern brushes.

19.21

Thumbnail View

This option sets the palette to display small proxies of each brush. This enables you to get a sense of the brush before selecting it. Hold your cursor over the brush thumbnail to see the name of the brush as a pop-up tool tip.

19.22

List View

This option sets the palette to display the names of the brushes and an icon indicating their types. Calligraphic brushes display a flat brush stroke. Scatter brushes display a random series of spots. Art brushes display a paintbrush and pattern brushes show a dashed line.

19.23

Options for Selected Object

This command functions the same as the button. *(For more information, see 19.8, Options for Selected Object.)*

19.24

Brush Options

This command functions the same as double-clicking a brush. The set of brush options opens for editing.

The Color Palette

Color Palette Overview

The Color palette is almost constantly in use. It is used to display fill and stroke attributes, to define fills and strokes for objects, to convert colors, to set colors stops for gradients and color points for meshes. It changes contextually, based on the color mode of the document and the current selection.

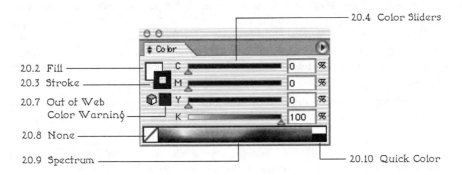

It is important to remember that while the Color palette enables you to define colors in five color models, the document may be in only one color mode. Mixing an HSB color in a CMYK document describes a CMYK color with HSB numbers.

20.2

Fill

Click the solid box to bring the Fill icon forward. Either fill or stroke may be edited at a given time. The swatch that is in front is active and available for editing. These swatches are the same as the fill and stroke swatches in the Tools palette. *(For more information, see 5.2, Fill.)*

The fill icon displays the current fill, whether it is a color, gradient or pattern. It does not display transparency. In the event that color stops in a gradient are being edited, the stroke attribute is temporarily hidden. This makes it clear that it is part of the gradient that is being edited and not the entire fill of the object.

20.3

Stroke

Click the outlined box to bring the Stroke icon forward. When forward, the stroke color may be edited.

20.4

Color Sliders

The principal feature of the Color palette is its sets of color sliders. The sliders are set to the color model selected in the Color palette menu. There is one slider for each component of the color. Each slider consists of a color ramp with a triangle below it. The ramp sets the value for the color component from left to right and the triangle indicates the current value. Each color component may be set individually using either the slider or the fields. To move a slider, click on the ramp above it or drag it into a position.

When dragging a color slider, move the other sliders proportionally by holding down the Shift key as you drag. Moving all of the sliders together creates a tint of the color.

If a spot color or global swatch is selected, the sliders are replaced with a single color ramp. The name of the swatch will be displayed below the ramp. Drag the slider to set a percentage value of the color.

Mistakes to Avoid

Picking colors for printing based on what you see on-screen. Even in color-managed environments, the monitor cannot completely forecast color correctly. Pick colors based on printed samples such as those found in PANTONE Process Guides.

20.5

Color Picker

Double-click on either fill or stroke icon to open the color picker dialog box. The color picker is a color conversion calculator you can use to specify colors. Its counterpart in Photoshop has much wider use than the Illustrator version. Often it is used to see the relationship between colors.

Color Picker Dialog Box

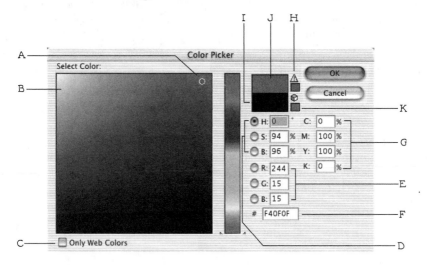

A. Color Indicator

This round marker indicates the position of the current color in the color field. Click anywhere in the Color Field to reposition the indicator. The position of the marker also changes as you enter new values into fields.

B. Color Field and Slider

The large color field and the color ramp work together to chart a large array of color. The contents of the two chart colors depends upon the radio buttons selected. The slider displays the range selected with the radio button, the Color Field displays the remaining colors. Drag the arrows bracketing the slider to adjust color. As you click in the Color Field, the color range in the slider is adjusted to reflect the change.

C. **Only Web Colors**

This option restricts the Color Field and Slider to the 216 "web safe" colors. Web safe colors are those that every monitor can predictably display. They are used to ensure that all viewers of a web page are having the same color experience.

Since the web safe palette is very small, this option posterizes the Color Field and Slider. Selected colors are pushed to their nearest web-safe equivalent. This is often a large change. Releasing this option does not reposition the color indicator to its original position.

D. **HSB Colors**

Choosing any of the HSB buttons sets the color field and slider to the HSB model.

H (Hue)

This setting is the default. It sets the slider to the visible spectrum of color. Move the arrows to set a particular color, such as red or blue. The color field then charts the possible combinations for the other two color components. Saturation is set left to right, brightness is set top to bottom.

S (Saturation)

This option sets the slider with the saturation possibilities for the selected color. The ramp shows the values between the color and gray. The Color Field charts hue left to right and brightness top to bottom.

B (Brightness)

This option sets the slider to the brightness possibilities for the color. The ramp shows the values between the color and black. The Color Field charts hue left to right, saturation top to bottom.

E. **RGB Buttons**

Choosing any of these buttons sets the slider and color field to the RGB model. The effects are:

R (Red)

This option sets the slider to the color's red range. The top of the slider shows the color with the red component boosted to the maximum (255), the bottom of the slider shows the color without any red (0). Use the slider to push red in or pull it out of the color.

In the color field, colors on the right contain maximum blue values; those on the left contain the minimum. Colors on the top contain maximum green, colors on the bottom have no green.

G (Green)

This option sets the slider to the color's green range. The top of the slider shows the color with the green component boosted to the maximum (255), the bottom of the slider shows the color without any green (0).

In the color field, colors on the right contain maximum blue values, those on the left contain the minimum. Colors on the top contain maximum red, colors on the bottom have no red.

B (Blue)

This option sets the slider to the color's blue range. The top of the slider shows the color with the blue component boosted to the maximum (255), the bottom of the slider shows the color without any blue (0).

In the color field, colors on the right contain maximum red values, those on the left contain the minimum. Colors on the top contain maximum green, colors on the bottom have no green.

F. #

This field displays the current color in hexidecimal notation. Hexidecimal code is a way of writing RGB colors that is typically used in web page development. This does not mean that all hexidecimal color numbers are web safe. To select a web safe color, be sure to select the Only Web Colors option.

G. **CMYK Values**

Use these numbers to enter specific values when you know the color numbers you need.

H. **Warning: Out of Gamut Color**

The Gamut Alter Triangle appears when you have selected a color that falls outside the currently printable range. The small swatch below the triangle indicates the nearest printable color. Click the triangle or the swatch to select that value.

I. **Current Color**

This swatch displays the currently selected color. It updates constantly as edits are made to color.

J. **Previous Color**

This swatch displays the initial color value before any changes were made. Compare this swatch with the Current Color swatch to judge the changes made to a color.

K. **Warning: Not a Web Safe Color**

The cube-shaped gamut warning appears whenever you specify a color that isn't one of the 216 browser-safe colors. Since most of the color range is not in this set of colors, this warning is often visible. Click the small swatch below the warning to select the nearest web safe color.

20.6

Out of Web Color Warning

The cube-shaped gamut warning appears whenever you specify a color that isn't one of the 216 browser-safe colors. Since most of the color range is not in this set of colors, this warning is often visible. Click the small swatch below the warning to select the nearest web safe color.

20.7

Out of Gamut Warning

The gamut alert triangle appears when you have selected a color that falls outside the currently printable range. This most commonly occurs when you are defining colors in RGB and HSB. The small swatch below the triangle indicates the nearest printable color. Click the triangle or the swatch to select that value. Switching the color model in the palette to CMYK will also bring the color into the printable range. This may significantly change the appearance of the color.

20.8

None

Click this button to set the current fill or stroke to None. This makes the attribute transparent. This commonly used option is always available in the palette.

20.9

Spectrum

The spectrum displays all of the colors available in the current color model. Click in the spectrum to select a color. Use the following techniques:

- Shift-click to switch the spectrum to the next color model. The sliders and spectrum change to the next color model in the Color palette menu.

- To set a color value for the fill when the stroke is active (and vice versa) (Option) [Alt]-click on the spectrum.

- To set a color to its inverse color, (Command) [Ctrl]-click anywhere in the spectrum.

- To set the inactive color to its inverse color, (Command-Option) [Ctrl-Alt]-click anywhere in the spectrum. The inactive color is the fill or stroke that is not forward.

20.10

Quick Color

Click these swatches to select the darkest and lightest colors of the current model. This is black and white except when a spot color or global swatch is selected. In those cases the swatches apply 100% and 0% tints of the color.

20.11

Spot/Process Color

Use these icons to convert global swatches and spot colors to their color equivalents. When a spot color is selected, a gray circle in a white square is displayed. When a non-spot global swatch is displayed a gray box is displayed. Click the icon to convert the color to the default color of the document (RGB or CMYK). This option will convert the color definitions of selected objects and break the connection to the swatch.

20.12

Document Color Space

Use these icons to convert global swatches and spot colors to their color equivalents. In an RGB document, red, green, and blue color bars are displayed. In a CMYK document, cyan, yellow, magenta and black triangles come together to form a box. Click the icon to convert the spot color or global swatch to the default color of the document (RGB or CMYK). This option will convert the color definitions of selected objects and break the connection to the swatch.

20.13

Color Palette Menu

The options in the Color palette menu modify the palette's appearance and convert colors.

20.14

Hide Options

Use this command to shrink the Color palette so that it only displays the None, Spectrum, and Quick Color options. When the palette is so minimized, the command may be used again to restore the options.

20.15

Grayscale

Use this command to set the sliders to the grayscale model. Grayscale is based on the colors that can be printed with varying amounts of black ink. Colors set in this mode are printed with black and displayed with equal amount of red, green, and blue. Choosing this converts the current colors to their gray equivalent.

20.16

RGB

Use this command to set the sliders to the RGB (red, green, blue) model. RGB is based on the values used to display color on-screen. This model is most frequently used when preparing web graphics and graphics for composite printing only.

20.17

HSB

Use this command to set the sliders to the HSB (Hue, Saturation, and Brightness) model. This model is commonly used when preparing display graphics. Often, it's used as an alternative to RGB because of the more intuitive nature of the sliders. For example, you may start out picking a red in the RGB sliders, but decide that you want a slightly less intense version of the same color. You can switch to HSB and adjust the Saturation slider rather than trying to figure out the correct RGB combination.

20.18

CMYK

Use this command to set the sliders to the process color model. This model is based on the color inks used in most full color commercial printing. CMYK stands for Cyan, Magenta, Yellow, and Black. Black is abbreviated with a K because it is the "Key" color for printers. These colors are used because they produce the widest range of color combinations in print with the fewest color components, and therefore the most cheaply.

20.19

Web Safe RGB

Use this command to set the sliders to the web-safe RGB model. This model is based on the 216 colors that can be predictably displayed on all monitors. It is a web standard for its ability to give a broad audience the same color-viewing experience.

20.20

Invert

Use this command to invert a color. Illustrator inverts a color by first considering the color's RGB equivalent color and then flipping each color sliders position. RGB colors run from 0 to 255. A color value of 0 would convert to 255, a color of 50 would become 205. Because RGB is based on light, this tends to lighten dark colors and darken light ones.

Mistakes to Avoid

Trying to convert multiple objects of different colors. This command is intended to convert a color value, not to convert objects. Doing this will make all the colors the inverse of the last selected color. To invert a series of objects, use Filter: Colors: **Invert Color**.

20.21

Complement

This command is similar to Invert, except that it retains the color's tone. It converts the selected color to the color's true complement. The complement of a color is the color that you would add to it to produce gray.

Complementary colors oppose each other on the color wheel. The color will be similar to the ones produced with Invert, except that the tone is truer to the original. Black and white have no complements and are not affected by this command.

The Document Info Palette

Document Info Overview

Use this palette to review a list of informational details about a document or selection. The topics covered are those that are usually of concern to prepress professionals or people who are receiving files from clients. The palette is often used as a basic preflight tool.

The palette can be set to provide details about an entire document or only the current selection. Details are provided about the document, the kinds of objects in the document and nine categories of detail about the object. The palette menu enables you to set the category of information displayed.

To use this palette to review a document, start with the palette in Document mode. Check the document category for anything odd like Split Long Paths being activated. Next, check the objects category to learn what kinds of objects are used in the document. The objects category can be thought of as a table of contents for the remaining categories. Upon noticing an item of interest in the document, go to the category to get more details about those objects. Later, switch the palette to selection mode to get quick details on objects in the document.

21.2

Selection Only

Select this option to restrict the information displayed to information about the current selection. This is commonly used to review a variety of objects without other palettes. Once set, this option becomes the default. Be sure to switch this option off when attempting to review a complete document.

21.3

Document

This category provides general information about the file. Most users note the color space the document is in, the size of the artboard, and move on to the objects section.

Issues to Consider

Split Long Paths is a red flag. The Split Long Paths option is off by default and is usually only activated in documents with very complex paths. If someone has turned it on, they expect that there are very long paths in the document that may cause printing difficulties. Splitting paths may change the appearance of the object as well. *(For more information, see 7.44, File: Document Setup.)*

21.4

Objects

This category reviews the number of objects and used in the document. Pay attention to the objects listed here, as each kind of object has its own particular issues and requirements. The first block of information reviews the number and kinds of paths in the document. The second details the use of color. Notable attribute types, such as patterns and brushes occupy the fourth block. Fonts and image objects are counted last.

Issues to Consider

Use the objects section as a table of contents. This section is often used to get a quick overview of the flavor of the document. You can see from here the kinds of objects used in the document and then go to that objects section in the palette for more details. For example, you may note in the objects section that a document uses spot colors. From there you can set the palette to spot colors to see the names of the colors used.

21.5

Styles

This section details the names of styles in use in the document and the number of objects that utilize them. You should be aware of styles for two reasons. Styles often contain effects or multiple fills and strokes. Objects that use styles may not be immediately obvious when inspected. For example, a circular path may have a style that makes it appear as a square. Secondly, styles often contain features, such as transparency, that have special printing considerations. You will want to be prewarned that styles exist and then go about inspecting them.

21.6

Brushes

This section details the names and types of brushes in use in the document and the number of objects that utilize them.

Brushes are not often a cause for printing problems, but can cause confusion. Since brushes do not appear the same in preview and outline modes, they can disturb some users. Also, if you need to manually adjust objects for printing (such as applying a trap), you will want to know about any existing brushes so so you can expand and adjust them.

21.7

Spot Color Objects

This section details the names and alternate color spaces of spot colors in use in the document and the number of objects that utilize them.

Issues to Consider

The use of color should be consistent with the printing manner chosen. Check the color usage to be sure it matches the printing called for. Spot colors of the correct names should be exactly those called for in the print job. The number of colors should also be considered. Some users duplicate and rename the same spot color, incorrectly assuming that they will print on the same plate. If you notice spot colors and process colors used together, be sure that the job is intended that way.

21.8

Pattern Objects

This section details the names of patterns in use in the document. It does not state the number of objects that use the pattern. Patterns used in styles that are applied to objects in the document are included here.

While patterns are mostly benign, they have been known to cause printing problems in some rare circumstances. Being aware that they exist gives you more places to look in the event things go wrong.

21.9

Gradient Objects

This section details the names, kind, and color modes of gradients in use in the document. Gradients used in styles that are applied to objects in the document are listed here.

Gradients occasionally cause printing to fail, but are often a source of client complaints. Gradients may print in noticeable color steps instead of a smooth transition. If gradients are used in the document, you should check the size and colors used. You should also be sure that gradients are not defined with mixed color spaces, such as spot color and process color in the same gradient. *(For more information, see 23.1, Gradient Palette.)*

21.10

Fonts

This section details the names and technologies of fonts in use in the document. It does not state the number of objects that use the font. Compare these with any fonts supplied to be sure you have the files required to print the file.

21.11

Linked Images

This section details the names and locations of files linked to the document. If is the link isn't an EPS, PDF, or other locked file format, the Document Info palette can also provide details about the image pixels. Details about raster links are actually richer in this palette than they are in the Links palette. From this section you can see the link's color mode, bit depth, and number of channels as well as file size, pixel dimensions and resolution. With this information you can assess the viability of the object for printing.

21.12

Embedded Images

This section details the embedded raster images in the file. No names are used on embedded art, but all of the pixel data is available, regardless of the original file's format.

21.13

Font Details

This section provides additional information about the fonts used in the document including the name of the associated fonts files. This can be quite useful when searching for fonts, particularly on PC systems where font files may be named counterintuitively.

21.14

Save

This command saves the contents of the Document Info palette as a text (.txt) file. This is sometimes used to create a report for submission with a file.

The Flattening
Preview Palette

22.1

Flattening Overview

Most printers and many file formats do not support Illustrator's transparent objects. To accommodate this, transparency must be flattened.

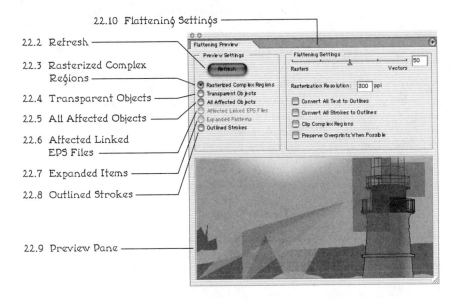

22.10 Flattening Settings

22.2 Refresh

22.3 Rasterized Complex Regions

22.4 Transparent Objects

22.5 All Affected Objects

22.6 Affected Linked EPS Files

22.7 Expanded Items

22.8 Outlined Strokes

22.9 Preview Pane

Flattening is the act of describing the appearance of the image without using transparent objects. Objects are broken into pieces and recolored where transparent objects overlap. The pieces may be vectors, rasters or a combination of the two, depending upon the nature of the image.

You may intentionally choose to flatten artwork, or it may happen automatically. Flattening occurs in the following circumstances:

- When a file with transparency is printed. This does not affect the saved version of the file. Rather, a flattened version of the file is temporarily substituted for the purposes of printing.

- When you save or export to a file format that doesn't support transparency. File formats that do not support transparency include the Illustrator 8 native and EPS formats, the Acrobat 4 PDF, and most exported file options.

- When you execute the command Object: **Flatten Transparency**

- When you place an Illustrator 10 EPS file into an application that does not support transparency. Illustrator 10 EPS files include both transparent and flattened versions of the art. If the application they placed in does not support transparency, the flattened version is used. This does not affect your ability to open and edit the transparency in Illustrator.

The Flattening Preview palette provides a dynamic way to establish and forecast the effect flattening will have on a file. Flattening options are set using the command File: **Document Setup**. You may also set those options in this palette. *(For more information, see 7.45, File: Document Setup: Transparency.)*

Flatten Preview is an optional palette that does not load by default. To add this functionality to Illustrator, the file Flattening Preview must be moved from Illustrator 10: Utilities: Flattening Preview to the directory Illustrator 10: Plug ins. Once you have done this, relaunch Illustrator to make the palette available.

Mistakes to Avoid

Confusing Flattening with Rasterizing. Flattening and rasterizing are related, but are not the same thing. Rasterizing is the act of converting to pixels. It may be an outcome of flattening. Flattening often involves rasterizing but might not. Flattening could produce vector shapes, depending upon the objects used.When you export to pixel formats, such as the Photoshop format, your work will be rasterized.

22.2
Refresh

Click this button to update the preview pane in the palette. Parts of the document that are affected are highlighted in red in the preview, the rest of the document is grayscale. If you alter the Flattening Settings or the document you will need to refresh the preview. This includes noninvasive changes to the document, such as zooming in.

22.3
Rasterized Complex Regions

This setting highlights any areas that will be converted to pixels if the document is flattened. This may be more than the transparent objects. The areas of the document affected will vary with the settings chosen in the Raster/Vectors slider in the Flattening Settings section of the palette. For example, if the document contains transparency and is set to a 0 Raster/Vector setting, all of the objects may be printed as pixels, whether or not they are affected by the transparency.

22.4
Transparent Objects

This option highlights all of the objects that contain transparency. This includes the following:

- Objects with opacity settings less than 100%.

- Objects that use blend modes other than normal.

- Objects that use opacity masks.

- Objects that are set to overprint. If overprinting objects are the only transparent objects in the document, they will not be highlighted.

When problem solving, this option enables you to quickly identify the objects that are creating the transparency issues.

22.5
All Affected Objects

This option highlights the objects that contain transparency and the objects they overlap. This differs from the Transparent Objects option in that it shows not only the objects that contain the transparency, but also the objects impacted by the transparency. Since flattening may involve changing both objects, this is a good option to employ. Many users will toggle between the two options to see the impact of transparency in the document and the objects that are causing it.

22.6

Affected Linked EPS Files

This option highlights linked EPS files that contain transparency or are affected by transparency. Once identified, it is good idea to embed these objects. Illustrator may fail to set the stacking order of linked transparent EPS files correctly.

22.7

Expanded Patterns

This option highlights objects that use pattern fills and strokes that will be expanded because of their interaction with transparency.

22.8

Outlined Strokes

This option highlights all of the strokes that will be converted to filled paths due to their interaction with transparency. If the Convert All Strokes option is active, all of the strokes in the document will be highlighted. This does not include brushed strokes.

22.9

Preview Pane

This panel provides a preview of the objects in the document. The preview is not intended to forecast color accurately and should be regarded as mildly dubious in that regard. Click in the preview to zoom in about the point clicked. (Option) [Alt]-click to zoom out. You cannot drag a marquee to enlarge an area. Reposition the preview area by holding down the spacebar to switch to the Hand tool.

22.10

Flattening Settings

The settings found in this section are the same as those in File: Document Setup: Transparency. Settings may be adjusted in either location. *(For more information, see 7.45, File: Document Setup: Transparency.)*

22.11

Flattening Preview Palette Menu

The settings in the Flattening Preview palette menu adjust the quality of the preview pane and load commonly-used flattening options.

22.12

Quick Preview

This option sets the palette to display a lower-quality preview that is speedier to display.

22.13

Detailed Preview

This option sets the palette to display a higher-quality preview that is slower to display. Many users employ the Quick Preview option by default and switch to this option only for complex work or when there is a concern about the accuracy of the preview.

22.14

Preview for Composite Output

This setting activates the Ignore Overprinting in Composite Output option by default. This option disregards the overprinting status of objects for purposes of previewing and composite printing. This setting is correct when preparing a file to be printing to a composite printer, such as an inkjet. This setting is carried to the Adobe Illustrator section of the print dialog box. *(For more information, see 7.50, File: **Print**.)*

22.15

Preview for EPS Output

This setting changes the Ignore Overprinting in Composite Output option to Preserve Overprints when Possible. This instructs Illustrator to maintain the overprinting status of objects for high-resolution printing. This option should be used whenever you intend to place EPS files in page layout applications for that purpose.

22.16

Preview for Legacy Output

This setting activates and disables the Convert All Text to Outlines option. It is intended for use when you will be saving to an earlier file format that does not support embedding fonts.

The Gradient Palette

Gradient Overview

Use the Gradient palette to define and apply gradients. A gradient is a smooth progression between at least two colors. The colors may be spot or process and can change in a linear or circular progression. Gradients can only be applied to fills. Typically, they are also saved as swatches.

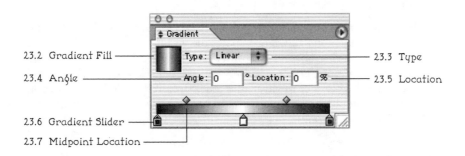

23.2 Gradient Fill — | Type: Linear | — 23.3 Type
23.4 Angle — | Angle: 0 ° Location: 0 % | — 23.5 Location
23.6 Gradient Slider —
23.7 Midpoint Location —

Gradients are defined by setting color values for different positions in the gradient. When applied to an object, locations in the document are connected these positions and color is applied to the object between these two points. Gradients are defined using Gradient Sliders. Sliders have a color and a location. The location of the sliders in the gradient is expressed as a percentage of the overall gradient. For example, a gradient may be defined by a slider with a white color at the beginning of a gradient (0%) and a black color at the end (100%). By default, the 0% position of a gradient is set to the far left of an object, the 100% at the far right. These positions may be adjusted using the Gradient tool.

Gradients in print are a common source of disappointment. Differing tones printed next to each other create a gradient. The amount of tones that are printed, and the area that they are printed in determine whether the difference between the tones are noticeable. The factors that influence whether a gradient will band when printed are as follows:

- **The kind of printer used.** PostScript Level 2 printers can create 256 different tones. This is the theoretical maximum number of steps in the gradient it could produce. In the real world, the amount printable is usually less. PostScript Level 3 printers can print gradients much more efficiently.

- **The paper-press combination used.** Tone is a function of the press, paper and line screen used in a print job. Although your imagesetter may be able to produce 256 tones, the paper used may drop off the lightest tones and clog up the darkest ones. This could leave you with only a fraction of those tones to work with.

  Also, printing at a high line screen may limit the printable tones. To calculate printable tones, divide the printer's resolution by the line screen used and square the result. Add 1 and discard any result higher than the maximum tones your printer can create. For example, printing a 150 line screen on a 1200 dpi imagesetter yields only a possible 65 tones ($1200/150 = 8$. $8 \times 8 = 64 + 1 = 65$).

- **The difference between the colors used.** The greater the difference between the colors, the more space the gradient can occupy without banding. In terms of tone, the difference between the colors limits the tones used. If your gradient is between 50% black and 25% black, you are only using 25% of the available tones. In a Postscript level 2 environment, you would be printing with about 64 different tone steps (25% of the 256 possible tones).

Blending between very similar colors is difficult. In cases where gradients that use similar colors are critical, many users employ spot colors. This provides a full range of tones to work with, while still appearing visually similar.

- **The size of the gradient.** The amount of distance the color changes over is the size of the gradient. The greater the distance of the gradient, the more likely it is to band, Many users rely on a 1 to 2 point rule for gradients. The rule states that the size of a gradient should be no more than 1 to 2 points for every tonal step it occupies. In the previous example, the gradient used 64 tones. A 1-point rule would limit the size of the gradient to 64 points, or less than an inch. The more liberal 2-point rule would let the gradient occupy 128 points.

- **The presence of other objects in the design.** When designs call for large gradients, many users try to break up the gradient with intermediate objects. This makes it harder to notice any banding that may occur. Similarly, some users produce gradients in Photoshop and use filters to create noise, breaking up the gradient.

Mistakes to Avoid

Mixing spot and process colors. When creating gradients, do not mix color models. This often happens when users confuse process white with 0% of a spot color. Both definitions mean the same thing (paper), but they cannot be used interchangeably. Gradients built in this way will print process colors and the spot color. To keep the gradient on a single color plate, be sure to blend between tints of the same spot color.

Failing to save gradients as swatches. Once a gradient has been defined, it should be saved as a swatch. Many users prepare a gradient and then select another object that contains a gradient. This replaces the prepared gradient in the Gradient palette with the selected one, forcing the user to Undo. Although this can be worked around, saving gradients is better tradecraft and results in cleaner workflow.

23.2

Gradient Fill

Use this swatch to preview gradients, to apply gradient fills to objects and to save gradients as a swatch.

This swatch displays a thumbnail of the current gradient. Apply the gradient to an object in the document by dragging this swatch directly onto the object. Objects do not need to be selected to execute this change.

To save a gradient, drag this item directly into the Swatches palette. A black box will highlight the Swatches palette as you do this, to indicate the gradient will be saved.

23.3

Type

Use this menu to set the current gradient to a linear or radial gradient.

Linear gradients change color as a series of lines. They start in one position (0%) and progress to another (100%). Areas on either side of those positions are given solid versions of the 0% and 100% color values.

Radial gradients change color as a series of ellipses radiating from one place outward. The starting (0%) point of the gradient is the smallest ellipse in the center. The ending point (100%) is the largest ellipse on the outside.

Issues to Consider

Additional types can be created as blends. Since the choices for blend types are limited, many users create their own gradient shapes manually using blends.

23.4

Angle

Use this field to set the direction in which a linear gradient progresses. The measure is set in degrees from the starting (0%) position. This value may be set numerically, or be set when using the Gradient tool. This field does not give information about the distance the gradient travels, or where it stops and starts. Although you can enter values between 32768° and 32767°, the equivalent 0–360° value is used.

23.5

Location

Use this field to set the position in the gradient of selected gradient sliders and midpoint diamonds. This field may be set numerically or by manually dragging the sliders or midpoints.

To select a gradient slider or midpoint diamond, click on it. The field will display its position within the gradient. Gradient sliders are expressed as a percent of the overall distance of the gradient. Midpoint diamonds express the distance between two sliders. The location field establishes where in the gradient the colors change and the rate that they change.

Setting the position of a slider or midpoint changes the rate that colors change in the gradient. For example, changing a midpoint slider's position from 50% to 25% causes the color to change more rapidly from the first color to the second. Changing a midpoint from 50% to 75% causes it to change more slowly.

23.6
_____

Gradient Slider

Use the gradient sliders to set the colors in a gradient. Each gradient slider sets one of the color values used in a gradient and has a location in the gradient. There must be at least two sliders in each gradient. The resulting gradient is previewed in the palette between the sliders.

To set the color value of a slider manually, click on it. The slider icon appears in the color palette. Set the color palette to the values you require. To set a color for a slider from an existing swatch, drag the swatch out of the swatches palette (or a swatch library) directly onto a slider. A small diamond appears in the slider to indicate you are about to change it.

To reposition a slider, click drag it into the position you require. As you drag, the location field updates to indicate the new position of the slider.

Duplicate a slider as you drag it by holding down the (Option) [Alt] key as you drag.

To create a new slider, click in the gradient ramp in the palette. A new slider is created using the color values that are associated with that location in the gradient. To create a gradient slider with new color values, drag a swatch from the swatches palette (or a swatch library) directly into the gradient ramp. A vertical line indicates the position the slider will be placed when then mouse is released.

23.7
_____

Midpoint Location

Use this slider to indicate the position in the gradient where the values of two gradient sliders are evenly mixed. By default, the midpoint is positioned halfway between gradient sliders, creating an even color transition. Position the slider between 13% and 87%.

Click drag a midpoint to change its position between two sliders. Alternatively, click to select the midpoint and set its position with the location field. As the midpoint gets nearer to a slider, color transitions more quickly away from that color. The result is less of that color in the mix. This is sometimes used to create sharp color transitions in a gradient.

23.8
___

Gradient Palette Menu

The Gradient palette menu only has one function: Show/Hide Options. Hide Options temporarily removes all of the fields from the Gradient palette, leaving only the gradient sliders, ramp and midpoints. This is not commonly activated, but it can be useful for reducing monitor clutter. Choose the command again to reveal the hidden options.

The Info Palette

Info Palette Overview

The Info palette provides basic data about objects. When nothing is selected, the palette displays the position of the cursor interactively. When objects are being transformed, the palette displays information about the change. The details provided are informational in nature and cannot be edited using this palette.

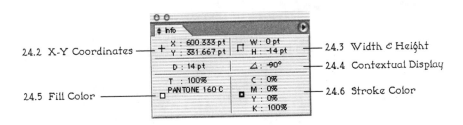

24.2 X-Y Coordinates

24.3 Width & Height

24.4 Contextual Display

24.5 Fill Color

24.6 Stroke Color

Issues to Consider

The Use Preview Bounds preference affects this palette. Activating this preference bases the displayed information on the actual printing size of the object, rather than its underlying vectors. *(For more information see 8.12, Edit: Preferences: **General**)*

Changes in the zero origin of the ruler are not updated automatically. If you change the zero origin position of the ruler after selecting an object, the Info palette does not update to reflect this automatically. To update the information, deselect and reselect the object.

The Appearance palette and the Transform palette provide much of the same information. Further, those palettes enable you to edit attributes. The key information not available in those two palettes is the dynamic readout the info palette provides as objects are transformed and the cursor is repositioned.

24.2

X/Y Coordinates

These two readouts display the X and Y coordinates of selected objects or the position of the cursor. The X measure displays the horizontal position; the Y measure displays the vertical position. The measures are relative to the zero position of the rulers. Positive numbers are above and to the right of the zero position. Negative numbers are to the left and below the zero position.

If an object is selected, the readouts display the upper-left corner of the selection's bounding box. This measuring location cannot be altered.

If nothing is selected, the readouts display the current position of the cursor.

24.3

Width & Height

These two readouts display the width and height of the current selection's bounding box. The bounding box is the total area of the widest and tallest points in the selection. If nothing is selected the readouts display zero.

24.4

Contextual Display

These two displays change contextually. If the Paintbrush tool is selected, the current brush is displayed. If an object is being transformed, transformation details are displayed. If an object is being moved, the distance and angle the object is being moved is displayed. If an object is being scaled, the scale width and height percent are displayed. If an object is being rotated or reflected, the angle of transformation is displayed. If an object is being sheared the angle of rotation and shear is displayed. When the Free Transform tool is being used, the angle of rotation and scaling percentage is displayed.

24.5

Fill Color

This readout displays the color values of the current fill. The display is in the color mode of the document. If the fill is a saved gradient or pattern, its name is displayed. Patterns are indicated with a (P:). Gradients are indicated with a (Gr:)

24.6

Stroke Color

This readout displays the color values of the current stroke. The display is in the color mode of the document. If the fill is a saved pattern, its name is displayed. If the stroke contains a brush, the underlying stroke color is displayed. Brush names are not displayed in this field.

24.7

Info Palette Menu

The Info palette menu contains only one function: Show/Hide Options. Hide Options temporarily removes the Fill and Stroke readouts. Choose the command again to recall the readouts once they have been hidden.

The Layers Palette

25.1

Layers Palette Overview

Use the Layers palette to organize documents, to lock and hide items, to target layers and groups, to create customized special effects, to simplify the task of redrawing raster art to select objects, and to prepare documents for exporting as animation.

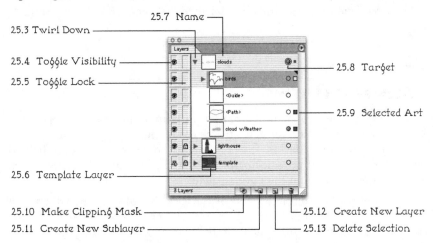

25.7 Name

25.3 Twirl Down

25.4 Toggle Visibility

25.5 Toggle Lock

25.8 Target

25.9 Selected Art

25.6 Template Layer

25.10 Make Clipping Mask

25.11 Create New Sublayer

25.12 Create New Layer

25.13 Delete Selection

Layers are used to organize documents is by simplifying the stacking order. Every object in an Illustrator document has a front-to-back position relative to every other object. In complex documents, this can add up to thousands of objects. Layers have their own stacking order and position relative to each other on the Z-axis. Each layer is in front of or behind the other layers. Objects on each layer are likewise in front of or behind all other objects on other layers. Further, placing objects on layers results in a series of smaller stacking orders, rather than one comprehensive one for the entire document. This makes it easier to find and select objects.

Layers are also used to organize logically connected items. Items that belong together are often placed on a single layer. They can then be locked, hidden, or changed as a unit by editing the properties of the layer. For example, while working on a logo against a background, the items in a logo may be collected on one layer and the background items on another. As the background art is adjusted, the logo layer may be locked to prevent accidental altering or hidden completely.

The Layers palette is essential for applying attributes to layers and groups. Layers and groups can have effects, styles, and transparency. When a layer or group has an attribute, all of the items in the layer or group display that attribute as well. If the items are moved to a different layer or are taken out of the group, they no longer display the attribute.

Layer palette commands are found in the Layers palette menu and buttons. Multiple items may be highlighted so that they can be edited collectively. To choose an item, click on its name. The object is highlighted in the Layers palette. The objects themselves need not be selected in the document, only highlighted in the Layers palette. To highlight multiple, contiguous items in the Layers palette, Shift-click on a second item. All items between the two objects are highlighted. (Command) [Ctrl]-click to highlight non-contiguous items. You cannot highlight items in different groups or layers. Once highlighted, the objects are subject to commands in the Layers palette. This is a common way to duplicate, delete, move, hide, and reorder multiple items.

25.2

Stacking Order

The Layers palette is organized from top to bottom. Items at the top of the Layers palette are in front of items below them. This is the case for layers as well as items within the layers. The positioning of objects in front of or behind other objects is called the stacking order. Reorder objects by dragging them into new positions within the Layers palette.

To reposition an item in the Layers palette, click-drag the name or thumbnail of the item to be moved. As you drag, a black bar with two triangles on the left appears in between other items in the palette. This indicates the position the item would occupy if you were to release the mouse.

When moving an item in the Layers palette, it may be dragged into a layer or group. Dragging an item into another places that item in that layer or group at the top of its stacking order. Layers may be dragged into other layers; groups and objects may be dragged into other groups or layers. When an object is dragged into a layer or group, a large black triangle highlights the item, indicating where the dragged item will be placed.

Mistakes to Avoid

Nesting layers accidentally. Layers can reside inside other layers. This is called a nesting. Be careful when repositioning layers, particularly when dragging one to the top of the stacking order, that you do not accidentally drag it into another layer. Watch for the presence of the black line to indicate the new position, rather than the black triangle, indicating you are nesting a layer.

Issues to Consider

Objects can be dragged into special groups. Some special objects have a group structure. For example, Clipping masks are a really a group with special instructions. Dragging an object into that group makes it clipped as well.

25.3

Twirl Down

Click these arrows to open and close the contents of an item in the Layers palette. Layers and groups may contain many items. The twirl down arrows reveal the contents of a layer or group so that you can inspect it or modify it. In instances where you do not need to see the contents of an item, you can reset the twirl down to hide the items, and reduce the clutter on the monitor.

Twirling down items is essential to accessing individual objects through the Layers palette. Once revealed, each item can be shown, hidden, locked, and repositioned in the stacking order.

To twirl down an item and all of the items it contains, (Option) [Alt]-click on the twirl down triangle. Repeat the process to close a twirl down and all of the items it contains. This is often handy when a layer contains many open groups you would like to close quickly.

Issues to Consider

Objects can be dragged into twirled down Compound Shapes and Envelopes. Compound Shapes and Envelopes are not groups. You cannot add items to these objects by dragging them onto the object in the Layers palette. However, if you twirl down the item and drag the object between items, it will be added to the object. Envelopes are only available to be twirled down if the Edit Contents option is activated.

25.4

Toggle Visibility

Click this button to switch the visibility status of items. Visible items have a solid eye icon next to them. Hidden items have an empty column. Changing the visibility of an item also changes the status of all subordinate objects. That is, hiding a layer hides all the items on that layer, including any sublayers or groups. Items retain their own, independent visibility however. When a layer or group is hidden, the visibility icons of all the items on the layer are dimmed and cannot be changed. If an item is hidden and then the layer it is on is hidden, and later revealed, the hidden item stays hidden.

To show or hide a series of layers, click drag across the toggle visibility icons. The visibility of the first icon is switched and all of the other dragged icons are switched to match.

When all of the layers are visible, to hide all of the layers except one, (Option) [Alt]-click on the visibility icon. When some layers are hidden, to reveal all of the layers, (Option) [Alt]-click on any layer's visibility icon.

To set a layer to outline view (Command) [Ctrl] click on the visibility icon. To set all of the other layers to outline mode, (Option-Command) [Alt-Ctrl]-click on the visibility icon. Reverse the process by repeating it.

Issues to Consider

Hidden Layers are discarded when layers are flattened. Layers that aren't visible are discarded when layers are flattened or merged. Hidden objects on visible layers are retained, but hidden layers are not.

Hidden Layers are not included when exporting. Exporting art to another format, such as the Photoshop native format, discards hidden layers.

Hidden layers do not print. Hidden layers don't print from Illustrator or from EPS files created from the document.

25.5

Toggle Lock

Click this button to switch the lock status of items. This is done to prevent an item from being modified. When applied to an object, this is the same as choosing Object: Lock: **Selection**. Changing the lock status of an item also changes the status of all subordinate objects. That is, locking a layer locks all the items on that layer, including any sublayers or groups. Items retain their own, independent lock status however. When a layer is locked, all of the items in the layer display dimmed lock icons. If an object is locked independently, the lock icon is solid. You cannot unlock a specific item on a locked layer.

To lock or unlock a series of layers, click-drag across the toggle lock icons. The lock status of the first icon is switched and all of the other dragged across icons are switched to match. *(For more information, see 9.18, Object: **Lock**.)*

When all layers are locked, to lock all of the layers except one (Option) [Alt]-click on the visibility icon. When some layers are locked, to unlock all of the layers, (Option) [Alt]-click on any layer's lock icon. Be certain that this does not unlock layers that should be locked accidentally. Special care should be given when unlocking template layers.

25.6

Template Layer

This icon indicates that a layer is a template. Templates are layers used to make it easier to trace images. Tracing is done to convert existing raster art into vector graphics. The art that is being traced is placed by itself on a layer and new art is created atop it on a separate layer. After the art is traced, the template layer is typically discarded.

Templates can be created in two ways: by choosing the template option when placing art or by choosing the template option in the Layers palette. When importing art that will be made into a template, it is usually better to create the template. This saves the step of creating an additional layer and repositioning it. *(For more information, see 25.7, Name.)*

Templates are better for tracing than regular layers because raster art on templates are visible in both preview and outline mode. Template layers have the following options by default:

- **Show (On).** The layer is visible. This option is not editable on a template.

- **Preview (On).** The layer is in preview mode rather than outline. This option is not editable on a template.

- **Lock (On).** The layer is locked so that it cannot be edited or moved. This option is not editable on a template.

- **Print (Off).** The layer doesn't print and cannot be exported. This option is not editable on a template.

- **Dim Images To (50%).** The raster art on the layer is ghosted, as if transparent) by the specified amount. This option is modifiable. The amount of dimming required will vary depending upon the tone of the original. Darker images often need to be dimmed more than lighter ones.

25.7

Name

Use the name to identify an item, to move an item and to select items. Both objects and layers have names. Change the name of an object with the Options dialog box. Change the name of a Layer with the Layer Options dialog box. Open the Options for an object or Layer by double-clicking its name or selecting the item in the Layers palette and choosing Options from the Layers palette menu. The Layer Options dialog box opens automatically when you choose New Layer from the Layers palette menu or when you (Option) [Alt]-click on the new Layer button.

Illustrator names objects by their object class. The name of each object by default is its object class in brackets. For example, paths are named <Path>; envelopes are named <Envelope>.

Illustrator names layers sequentially by default. The first layer in a document is named "Layer 1" and the second one created is named "Layer 2." In some cases, layers are given different default names. For example, template layers made from linked files are named for the file that created them.

To select all of the items on a Layer (Option) [Alt]-click on the Layer's name. To select an individual object, (Option) [Alt]-click on its name. To add or subtract an item to the selection, (Option-Shift) [Alt-Shift]-click on the object's name. It should be noted that selecting all of the items in a layer is different than targeting a layer. *(For more information, see 25.8, Target.)*

Layer Options

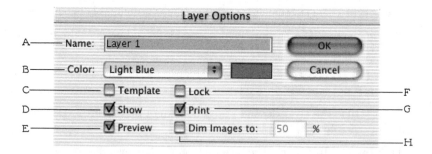

A. **Name**

Use this field to affix a name to a layer. Layer names should be as descriptive as possible. The name for the layer appears in the Layers palette.

B. **Color**

Use this option to set the highlight color of the layer. The highlight color is used to indicate selected objects. Objects that are selected appear highlighted with the color. The Layers palette indicates selected objects and layers that contain selections by placing boxes of this color next to them in the palette.

Choose a color for the layer by selecting a commonly chosen color from the menu or choose a custom color by clicking the color swatch to the right of the menu. Layers are given colors from the menu sequentially as they are created. That is, the first layer in the document uses the first highlight color on the list: light blue. The second layer created will have the second highlight color on the list: red.

C. **Template** (Default: Off)

Use this option to convert the selected layer into a template. Template layers are commonly used to trace imported art. *(For more information, see 25.6, Template Layers.)*

D. **Show** (Default: On)

This option sets the visibility of the layer to on. It is the same as activating the show layer icon *(For more information, see 25.4, Toggle Visibility.)*

E. **Preview** (Default: Current document setting)

This option sets the view mode of a Layer to Preview. Unchecked, a layer is set to outline mode.

F. **Lock** (Default: Off)

This option sets a layer to locked. Locked layers cannot be selected. *(For more information, see 25.5, Toggle Lock.)*

G. **Print** (Default: On)

This option enables the contents of a layer to be printed and exported. This option is used when you want to able to preview a layer's contents without printing it. The most common example is the template layer *(For more information, see 25.4, Template Layer.)*

H. **Dim Images to:** (Default: Off)

Use this option to fade the display of raster images on the layer. This is most commonly used when tracing images on template layers.

Object Options

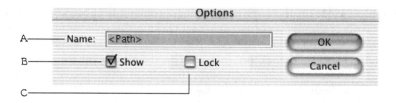

A. Name

Use this field to affix a name to an object. Object names are most commonly used when creating variables. Giving an object a name makes it easier to find and understand in a variable list. The name for the item appears in the Layers palette.

B. Show

This option sets the visibility of the object to on. It is the same as activating the show icon in the Layers palette. *(For more information, see 25.4, Toggle Visibility.)*

C. Lock

This option sets an object to locked. It is the same as selecting the object and choosing Object: Lock: Selection. Locked items cannot be selected. *(For more information, see 25.5, Toggle Lock.)*

25.8

Target

Use this circle to identify styled items, to select objects and to target Layers and Groups.

Items that contain transparency, Effects, Styles, or Brushes are indicated with a gradient icon in this location. To remove the appearance from one item and give it to another, click-drag the gradient from one item to another item's target circle. To copy the appearance from one item to another, hold down the (Option) [Alt] key as you drag. To clear the Appearance from an item, drag the gradient into the Trash button on the Layers palette.

Select objects and target layers by clicking on the target icon. For objects, being selected and being targeted is the same thing. Selected items are indicated with both a selection marker and a large circle surrounding the target icon. Target Objects directly by clicking on the target icon. *(For more information, see 25.9, Selected Art.)*

Target layers by clicking on the target icon next to the layer's name. When this happens, the targeting is indicated with a large circle around the layer's target icon. All of the items on the layer become selected, but not targeted. Once targeted, a layer is available to have transparency, effects and styles applied to it. To alter settings applied to a layer, the layer must once again be targeted.

Issues to Consider

Transferring Appearance is usually done between objects and groups, or objects and layers. This may happen when you decide that an effect is better suited applied to individual objects, rather than groups or layers. This might be done to apply the effect based on an object's bounding box, rather than the collective bounding box of a group.

Targeting a layer selects locked and hidden objects. Objects that you've protected by locking or hiding are selected when a layer is targeted and will be affected by edits that you make. For example, if you target a layer and then apply a new fill color, hidden objects will receive that fill as well. Targeting should be reserved for applying styles, transparency and effects to layers.

25.9

Selected Art

Selected objects are indicated with a large box of the layer's highlight color to the right of their name. Layers and groups that contain selections are indicated with a smaller highlight-color box.

Objects may be moved in the stacking order by dragging the highlight box into a new position. Move multiple objects between layers by dragging the layer selection icon onto another layer.

Mistakes to Avoid

Trying to drag multiple objects between layers by object selection icons. If you have more than one object selected and you attempt to drag all of them to another layer by dragging an individual object's selection icon, only the object dragged will be moved. Either drag the selection icon next to the layer or highlight the objects to be moved by (Command) [Ctrl]-clicking on each item in the Layers palette.

25.10

Make Clipping Mask

Use this button to create or release a clipping mask for a layer. This command is similar to Object: **Clipping Mask**, except that it affects all of the objects on a layer, rather than only selected items. This option is only available when a layer is highlighted in the Layers palette and the top object in the layer is a path, compound shape, text object, or a group comprised of those elements. No objects need be selected to execute this command. *(For more information, see 9.68, Object: Clipping Mask.)*

When this option is activated, the top object in the layer becomes a bounding area for all the other objects in the layer. This means that the only parts of objects that are visible are those that fall within the boundaries of the top object. The top object in the layer is set to a fill and stroke of none. The name of the object in the Layers palette is underlined to indicate it is the mask and the lines between all of the items in the Layers palette are replaced with dotted lines.

The mask shape clips new objects added to the layer as well as old ones. Objects can be in front of the mask without affecting its function.

Layer clipping masks are commonly used in lieu of clipping mask groups in the following circumstances:

• When you want to crop an entire illustration quickly.

• When you are designing to fit a specific size and do not know what the illustration will look like.

• When you want to crop and organize a series of existing illustrations to size. For example, you may need to set up a series of boxes each containing cropped art and frame the series with text. Setting each piece of art as a layer makes it easier to crop, style and select the set of art.

Mistakes to Avoid

Flattening or merging layers that each contain clipping paths. When layers that contain clipping paths are merged, all of the objects disappear. Only one object can be the clipping mask, and a layer with two, such as when two layers with clipping paths are merged, cannot resolve itself. To rectify the problem, delete all but one of the clipping paths for the layer.

25.11

Create New Sublayer

Use this button to create a new layer, nested with the current one. This option is only available when a visible, unlocked layer is highlighted in the Layers palette.

Sublayers are layers that reside inside another layer. As long as they are inside another layer they are subordinate to the layer they are on and are affected hiding and locking the parent layer and by any layer styles, transparency or clipping masks the parent layer may have. Sublayers may be moved out of the layer they are on to become independent layers or moved to another layer.

When this command is executed, a new, empty sublayer is created at the top of the stacking order of the selected layer. To create a new sublayer at the bottom of the stacking order, hold down the (Option-Command) [Alt-Ctrl] keys when clicking the command. The new layer will be highlighted in the Layers palette upon creation.

Sublayers are similar in function to groups. They are subordinate to layers but can support their own transparency and effects. Typically, they are used when you want to keep the option of making the layer independently available.

25.12

Create New Layer

Use this button to create new layers and to duplicate items.

To create a new layer, click the button. A new layer is created with the default options above the currently highlighted item in the Layers palette. To open the Layer Options dialog box upon as you create the new layer, (Option) [Alt]-click the button. *(For more information, see 25.7, Name.)*

To create a new layer on top of all the other layers, (Command) [Ctrl] click the button. To create a new layer below the current layer, (Option-Command) [Alt-Ctrl]-click on the button.

To duplicate an item, drag it onto this icon. A plus (+) sign appears on the icon when the cursor is on it, indicating the items will be duplicated. Duplicated items share all of the attributes of the original and appear atop the originals in the stacking order. Layers that are duplicated are named with word "copy" added. Duplicate multiple items by highlighting more than one object in the Layers palette. *(For more information, see 25.1, Layers Palette Overview.)*

Issues to Consider

Sublayers may be created with this button. If the highlighted item in the Layers palette is not a layer, the new layer will be created as a sublayer above the current selection. To create an independent layer, click on a layer in the palette before executing the command.

25.13

Delete Selection

Use this button to delete highlighted items in the Layers palette. To delete an object, layer, or group, highlight it in the Layers palette and click this button. Alternatively, drag the item directly onto this icon. If the selected item is a layer that contains objects, you will be prompted with an alert, warning you of the situation. If the highlighted items are objects or groups, they will be deleted without warning. To bypass the alert when deleting a layer, hold down the (Option) [Alt] key while hitting the button or drag the layer directly onto the Trash icon. Delete multiple items by highlighting more than one object in the Layers palette. *(For more information, see 25.1, Layers Palette Overview.)*

25.14

Layer Palette Menu

The Layer palette menu repeats some of the commands available as buttons in the Layers palette, and provides commands for managing layers and objects.

25.15

New Layer

This command is the same as the New Layer button except that it displays the Layer options dialog box by default. *(For more information, see 25.12, Create New Layer.)*

New layers are created atop the last or currently highlight item in the Layers palette. Holding down the (Option) [Alt] key before choosing the command spells out which item the layer will be created atop. For example, if the highlighted item in the Layers palette were named "border _art", holding down the (Option) [Alt] key would cause the command to read "New Layer Above 'border_art.'"

To create a new layer at the top of the stacking order of the document, hold down the (Command) [Ctrl] key before choosing the command. To create a layer below the selected item in the Layers palette hold down the (Option-Command) [Alt-Ctrl] keys before executing the command.

25.16

New Sublayer

This command is the same as the New Sublayer button, except that it displays the Layer options dialog box by default. *(For more information, see 25.11, Create New Sublayer.)*

25.17

Duplicate Item

Use this command to copy highlighted items in the Layers palette. If a single item is selected in the palette, it is listed by name in the menu. For example, if a layer named "border_art" is highlighted, the command will read "Duplicate 'border_art'." If more than one item is selected, the command will read Duplicate Selection. Duplicated items are created atop the original items in the stacking order. This command is the same as dragging highlighted items onto the New Layer button.

25.18

Delete Item

Use this command to delete highlighted items in the Layers palette. If a single item is selected in the palette, it is listed by name in the menu. For example, if a layer named "border_art" is highlighted, the command will read "Delete 'border_art'." If more than one item is selected, the command will read "Delete Selection." When deleting a layer that contains art, you will be warned with an alert dialog before the layer is removed. This command is the same as dragging highlighted items onto the Delete button in the front of the Layers palette.

25.19

Options for Item

Use this command to open the options dialog box for highlighted items in the Layers palette. If the highlighted item is an object, the Options dialog is opened; if the item is a layer, the Layer Options palette is opened. If more than one object is highlighted, the Options dialog opens, but the name field is dimmed. This enables you to set the options for multiple objects at the same time. The same is true when multiple layers are selected. When Layers and objects are selected together, the Layer Options dialog opens with the layer-specific options set to neutral. Neutral is indicated with a dash. Leaving options set to neutral doesn't override any existing settings. *(For more information, see 25.7, Name.)*

25.20

Make Clipping Mask

This command is the same as the Make/Release Clipping Mask button on the front of the Layers palette. *(For more information, see 25.10, Make/Release Clipping Path.)*

25.21

Locate Object

Use this command to set the Layers palette to display the currently selected object. This is useful in complicated documents to quickly find a selected object. Finding an object in the Layers palette can provide information about the group the object is in and where the item takes its styling from. If more than one object is selected, the topmost object is positioned at the top of the Layers palette display.

25.22

Merge Selected

Use this command to collapse multiple layers into a single one. To execute the command, at least two layers must be highlighted in the Layers palette. The last layer to be selected is the one the other layers are merged into. The other layers are deleted and all of the objects on those layers are added to the retained layer. The stacking order of the objects remains the same. Any transparency or effects applied to the retained layer are applied to the new objects as well. Care should be taken when merging layers to select the correct layer to be retained.

25.23

Flatten Artwork

Use this command to collapse all of the layers in the document into a single one. The last layer to be highlighted is the layer that will be retained. All of the other layers are deleted and the objects on the layers are placed on the retained layer. The stacking order of the objects is retained.

Issues to Consider

Sublayers are removed but not deleted. Sublayers in a document are no longer seen as layers in the document after this command is executed. However, they still display in the Layers palette as sublayers. This can be confusing, since the sublayers appear the same, but cannot be moved or styled as layers.

25.24

Collect in New Layer

Use this command to create a new sublayer from highlighted items in the Layers palette. If the selected items are objects, they will become a new sublayer in their current layer. If the selected items are layers, a new layer is generated and the selected layers become sublayers inside the new layer. This command is usually used to save the steps of creating a new layer and dragging selected items onto that layer.

25.25

Release to Layers (Sequence)

Use this command to create a new sublayer for every item in a layer and distribute each object onto its own layer. This command is usually used as part of the process of preparing a file for web animation in another application. For example, a series of sequential objects may be created on a layer, perhaps after a blend was expanded. From there the objects are released to their own layers and the file is exported to the Photoshop format. The file is opened in Adobe ImageReady (which uses the Photoshop native file format) and the layers are processed as frames of an animation. Illustrator layers may also be exported as frames in a flash animation directly.

When this command is executed, each object is placed on a discrete sublayer. The stacking order of the objects is reflected in the positions of the new layers. To use these layers as described above, the layers will need to become independent layers.

This model of releasing to layers works best when you are preparing an animation where things change or move.

Related Topics

7.13   *File: Save As: SVG*

7.25   *File: Export: Macromedia Flash (SWF)*

25.26

Release to Layers (Build)

This command is similar to Release to Layer (Sequence). The only difference is that the animation it is intended to prepare for adds items each frame instead of replacing them. For example, a build animation might spell out a word by adding a letter each time, or reveal a logo one piece at a time.

What this means in Illustrator is that each sublayer contains all of the objects before it plus one new object. The sublayer at the bottom contains only the last item. The next sublayer contains that item and the next one atop it. This way, as frames in the animation progress, each object is retained.

25.27

Reverse Order

Use this command to reverse the stacking order of highlighted items in the Layers palette. The top object becomes the bottom object and so forth. The highlighted items may be layers, objects, or objects and sublayers. Commonly, this command is used to quickly reverse the order of layers to be exported for an animation.

25.28

Template

Use this command to activate the template option of a highlighted layer. Choose the command again to release the template or double click on the layer to open the Layer Options dialog box and release the template manually. A layer must be highlighted in the Layers palette to use this command. *(For more information, see 25.6, Template.)*

25.29

Hide Others/Show All Layers

Use this command to hide all layers in the document except the one that is highlighted. If any layers are already hidden, the command reveals all layers. If the highlighted layer is a sublayer, every layer except the parent layer and its subordinates are hidden. This command is the same as (Option) [Alt]-clicking on the visibility icon of a layer. *(For more information, see 25.4, Toggle Visibility.)*

25.30

Outline Others/Preview All Layers

Use this command to set all layers in the document except the one that is highlighted to Outline mode. If any layers is already in Outline mode, the command sets all layers to preview mode. If the highlighted layer is a sublayer, every layer except the parent layer and its subordinates are set to outline. This command is the same as (Option-Command) [Alt-Ctrl]-clicking on the visibility icon of a layer. *(For more information, see 14.2, View: **Outline/Preview** and 25.4, Toggle Visibility.)*

25.31

Lock Others/Unlock All Layers

Use this command to lock all layers in the document except the one that is highlighted. If any layers are already locked, the command unlocks all of the layers. If the highlighted layer is a sublayer, every layer except the parent layer and its subordinates are hidden. This command is the same as (Option) [Alt]-clicking on the lock icon of a layer. *(For more information, see 25.5, Toggle Lock.)*

25.32

Paste Remembers Layers

Use this setting to include information about where an object's layer when it is copied and pasted. By default, objects may be copied and pasted freely between layers. When this option is activated, pasted objects are returned to the layer where they were copied or cut. This has the following uses:

Helps maintain organization of layers. Although not always useful, when a document is highly structured and organized, this option can prevent you from fouling that organization with copy and paste errors.

Duplicating layer organization to other documents. When Paste Remembers Layers is active, objects pasted into other documents carry their layers with them. If a layer of the same name already exists, the objects are pasted onto that layer. This works well in template-driven workflows. If no such layer exists, a new layer is created of that name in the new document. Layer effects and appearance are not retained upon copying.

Paste Remembers Layers is an application preference. Once activated it becomes the default preference until deactivated.

25.33

Palette Options

Use these options to affect the appearance of the Layers palette.

Layers Palette Options

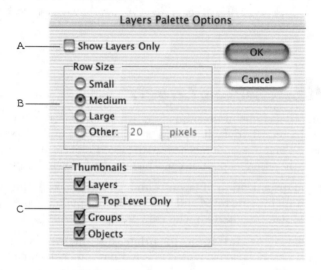

A. **Show Layers Only**

Activating this preference hides everything in the Layers palette except the layers themselves. This destroys access to group-level styling and disables many of the Layers palette's functions. Unless documents are very simple or the user is easily overwhelmed, it is not recommended that you activate this option.

B. **Row Size**

Use this option to set the height of each row in the Layers palette. Many users find that increasing the size from medium, the default, begins to eat up too much monitor space quickly.

C. **Thumbnails**

This option controls the presence of the thumbnails used for visual cues in the palette. The presence of thumbnails increases the memory requirements on the document. By default, Illustrator creates thumbnails of everything. As documents increase in complexity, consider disabling some of the thumbnails to increase performance.

Layers

> Check to create thumbnails for layers.

Top Level Only

> This option creates thumbnails from only the layer and not from sub-layers in the layer.

Groups

> Check to create thumbnails for groups

Objects

> Check to create thumbnails for objects. Consider disabling this option first as performance decreases. It is easier to identify objects by selecting them and there are far more objects than groups or layers typically.

The Links Palette

Links Overview

Use the Links palette to manage all raster art in a file and the external files placed into Illustrator documents.

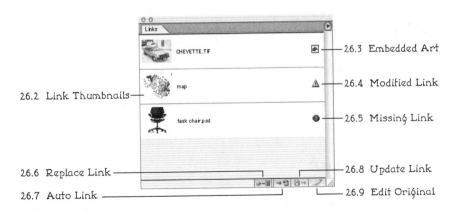

26.2 Link Thumbnails

26.3 Embedded Art

26.4 Modified Link

26.5 Missing Link

26.6 Replace Link

26.7 Auto Link

26.8 Update Link

26.9 Edit Original

Illustrator lists all raster art in a document in the Links palette. It also lists all files that are linked into the document from external files, whether those files are rasters or vectors. In this chapter, the term *link* is used to mean anything in the Links palette. *(For more information, see 7.16, File: **Place**.)*

26.2

Link Thumbnails

Use thumbnails to get a quick sense of what the link looks like. The name of external files that have been placed will be listed here as well. Objects rasterized in Illustrator do not have names, even if they were given custom names in the Layers palette.

Click on a link to highlight it in the Links palette. Items activated in this way are not necessarily selected, but are available for Links palette commands. Shift-click to select multiple contiguous items, (Command) [Ctrl]-click to select noncontiguous files. (Option-Command) [Alt-Ctrl]-click on the palette to select it, enabling you to highlight items in the palette by typing their names. Double-click on a link to open the Link Information window. *(For more information, see 26.19, Information.)*

26.3

Embedded Art

This icon indicates that the item is embedded and not linked. *(For more information, see 7.16, File: **Place**.)*

26.4

Modified Link

This icon indicates that the file for the external link has been altered since it was placed into the document. The link has the capacity to print, but it will likely print differently than it appears in the file. Modified links ought to be updated without delay. *(For more information, see 26.8, Update Link.)*

26.5

Missing Link

This icon indicates that the link cannot be located and the document cannot print as intended. This usually happens when external files are placed in a different directory, or when linked files are not included when a file is handed off. Missing links must be replaced. *(For more information, see 26.6, Replace Link.)*

26.6

Replace Link

Use this button to swap a selected item in the Links palette with an external file. Both linked and embedded art may be replaced. Once the command is executed, the Place dialog box opens. Replacement links may be linked or embedded freely. The replacement art is aligned about the center of the original link's bounding box.

Issues to Consider

Transformations applied to links are applied to replacements. If you have scaled or in some other way transformed embedded art, the replacement will be transformed in the same way. If your chose to link when you replaced, you can change the way the transformations are treated using the Placement options preference. *(For more information, see 26.15, Placement Options.)*

Objects may be replaced using the Place command. You may replace selected items in the Links palette by enabling the Replace option in the Place dialog box. *(For more information, see 7.16, File: Place.)*

Multiple Objects may be replaced at once. If more than one object is selected in the Links palette, you can replace more than one file at a time. Illustrator will offer you a different dialog box for each item to be replaced. The items will be replaced from the top of the Links palette down. Unless you are replacing all of the links with the same file, it's usually easier to replace art one at a time.

26.7

Go To Link

Use this button to select the highlighted link in the document and switch the view location of the document to place the item in the center. This command is useful for finding the link objects in a document quickly. This command is often used while inspecting links for print viability.

Hold down the (Option) [Alt] key while clicking the button to enlarge view depth to fit the link in the window.

26.8

Update Link

Use this button to refresh the connection to an external linked file. This command is only available when linked files are highlighted in the Links palette. When the command is executed, the preview of the link is redrawn to indicate any changes in the source file.

Issues to Consider

You may be prompted to update links automatically. If you are working on link source files during your working Illustrator session, you may be prompted to save automatically as Illustrator notices the changes in the files modification date. This will come in the form of an alert dialog box.

This option is not available to embedded art. Embedded art has no connection to external files. To be updated it must be replaced.

26.9

Edit Original

Use this button to open the selected link in its authoring application. This is usually done to make changes in the link to better suit the design. The authoring application is the one associated with the file by the system. Commonly, the authoring applications are Photoshop for raster art and Illustrator for vector art.

If changes are made to the external file in the authoring application, you will be prompted to update the links upon returning to Illustrator.

26.10

Links Palette Menu

Use the commands in the Links palette menu to change the appearance of Links palette and to replicate the button commands on the front of the palette.

26.11

Go To Link

This command is the same as the button of the same name. *(For more information, see 26.7, Go to Link.)*

26.12

Update Link

This command is the same as the button of the same name. *(For more information, see 26.8 Update Link.)*

26.13

Edit Original

This command is the same as the button of the same name. *(For more information, see 26.9, Edit Original.)*

26.14

Replace

This command is the same as the button of the same name. *(For more information, see 26.6, Replace Link.)*

26.15

Placement Options

Use this command to set how transformations applied to a link are applied. This is especially useful when links are replacing other links and have inherited transformations. This command is not available for embedded art.

Issues to Consider

This command may result in art that overlaps its bounding box, or the creation of a "mask" that is not apparent in the Layers palette. This can be confusing because it creates art that does not fit its bounding box. The mask isn't immediately visible in the Layers palette and cannot be released directly. To access the clipping mask you will first need to choose Object: **Flatten Transparency**. Any Raster/Vector Balance setting may be used. The group that results will contain a clipping path that can be released.

These options are discarded when links are embedded. If you embed linked art, these settings are removed. This is a concern if you are using these options to create a specific visual effect. Since linked art is often embedded upon saving, this may cause unwanted changes in the appearance of your art.

Placement Options Dialog Box

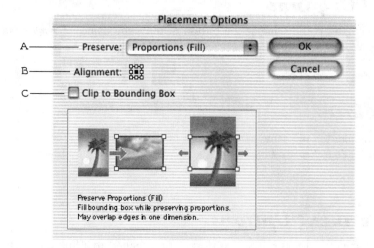

A. Preserve

When linked art is transformed, its bounding box changes size. The source art has its own dimensions, though. These options determine how the source file should fit its transformed bounding box.

Transforms

This option leaves the art transformed as it is. This choice is the default. It enables you to edit the link freely.

Proportions (Fit)

This option transforms the original file to fit into the dimensions of the bounding box while maintaining the proportions of the original. This maintains the appearance of the link while sacrificing exact fit into the bounding box. The Align option is available with this choice.

Proportions (Fill)

This option transforms the original to fill the bounding box using the smaller dimension while maintaining the object's original proportions. The result is that the original will typically overlap the bounding box unless they are the same proportions. The Align and Clip to Bounding Box options are available with this choice.

File Dimensions

This option ignores the transformations and uses the link at its original size. The Align and Clip to Bounding Box options are available with this choice.

Bounds

This option scales the link however required to fit into the bounding box space. Typically this sacrifices the proportions of the object, scaling the width and height differently.

B. **Alignment**

Use this wire frame to set the position the link is scaled from, relative to bounding box.

C. **Clip to Bounding Box**

Use this option to omit parts of the link that fall outside of the bounding box areas. This essentially creates a mask. The masking shape cannot be accessed unless you first choose Object: **Flatten Transparency**.

26.16
Verify Workgroup Link

Use this command to check the update status of a links placed in the document from WebDAV servers. This function is only available when using the Workgroup Server function. *(For more information, see 8.20, Edit: Preferences: Workgroup.)*

26.17
Save Workgroup Link

Use this to write a copy of a file linked from a workgroup server to your local hard drive. This function is only available when using the Workgroup Server function. *(For more information, see 8.20, Edit: Preferences: Workgroup.)*

26.18
Embed Image

Use this command to embed a linked file. This breaks the connection between the art and the source file. If the link is to a vector file, the art becomes editable vector shapes. If it is raster images, the art is added to the document and appears in the Links palette as an embedded object.

Issues to Consider

Transparency in linked art isn't always translated correctly on embedding. Commonly, transparency is flattened to raster art. If you need to add vector art to a document reliably, copying and pasting the art is more sensible.

26.19

Information

This command provides useful details about linked and embedded art. The command opens the Link Information window. Few details are available for embedded art, but good information is available about linked files. The Link Information window is strictly informational and contains no editable options.

For placed files, details include the file's name, directory, size, file format, creation and modification dates, transformation details, and workgroup server location. For art rasterized in Illustrator, only transformation details are provided.

Issues to Consider

The Document Info palette provides better information for embedded art. Details are available there about resolution and such that is of more use than the info in the Links palette.

26.20

Show All

This command shows all of the linked files and raster images in a document, whether they are linked or embedded. Use this command to get a complete picture of link usage in the document.

26.21

Show Missing

This command displays only the missing links in the document. Embedded art is omitted. Use this command to quickly locate large problems in the file.

26.22

Show Modified

This command displays only the modified links in the document. Embedded art is omitted. Use this command to quickly locate minor problems in the file.

26.23

Show Embedded

This command displays only the embedded rasters in the document.

26.24

Sort by Name

This command displays links in alphabetical order. Embedded art is unnamed, and therefore listed first.

26.25

Sort by Kind

This command displays all of the embedded art first, and then all of the linked art.

26.26

Sort by Status

This command displays all of the missing art first, then all of the modified art, followed by art links that are fine.

26.27

Palette Options

Use the palette options to set the size of thumbnails used and to set the interaction of transparency. Choose from the following options:

- **Thumbnail Size.** Select a radio button to choose the size of the thumbnails displayed in the Links palette. Larger thumbnails can impact performance mildly in documents with many links.

- **Show Transparency Interactions.** Enable this option to display the interaction of transparency in linked EPS files. Files that are affected by this option display a yellow embedded art icon in the Links palette. Linked transparency files may not output as anticipated and should be regarded with some suspicion.

The Magic Wand Palette

Magic Wand Palette Overview

The Magic Wand tool selects multiple objects based on their similarity to an object clicked on. The options in this palette are used to set the criterion by which objects are selected. When selecting with the Magic Wand, keep the Magic Wand palette nearby. Options should be set and adjusted frequently to make the selection you want. By adjusting the combinations of items searched for, you can fine-tune your selection. For example, you may want to select all of the objects with the same fill color and a specific stroke weight. Activating both the fill and stroke weight options will limit the Magic Wand's selection to just those objects that meet the criterion. *(For more information, see 1.7, The Magic Wand.)*

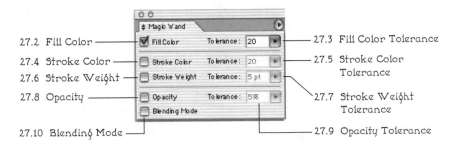

27.2 Fill Color

27.3 Fill Color Tolerance

27.4 Stroke Color

27.5 Stroke Color Tolerance

27.6 Stroke Weight

27.7 Stroke Weight Tolerance

27.8 Opacity

27.9 Opacity Tolerance

27.10 Blending Mode

Each search criterion has a tolerance setting. The lower the tolerance setting for each criterion, the closer the match must be for an object to become selected. Each search criterion has its own tolerance setting. Tolerance sets the amount of leeway both high and low is given when selecting. Clicking on objects with middle values tends to result in more objects selected. For example, if you are selecting objects by stroke weight and decide on a 2-point tolerance, objects with strokes 2 points higher or lower than the object clicked on will become selected. Clicking on the object in the document with the thinnest stroke will only select objects with thicker values. Clicking on an object with a middle range stroke in the document selects objects with strokes both thinner and thicker.

Each color model is selected separately. Spot colors are not the same as process colors and do not match process color searches, even if the spot color's alternate color build is the same. Different color descriptions of the same process color are considered the same, however. So, an RGB and a CMYK description of the same color are selected together using the Magic Wand.

Issues to Consider

Cardinal attributes are compared. When considering objects with more than one fill and stroke, the Magic Wand compares cardinal attributes only. This may differ greatly from the actual visual appearance of the color. *(For more information, see 17.6, Attribute Appearance.)*

Global swatches are considered different colors. Global swatches are different colors than process color swatches. At low tolerance settings, clicking an object that uses global swatches will not select objects that use process colors, even if the process colors are the same colors as the global swatch. At higher tolerance settings, global and nonglobal swatches may be selected together.

27.2

Fill Color

Check this option to select objects with fill colors similar to the initially clicked object. The level of similarity required for selection is determined by the Tolerance setting to the right of this option.

27.3

Fill Color Tolerance

Fill Color tolerance is based upon the color mode of the document. In RGB Color Mode documents this is set from 0–255, in CMYK documents 1–100. In both cases, the lower the value, the closer objects must be to the original to become selected. At 0 or 1, the Magic Wand only selects exact color matches. At 100 or 255, almost any color commonality is acceptable for selection.

27.4

Stroke Color

Check this option to select objects with stroke colors similar to the initially clicked object. Other stroke options, such as dashed line, are not compared. The level of similarity required for selection is determined by the Tolerance setting to the right of this option.

27.5

Stroke Color Tolerance

Stroke Color tolerance is determined and set the same as Fill Color tolerance. *(For more information, see 27.3, Fill Color Tolerance.)*

27.6

Stroke Weight

Check this option to select objects with stroke weights similar to the initially clicked object.

27.7

Stroke Weight Tolerance

Stroke Weight tolerance is the amount greater or less than the original object's stroke weight an object can be to become selected. At a setting of 0 strokes must be exactly the same to become selected. At a setting of .5 clicking on a 2-point stroke would select items with strokes between 1.5 and 2.5 points thick. This setting is purely mathematical and does not round up or down.

27.8

Opacity

Check this option to select objects with opacity similar to the initially clicked object. This compares the opacity attribute of the object. It does not consider any opacity attached to an object due its group or layer affiliation. *(For information, see 36.3, Opacity and 17.2, Hierarchical Appearance.)*

27.9

Opacity Tolerance

Opacity tolerance is the amount greater or less than the original object's opacity an object can be to become selected. For example, at a tolerance of 10% clicking an object with a 60% opacity selects objects with 50% to 70% opacities. At a setting of 0 the opacity must be exactly the same to become selected.

Issues to Consider

This option can be used to select everything that is not the default. Most objects have the same transparency, 100%, by default. Clicking on an object like this selects everything in the document that has not been changed from the default. You can then choose Select: **Inverse** to select all of the other objects.

27.10

Blending Mode

Check this option to select objects with the same blending mode as the original object. This option compares blend modes attached to the object, not the layer or group an object belongs to.

Issues to Consider

This can be used to select everything that is not Normal. Most objects have the same blend mode, Normal, by default. Clicking on an object with a Normal blend mode selects everything in the document that has not been changed from the default. You can then choose Select: **Inverse** to select all of the other objects.

27.11

Show Stroke Options

Use this command to toggle the visibility of the Stroke Color and Stroke Weight selection options.

Issues to Consider

Hiding stroke options does not deactivate them. For example, if you turn on stroke weight and then hide the stroke options, the Magic Wand will still consider the stroke weight when making a selection.

27.12

Show Transparency Options

Use this command to toggle the visibility of the Opacity and Blending Mode selection options.

Mistakes to Avoid

Activating an opacity option and hiding it. If you turn on a transparency option and then hide it, the Magic Wand will still use the setting when making a selection. This can lead to confusion.

27.13

Reset

Use this command to reset the options in the Magic Wand palette to their default settings. By default, the Fill Color option is activated and given a tolerance of 20 (CMYK) or 32 (RGB). No other option is active. The settings in this palette are stored differently for RGB and CMYK documents. If you switch color modes, you will need to reset the palette.

27.14

Use All Layers

Activate this option to make objects on all unlocked, visible layers available for selection. When deactivated, only objects on the same layer as the initially clicked object may be selected by the Magic Wand.

The Navigator Palette

28.1
Navigator Palette Overview

Use the Navigator palette to change the view depth and location of a document, based on a low-resolution proxy.

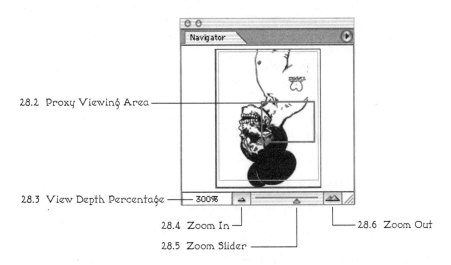

28.2 Proxy Viewing Area

28.3 View Depth Percentage — 300%

28.4 Zoom In

28.5 Zoom Slider

28.6 Zoom Out

Some users prefer the Navigator palette to the Zoom tool and Hand tools because of its ability to show the entire document and to intuitively reposition the view area, and because it behaves identically to the palette of the same name in Photoshop. Although it can be handy, most experienced users find it more efficient bypass the palette in favor of commonly used keyboard shortcuts and saving views. *(For more information, see 14.34, View: New View.)*

The Navigator palette displays a proxy of the entire document in preview mode. The View Box, a highlight rectangle, indicates the part of the document currently displayed. Repositioning and resizing the View Box resets the view depth and location of the document.

Issues to Consider

The Navigator palette is always in preview mode. Regardless of the view settings in the document, the Navigator palette always displays in preview mode. This provides useful perspective when working on a small, complicated section of the document. *(For more information, see 14.2, View: Outline/Preview.)*

In complicated documents, the Navigator may display slowly. This is especially true if the Navigator has been enlarged substantially. If the slowdown is excessive, consider hiding some objects or layers or closing the Navigator palette.

28.2

Proxy Preview Area

This area displays the active document in preview mode, including the artboard and page tiling. As the document changes, the preview is updated to match. The View Box (by default it is red) displays the portion of the file currently visible in the document window. Repositioning the View Box changes the view location of the document. Resizing the box changes the view depth. The smaller the box is, the greater the zoom percentage. As you edit the View Box, the view in the document is updated on-the-fly.

Click in the Proxy Preview area to position the center of the View Box in the position clicked. Click-drag and the highlight box follows the cursor. Hold down the (Command) [Ctrl] key and drag in the Proxy Preview area to create a new highlight marquee around an area you wish to enlarge.

Issues to Consider

Page tiling can be hidden, the artboard cannot. If you hide the page tiling it will be hidden in the Navigator palette as well. If you hide the artboard, it is still displayed in the palette.

Selection edges are not displayed. You cannot tell which objects are selected and which are not by looking at the Proxy Viewing area.

28.3

View Depth Percentage

Enter a value into this field (between 3.13% and 6400%) to change the view depth of the document. To accept a value, hit Enter or Return to change the zoom of the document. View depth is changed about the center of the current display.

28.4

Zoom In

Click this button to set the view depth percentage to the next highest default value. Default values are found in the view depth percentage field in the lower left corner of the document.

28.5

Zoom Slider

Click-drag this slider to set the view depth percentage to a custom amount. Drag to the right to increase the view depth, drag to the left to decrease it. As you drag, the document preview updates on-the-fly. Clicking on the slider sets the value to the position clicked.

28.6

Zoom Out

Click this button to set the view depth percentage to the next smaller default value. Default values are found in the view depth percentage field in the lower-left corner of the document.

28.7

Navigator Palette Menu

Use the commands in this menu to alter the behavior of the Navigator palette.

28.8

View Artboard Only

This option restricts the Proxy Preview area to only the artboard. Without this option on, the Proxy Preview will expand to include objects on the pasteboard.

28.9

Palette Options

Use this dialog box to set preferences for the palette.

Palette Options Dialog Box

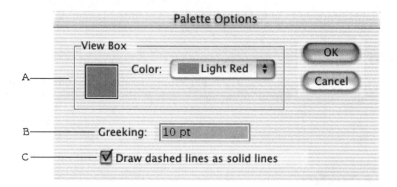

A. View Box Color

This option sets the color for the highlight View Box. By default it is red, and few users change this option. The only good reason to change it would be if your document contained a lot of red objects that made it difficult to see the View Box. Choose a color by double-clicking on the swatch to the left or choosing a color from the menu.

B. Greeking

Use this option to display text below this point size as gray bars in the Proxy Preview. This helps performance by not forcing the palette to pay attention to type.

C. Draw dashed lines as solid lines

Use this option to display dashed lines as solids in the Proxy Preview. This helps performance by not forcing the palette to draw each dash.

The Pathfinder Palette

Pathfinder Overview

The Pathfinder palette is used to create new paths based on the areas of at least two other shapes. Paths may be combined with other paths or used to chop each other into pieces. This simplifies the process of creating custom shapes. For example, instead of drawing a crescent moon shape with the Pen tool, you could create two overlapping circles and knock one out of the other. The Pathfinder palette has two separate sets of functions: shape modes and pathfinders.

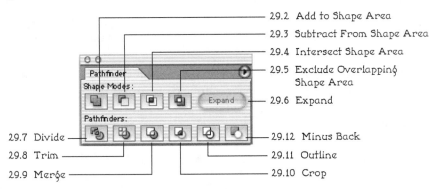

- 29.2 Add to Shape Area
- 29.3 Subtract From Shape Area
- 29.4 Intersect Shape Area
- 29.5 Exclude Overlapping Shape Area
- 29.6 Expand
- 29.7 Divide
- 29.8 Trim
- 29.9 Merge
- 29.12 Minus Back
- 29.11 Outline
- 29.10 Crop

Shape Modes

The shape mode commands create compound shape objects. Compound shapes have the following characteristics:

- Simple paths, blends, envelopes, compound paths, symbol sets, text objects, and other compound shapes may be used to create them.

- Each item in a compound shape has a shape mode. The overall shape of the object is determined by the interaction of the individual shapes and their modes. The component shapes remain independently editable. Changing the shape of component objects changes the compound shape. For example, two paths could be combined with a third shape that took away from the shape area.

- Once a compound shape is made, you can switch the mode of any component at any time. For example, you could convert one of the objects in the shape to the Subtract mode while all others were in Add. To do this, use the Direct Selection tool to select one of the component shapes and click on a new Shape Mode in the Pathfinder palette. You cannot change the mode of the rear-most object in the compound shape.

- When items in a compound shape have different modes, the stacking order of the shapes is important. The mode of each item is applied to the shapes below it. This creates a cumulative effect. Changing the order of items in a compound shape can produce very different effects.

- A compound shape is a single object. They are styled and treated as a unit with respect to fill and stroke and may be used as a mask.

- The top component item's fill and stroke are applied to the compound shape. If the object has more than one fill or stroke, all of them are applied. Although transparency is carried over to the compound shape, effects are not. Effects and styles can be applied or moved to the compound shape after it is created.

- Compound shapes may be turned back into individual shapes (released) or converted into a simple path shape without components objects (expanded).

- Component objects return to their original attributes in the event that the compound shape is released.

- The Layers palette displays the items in a compound shape. You can inspect, add and remove component objects there.

Pathfinders

Pathfinder commands also creates shapes based on the interaction of paths, but do not create compound shapes. At least two paths must be selected to use these commands. Once the command is executed, new paths are created. You cannot adjust components or change your mind once you have applied a pathfinder. When using pathfinders be aware of the following:

• Pathfinders don't work on complex objects. Text must be converted to outlines to be used in a pathfinder command. Envelopes and symbol sets must be expanded. *(For more information, see 9.28, Object:* **Expand***.)*

• Pathfinders may create groups automatically. If more than one path is created as a result of a pathfinder command, the items created will be grouped.

• The shape mode commands can be executed as pathfinders. Hold down the (Option) [Alt] key as you press a shape mode button to execute it as a pathfinder.

• The attributes of the paths created by these commands differ depending upon the command.

Issues to Consider

Compound shapes may be copied and pasted to Photoshop as shape layers. Photoshop 6's shape layers are a kind of compound shape. If you copy a compound shape in Illustrator, you may paste it into Photoshop as a shape layer. To do this you must choose Edit: **Copy** in Illustrator and then Edit: Paste in Photoshop. In the dialog box that results, choose Shape Layer. If you drag and drop into a Photoshop document you will produce a raster layer. Likewise, you can paste copied shape layer paths into Illustrator and continue working on them as compound shapes. To paste as a shape layer it must have copied with the AICB option in the Files & Clipboard preference. *(For more information, see 8.19, Edit: Preferences:* **Files & Clipboard***.)*

Compound shapes can be written as shape layers when exporting to the Photoshop file format. Strokes on compound shapes are converted to stroke layer styles. For this to happen correctly, you must be sure to use round joins on the strokes. Also, compound shapes that contain effects or styles will not be converted to shape layers. *(For more information, see 7.27, File: Export:* **Photoshop (PSD)***.)*

Many different modes in a compound shape reduces efficiency. Where possible, it's better to combine compound shapes of different modes rather than setting each object to a different mode. This is less complex and results in greater efficiency.

You can't change individual fonts with the Direct Selection tool. If you select a type object used in a compound shape with the Direct Selection tool and change its font, it will not affect the object overall. You must either select the entire Compound Shape or use the Type tool to select the text. In cases where different fonts are used in the same Compound Shape you will need to use the Type tool.

You cannot use the buttons to convert single objects to compound paths. The buttons require that you select at least two objects. Some single objects, like groups blends and objects that have effects that give them multiple shapes, may still become compound shapes. To convert these objects, you must use the Create Compound Shape command. *(For more information, see 29.17, Make Compound Shape.)*

29.2

Add to Shape Area

Click this button to create a compound shape from the selected objects using the Add filter. Add unites, or merges the shapes, leaving only the outside edges. (Option) [Alt]-click to apply this command as a pathfinder.

29.3

Subtract from Shape Area

Click this button to create a compound shape from the selected objects using the Subtract filter. Subtract removes the shape from objects behind it. (Option) [Alt]-click to apply this command as a pathfinder.

29.4

Intersect Shape Areas

Click this button to create a compound shape from the selected objects using the Intersect filter. Intersect preserves areas where shapes overlap and discards the rest. (Option) [Alt]-click to apply this command as a pathfinder.

29.5

Exclude Overlapping Shape Areas

Click this button to create a compound shape from the selected objects using the Exclude filter. Exclude discards areas where shapes overlap and preserves the rest. (Option) [Alt]-click to apply this command as a pathfinder.

29.6

Expand

Use this command to convert a compound shape into a path. This renders all members of the shape as paths. Text is converted to outlines, envelopes, blends, and symbol sets are all expanded.

Issues to Consider

Expanding does a better job on compound shapes than expand appearance. Compound shapes can be converted to paths by choosing Object: **Expand Appearance**. This command tends to create separate objects for every object component, including separating fills and strokes. Expand typically renders the item a compound path and passes the object attributes over directly.

29.7

Divide

Click this button to create a new shape everywhere paths overlap each other. Each object created retains its original fill and stroke.

Issues to Consider

Use this pathfinder if you are totally confused about which option to use. Divide creates objects everywhere paths overlap. You can then manually delete and combine the shapes created to get the effect you want. It may be messy, but it can often solve problems.

29.8

Trim

Click this button to remove all of the hidden parts of the paths and remove all of the strokes. Each object created retains its original fill color. Trim is often used to clear out parts of objects that are in back of other objects. This is done before applying other pathfinders, envelope distorts or transparency so that unwanted parts do not interfere.

29.9

Merge

This command is the same as Trim except that adjoining object of the same color are combined into a single object.

29.10

Crop

Click this button to delete all parts of paths that do not overlap the topmost object. Strokes are removed, and hidden parts of objects are removed.

29.11

Outline

This command creates a new open path everywhere objects overlap each other. The paths are stroked in the original color of the object and filled with none. Outline is often used in manual trapping techniques. *(For more information, see C.9, Basic Trapping.)*

29.12

Minus Back

Click this button to knock all other selected object's shapes out of the front most object. The path areas of objects that intersect the top object become the new border for the front path.

29.13

Pathfinder Palette Menu

Use the commands in the Pathfinder palette menu to adjust the functioning on some pathfinders, to manually execute commands, to apply a specialized pathfinder and to repeat previous commands.

29.14

Trap

Use this Pathfinder to create traps in preparation for high-end printing. Traps are thin overprinting objects used to compensate for potential misregistration on a printing press. This pathfinder creates new paths based on areas of different abutting colors in selected objects. The shapes themselves are not affected by this command. *(For more information, see 18.2, Overprint Fill.)*

The Trap item bases the creation of shapes on color differences and the need for trapping. When applying the command to process colors that have color components in common, Trap typically produces no new shapes. This is because colors with common values typically require no trapping.

Issues to Consider

Trap produces shapes in a specific direction. Shapes generated by this command overlap the darker of the two colors. This is called a spread or a choke, depending upon which way the trap goes. It is important to note that the trap goes in a specific direction, because you must trap with the lighter color. If you change your mind about the color you want to trap with, you will need to rebuild the traps. This usually involves activating the Reverse Traps option.

The trapping objects are set to overprint. The fills of the traps made are set to Overprint. Changing the color of the fill does not affect the overprinting status.

The trap shapes are fills, not strokes. The traps made are filled, closed paths set to a specific size. This is important to note because you cannot change the trap size easily. Other trapping models (such as those employed using the Outline command) use overprinting strokes. These may be adjusted for size by changing stroke width. The traps produced here are not easily adjustable.

This filter is not foolproof. This command may or may not trap things. It is based on Illustrator's perception of what requires trapping. In some cases, it will report that it has produced no results, even when trapping is clearly required. You should be prepared to manually trap in the event that this fails. *(For more information, see C.9, Basic Trapping.)*

Pathfinder Trap Options Dialog Box

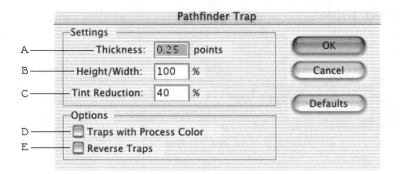

A. Thickness

Use this field to set the width of the trapping area. Most paper-press combinations call for a specific trap size. Your printer should be able to tell you the trap size to use. That value should be entered here. If you do not know the value to use, consider a .3-point setting. Although somewhat large, this size accommodates most uses.

B. **Height/Width**

Use this field to adjust the height to width ratio of the traps. In some cases, trapping needs are based on film being pulled off a take-up roll at the incorrect speed. This results in distended images and requires a different sizing ratio. Unless you know this to be the case, leave this field at the 100% setting.

C. **Tint Reduction**

Use this field to trap with a lighter tint of the color. The value of this field is the percentage of the original color. When trapping a 100% tint of a spot color with a 40% tint reduction, the trap object is styled with 40% of the color. When trapping an 80% tint, with the same 40% reduction, the trap object is styled 32% ink (80% × .4). Tinting traps is done to make it less noticeable by screening it. Not everyone does this. Different shops prefer to trap in different ways.

D. **Traps with Process Color**

Activate this option to create a trap objects that use a process color fill. Normally, Illustrator will trap with the lighter spot color that it sees in the objects used. In the event that you were producing a job with both spot and process colors, you could use this option to build the trap with the process colors instead of the spots.

E. **Reverse Traps**

Activate this option to trap with the darker color instead of the lighter one. Use this option only if you know Illustrator has picked the wrong color to trap with.

Related Topics

C.11   Using the Trap Pathfinder

29.15

Repeat Pathfinder   *(Command) [Ctrl]-4*

Use this command to repeat the last pathfinder or shape mode command executed. The Trap pathfinder is not repeated with this command.

29.16

Pathfinder Options

Use these options to modify how the pathfinder commands are executed.

Pathfinder Options Dialog Box

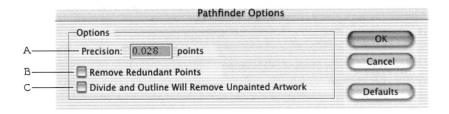

A. **Precision** (.001 to 100 pts)

Use this option to control how closely the pathfinder commands follow the original shapes. At high values, shapes are distorted. At low values, the path is followed closely, but more points are produced and the filter takes longer to execute. Most users do not change this setting from the default.

B. **Remove Redundant Points**

Use this option to delete unneeded points from the paths created.

C. **Divide and Outline Will Remove Unpainted Artwork**

Use this option to automatically delete objects with no fills and strokes created by the Divide and Outline pathfinders. This option often saves time and confusion by removing invisible objects.

29.17

Make Compound Shape

Use this command to convert selected items into a compound shape. By default, shapes made this way use the Add shape mode. This command is useful because it can convert a single object into a compound shape. The buttons in the palette require that at least two objects be selected. For example, you may wish to track text in on itself and combine the letters. Since you are combining a single object, you cannot use the Add button in the palette. You must use the Make Compound Shape command. This is also useful for converting a single group into a compound shape.

29.18

Release Compound Shape

Use this command to convert a compound shape object into its component objects. Objects are returned to their original states with the attributes they had before joining the compound shape.

29.19

Expand Compound Shape

This command is the same as the Expand button on the face of the Pathfinder palette. *(For more information, see 29.6, Expand.)*

The Stroke Palette

Stroke Palette Overview

Use the Stroke palette to set the width and style of strokes on selected objects. Many of the options in this palette are hidden by default. To show all the fields, choose Show Options from the Strokes palette menu. *(For more information, see 30.7, Show/Hide Options.)*

Strokes straddle vector paths, half on one side, half on the other. By default they appear in front of fills. (For more information, see *5.2, Stroke, 17.1, Appearance Palette Overview, and 20.3, Stroke.)*

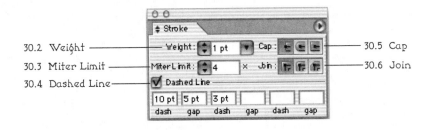

30.2

Weight

Use this field to set the width of the stroke. You can set a width in three ways. You can type a value directly into the field. You can choose one of the values from the pop-up menu to the right of the field or you can use the up and down buttons to increase or decrease the stroke weight incrementally.

Issues to Consider

The incremental arrows use different values depending upon the Stroke units preference. This setting is found in the Edit: Preferences: **Units & Undo** dialog box. When set to points and pixels, the arrows change the stroke weight by 1 point or pixel. When set to other measures, the arrows change the stroke weight by around 3 points.

Very thin stroke weights may not print. Setting strokes to very thin weights may not print correctly in some paper-press combinations. This is especially true when strokes are set to color values different that 100% of an ink. Consider also any scaling that may be applied to the art in a page layout application. An effective stroke weight of less than .5 points should be regarded as a potential printing problem.

A stroke weight of 0 is a stroke of None. If you set the stroke weight to 0 the stroke color is set to None. This often happens accidentally when using the down buttons to set stroke weight. If you reset the stroke width to a positive number, it is assigned the current color in the Color palette. Often, this will return the stroke to its original color, but if the Fill swatch is forward in the palette it will be assigned that color.

30.3
___

Miter Limit

Use this option in conjunction with miter joins on strokes. *(For more information, see 30.6, Join.)* Choose a value between 1 and 500.

Miter joins are sharp, pointed corners on anchor points with no curve handles. When angles are tight, these miters can get long. Miter limit sets the upper limit the stroke width can be before Illustrator converts the corner to a bevel join. A bevel join is a flat corner. Multiply the stroke weight by the miter limit to set the width a stroke may be at a corner. If stroke becomes thicker than this amount at the corner, the join is beveled. The higher the miter limit, the more apt a corner is to remain a miter join. This option may result in paths that have both miter and bevel joins.

Issues to Consider

A miter limit of 1 is the same as a bevel. Setting this to 1 results in every miter being converted to a bevel.

The more acute the angle of a corner, the more important is the miter limit. Sharp turns often result in long, spindly joins. If your path has many of tight corners,consider adjusting miter limit.

30.4
___

Dashed Line

Activate this option to convert a solid stroke into a dashed one. Enter a value between 0 and 1000 pts.

Set the size of the dashes and gaps with the dash and gap fields that are enabled when this option is activated. Up to three sizes of dash and gap may be set to create an irregular pattern. It is not necessary to fill all the fields, but at least the first dash field must be completed. If you delete the value in first field, the dashed line option deactivates itself.

Each dash uses the cap setting for the stroke. You can use this to create rounded dashes or to thicken the dashes by adding projecting caps. The size of the dash is set prior to the addition of caps. Make circular dashes by giving the stroke a dash of 0 and using rounded caps.

30.5

Cap

Use this setting to establish how the ends of open paths and dashes are treated.

Cap Options

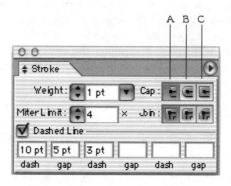

A. **Butt**

Butt caps end the stroke cleanly at the end of the path. No additional distance is used.

B. **Round**

Round caps end paths in semicircles.

C. **Projecting**

Projecting caps continue the stroke one half of the stroke weight after the end of the path. This sets the stroke the same distance in all directions away from the path.

30.6

Join

Use this setting to establish how the corners of paths are treated.

Join Options

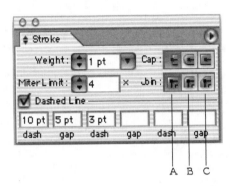

A. **Miter Join**

This option creates pointed corners. If the point extends past the distance set in miter limit, the corner is switched to a bevel. *(For more information, see 30.3, Miter Limit.)*

B. **Round Join**

This option creates curved corners.

C. **Bevel Join**

This option creates squared corners.

30.7

Show/Hide Options

Use this command to toggle the visibility of all of the fields except stroke weight. This is commonly done when you are creating basic strokes that do not require adjustment. Hiding the options does not deactivate them.

The Style Palette

31.1
Style Palette Overview

Use the Style palette to store and apply object appearances.

The contents of the Appearance palette may be stored as a style. The Appearance palette contains all of the information about an object's fill, stroke, effects, and transparency. The Appearance palette is also used to edit and redefine styles. *(For more information, see 17.1, Appearance Palette Overview.)* The style may then be applied to other objects, similar in effect to using the Eyedropper to copy and paste attributes between objects.

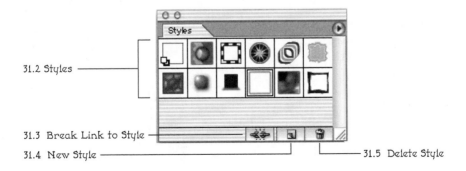

31.2 Styles

31.3 Break Link to Style

31.4 New Style

31.5 Delete Style

Styles are linked to the objects that use them. As styles are edited, the objects that use them are updated to match. This automatic connection is an important feature of styles and should be considered when employing them.

Styles tend to fall into one of two uses:

- **For special effects.** These styles are complex, often involving multiple fills and strokes with nested effects and transparency. Many of the default styles fall into this category. They are often used when the object is the center of attention or to create a specific design effect.

- **For production.** They are basic fill and stroke combinations. For example, a corporate spot color fill and 1-point black stroke can be saved and applied to objects as needed.

Issues to Consider

The default style is a quick way to remove complex Appearance. Many users, especially those new to Styles, apply styles and effects accidentally and wish to remove them. Clicking the default style removes effects and extra attributes from the object without having to use the Appearance palette.

The default fill and stroke in the toolbox are actually a style. Since styles can be edited and changed, you can switch the default settings to ones of your choice. The default style is the first one in the Swatches palette. It contains the same "white fill black stroke" icon that appears in the toolbox. To do this, (Option) [Alt]-drag an existing style atop the default style swatch. This makes it easier to apply a commonly used style, because you can use the "d" keyboard shortcut to set objects to the default style.

If you change the default style in the startup document, the default style is changed. For example, you could set up a 2-point default fill instead of a 1-point. *(For more information, see A.3, Customizing Illustrator's Defaults.)*

Styles are a document resource. Styles are saved with a document. Document styles may be loaded as libraries. Since styles take up disc space many users delete all unused styles after completing work on a file.

Related Topics

31.2

Styles

Styles in the document are displayed in this portion of the palette. Styles can be displayed by name or as a thumbnail. Thumbnails are a low-resolution proxy of what the style looks like applied to a square. Smaller thumbnails are also displayed with the name of the style.

To apply a style to selected objects, click on the style in the palette. Alternatively, drag a style directly onto an object. When a style is applied to an object, the style is indicated with a square around the style. Styles may also be selected in the palette for editing, duplicating, and deleting. To select multiple continuous styles, click on a style and then Shift-click on a second style. To select multiple noncontiguous styles, click on a style and then (Command) [Ctrl]-click a second style. Highlight the palette by (Option-Command) [Alt-Ctrl]-clicking on the palette. Once the palette is highlighted, you can select styles by typing their names.

Replace a style by (Option) [Alt]-dragging a style on top of it in the palette. The style will be surrounded by a black box to indicate the style is to be replaced. Reposition a style in the palette by dragging it into a new position. A black bar indicates the new position the style will occupy in the palette.

Double-click on a style to set its options. The only option styles have are their names. Style names appear when the palette is in list view or as tool tips when in thumbnail view.

31.3

Break Link to Style

Click this button to sever the connection between an object and a style. The object retains its appearance, but is not updated as the style changes. You might use this command before altering the definition of a style in order to preserve the appearance of objects.

Any time you alter the attributes of an object that uses a style, the link to the style is broken automatically.

31.4

New Style

Use this button to create new styles and to duplicate existing styles.

Click this button to record the appearance of a selected object as a style. When you do this, a new style with a default name is created. To name a style as you create it, hold down the (Option) [Alt] key as you click the button. Drag selected styles onto this button to duplicate them.

31.5

Delete Style

Use this button to delete styles. Click this button to delete selected styles in the palette. Alternately, drag selected styles onto the button. When clicking the button, you will be warned with an alert dialog box. (Option) [Alt]-click the button to bypass the warning.

Deleting a style does not change the appearance of objects that use the style.

31.6

Style Palette Menu

Use the commands in the Style palette menu to change the appearance of the Style palette and to edit styles.

31.7

New Style

This command is the same as the button of the same name. *(For more information, see 31.4, New Style.)*

31.8

Duplicate Style

Use this command to copy selected styles. Duplicated styles are named the same as the originals with the addition of a number at the end to differentiate it. Selecting this command is the same as dragging existing styles in the palette on to the New Style button.

31.9

Merge Styles

Use this command to create a new style that contains the appearance settings of at least two existing styles. This is usually done to create style variations. To merge styles, select the styles in the palette you want to merge and choose the command. A dialog box will prompt you to name the new style.

The new style will contain all the attributes of the styles used to generate it. This usually results in a style with multiple fills and strokes. The items will be added from top to bottom in the order the original styles were in the palette.

31.10

Delete Style

This command deletes selected styles in the palette. It is the same as the button of the same name.

31.11

Break Link to Style

This command is the same as the button of the same name. *(For more information, see 31.3, Break Link to Style.)*

31.12

Select All Unused

Use this command to select all of the styles in the palette that have not been applied to objects. This is usually done so that you can delete all the unnecessary styles at once.

31.13

Sort by Name

Use this command to put the styles in the palette in alphabetical order. This works whether the palette is in thumbnail or list view.

31.14

Thumbnail View

Use this command to display styles as square swatches. This is the default view and it takes up the least monitor space. The swatches show an approximation of what the style would look like when applied to a square. Hold the cursor over a style to see its name as a pop-up tool tip. Styles fill the palette left to right, top to bottom in this view.

31.15

Small List View

Use this command to display styles as small square swatches with their names next to them. The small swatches show an approximation of what the style would look like when applied to a square. Styles fill the palette top to bottom in this view.

31.16

Large List View

This command is the same as small list view except that larger swatches are used. The swatches are the same size as those used in thumbnail view. This view takes up a lot of monitor space but provides a complete view of the thumbnail and the style name.

31.17

Override Character Color

Use this option to set the fill and stroke of characters to none when applying a style to text. Activating this option makes the style appear the same when applied to type as it does when applied to other objects. Deactivated, the attributes of the type are retained.

This option affects colors applied to characters, not to text objects. You must select characters with one of the Type tools to edit the attributes of the of the characters.

31.18

Style Options

Use this command to open the Style options dialog box. Styles only have one attribute name. Use this command to open the dialog box to change the name of styles.

The SVG Interactivity Palette

SVG Interactivity Overview

Use the SVG palette to add interactivity to your document when exported as an SVG file. Interactivity is basically a response to a user's actions. A rollover button is a common example. When the user does something (placing the cursor in a specific position) something happens (a graphic changes). The thing the user does is called an event. Events trigger a response and the interaction is written as JavaScript into the SVG.

32.2 Event

32.3 JavaScript

32.4 JavaScript Text Box

32.5 Link JavaScript Files

32.6 Remove Selected Entry

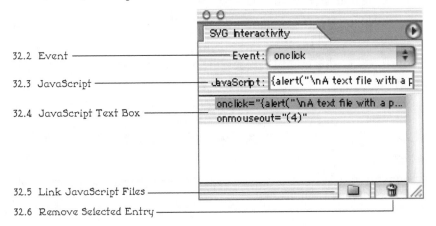

To begin the process of creating interactivity, first select or target an item. The item could be an object, layer, or group. Next, choose an event for that object and associate a JavaScript with it. For example, you might create a box you want to act as a button. You would select the box, and then choose an event and code in the JavaScript that went with that event.

Issues to Consider

Interactivity doesn't work in Internet Explorer for the Mac. Because the Microsoft browser doesn't give JavaScript access to plug-ins, SVG interactivity does not work in the current (5.1) version of IE. There is currently no work-around for this.

Illustrator includes sample SVG and JavaScripts. You can find sample SVG and a JavaScript events file in the directory Adobe Illustrator 10/Sample Files/Sample Art/SVG. There are also a number of samples available online at *www.adobe.com/SVG*.

32.2

Event

Use this menu to set the behavior that triggers the interactivity. The Event menu contains the following items:

- **onfocusin.** Use this event to trigger the action when the item gets focus, such as being selected.

- **onfocusout.** Use this event to trigger the action when the item loses focus, such as another item being selected.

- **onactivate.** Use this event to trigger the action when a key is pressed or the mouse is clicked.

- **onmousedown.** Use this event to trigger the action when the mouse button is held down over the item.

- **onmouseup.** Use this event to trigger the action when the mouse button is released over the item.

- **onclick.** Use this event to trigger the action when the mouse button is clicked over the item.

- **onmouseover.** Use this event to trigger the action when the mouse is over the item.

- **onmousemove.** Use this event to trigger the action when the mouse moves.

- **onmouseout.** Use this event to trigger the action when the mouse button is moved away from the item.

- **onkeydown.** Use this event to trigger the action when a key is pressed down.

- **onkeypress.** Use this event to trigger the action when a key is pressed.

- **onkeyup.** Use this event to trigger the action when a key is released.

- **onload.** Use this event to trigger the action when the entire SVG file has been loaded into memory. This is usually used to set up functions and variables at the beginning of the interaction.

- **onerror.** Use this event to trigger the action when an error happens, such as something loading incorrectly.

- **onabort.** Use this event to trigger the action when the page loading is stopped before the item is loaded.

- **onunload.** Use this event to trigger the action when the SVG is removed from the window.

- **onzoom.** Use this event to trigger the action when the view depth of the document is changed.

- **onresize.** Use this event to trigger the action when the view of the document is resized.

- **onscroll.** Use this event to trigger the action when the scrollbars are used or if the view location is changed.

32.3

JavaScript

Enter JavaScript to be executed directly into this field. As you do, the script and the event that trigger it are written into the JavaScript Text Box.

Many users copy and paste JavaScript text from other authoring applications rather than entering it directly here.

32.4

JavaScript Text Box

Each event and response for an item is listed here as a separate item. Text continues on in a straight line until the argument is complete. Select items on the list by clicking them. Selected items appear in the JavaScript field where they may be edited. Shift-click to select multiple items next to each other, (Command) [Ctrl]-click to select multiple items that aren't next to each other in the list. Selected items may be deleted.

32.5

Link JavaScript Files

Click this button to attach external JavaScript, SVG, or HTML files to the document. This is commonly done to use existing functions and commands built into other documents.

JavaScript Files Options Dialog Box

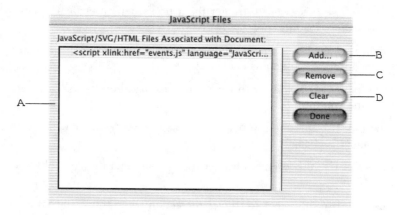

A. Associated Files

This field lists all of the external files attached to the document. Select an entry by clicking on its name.

B. Add

Click this button to add external files to the document.

C. Remove

Click this button to remove a selected file from the Associated files list.

D. Clear

Click this button to remove all of the associated files from the list.

Add JavaScript Files Dialog Box

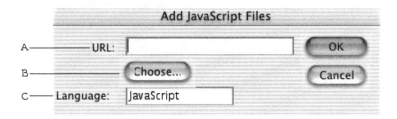

A. URL

This field lists the path to the external file. If you know the web address of the file to be linked, you can enter it here.

B. Choose

Click this button to navigate to a local file. An Insert dialog box opens, enabling you to find and attach local files.

C. Language

Use this field to enter the format of linked files. By default, the language is JavaScript.

32.6

Remove Selected Entry

Click this button to delete selected events from the JavaScript Text Box. Unlike other palettes, no warning is given when deleting events.

32.7

Delete Event

Use this command to delete selected events from the JavaScript Text Box.

32.8

Clear Events

Use this command to remove all of the events for an object.

32.9

JavaScript Files

This is the same as the Link JavaScript Files button. *(For more information, see 32.5, Link JavaScript files.)*

The Swatches Palette

Swatches Palette Overview

Use the Swatches palette to save colors, gradients, and patterns, to apply color, and to manage swatches. Swatches are a key part of most workflows. Use them to select and edit colors consistently and to organize your choices.

Swatches are a required part of a spot color workflow. Whether you are defining your own new spot colors or loading them from libraries, spot colors must be defined as a swatch.

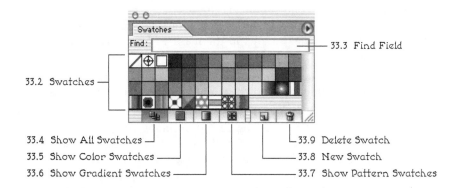

33.3 Find Field

33.2 Swatches

33.4 Show All Swatches
33.5 Show Color Swatches
33.6 Show Gradient Swatches

33.9 Delete Swatch
33.8 New Swatch
33.7 Show Pattern Swatches

Some users disregard swatches and define and apply color in an object-by-object basis. Using swatches has the following advantages:

- **It organizes the items used** and makes them easily available for other objects.

- **It encourages a printed swatch workflow.** When working for print it is best to pick colors from printed swatch books. This helps you forecast color based on real paper samples. Entering process color numbers from these swatch books is often done as a swatch.

- **It enables global color replacement.** If you later decide that all of the greens used should be blues, you can switch them quickly using swatches. You could switch them without swatches, but the process is more time consuming.

- **Provides color communication with service bureaus.** When others are inspecting your work for processing, it is easier for them if you have organized your work and included only the swatches used.

- **Prevents you from choosing incorrect colors.** If you are working on a web-safe color palette, or with a set of corporate colors, using swatches helps prevent you from choosing out-of-gamut or incorrect colors.

33.2

Swatches

Swatches in the palette may be viewed as thumbnails or by their names. To apply a swatch to a fill or stroke, select the object and confirm the attribute you want to set is forward in the Tools or Color palette. Click a swatch to apply it to the selected fill or stroke. A highlight box surrounds the swatch, indicating its use. Alternatively, drag a swatch out of the palette and onto an object. The cursor becomes a crosshair as you do. The swatch is applied to the fill or stroke of the object, whichever is forward in the Color palette and Tools palette.

When dragging a swatch onto a gradient mesh, swatches can color individual mesh points or areas of color. Drag the swatch directly atop a mesh point to color it. Drag a swatch into an area in the mesh without points and all the points surrounding it are colored with the swatch.

Swatches may also be dragged into the Gradient palette to create a gradient slider. Drag a swatch into the gradient ramp to create a new slider, (Option) [Alt]-drag a swatch onto an existing slider to replace it.

Reposition a swatch in the palette by click-dragging it into the position you want. A black bar indicates the position the swatch will occupy as you drag. Select a swatch to be edited, duplicated, or deleted by clicking on it. To select multiple contiguous swatches, click on a style and then Shift-click on a second swatch. To select multiple noncontiguous swatches, click on a swatch and then (Command) [Ctrl] on a second one. Highlight the palette by (Option-

Command) [Alt-Ctrl]-clicking on the palette. Once the palette is highlighted, you can select swatches by typing their names.

Replace a swatch by (Option) [Alt]-dragging a style on top of it in the palette. The swatch will be surrounded by a black box to indicate the style is to be replaced. If the swatch is replacing a different kind of swatch (for example, a pattern swatch replacing a gradient) you will be prompted with an alert dialog box.

Start Up Swatches

Swatches are a document level resource. They are saved with the document. Any changes you make to the swatches only affect that document. Each time you create a new document, Illustrator resets the swatches to the default set.

The default set of swatches comes from two documents: Adobe Illustrator Startup_CMYK and Adobe Illustrator Startup_RGB. There is a different start up document for each of the two color modes Illustrator supports. When a new document is created, Illustrator reads the swatches in the appropriate document and populates the new file with them.

Changing the contents of the Swatches palette in either of these documents changes the default sets. Both files live in the directory Adobe Illustrator 10: Plug-ins. They are loose in this directory. Change the swatches in either of these documents and relaunch Illustrator. New documents created after that will use the edited default swatch set.

Default Swatches

Illustrator has two swatches you can't edit, duplicate or delete. The [None] and [Registration] swatches are used by the application and cannot be altered. Theses swatches are first and second by default in the palette, but can be repositioned.

The [None] swatch is used for objects with negative space. It is the first one in the palette by default and has a red diagonal line through it. [Registration] is a color used for registration and printers marks when making separations from Illustrator. It is the second swatch in the palette by default and has a crosshair in it. [Registration] prints 100% on all printing plates, including the four process color plates. It should not be used for anything except registration marks.

Color Swatches

There are three kinds of color swatches: color, global color, and spot color. They differ in the model they use for printing and in their connection to the objects that use them. Swatches you create from scratch are standard color swatches by default. To create a global or spot color, you must edit the swatch's options.

Standard color swatches are repositories for saving color definitions. There is no special connection between the swatch and the object that uses the swatches. If you change the definition of the swatch, objects are not updated to match unless they are selected when you alter the definition.

To change a swatch's options double-click it, or select it and choose Swatch Options from the Swatches palette menu.

Spot Color

Spot colors are printed with a custom printing ink on press. The color comes from a single colored ink rather than from a combination of multiple colored inks. This is usually done to reduce printing costs or to create a color not reproducible with the standard process inks. Spot colors are also used to keep specific colors, such as colors in logos, consistent over a press run. Objects colored with a spot color swatch may be styled with tints of the color and change colors automatically if the swatch is redefined.

Once a spot color swatch is defined, you may define swatches from tints of the spot color. That is, if you create a percentage of the color in the color palette and then create a new swatch, the new swatch will be a saved tint of the first spot color, not a new spot color.

Spot color swatches are indicated in small and large thumbnail view by a white triangle with a black spot in the lower-right corner. In list view they are indicated by a gray spot in a white box next to their name.

Issues to Consider

Spot colors may be converted to process automatically. Some techniques result in spot colors being converted to process color equivalents. These techniques include: making a spot color object transparent; giving spot color objects a blend mode; and mixing spot with process colors or different spot colors in a gradient, a gradient mesh, or a blend.

Global Color

Global colors are process color swatches that have a connection to the objects that use them. Create one by choosing the Global option in the Swatch Options dialog box. Objects that are styled with global colors may be given tints of the color. The Color palette displays a tint slider instead of the standard process sliders. Further, if the swatch definition changes, the color change is updated in the objects automatically. Styles that use the global swatch are likewise updated. Global colors tend to be used in color-controlled environments where only certain colors are allowed.

Global color swatches are indicated in thumbnail view by a white triangle in the lower-right corner. In list view they are indicated by a gray box next to their names.

Gradient Swatches

Gradient swatches store gradient definitions. They have no special connection to the contents of the gradient palette. Changes made in the gradient palette do not affect gradient swatches. To change an existing gradient swatch, you must replace it. Replace a gradient swatch by (Option) [Alt]-dragging another gradient swatch on top of it. Objects that use replaced gradients are updated automatically.

Double-click the swatch in the Swatches palette to open the Swatch Options dialog box. The only editable option a gradient swatch has, though, is its name.

Pattern Swatches

Pattern swatches store pattern tiles. Pattern tiles cannot be edited, but must be replaced. Replace a pattern swatch by (Option) [Alt]-dragging another pattern swatch on top of it. Objects that use replaced patterns are updated automatically. *(For more information, see 8.7, Edit: **Define Pattern**.)*

Double-click the swatch to open the Swatch Options dialog box. The only editable option a pattern swatch has is its name.

Swatch Options Dialog Box

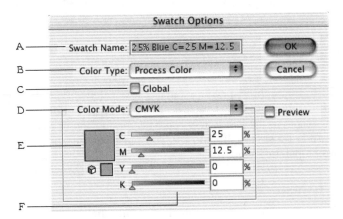

A. Swatch Name

Use this field to attach a name to a swatch. By default, new swatches are given sequential names. Swatch names appear when the palette is in list view or as tool tips when the cursor is over a swatch. This is the only editable field for pattern and gradient swatches.

B. **Color Type**

Use this menu to set the color separation model of the swatch. Colors may be spot or process.

C. **Global**

Use this option to create a global swatch. Global swatches are viewed as a single tint slider in the Color palette and automatically update objects that use them as they change. Spot colors are global by default. This cannot be changed.

D. **Color Mode**

Set the color mode used to describe color. *(For more information, see 20.1, Color.)*

E. **Color Swatch**

This swatch previews the colors chosen with the sliders. Shift-click on it to cycle through the color modes. (Command) [Ctrl]-click on it to choose the current color's compliment. If the color is out of the web safe color set, a small swatch with a cube next to it is displayed. Click either to shift the color to the web-safe version of the color.

F. **Color Sliders**

Use these sliders to adjust the colors of the swatch. Add the Shift or (Command) [Ctrl] key as you drag to move all of the sliders together.

33.3

Find Field

Use this field to highlight a specific swatch in the palette. Type the name of the swatch you want in the field rapidly. You must type rapidly as the field highlights any match to the first letters you type, forcing you to start over. This field is not visible by default. To show it, you must choose Show Find Field from the Swatch palette menu.

Issues to Consider

Highlighting the palette lets you navigate with the arrow keys. If you (Option-Command) [Alt-Ctrl] click on the Swatches palette it becomes highlighted. You can then use the up and down arrow keys on the keyboard to navigate through the palette.

33.4

Show All Swatches

Click this button to display a complete list of all the swatches in the document.

33.5
Show Color Swatches

Click this button to display only the color swatches in the document.

33.6
Show Gradient Swatches

Click this button to display only the gradient swatches in the document.

33.7
Show Pattern Swatches

Click this button to display only the pattern swatches in the document.

33.8
New Swatch

Use this button to create and to duplicate swatches. Click this button to create a new swatch from the current fill or stroke attribute. This is done without a dialog box by default. To create a new swatch and open the Swatch Options dialog box, (Option) [Alt]-click on the button.

Duplicate selected swatches by dragging them directly onto this button.

33.9
Delete Swatch

Click this button to delete the currently selected swatches. You will be warned with a dialog box before the swatch is deleted. To bypass the warning, (Option) [Alt]-click on the button. Deleting swatches does not directly affect the appearance of objects that utilize them.

33.10
Swatches Palette Menu

Use the commands in the Swatches palette menu to modify the appearance of the palette and to perform some of the same functions as the palette's buttons.

33.11

New Swatch

This command is the same as the New Swatch button except that it opens the Swatch Options dialog box by default.

33.12

Duplicate Swatch

Use this command to duplicate selected swatches. Be careful when duplicating spot color swatches. Each spot color with a different name prints on its own separation plate.

33.13

Merge Swatches

Use this command to merge multiple swatches into one. Swatches must be the same kind of swatch to be merged. Spot, global, gradient, and pattern swatches may be merged. When swatches are collapsed together, all of the swatches except one are deleted. Objects that used the swatches are styled with the remaining swatch. The first swatch selected in the palette is the one that is retained.

Swatches are often merged to resolve multiple versions of the same spot color. Duplicate versions of the same color may be created accidentally as files that use the same color are placed, or by users who duplicate and rename swathes for their convenience.

33.14

Delete Swatch

Use this command to clear selected swatches. You will be warned with an alert dialog box before the command is executed.

33.15

Select All Unused

Use this command to select all of the swatches in the palette that aren't applied to any objects. This command is usually used to select unwanted swatches before deleting them.

33.16
Sort by Name

Use this command to place the swatches in alphabetical order.

33.17
Sort by Kind

Use this command to reorder the swatches in the palette from top to bottom by type. Color swatches are first, gradients and patterns follow. This command is only available when all of the swatches are displayed.

33.18
Show Find Field

Use this command to toggle the visibility of the Find field at the top of the palette.

33.19
Small Thumbnail View

Use this command to display the swatches as small squares. This reduces the amount of monitor space the palette takes up. Swatch names are only visible as tool tips. When the cursor lingers over a swatch for a moment, the name of the swatch appears in a small floating box next to it.

33.20
Large Thumbnail View

This command sets the palette to display swatches as larger thumbnails.

33.21
List View

Use this command to display the swatches by name. Small thumbnails appear to the left of the swatch's name. Color models icons are displayed to the far right of the name. Global and spot color icons are displayed to the near right of the swatch name.

33.22

Swatch Options

Use this command to open the Swatch options dialog box. *(For more information, see 33.2, Swatches.)*

The Symbols Palette

34.1
Symbols Overview

Symbols are objects that are stored in the Symbols palette. Once stored, you can reuse symbols in the document either as individual instances or as groups of instances called symbol sets. Instances can be placed by dragging them directly into the document from the palette, using the Place Instance button or command or by using the Symbol Sprayer tool. *(For more information, see 4.2, Symbol Sprayer Tool.)*

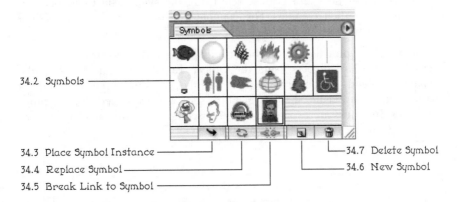

34.2 Symbols

34.3 Place Symbol Instance

34.4 Replace Symbol

34.5 Break Link to Symbol

34.7 Delete Symbol

34.6 New Symbol

Symbols are saved once in the document, and each instance refers back to the definition. This accomplishes several things:

- **Symbols reduce file size.** Since symbols are only coded once in the document, having many instances of the symbol takes up less file size than having many individual objects.

- **Symbols easily integrate with SWF and SVG.** Since these file formats also use a symbol workflow, preparing symbols in Illustrator helps streamline exporting to those formats.

- **Instances are updated automatically.** If you redefine a symbol, all of the instances of the symbol are changed automatically.

- **Instances can be edited using the symbolism tools without greatly impacting file size.** Instances can be transformed, colored, and given styles while still maintaining their link to the symbol. This enables you to create variations on symbols without creating additional objects.

- **Instances can be connected to different symbols and still maintain their transformations.** For example, if you scale an instance and then decide to replace it with a different design element completely, you can switch the symbol the instance represents without losing the scaling. This is often used to create variations on designs without making multiple layouts.

Virtually any object except linked files and graphs can become a symbol. This includes raster art, type, clipping masks, blends, meshes, envelopes, brush strokes, objects with opacity masks, and other symbols. Instances differ from other objects in the following ways:

- **They are based on a rectangular bounding box.** You can't transform them in a way that would alter that rectangle. For example, you can't twirl them, use the liquify tools on them or edit their anchor points with the Direct Selection tool. You can scale, reflect, rotate, and shear them.

- **You can't edit them for content on the page.** You can transform the contents of instances and symbol sets using the symbolism tools, but you cannot edit their contents. For example, you can't edit the text inside a placed symbol set or instance.

In cases where you need to edit their contents, instances and sets can be converted to standard objects using the Object: **Expand** command. Much like expanding blends or converting type to outlines, you can be replace instances with their component shapes. Symbol sets are expanded into symbol instances. Instances are expanded into their component objects. This enables you to edit them using tools unavailable to symbols.

Symbols are document resources. They get saved with document, Changes made to the palette are returned to the defaults when a new document is created. The default symbols are determined by Illustrator's start up documents. You can load the symbols in another document as a library. *(For more information, see 33.2, Swatches, 42.5, Symbol Libraries, and A.3, Customizing Illustrator's Defaults.)*

Related Topics

4.2   *Symbolism Tools*
7.25   *File: Export:* **Macromedia Flash (SWF)**
7.13   *File: Save As: SVG (SVG)*
33.2   *Swatches*
42.5   *Symbol Libraries*

34.2

Symbols

This main part of the palette displays all of the symbols in the document. As with other palettes, they can be displayed as square thumbnails or as a list. Choose the way its displayed from the Symbols palette's menu.

Select a symbol by clicking on it. Once selected, a symbol can be added to the document using the Symbol Sprayer tool, placed in the document as an instance, switched with another symbol, redefined, deleted, or duplicated. Select more than one contiguous symbol by Shift-clicking a second item. Select multiple noncontiguous symbols by (Command) [Ctrl] clicking on additional symbols. If more than one symbol is selected, only the first one selected is used when adding symbols to the document. Change the position of a symbol in the palette by dragging it into a new place in the palette. A black bar indicates the position the symbol will occupy. Hold down the (Option) [Alt] key and drag a symbol onto another to replace the symbol. A black box highlights the symbol that will be replaced.

Add an instance of the symbol to the document by dragging it out of the palette and onto the document or clicking the Place Symbol Instance button.

Double-click on a symbol to edit its options. The only option symbols have, though, are their names.

34.3

Place Symbol Instance

Click this button to place an instance of the symbol in the center of the document. Do this when you want a single version of the art, rather than a set. To place a single instance in a specific location, drag the symbol directly into the document. The instance will be centered about wherever you release the mouse. The document view does not scroll as you drag, so you'll want to set the view to the approximate position you want the instance.

Instances can be edited with the symbolism tools and with some transformation tools. *(For more information see, 4.1, Symbolism tools and 34.1, Symbols Overview.)*

34.4

Replace Symbol

This button swaps the symbol for selected instances and sets from their current ones to the one highlighted in the Symbols palette. This is a powerful tool. It enables you to place and adjust an instance in a design and then switch it with another symbol. For example, let's say you needed to switch all of the logos in a design with a new version. The logos appear at different sizes and at different rotations. If the logo was placed as a symbol, you can select the instances and switch them in one click with a symbol of the new logo.

To replace a symbol, select first instances or symbol sets and then highlight the replacement symbol in the palette. Click the Replace Symbol button and they switch. The replacement's center is aligned about the old instance's center. Any transformations applied to the instance or set is maintained. If this command is used to replace symbols in a set, all of the instances are switched, even if they are connected to different symbols.

34.5

Break Link to Symbol

Use this command to convert selected instances or symbol sets to standard objects. The items lose their connections to the symbols and become editable as objects. Any styling or transformation applied to the instances is maintained in the new objects.

This command always creates groups. Even if the symbol is a single path, the results of this command will be a group. If the Symbol Styler was used to edit instances, styles will be applied to the group created when they are converted, rather than the individual items.

Issues to Consider

This command is often used to create new symbol variations. You may start with a symbol, place an instance in the document, and then convert it to objects using this command. After editing the objects, they may be converted into a new symbol, perhaps even replacing the original one.

Use this command to create new symbols and duplicate existing ones. Click this button to create a new symbol from selected items. A new symbol with a default name will be created. To add a name as the symbol is created, (Option) [Alt]-click on the button.

Another way to create a new symbol is to drag selected items directly into the Symbols palette. The palette becomes highlighted with a black box to indicate that a new symbol is about to be created.

To duplicate an existing symbol, drag it directly onto this button. The symbol is duplicated and given a default name.

34.6

Delete Symbol

Click this to delete selected symbols in the palette. You will be warned with an alert dialog when doing this. Bypass the warning by (Option) [Alt]-clicking on the icon. Alternatively, drag selected items directly onto this button.

34.7

Symbol Palette Menu

Commands in the Symbols palette menu duplicate commands available as buttons on the palette and help organize the palette.

34.8

New Symbol

This is the same as the New Symbol button on the palette except that it opens the symbol options dialog box by default.

34.9

Redefine Symbol

Use this command to discard a selected symbols current definition and replace it with the selected objects in the document. This is commonly done to edit a symbol for content, such as changing some of the objects in it. To use this command, you need to have both objects selected in the document and a symbol highlighted in the palette.

Once a symbol is redefined, all of the instances and symbol sets that use the symbol are automatically updated to reflect the change.

34.10

Duplicate Symbol

This command creates copies of symbols selected in the palette. The new symbols are given default, sequential names and placed at the end of the list in the palette.

This command can also be executed by dragging a symbol onto the New Symbol button.

34.11

Delete Symbol

This command is the same as the button of the same name. *(For more information, see 34.7, Delete Symbol.)*

34.12

Place Symbol Instance

This command is the same as the palette button of the same name. *(For more information, see 34.3, Place Symbol.)*

34.13

Replace Symbol

This command is the same as the palette button of the same name. *(For more information, see 34.4, Replace Symbol.)*

34.14
Break Link to Symbol

This command is the same as the palette button of the same name. *(For more information, see 34.5, Break Link to Symbol.)*

34.15
Select All Unused

Use this command to select all of the symbols that aren't being used in the document. This command is usually used to select unneeded symbols so that they can be deleted.

34.16
Select All Instances

Use this command to select all of the instances of a selected symbol in the document. This is often done before using the Replace Symbol command. *(For more information, see 34.4, Replace Symbol.)*

This command does not select symbol sets that use an instance, even if the set uses the symbol exclusively.

34.17
Sort by Name

This command sorts the contents of the palette in alphabetical order from top to bottom. This option is usually most useful when the palette is in one of the list views. *(For more information, see 34.20, Small List View.)*

34.18
Thumbnail View

Use this command to set the palette to display Symbols as square swatches. This is the default view for the palette. To see an item's name in this view, hold your cursor over a swatch and wait for the name to appear as a tool tip.

34.19
Small List View

Use this command to set the palette to display symbols by name. A small thumbnail of the symbol appears to the left of the symbol's name.

34.20

Large List Symbol

Use this command to set the palette to display symbols by name. A thumbnail of the symbol appears to the left of the symbol's name. The thumbnail in this view is as large as those in thumbnail view. This option takes up the most monitor geography.

34.21

Symbol Options

Use this command to open the Symbol Options dialog box. The only option symbols have is their name. You can also open that dialog box by double-clicking on the symbol itself.

The Transform Palette

35.1

Transform Palette Overview

Use the Transform palette to make basic transformations to selected objects. These transformations are numeric and in relation to a specific point on the item's bounding box.

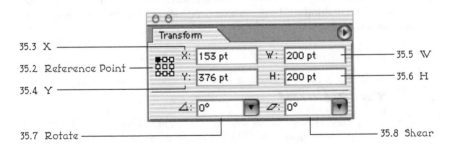

35.3 X

35.2 Reference Point

35.4 Y

35.7 Rotate

35.5 W

35.6 H

35.8 Shear

Issues to Consider

The Use Preview Bounds preference affects this palette. The fields in this
palette will reflect either the size of the path or the size of the object,
depending on whether this preference is activated. Due to strokes and
effects, there may be a great difference between the two. This is a useful
way to set something to a specific size and don't want to do math. For
example, if you need a box with a stroke on it to be a certain size, you can
activate the preference and dial the size directly, rather than subtracting
the stroke weight from the object size. *(For more information, see 8.12, Edit:
Preferences: General.)*

Transformations can be applied to copies. To copy an item as you transform
it, hold down the (Option) [Alt] key as you press Enter or Return to apply
the transformation. The changes are made on a copy of the object.

Math and percentages may be used in the fields. As with most fields in
Illustrator, the fields in this palette support alternate measurements and
math. To enter a width or height as a percentage of current size, key in
the amount of scaling you want and add the percent (%) sign. To multiple the current value in a field be some number, position the cursor after
the value and type the asterisk (*) and the number to be multiplied by.
To divide the value in a field, type the forward slash (/) followed by the
amount after the value. Add and subtract in the same manner, using the
plus (+) and minus (-) symbols.

The transform palette only affects entire objects. You cannot use it to
adjust the positions of anchor points or segments.

Many of these transformations can also be applied as an effect. Except for
shear, you can apply all of the transformations available here as an effect
(by choosing Effects: Distort & Transform: **Transform**). Typically, these
transformations are used to set transformations when an exact position
and size are needed and effects are used when style is more important
than exactness.

35.2

Reference Point

Transformation takes place about a reference point. Illustrator divides the
bounding box of a selection in half horizontally and vertically and places an
imaginary point at each corner, center point, and the center of the bounding
box itself. Each transformation is made in reference to one of these nine
points. For example, if an item is rotated about the upper-left corner, that
point is held stationary and the rest of the object rotates around that point.

The reference point is indicated by a solid black square in the wire frame. The remaining points are all white. To select a new reference point, click one of the white points. Once you do, the X and Y fields adjust to indicate the position of the reference point.

35.3

This field indicates the horizontal position of the reference point on selected items. Enter a value between -16384 and 16384 pts. Positive values are to the right of the document ruler's zero position; negative values are to the left. *(For more information, see 35.2, Reference Point.)*

Changing the values in this field repositions selected items. Press (Option) [Alt] as you press Return to move a copy of the object.

35.4

This field indicates the vertical position of the reference point on selected items. Enter a value between -16384 and 16384 pts. Positive values are above the document ruler's zero position; negative values are below. *(For more information, see 35.2, Reference Point.)*

Changing the values in this field repositions selected items. Press (Option) [Alt] as you press Return to move a copy of the object.

35.5

Use this field to change the width of selected items. Enter a value between 0 and 16384 pts.

If more than one item is selected, this field displays their collective size. Enter a new value to scale the objects horizontally. Press (Option) [Alt] as you press Return to resize a copy of the object.

35.6

Use this field to change the height of selected items. Enter a value between 0 and 16384 pts.

If more than one item is selected, this field displays their collective size. Enter a new value to scale the objects vertically. Press (Option) [Alt] as you press Return to resize a copy of the object.

35.7

Rotate

Use this field to rotate selected items about the reference point. Enter a value between 0 and 360°.

Choose from one of the 15 angles in the pop-up menu or enter a custom value. The default values are not based on the document's default angles and do not change when that preference is altered Press (Option) [Alt] as you press Return to rotate a copy of the object. *(For more information, see 8.12, Edit: Preference:* **General.***)*

Once the command is executed, the field resets itself to 0°. You will not be able to tell how much the object has been rotated from its original position.

35.8

Shear

Use this field to shear selected items about the reference point. Chose from one of the 11 angles in the pop-up menu or enter a custom value. The default values are not based on the document's default angles and do not change when that preference is altered. Press (Option) [Alt] as you press Return to rotate a copy of the object. *(For more information, see 8.12, Edit: Preference:* **General.***)*

Once the command is executed, the field resets itself to 0°. You will not be able to tell how much the object has been rotated from its original position.

35.9

Transform Palette Menu

Use the commands in this menu to perform additional transformations and to alter the options for the palette.

35.10

Flip Horizontal

Use this command to Reflect selected items horizontally about the reference point. Since the objects are flipped 180°, the only important information the reference point provides is whether to flip the items about their left edge, right edge, or center.

35.11

Flip Vertical

Use this command to reflect selected items vertically about the reference point. Since the objects are flipped 180°, the only important information the reference point provides is whether to flip the items about their top edge, bottom edge, or center.

35.12

Scale Strokes & Effects

Activate this option to include stroke weight and effects when scaling objects. This gets turned on and off depending on whether you want to preserve the appearance of the object as you scale it. For example, you may not want to use this option when scaling down objects that already have thin strokes. Although the appearance of the objects will change, the stroke weights are protects. When the option is activated, a check mark appears next to it in the menu.

Issues to Consider

Setting this option sets the preference for the document. If you activate this option for the Transform palette, it will also be the default for the Scale tool, the Selection tool and the Free Transform tools. This option may also be reset by choosing Edit: Preferences: **General**.

35.13

Transform Object Only

Use this option to set the transform palette to disregard pattern fills when transforming items. When this option is activated, patterns are unaffected by scaling, rotating, shearing, or moving objects. Setting this option also sets the default for the other transformation tools.

35.14

Transform Pattern Only

Use this option to set the Transform palette to only affect pattern fills when transforming items. When this option is activated, only patterns are affected by scaling, rotating, shearing, or moving objects. Setting this option also sets the default for the other transformation tools.

35.15

Transform Both

Use this option to set the Transform palette to affect items and pattern fills together when transforming items. Setting this option also sets the default for the other transformation tools.

The Transparency Palette

36.1
Transparency Palette Overview

Use the Transparency palette to set the opacity and blend modes of items, to create opacity masks, and to modify the way transparent items in groups affect each other.

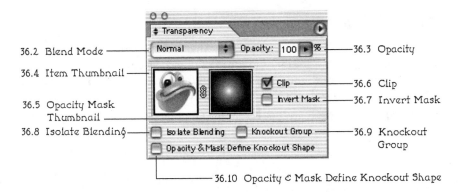

36.2 Blend Mode

36.4 Item Thumbnail

36.5 Opacity Mask Thumbnail

36.8 Isolate Blending

36.3 Opacity

36.6 Clip

36.7 Invert Mask

36.9 Knockout Group

36.10 Opacity & Mask Define Knockout Shape

The use of transparency (opacity, blend modes, or opacity masks) may lead to objects being printing as rasters. Whether or not they are depends upon the settings used in the Document Set Up and kinds of objects used. *(For more information, see 7.45, File: Document Setup: Transparency.)*

Regardless of the settings used, transparency will create rasters in the following circumstances:

- **When using an effect that creates diffuse transparent edges.** Soft, fuzzy edges can't be printed as vectors and must be flattened. The drop shadow, feather, and gaussian blur effects are common examples of effects that must print as raster art.

- **When transparent gradients are atop other gradients.** Gradients on top of solid colors may not result in flattened art, but gradients on other gradients will.

- **When gradient meshes are transparent.** Even if the mesh doesn't interact with anything else, if it is transparent, it will need flattening to print.

- **When spot colors are given transparency.** Spot colors convert to process when they are made transparent. Technically, this isn't a flattening issue, but it is worth noting when working on spot color jobs.

Related Topics

36.2

Blend Mode

Blend modes are a type of transparency that mixes colors that cross each other. When you apply a blend mode to an object or attribute, the colors of an object change based upon the color in the object, the color below it and the blend mode applied. Three values are involved:

- **Blend colors.** These are the colors in the object that has been given the blending mode.

- **Base colors.** These are the colors of the underlying objects.

- **Result colors.** These are the values that are ultimately produced by the blending mode. The value changes whenever you change the blend color, base color, or blend mode. If transparency is flattened, the results become fixed and do not change dynamically.

The math behind blend modes makes them seems obscure and difficult to anticipate. While many users report a hit-or-miss strategy of trying different modes until they find an effect that pleases them, it is important to remember that each mode was created as a production aid. When used correctly, blend modes are often part of a more focused technique.

Issues to Consider

Blend modes compare brightness values. The same colors using the same blending modes may produce different results in different color mode documents. This is because the math works by comparing the brightness of each color component. Since the two color modes use a different number of channels and mix together differently, the underlying math behind blending works differently.

Color management can complicate the math. If you are using color management, it is important to remember that the same color numbers in the color palette do not necessarily represent the same colors in different modes. As a result of this, blend modes may behave differently when color management is on or off.

Most blend modes have a neutral color. The neutral color for a mode is the color that produces no effect on objects beneath them when used. For example, the neutral color of Multiply is white. If you apply multiply to a white object, objects below it show through as though the object were transparent. There are three possible neutral blend colors: black, white, and 50% gray.

Overprinting is similar to a blend mode. Overprinting adds the color values of the blend and base colors directly, resulting in a darker color, often black. Although not technically a blend mode, it behaves similarly and may be flattened as transparency. *(For more information, see 18.2, Overprint Fill.)*

Blend modes behave differently in different color modes. When working on files in the CMYK and RGB document color mode, you may notice a difference in how blending modes behave. This is because blending modes compare individual color component's values. CMYK colors have a different set of color values than RGB and will act slightly differently. Also rich blacks, since they have values in all four color channels behave differently than blacks made purely from black ink.

Normal

This is the default blend mode for most objects. This mode displays the full values of blend colors. Nontransparent colors conceal those beneath them.

Multiply

The resulting color is always darker than the blend and base colors when using this mode. For this reason, this mode is used almost exclusively when creating drop shadows. It handles grays especially well, creating a natural-looking shadow effect.

White is the neutral color for Multiply.

Screen

Screen is essentially the essentially the opposite of Multiply. The result colors it produces are always lighter than the blend and base colors. Screen is sometimes used with gray base colors to produce a light-monotone effect.

Black objects set to Screen become white except when atop other black objects.

Overlay

Overlay is the same as either Screen or Multiply, depending upon the brightness of the base color. Light colors are screened; dark colors are multiplied. The result colors will differ, depending upon the use of grays and colors in base and blends:

- **Blend is full color, base is full color.** Result color is similar to reducing opacity with exaggerated highlight and shadows.

- **Blend is grayscale, base is full color.** Result color is lightened or darkened version of the base color. The result color is lightened or darkened based on the tone of the grayscale image. Darker values multiply, lighter values screen.

- **Blend is solid color, base grayscale.** The blend color colorizes the grayscale underlying color.

Soft Light

The results of soft light are similar to overlay, but less intense.

Hard Light

The results of soft light are similar to overlay, but more intense.

Color Dodge

Color Dodge lightens the base colors. Dodging is a darkroom technique that prevents light from exposing film, producing a lighter image. The hues of colors are shifted toward the blend colors.

Color Burn

Color Burn darkens the base colors. Burning is a darkroom technique that adds extra light to parts of an image while exposing film, producing a darker image. The hues of colors are shifted toward the blend colors.

White is the neutral color for color burn; in both color modes it becomes transparent.

Darken

This mode compares the brightness values of each color component and produces a result color with the darkest version of each.

White is the neutral color for darken. White items with this blending mode become transparent in CMYK and RGB.

Lighten

This mode compares the brightness values of each color component and produces a result color with the lightest version of each component.

Black is the neutral color for this mode. It disappears in RGB mode files. In CMYK flat black produces white. Only 100% of each process color ink makes the color behave as a neutral blend.

Difference

Difference compares the brightness values of each component of the blend and base color. Subtracting the smaller from the larger value of each component produces the resulting colors. So a blend color R: 255, G: 10, B: 10 and a base color R: 55, G: 20, B: 20 would produce a result color R: 200, G: 10, B: 10.

Exclusion

Exclusion produces resulting colors similar to difference but they tend toward neutral grays. Black is the neutral color for Exclusion. As with lighten, only 100% of each process color ink makes the color behave as a neutral blend in CMYK mode.

Hue

Hue replaces the Hue values of the base colors with the values of the blend colors. Saturation and Brightness are not affected. There is no neutral color for this mode.

Saturation

This mode replaces the Saturation values of the base colors with the values of the blend colors. Hue and Brightness are not affected. There is no neutral color for this mode.

Color

This mode replaces the Hue and Saturation values of the base colors with the values of the blend colors. Brightness is not affected. There is no neutral color for this mode.

Luminosity

This mode replaces the Brightness values of the base colors with the values of the blend colors. Hue and Saturation are not affected. There is no neutral color for this mode.

36.3

Opacity

Opacity is the ability of light to pass through an object. Enter a value between 0 and 100%.

You can see through things that are partially opaque. Because of this, the terms opacity and transparency are often used interchangeably. Almost all objects and attributes support transparency. Transparency may also be applied to individual object attributes, or to layers and groups. Because of this, an object's transparency can come from itself, the group that it is in, the layer that it is on, or be limited to only its fill or stroke. This can lead to confusion, but is usually easily managed by the Appearance palette *(For more information, see 17.1, Appearance Palette Overview.)*

Opacity can range from 100% (no transparency) to 0% (completely transparent). As an object become less opaque, its color becomes lighter and you can see more of the objects behind it

Set the opacity of a selected object, either by entering a value in the field and hitting return or enter, or by clicking on the triangle next to the field and then using the opacity slider. The opacity slider is often used when making visual assessments as you apply opacity because it previews the transparency as it is being applied. To set the opacity of a group or layer it must be targeted. Target an item by clicking in the circle to the right of its name in the Layers palette.

Objects on transparent layers or groups affect each other normally unless they have their own transparency setting. It is as though the entire set of objects is considered as a single image and that image is transparent. For example, two overlapping objects with 100% opacity on a 50% transparent layer do not change appearance as they cross each other. Objects on layers below them are shown through them both. This is different than selecting all of the objects and making them each 50% transparent. You should familiarize yourself with the visual difference and know when to use which technique.

Item Thumbnail

The thumbnail displays a low-resolution proxy of the current selection. The thumbnail shows the image without transparency, blend modes, or opacity masks applied to it. This provides a reference to the base appearance and color of the object. The thumbnail is most commonly used when an object has an opacity mask. When a selection uses an opacity mask, you may edit either the items or the mask. When you are editing an opacity mask, the mask's thumbnail will be highlighted with a black box. To begin editing the items, click on the item thumbnail. *(For more information, see 36.14, Make Opacity Mask.)*

Opacity Mask Thumbnail

This box shows a low-resolution proxy of the opacity mask of the current selection or target. An opacity mask instructs objects where to be transparent and how transparent they should be. *(For more information, see 36.14, Make Opacity Mask.)*

When selected objects are masked, a thumbnail of the masking shapes appears here. To edit the mask, click on the thumbnail. When the mask is being edited, no other shapes may be affected. Objects that are added are added to the mask. When the thumbnail is selected, a black box highlights it and the document title bar changes to indicate that the mask is being edited. The title bar puts the name of the masking object or group followed by a slash and the words "Opacity Mask" in parentheses. By default, opacity mask objects are named <Opacity Mask>, but they can be renamed in the layers palette. Once you have finished editing the mask, click on the item thumbnail to return to editing objects.

When editing an opacity mask, only the original objects are displayed. This can make it difficult to find and select objects in the mask. To switch the display to a grayscale version of the masking shapes, (Option) [Alt]-click on the Opacity Mask thumbnail. A grayscale version is displayed because it is the tone of the objects that determines the transparency of the masked objects. To return to previewing the affects of the mask, (Option) [Alt]-click on the Opacity Mask thumbnail again, or click on the Item Thumbnail.

To temporarily disable a mask, Shift-click on the opacity mask thumbnail. A large, red "x" crosses out the thumbnail, indicating the mask is disabled. The masked objects display as they did before they were masked. This provides information about the underlying objects and may give visual clues when problem-solving mask issues.

By default, opacity masks are linked to the objects they affect. This means that as one item is moved, the other moves with it. This way you can adjust the position of masked objects without destroying the mask effect. A chain icon between the item and mask thumbnails indicates their linked status. You may want to unlink the items to adjust the position of one or the other. This is usually done to reposition the masked areas. When the item thumbnail is highlighted, toggle between linked and unlinked by clicking the chain icon. If the icon is missing, the items are unlinked and moving one or the other changes the visibility of the objects.

36.6

Clip

Check this option to make a selected opacity mask act as a clipping mask as well. Parts of masked shapes not directly under masking shapes are made invisible. When the clip option is activated, the thumbnail displays solid black on those areas to indicate they are clipped. If more than one object is used in the opacity mask, all mask shapes are used for clipping. The Invert Mask option has no affect on the clipping bounds. *(For more information, see 9.68, Object: Clipping Mask.)*

Opacity masks may clip by default, based upon the setting of the New Opacity Masks are Clipping option in the Transparency palette menu. *(For more information, see 36.17, New Opacity Masks are Clipping.)*

36.7

Invert Mask

By default, light tones in a clipping mask make objects opaque and dark tones make objects transparent. The darker an object is, the more transparent objects become. Gray values are partially transparent.

Use this option to invert the defaults. When activated, light tones in a masking object become transparent and dark tones become opaque.

36.8

Isolate Blending

Use this option to restrict the effect of blend modes of items in a selected group to other members of the group. This option is applied to groups when members of a group use blending modes. When the option is activated, the effects of the blend mode are only applied to objects that are in the same group. For example, you may wish to items in a group to darken when they cross each other, but not when they cross other objects in the document. Setting the objects to multiply and the group to isolate blending causes this to happen. To activate this option, select or target the group and check the option. Be careful to get it right—the items within the group or layer will have the blending mode, the group will have the isolate option.

36.9

Knockout Group

Use this option to restrict the effect of blend modes of items in a selected group to objects outside of the group. This option is essentially the reverse of Isolate Blending. When objects in a group have blend modes, this option disregards other members of the group when applying the mode. This treats objects in the group as though no blending mode were applied where they cross each other.

There are three states that this option can be set to, on, off and neutral. On is indicated with a check, off is blank and neutral is indicated with a dash. Neutral is the state that comes up when a group or layer contains groups or layers that have a knockout group setting of their own.

36.10

Opacity & Mask Define Knockout Shape

Use this option to base the level of impact that the knockout group option has on the opacity of the objects involved. This option is most commonly used when an object that has both an overlay mode and an opacity mask is atop other objects it is grouped with and the group uses the knockout group option. Although this is a rare set of circumstances, this option usually makes the appearance of the object in those circumstances appear more as the settings applied to it imply. The blending mode follows the opacity, causing the blend effect to fade as the opacity fades rather than making a harsh transition.

This option is applied to the object that has the blending mode and the opacity mask, not the group that contains it. The group or layer that contains the item should beset to the knockout group option.

36.11

Transparency Palette Menu

Use the commands in this menu to manage opacity masks and to control the appearance of the palette.

36.12

Show Thumbnails

Use this command to toggle the display of the item and opacity mask thumbnails (and the clip and invert mask options). The thumbnails are usually hidden when they are not needed to reduce the amount of space the Transparency palette occupies.

When the both the options and the thumbnails are visible, hiding the thumbnails hides the options as well.

36.13

Show Options

Use this option to toggle the visibility of the isolate blending, Knockout Group, and the Opacity & Mask Define Knockout Shape options. These options cannot be visible without the thumbnails also being visible. If the thumbnails are not visible when this command is chosen, they will be made visible when the command is activated.

36.14

Make Opacity Mask

An opacity mask sets the opacity of masked objects based on the tone of the masking objects. This typically sets the opacity of objects differently in different parts. For example, half of an object could be transparent while the other half remains opaque. This is often used to make objects fade into each other or to solve stacking order problems.

The tone of the opacity mask instructs the masked objects how opaque they should be. The darker the tone, the more transparent the masked objects become. White areas in the mask make that area opaque. So if you mask an object with a white to black gradient, the opacity of the object will follow the gradient.

It is important to remember that it is the tone and not the color of the opacity mask that sets visibility. Objects used as a mask retain their colors but it is really the relative lightness or darkness of the color that sets the transparency level. Some users prefer to work with grayscale objects when making masks to clarify the tone of the object.

Objects and groups may be given opacity masks. In the event a mask affects that more than one object, a group will be made automatically. You can create an opacity mask based on existing objects or set up the mask and then add objects to it. To make an opacity mask based on existing objects, first be sure that the object that will become the opacity mask is on top of the objects it will mask. Next, select the objects and choose this command. To make a blank opacity mask select a single object and apply the command.

In either case, when an opacity mask is made, its thumbnail is added to the palette. *(For more information, see 36.5, Opacity Mask Thumbnail.)*

36.15
Release Opacity Mask

Use this command to convert an opacity mask back into standard objects. The objects used as a mask return to the appearance they had before becoming masks.

36.16
Disable Opacity Mask

This command hides the effects of an opacity mask. The mask is not released and may be shown by selecting the command again. You can also disable a mask by Shift-clicking on the opacity mask thumbnail.

36.17
New Opacity Masks Are Clipping

This option sets opacity masks to clip by default. When the command has a check next to it, it is activated. Select the command again to deactivate the option. *(For more information, see 36.6, Clip.)*

36.18
New Opacity Masks Are Inverted

This option sets opacity masks to be reversed by default. When the command has a check next to it, it is activated. Select the command again to deactivate the option. *(For more information, see 36.7, Invert Mask.)*

The Character Palette

Character Palette Overview

Use the Character palette to set the options for text. Open this palette by choosing Window: Type: **Character**. Some of these options are available as commands in the Type menu. However, since this palette has all of the character options in one place, it is more commonly used when all but the simplest type chores are being performed.

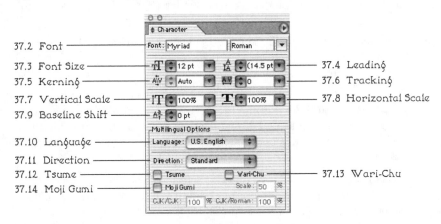

37.2 Font

37.3 Font Size

37.5 Kerning

37.7 Vertical Scale

37.9 Baseline Shift

37.10 Language

37.11 Direction

37.12 Tsume

37.14 Moji Gumi

37.4 Leading

37.6 Tracking

37.8 Horizontal Scale

37.13 Wari-Chu

As you set type in Illustrator, keep the following in mind:

- **Illustrator is not a typesetting application.** It isn't designed to be and it doesn't handle large amounts of type well. If you have a lot of type to set (more than a couple of paragraphs) consider using a page layout application instead.

- **Illustrator is not a custom typography application.** Although it is often used to customize short amounts of type and can create multiple master instances, Illustrator isn't designed to customize typefaces.

Character attributes can be set for individual characters selected with a type tool or for entire selected type objects. The following shortcuts are used in the palette:

- **Show and hide the palette.** Press (Command) [Ctrl]-T.

- **Reset a field to its default settings.** (Command) [Ctrl]-click the field icon.

- **Apply a value.** Press Enter or Return.

- **Apply a value and highlight the current.** Press Shift-Enter or Shift-Return.

- **Apply a value and highlight the next field.** Press Tab.

- **Apply a value and highlight the previous field.** Press Shift-Tab.

37.2

Font

(Option-Command-Shift) [Alt-Ctrl-Shift]-F

Use this field to connect a typeface to characters. Typefaces come in the form of fonts. Fonts are applications that instruct the system how to express the keystrokes you type in. As external applications, fonts have some special concerns when files are printed or handed off to a service provider. You have the following choices:

- **They may be given to the service provider for printing.** This way the fonts you used can be activated by the provider to print the file. The service provider must be given the exact font used. This usually means that the fonts are provided when the job is handed off.

- **They may be embedded in the file.** When a file is printed from an external application, such as Quark or InDesign, fonts can be embedded into an EPS or AI file. In this case, the fonts need not be activated or supplied. *(For more information, see 7.7, File: Save As.)*

- **They may be converted into objects.** Selected fonts may be converted to paths. In this case, fonts are not required to print the file. *(For more information, see 10.10, Type: Create Outlines.)*

The Font field is actually two fields, the first is the font family, the second the font style. You can set both fields at once by choosing a typeface from the pop-up menu at the right of these fields. You can also set either field by keying text directly in. As you type, Illustrator populates the field with matches from the active font set. Once enough of a face's name has been typed in, press Enter or Return to accept a choice.

Issues to Consider

Although type family and style are set in different fields, they are actually a single font. In some applications, you can create bold and italic styles for fonts even if there is no corresponding font. It is a good thing that Illustrator does not support this feature, since it commonly leads to printing problems.

Some styles must be created manually. Some font styles that are commonly available and do not create printing issues, such as superior and small caps, are not available in Illustrator. Using other font options you can manually create these effects.

37.3

Font Size

Use this field to set a point size for selected characters. Set a value between .1 and 1296 pts.

Font size varies from font to font. The same text at the same point size may be very different sizes in different fonts. This is due to the vagaries of the design process. Fonts are measured from ascender (the tallest point in a typeface) to descender (the lowest point in a typeface) plus however much white space the font designer thinks is necessary. Individual character sizes may vary considerably from face to face.

Type size can be increased incrementally using keyboard shortcuts. The amount is determined by Size and Leading preference. *(For more information, see 8.13, Edit: Preferences: Type & Auto Tracing.)*

When setting font size, use the following shortcuts:

- **Increase size by the preference-defined amount.** Press (Command-Shift) [Ctrl-Shift]->

- **Decrease size by the preference-defined amount.** Press (Command-Shift) [Ctrl-Shift]-<

- **Increase size by five times the preference-defined amount.** Press (Option-Command-Shift) [Alt-Ctrl-Shift]->

- **Decrease size by five times the preference-defined amount.** Press (Option-Command-Shift) [Alt-Ctrl-Shift]-<

Issues to Consider

Scaling text objects sets font size. If you scale a type object, the font size will be scaled appropriately.

37.4

Leading

Use this field to set the space between lines in a paragraph.Set a value between .1 and 1296 pts.

Leading (pronounced "ledding") is the vertical distance between the baselines of each line of type. A baseline is an imaginary line the characters sit on. When leading is less than the font size, lines of type may begin to crash into each other.

Set leading by choosing one of the popular choices from the pop-up menu or by keying a value directly into the field and pressing Enter or Return. By default, leading is set to the Auto option. This sets the leading to a 120% of the font size. Leading may be set incrementally using keyboard shortcuts. The amount is determined by Size and Leading preference. *(For more information, see 8.13, Edit: Preferences: **Type & Auto Tracing**.)* Use the following shortcuts:

- **Increase leading by the preference-defined amount.** Press (Option) [Alt]-up arrow.

- **Decrease leading by the preference-defined amount.** Press (Option) [Alt]-down arrow.

- **Increase leading by five times the preference-defined amount.** Press (Option-Command) [Alt-Ctrl]-up arrow.

- **Decrease leading by five times the preference-defined amount.** Press (Option-Command) [Alt-Ctrl]-down arrow.

- **Set leading to current point size.** Double-click the leading icon.

Issues to Consider

The highest leading in a line is used. If different leading values are set for the same line of type, the largest one is used. If you are trying to use leading to nudge individual characters closer together vertically, use baseline shift instead. *(For more information, see 37.9, Baseline Shift.)*

Large leading differences make paragraphs look bad. Be careful when setting different leading values for the same blocks of type. Type looks odd and unprofessional when the spacing is noticeably irregular.

37.5

Kerning

Use this field to set the distance between two characters. Set a value between -1000 and 10000 units.

To set kerning, there must be an insertion point between two characters. Kerning is measured in thousandths of em space units. An em space is the size of an em dash character, commonly the width of capital "M".

Set kerning by choosing one of the popular choices from the pop-up menu or by keying a value directly into the field and pressing Enter or Return. By default, kerning is set to the Auto option. This uses any kerning information that is built into the typeface. When a kerning value appears in parenthesis, the value is being supplied automatically. Kerning may be set incrementally using keyboard shortcuts. The amount is determined by Tracking preference. *(For more information, see 8.13, Edit: Preferences: Type & Auto Tracing.)* Use the following shortcuts:

- **Increase kerning by the preference-defined amount.** Press (Option) [Alt]-]

- **Decrease kerning by the preference-defined amount.** Press (Option) [Alt]-[

- **Increase kerning by five times the preference-defined amount.** Press (Option-Command) [Alt-Ctrl]-]

- **Decrease kerning by five times the preference-defined amount.** Press (Option-Command) [Alt-Ctrl]-[

- **Highlight kerning field while insertion point is active.** Press (Option-Command) [Alt-Ctrl]-K

37.6

Tracking

Use this field to set the distance between characters and words. Set a value between -1000 and 10000 units.

Tracking can be set for selected characters or entire type blocks. Like kerning, tracking is measured in thousandths of em space units. An em space is the size of an em dash character, commonly the width of capital letter "M".

Set tracking by choosing one of the popular choices from the pop-up menu or by keying a value directly into the field and pressing Enter or Return. By default, tracking is set to 0. Tracking may be set incrementally using keyboard shortcuts. The amount is determined by Tracking preference. *(For more information, see 8.13, Edit: Preferences: Type & Auto Tracing.)*

Use the following shortcuts:

- **Increase tracking by the preference-defined amount.** Press (Option) [Alt]-]

- **Decrease tracking by the preference-defined amount.** Press (Option) [Alt]-[

- **Increase tracking by five times the preference-defined amount.** Press (Option-Command) [Alt-Ctrl]-]

- **Decrease tracking by five times the preference-defined amount.** Press (Option-Command) [Alt-Ctrl]-[

- **Highlight tracking field while insertion point is active.** Press (Option-Command) [Alt-Control]-K

37.7

Vertical Scale

Use this field to adjust the vertical width of the characters relative to the baseline. Enter a value between 1 and 10000%.

Vertical scaling is given as a percentage of the characters designed size. Vertical scaling may be set incidentally when type is transformed using any of the transformation tools. This is usually done to create a visual effect, and not to assist in copy fit. This may be applied in conjunction with horizontal scaling.

To set vertical scaling, choose one of the 10 preset amounts from the pulldown menus or type the desired amount directly in the field and press Enter or Return. To reset horizontal and vertical scaling to 100% hit (Command-Shift) [Ctrl-Shift]-X. This field is only visible when Show Options is chosen from the Character palette menu.

37.8

Horizontal Scale

Use this field to adjust the horizontal width of the characters relative to the baseline. Enter a value between 1 and 10000%.

This is given as a percentage of the characters designed size. Horizontal scaling may be set incidentally when type is transformed using any of the transformation tools. This is usually done to create a visual effect, and not to assist in copy fit. This may be applied in conjunction with vertical scaling.

To set horizontal scaling, choose one of the 10 preset amounts from the pulldown menus or type the desired amount directly in the field and press Enter or Return. To reset horizontal and vertical scaling to 100% hit (Command-Shift) [Ctrl-Shift]-X. This field is only visible when Show Options is chosen from the Character palette submenu.

37.9

Baseline Shift

Use this option to set the vertical distance of characters relative to the baseline. Positive values lift characters above the baseline; negative numbers drop it below. This option is typically used to create type effects not automatically available in Illustrator. Superscript and subscript type are common examples. It is also commonly used to align the ascenders of path type to the path.

Set baseline shift by choosing one of the popular choices from the pop-up menu or by keying a value directly into the field and pressing Enter or Return. You may set values incrementally using keyboard shortcuts. The amount is determined by the Baseline Shift preference. *(For more information, see 8.13, Edit: Preferences: Type & Auto Tracing.)* Use the following shortcuts:

- **Increase by the preference-defined amount.** Press (Option-Shift) [Alt-Shift]- =

- **Decrease by the preference-defined amount.** Press (Option-Shift) [Alt-Shift]-hyphen

- **Increase by the preference-defined amount.** Press (Option-Command-Shift) [Alt-Ctrl-Shift]- =

- **Decrease by the preference-defined amount.** Press (Option-Command-Shift) [Alt-Ctrl-Shift]-hyphen

This field is only visible when Show Options is chosen from the Character palette menu.

37.10

Language

Use this option to connect languages to text. This is used when hyphenating words. The rules for hyphenation are different in different languages. Set the option for foreign language text to make it break according to the rules of the language. If more than one language is used in a selection, the setting lists "mixed." This field is only visible when Show Multilingual is chosen from the Character palette menu.

37.11

Direction

Use this option to change the orientation of characters in a vertical text block. This is principally used in Asian fonts, but can be used with Roman type as well. You have the following options:

- **Standard.** This option applies no rotation to the type.

- **Rotate.** This option rotates selected Roman characters 90°.

- **Tate Chu Yoko.** This option sets the type to horizontal within the vertical block.

This field is only visible when Show Multilingual is chosen from the Character palette menu.

37.12

Tsume

Use this option to convert monospaced fonts to proportionally spaced fonts. Most CJK (Chinese, Japanese, or Korean) fonts occupy the same block of white space. Each character is design to fit into the same space. Some include additional proportional spacing information to account for differing character sizes. If you are using one of these fonts or a monospaced Type 1 font that contains proportional data, you can use this option to proportional spacing.

This field is only visible when Show Multilingual is chosen from the Character palette menu.

37.13

Wari-Chu

Use this option to reduce the type size of selected characters and stack them atop each other inline. When the option is activated, the Scale field becomes available. This will proportionally scale characters the specified amount.

This option does not work on path type. It always creates a stack of only two lines of type. This field is only visible when Show Multilingual is chosen from the Character palette menu.

37.14

Moji Gumi

Use this option to change the default spacing between CJK (Chinese, Japanese, or Korean) characters and punctuation or between CJK characters and Roman characters. Enter a value between 0 and 200%.

This option is typically used when mixing languages in a file. Activate the option and then set an offset percentage for CJK characters and other CJK characters or between CJK and Roman type. 100% is the standard spacing. 0% removes extra space between characters, 200% doubles the space. This field is only visible when Show Multilingual is chosen from the Character palette menu.

37.15

Show Options

Use this command to toggle the visibility of the horizontal scale, vertical scale, and baseline shift options. If these options are hidden, the Multilingual options are hidden as well.

37.16

Show Multilingual

Use this command to toggle the visibility of the Language, Direction, Tsume, Wari-Chu, and Moji Gumi options. When these options are visible, the entire palette is available.

The MM Design Palette

MM Design Overview

Use this palette to create instances of Multiple Master fonts. These fonts are Type 1 fonts with editable widths and heights. Each one includes one or more axes you can edit. For example, one may have a weight axis, enabling you to create a custom bold version of the font.

When fonts are edited in Illustrator, they are only available for use in that document. Permanently available instances may be created using Adobe Type Manager Deluxe.

Since each font ships with different options, space prohibits a complete discussion here. For information on Multi Master fonts, consult the documentation that came with your font or visit *www.adobe.com/type*.

The Paragraph Palette

Paragraph Palette Overview

Use this palette to set options that apply to paragraphs. Open the palette by choosing Window: Type: **Paragraph**. Paragraphs are defined by hard returns (the Return key creates a hard return). All the type between hard returns (or a hard return and the start or end of a type block) is considered a paragraph.

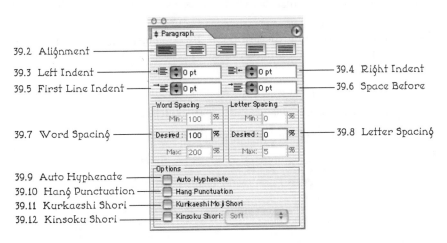

39.2 Alignment

39.3 Left Indent

39.4 Right Indent

39.5 First Line Indent

39.6 Space Before

39.7 Word Spacing

39.8 Letter Spacing

39.9 Auto Hyphenate

39.10 Hang Punctuation

39.11 Kurkaeshi Shori

39.12 Kinsoku Shori

To set paragraph options, the entire paragraph need not be selected. An insertion point anywhere in the paragraph is sufficient. Paragraph options can also be set for entire selected text objects.

Paragraph options all involve copy flow. The alignment of text, the margins, and spacing between words and letters can all be set in this palette. Press (Command) [Ctrl]-M toggle the visibility of the palette.

Mistakes to Avoid

Confusing soft and hard returns. A soft return breaks the line of type but does not create a new paragraph. Create a soft return by pressing Shift-Return.

Related Topics

4.29   Eyedropper Tool
Chapter 37, The Character Palette
Chapter 10, The Type Menu
Chapter 40, The Tab Ruler Palette

39.2

Alignment

Use these five buttons to set the alignment of a paragraph. Alignment determines which side of a text block is left ragged as type lines break to fit space. In left aligned type, the left side of a paragraph is flush and the right side is ragged. Right aligned text is set the opposite. In center-aligned type, both edges are ragged and in justify full lines, neither edge is. The Justify option adds space between words to keep both the right and left edges of a text block flush. The exception is the last line of type, which is left aligned. To add space to the text in the final line so that it is justified as well, use Justify All Lines.

Path type is aligned about the hot point. By default, the hot point is in the position clicked when the type was created. Likewise, point type is aligned about the position clicked when the type was created.

Use the following shortcuts to set paragraph alignment:

- **Left align.** Press (Command-Shift) [Ctrl-Shift]-L.

- **Right align.** Press (Command-Shift) [Ctrl-Shift]-R.

- **Center align.** Press (Command-Shift) [Ctrl-Shift]-C.

- **Justify full lines.** Press (Command-Shift) [Ctrl-Shift]-J.

Issues to Consider

Center align is often used with path type. When creating path type, such as type on a circle, many users prefer to center align type. This makes it easy to set type in a position of type with confidence that an equal amount of text falls on either side.

39.3

Left Indent

Use this option to offset text from the left margin. The amount can range from -1296 to 1296 pts. Depending on the indentation and alignment used, text may extend outside of its boundaries. When applied to left-aligned point type, text actually separates from its anchor point, leaving what appears to be a stray point behind.

Indenting is usually done when formatting text in columns or when using the text wrap option. It's also often done with area type to create text that is offset from its boundaries, often when the bounds are colored. When applied to Center Aligned text, half of the specified value is used. This option may also be set with the Tab Ruler palette. *(For more information, see 10.6, Type: **Wrap**.)*

39.4

Right Indent

This option is the same as Left Indent except that type is offset from the right side of the block. Enter a value between -1296 and 1296 pts.

39.5

First Line Indent

Use this option to indent the first of type in a paragraph. This option is often used in conjunction with tabs to create hanging indentations. Enter a value between -1296 and 1296 pts. *(For more information, see D.3, Creating a Hanging Indent.)*

39.6

Space Before Paragraph

Use this option to add white space between paragraphs by offsetting the selected paragraph. This is used instead of hard returns to open up copy spacing. Adding space in this way enables you to set custom amounts and avoids the type reflow problems caused by extra returns. Enter a value between -1296 and 1296 pts. The first paragraph in a text block does not support space before.

39.7

Word Spacing

This option sets the distance between words in paragraphs. This option is usually used with justified type to finesse the copy flow. It can be applied to non-justified type as well, though. Word spacing increases the default spacing amount without affecting letter spacing. It expresses the amount as a percentage of the default width of a space for the selected font and point size.

Enter a value between 0 and 1000%. At 100%, no extra space is added between words.

When setting justified type, you can choose from the following options:

Minimum

This option sets the smallest amount of spacing allowed. By default, this is set to 100%. At this value, space can only be added between words and not subtracted.

Desired

This option sets the preferred spacing. It sets the default for the paragraph and impacts the overall flow of the type.

Maximum

This option sets the upper limit for spacing. It defaults to 200%, which allows for up to twice the normal spacing.

For non-justified type, only the Desired option may be set. This is commonly used in lieu of tracking to set the copy flow for complete paragraphs. Many users set word spacing first and then use tracking to touch up bad breaks.

These fields are only available if Show Options is chosen from the Paragraph palette menu.

39.8

Letter Spacing

This option adjusts the distance between all the characters in a paragraph. This is usually used with justified text, particularly text set to Justify All Lines, to tweak the copy fit. As with Word Spacing, though, it can also be applied non-justified type. Letter spacing is measured as a percentage of the default spacing added between letters. Enter a value between -50 and 500%. A value of 0% adds no space.

When setting justified type, you can choose from the following options:

Minimum

This option sets the smallest amount of spacing allowed. By default, this is set to 0%. At this value, space can only be added between letters and not subtracted.

Desired

This option sets the preferred spacing. It sets the default for the paragraph and impacts the overall flow of the type.

Maximum

This option sets the upper limit for spacing. It defaults to 5%, which opens up the spacing slightly.

For non-justified type, only the desired option may be set. This is commonly used in lieu of tracking to set the copy flow for complete paragraphs.

These fields are only available if Show Options is chosen from the Paragraph palette menu.

39.9

Auto Hyphenate

Use this option to automatically hyphenate selected paragraphs. This option hyphenates words as needed based on the dictionary for the document and the hyphenation options for the paragraph. Without this option activate, Illustrator will not hyphenate text on its own. You may insert discretionary hyphens in words by typing (Command-Shift) [Ctrl-Shift]-Hyphen (-) where you want to break a word, but this can be time consuming.

The rules for how hyphenating words are based on the language the text is in. This option is set for a document overall. Selected text can also be set to a different language option in the Character palette. Lastly, individual paragraphs have their own hyphenation options that control the amount and placement of hyphens.

Related Topics

*8.16 Edit: Preferences: **Hyphenation***
37.10 Language
39.15 Hyphenation

39.10

Hang Punctuation

Use this option to place punctuation marks that fall at the end of a line of type outside of the type bounds. This usually makes for a cleaner, more pleasing margin.

When this option is activated, the following characters hang: single and double quotemarks, apostrophes, hyphens, em and en dashes, periods, commas, and semi-colons. Question marks and exclamation points do not hang. This option is available for text regardless of its orientation.

This option is only available if Show Options is chosen from the Paragraph palette submenu.

39.11

Kurikaeshi Moji Shori

Use this option when using Japanese fonts to substitute the repeated character option for duplicated glyphs that are next to each other. The characters
display as if you had broken the type line. This option is only available if
Show Options is chosen from the Paragraph palette menu.

39.12

Kinsoku Shori

Use this option when using CJK fonts to keep certain characters from breaking inappropriately. This option keeps characters like a closing parenthesis
with the word it encloses rather than allowing it to break to the top of a new
line. To do this, Illustrator condenses the spacing in the line to accommodate
the characters.

When the option is activated, choose which of the two sets of characters that
will not be allowed to break, Hard or Soft. The Hard set is larger; Soft is the
same set with fewer options. You should also set Kinsoku Shori options from
the Paragraph palette menu. This option is only available if Show Options is
chosen from the Paragraph palette menu. *(For more information, see 39.16,
Kinsoku Shori.)*

39.13

Paragraph Palette Menu

Use the commands in the Paragraph palette menu to customize the appearance of the palette and to set additional multilingual options.

39.14

Hide Options

This command toggles the visibility of the lower half of the palette. This
includes the word and letter spacing options and the choices in the Options
box.

39.15

Hyphenation

Use these options to control how hyphenation may be applied to a selected paragraph. Options may be set differently for each paragraph.

Hyphenation Options Dialog Box

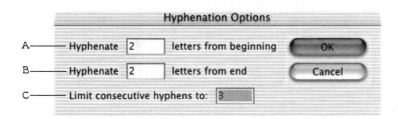

A. **Letters from Beginning** (0 to 255)

This option limits the distance a hyphen may be from the beginning of a word.

B. **Letters from End** (0 to 255)

This option limits the distance a hyphen may be from the beginning of a word.

C. **Limit Consecutive hyphens to** (1 to 127)

This option limits the number of hyphens in a row a paragraph may have. This is a good option, since excessive hyphenation makes text more difficult to read.

39.16

Kinsoku Shori

Use these options to modify the way the Kinsoku Shori option adjusts lines of type. *(For more information, see 39.12, Kinsoku Shori.)*

Kinsoku Shori Options Dialog Box

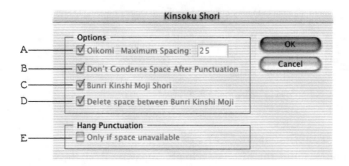

A. **Oikomi** (0 to 100)

This option adjusts the spacing on justified type evenly to fit on a line. All characters are condensed by the amount set in the Maximum Spacing field. If this option is not used, type is spaced evenly and text flows to the next line.

B. **Don't Condense Space After Punctuation**

This option omits condensing space on double byte font period characters.

C. **Bunri Kinshi Moji Shori**

This option adds characters to both the soft and hard sets. The double and triple period and em dash characters are added.

D. **Delete Space between Bunri Kinshi Moji**

This option adjusts the spacing when using the Bunri Kinshi Moji Shori additional characters.

E. **Hang Punctuation Only if space unavailable**

Use this option in conjunction with the Hang Punctuation option. Without this option, text hangs freely. When this option is on, text only hangs if space cannot be adjusted to fit. *(For more information, see 39.10, Hang Punctuation)*

The Tab Ruler Palette

Tab Ruler Palette Overview

Use the Tab Ruler palette to assist in placing custom tabs in a selected block
of type, to edit existing tabs, and to set the left and first line indents for a
selected paragraph. Open the palette by choosing Window: Type: **Tab Ruler**.
Tab placement sets the action that happens when you type the Tab key. Tabs
set a position and alignment for the characters that follow them. This is used
to set up common paragraph features such as tables and hanging bullets.

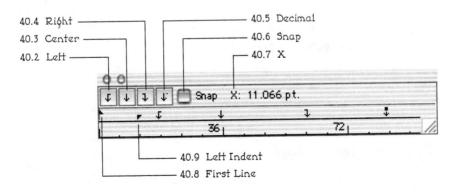

40.4 Right
40.3 Center
40.2 Left
40.5 Decimal
40.6 Snap
40.7 X
40.9 Left Indent
40.8 First Line

When you open the Tab Ruler palette and text is selected, the palette positions and sizes itself to cover the width of the text block. The palette orients itself horizontally or vertically to match the orientation of the selected text. Set the tabs you want by clicking directly on the tab ruler. As you do, a guide follows in selected text to indicate the position the tab will have. Reposition a tab by dragging it into a new position. The position of the tab is indicated in the X field. If you drag the tabs off the palette, it will be deleted.

Once a tab is set in the ruler, you can edit the alignment of the tab. Custom tabs appear in the palette as downward arrows. The top part of the arrow indicates the alignment of the tab. Left and right align tabs hook at the top to the left and right, respectively. Center align tabs have no change at the top and decimal tabs are indicated with a dot to the right of the top. Select a tab to edit it by clicking on it. Click a tab button to set the alignment or (Option) [Alt] click on the tab to cycle through the choices.

Mistakes to Avoid

Changing the view of the document after opening the palette. If you pan in or adjust the view of the document in any way, the Tab palette will no longer be aligned with the text block. On the PC, you can reset this using the Alignment option. On the Mac, you must reset it manually, or close and open the palette again.

Issues to Consider

Default tabs are indicated with a "t." Default tabs are placed every half-inch. If you place a tab, it will remove all the default tabs to the left of it.

You can move several tabs at once. Reposition all of the tabs to the right of the selected one by holding down the Shift key as you drag.

The palette can be shown and hidden with a keyboard shortcut. Press (Command-Shift) [Ctrl-Shift]-T to toggle the visibility of the palette.

40.2

Left-Justified Tab

Click this button to set a selected tab to left alignment. This is the default setting for tabs.

40.3

Center-Justified Tab

Click this button to set a selected tab to center alignment. Text centers in the line about the tab position provided space is available.

40.4

Right-Justified Tab

Click this button to set a selected tab to right alignment. Text is right aligned after the tab position.

40.5

Decimal-Justified Tab

Click this button to set a selected tab to decimal alignment. Text is aligned about a period. Text to the right of the period is left aligned, text to the left is right aligned. This is often used to line up rows of numbers or prices.

40.6

Snap

Use this option to snap the position of tabs being dragged to the hash marks in the ruler.

40.7

X:

This field displays the position of selected tabs and indents. As you drag a tab or indent, the value updates on-the-fly. If you drag a tab off the palette, the field reads *delete* to indicate the tab will be cleared. This field is informational only and cannot be used to reposition tabs.

40.8

First Line Indent

Use this triangle to set the first line indent of selected paragraphs. *(For more information, see 39.5, First Line Indent.)*

40.9

Left Indent

Use this triangle to set the left indent of selected paragraphs. *(For more information, see 39.3, Left Line Indent.)*

The Variables Palette

41.1

Variables Palette Overview

Use the Variables palette to prepare templates for data-driven graphics. The term "data-driven" means that the graphic takes information from an external data file. For example, data from a spreadsheet may be used to populate text fields in a template. This workflow usually involves a developer who writes a customized script. The script may load the data file into the Illustrator file and produce a series of different files based on the data all on its own.

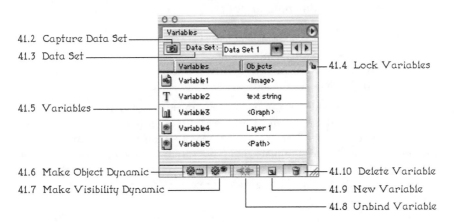

41.2 Capture Data Set

41.3 Data Set

41.5 Variables

41.6 Make Object Dynamic

41.7 Make Visibility Dynamic

41.4 Lock Variables

41.10 Delete Variable

41.9 New Variable

41.8 Unbind Variable

For example, scheduling data from a spreadsheet could populate a calendar template and generate a customized PDF file for each employee with their particular assignments. Or a series of sell sheets with different pricing and graphics could be created from a single template. The scripts the developer writes may perform these functions entirely on their own or use Illustrator actions as well. *(For more information, see A.12, Basic Short-Run XML.)*

Data driven graphics require three things: a data file, a template, and a script. Data files take the form of XML documents. These are often exported out of other applications (including Illustrator) or coded directly for use in this workflow. The template file is created in Illustrator and it connects objects to the data. Objects and data are connected by variables. For example, you may style and place type and then bind that type object to a variable. The variable data changes as the data streams to it, and the type changes to match. The script usually informs Illustrator to do something, such as create a PDF or web graphic, to change the variables and then to do it again until it is out of data. In this way many different files can be created automatically from a single template file.

Prepare templates in Illustrator by first setting up a design and then creating variables. The variables may come to you with the XML file, they may be opened as a library, or you may create them yourself. *(For more information, see 41.16, Load Variable Library.)* Illustrator supports the following types of variable:

- **Text String.** These variables change type information. Using these enables you to change copy in a template. For example, names could change from person to person. These may be connected to any kind of type.

- **Visibility.** This sets whether an item can be seen or not. This enables you to show or hide an item based on data. For example, logos built in the image can be shown or hidden as appropriate. You can set the visibility of entire layers and groups with this, enabling you to change backgrounds and such.

- **Linked File.** This variable connects to an external file, such as a photo. As variables change, different images can be linked in and replaced.

- **Graph Data.** This variable changes graph data.

- **No type.** This variable is not connected to one of the four other types until it is connected to an object. Then it becomes a variable based on the kind of object it is connected to.

Once you've set variables, many users temporarily populate them with data to preview the use of the template. The information that populates each variable at a given time creates a Data Set. There may be many data sets in a file. For example, a business card template may have variables for employee name, title and telephone extension. All three pieces of information together make a data set. A different data set would be used for each employee.

To save a data set, you modify the variable data and then save the collection of changes as a set. Repeating the process creates multiple sets quickly. Modify variables in the following ways:

- **Text String.** Key in new text. Edit the existing text using one of the type tools. The characters are the variables here, not the appearance of the text object.

- **Visibility.** Show or hide the item in the Layers palette or by using the command Object: Hide: **Selection**. Usually the Layers palette is used since individual objects may be shown and it gives access to showing and hiding layers and groups. *(For more information, see 25.4, Toggle Visibility.)*

- **Linked File.** Replace the link with another graphic. Use the Links palette to do this. *(For more information, see 26.6, Replace Link.)*

- **Graph Data.** Change the values by using the Object: Graph: **Data** command. *(For more information, see 4.11, Creating Graphs.)*

41.2

Capture Data Set

Use this button to save the current settings for variables as a data set. A new set containing the current settings will be created and given a default name. (Option) [Alt]-click to open the New Data Set dialog box. The only option in that dialog box is the name of the set.

41.3

Data Set

This field lists the current data set used for variables in the document. Change the name of the set by keying directly into this field. Cycle through the data sets in the document by clicking the forward and backward arrows to the right of this field or by choosing one from the drop-down menu to the right of the field. If there is only one set, the arrows are disabled.

If you change the values for any of the variables by editing objects the data set's name will be in italic. If you switch data sets without updating the current set or creating a new one, the changes you made will be discarded.

41.4

Lock Variables

Click this icon to toggle the lock status of variables. When the variables are locked, you cannot edit or add to them in any way. The data and objects may be changed, but the variables are fixed. This prevents you from adding variables or changing the names of them. This is important, since the names of variables are used in the scripts that process them. If you alter the names of variables after a developer has prepared a script that calls them, the script won't work.

41.5

Variables

This field lists the all variables and objects connected to them in three columns. Variable types are indicated by icons in the left column, followed by the variable name in the center and object name in the right. Objects may be listed here by the names that are given them in the Layer's palette or by their XML ID. To set this preference, choose Edit: Preferences: **Units & Undo**. Some developers prefer to look at the XML IDs for objects, which may be descriptive.

Use the following shortcuts when using variables:

- Click the variable to select it, Select variables to begin the process of binding or unbinding objects and deleting variables

- Double-click to edit the variable's options. This is done to change a variable's name or type.

- Click the column headers to sort variables. Click the blank space over the variable icons to sort by type. Click the Variables column header to sort the variables alphabetically. Sort the objects alphabetically by clicking on that column's header.

- Select the objects connected to the variable by (Option) [Alt] clicking on the item in the variables palette. Selecting objects this way enables you to edit the object connected to the variable with certainty that you have selected the correct item. Objects that are locked or hidden cannot be selected.

Variable Options Dialog Box

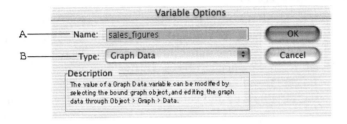

A. Name

Use this field to create a name for the variable. Tight coordination between developers and designers is important with respect to variable names. Be sure that you are in complete understanding of all of the variables used and the names of each.

B. Type

Use this menu to select the variable's type. Be aware that not every kind of object may be bound to all variables.

41.6

Make Object Dynamic

Use this button to make selected graphs, text objects and linked files dynamic objects. A dynamic object is one that is connected, or *bound*, to a variable.

When you click this button with nothing selected in the Variables palette, a new variable is created and connected to the selected object. The variable type is determined by the kind of object. Graphs become graphs, text becomes text and links become links. If a variable is selected, and it matches the type of object that is selected in the document, the button binds the object to the existing variable.

41.7

Make Visibility Dynamic

Use this button to connect the visibility of an item to a variable. Any object, group or layer can be bound in this way. This includes items that are already dynamic. This is usually done to switch visual elements that cannot be made dynamic. For example, you may want to switch between vector background images for different data sets. You can build both into the file as layers and connect the visibility of each to variables.

41.8

Unbind Variable

Use this button to break the connection between a variable and an object. When you do this, the object is no longer bound to the variable and it disappears from the palette. Variable information in data sets is not lost; it is just longer connected to that particular object. This enables you to connect the data to a new object. To connect a new object to the variable, select a suitable object to the variable type and click the Make Object Dynamic button.

41.9

New Variable

Click this button to create a new (no type) variable. Variables created in this way are not connected to objects and have no object type. They will become a specific type if you connect them to an object or assign one in the Variables Option dialog box.

41.10

Delete Variable

Click this button to clear highlighted variables from the document.

41.11

Make Object Dynamic

This command is the same as the button of the same name. *(For more information, see 41.6, Make Object Dynamic.)*

41.12

Make Visibility Dynamic

This command is the same as the button of the same name. *(For more information, see 41.7, Make Visibility Dynamic.)*

41.13

New Variable

This command is the same as the button of the same name. *(For more information, see 41.9, New Variable.)*

41.14

Delete Variable

This command is the same as the button of the same name. *(For more information, see 41.10, Delete Variable.)*

41.15

Variable Options

Choose this command to open the Variable Options dialog box for a selected variable. *(For more information, see 41.5, Variables.)*

41.16

Load Variable Library

Variable Libraries are XML documents that contain variable and data set information. Libraries are used to coordinate efforts between developers and designers. Commonly, developers write libraries and hand them to designers. This way the developer is sure that the variables used in the template will match the ones written into the script. The designer loads the library and connects objects to the variables contained. Typically, several data sets are included so that the designer can try out different presentations for the data.

Before loading a library, it is usually a good idea to discard any existing unused variables in the document to avoid confusion. Once the command is chosen, navigate to the library document and open it. The loaded variables appear in the palette. Connect the variables to appropriate objects. The data sets may appear blank at first. Check the data sets by picking one from the drop down menu next to the Data Sets field.

41.17

Save Variable Library

Use this command to write the variables and data sets in an Illustrator document to an XML file. This is usually done when it is the designer who is defining the variables. The designer may create a template and define variables there. Afterward, they export the XML and hand it to the developer who uses the variable names to write a script.

41.18

Unbind Variable

This command is the same as the button of the same name. *(For more information, see 41.8, Unbind Variable.)*

41.19

Capture Data Set

This command is the same as the button of the same name. *(For more information, see 41.2, Capture Data Set.)*

41.20

Delete Data Set

Use this command to clear the current data set from the document.

41.21

Update Data Set

This command saves the changes made to dynamic objects into the current set. Unless this command is used, changes made to dynamic objects will be discarded from the data set.

41.22

Rename Data Set

Use this command to change the name of the current data set. Alternatively, you can just key the name directly into the data set field.

41.23

Previous Data Set

This advances to the previous data set in the document. All variables are switched to the state in the next data set. If the current set is the first one, it moves to the last set.

41.24

Next Data Set

This advances to the next data set in the document. All variables are switched to the state in the next data set. If the current set is the last one, it moves to the first set.

41.25

Select Bound Object

Use this command to select the items connected to the current variable in the palette. Locked or hidden objects are not selected. Alternatively, (Option) [Alt]-click directly on the variable .

41.26

Select All Bound Objects

Use this command to select all objects in the document that are dynamic.

Libraries

42.1

Libraries Overview

Use libraries to load brushes, swatches, symbols, and styles from saved Illustrator files into the current document. Libraries are saved files that you can open as locked palettes. This enables you to use the document resources of the file without risking changing it.

Illustrator ships with a series of brushes, swatches, symbols, and styles that are not in the default sets. Load these or other Illustrator files as libraries to use them. When a library loads, it opens as a locked palette. Brushes, swatches, symbols, and styles each open as their own library. To add one of the items in the library to the corresponding palette of the current document, click the item in the library. If it is not added immediately, apply the item to an object or drag it directly into the palette.

Choose from one of the prebuilt libraries or navigate to another file by choosing Other Library from the bottom of the Library menu. Illustrator Native, EPS, and PDF files may be used as libraries.

Libraries have the same as the options as the palettes they correspond to except for the options that follow.

Issues to Consider

Libraries can be added and removed from the menus. The items in each Library menu are files that live in the presets folder. For example, the Brushes libraries are found in the directory Adobe Illustrator/Presets/Brushes. You can add your own files to this list or delete ones you do not want.

Persistent libraries must not be moved. If you use the persistent option for a library, be sure that you do not move the original document. For this reason, many users store libraries they wish to use in the corresponding presets folder.

To appear in libraries, colors must be saved as swatches. Libraries read the contents of palettes, not the objects in a document. This is not an issue for brushes, swatches, and symbols, but colors that are not saved as swatches are not available in swatch libraries.

You can load the defaults as a library. All of the library menus offer a default settings library. This is useful if you have edited the contents of a document's palette and you wish to recall the defaults.

Library Palette Options

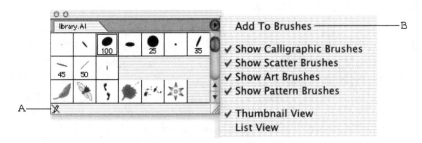

A. **Locked**

This icon indicates that the library is not a palette and cannot be written to. To edit a library, you need to open the source file and make changes to the palette contents of that document.

B. **Add To**

Use this command to add selected items in the library to the document's palette. This is usually done when many items are selected at once.

Related Topics

Chapter 19, "The Brushes Palette"
Chapter 33, "The Swatches Palette"
Chapter 31, "The Styles Palette"
Chapter 34, "The Symbols Palette"

42.2

Brush Libraries

Choose one of these nine prebuilt files to load as a library or select a custom file by choosing Other Library.

42.3

Style Libraries

Choose one of these eight prebuilt files to load as a library or select a custom file by choosing Other Library.

Issues to Consider

These styles may create large documents. Some of these styles result in complex documents that may take some time to image. The Strokes and Strokes (RGB) libraries contain several such styles.

42.4

Swatches Libraries

Choose one of these twenty-five files to load as a library, including the popular PANTONE swatches, or select a custom file by choosing Other Library. The following files are supplied:

- **Default_CMYK.** These are the color swatches that load by default when you create a new CMYK document. Use this library in the event that you have edited or deleted default swatches you wish to recall.

- **Default_RGB.** These are the color swatches that load by default when you create a new RGB document. Use this library in the event that you have edited or deleted default swatches you wish to recall.

- **DIC Color.** DIC is Dainippon Ink & Chemicals. This company produces the DIC Color Guide and the corresponding 1280 spot color swatches. This color system is popular in Japan.

- **Earthtones_1.** These are process color swatches of browns, reds, and greens. This set is provided because earth tones can be difficult to mix manually.

- **FOCOLTONE.** These 763 CMYK colors are produced by the UK company Focoltone International, Ltd. The set is intended for use with the company's printed guide.

- **Harmonies_1.** These six rows of eight CMYK colors are provided with the intention that they be used together. Each row represents a group of colors that balance well together. You could use the colors in a row to simplify color choices in a design.

- **HKS E.** These spot colors come from the German company HKS-Farber. They are intended for use with BASF inks on continuous forms papers.

- **HKS K.** These spot colors are intended for use with BASF inks on glossy paper.

- **HKS N.** These spot colors are intended for use with BASF inks on uncoated paper.

- **HKS Z.** These spot colors are intended for use with BASF inks on newsprint.

- **PANTONE Coated.** Use these colors in conjunction with the printed PANTONE swatch guide to specify exact colors on press. This particular set is to be used when printing on coated paper. Coated paper has a finish, such as the glossy finish on most magazines. The colors here are spot colors with CMYK alternate values. This set is widely used in the United States.

- **PANTONE Process.** Use these swatches in conjunction with the printed PANTONE process color guide. These swatches are process colors, designed for use with a four-color printing system. This is a great way to specify colors since you can choose based on actual printed samples, rather than on-screen approximations.

- **PANTONE Uncoated.** Use these swatches in conjunction with the printed PANTONE swatch guide for use on uncoated papers.

- **Pastels.** These swatches are a series of pastel process colors.

- **System (Macintosh).** These are the 256 standard colors used by the Mac operating system. You can use these when preparing on-screen work for a strictly Mac audience and know that they will see what you see.

- **System (Windows).** These are the 256 standard colors used by the Windows operating system. You can use these when preparing on-screen work for a strictly PC audience and know that they will see what you see.

- **Toyo.** These spot colors are used in Japan as the PANTONE colors are used in the United States. A printed guide is used to specify colors, ensuring clear color communication between designer and printer.

- **Visibone2.** These swatches are the 216 web-safe colors arranged in a color wheel format. When using this library, resize the palette so that a white swatch is in all four corners of the palette. This will make the arrangement of the colors in the palette more intuitive.

- **Web.** These 216 colors are the ones that can be viewed reliably on all monitors. The Mac and Windows system palettes are the same except for forty colors. The colors they have in common make up this set.

42.5

Symbols Libraries

Choose one of these six files to load as a library or select a custom file by choosing Other Library.

Document Management Techniques

Selecting Locked and Hidden Objects

Locked and hidden objects are not selected when clicked with selection tools. This does not mean that they cannot be transformed, colored, or deleted. When a group is selected or targeted, locked and hidden members of the group are available to be edited. Also, when a layer is targeted, locked and hidden items on the layer become available. This will be indicated in the Layers palette with a highlight square next to the locked or hidden item.

An exception occurs when layers or groups contain only one object. In this case, the layer or group cannot be targeted and the object will need to be unlocked to be edited.

A.2

Selecting with Actions

Specific objects can be selected using actions. To select predefined objects you will need to create two actions. The first will tag a selection and the second will recall it. This is used in lieu of simply saving a selection because it can be done completely with keyboard shortcuts. To set an action that records a selection:

1. Select an object to use as you create the action.

2. In the Actions palette menu, choose New Action and begin recording. Be sure to give the action a keyboard shortcut.

3. In the Attributes palette, add a note such as "select." Stop recording the action.

4. Create a second action. In the actions palette menu, choose Select Object. This action should also have a keyboard shortcut.

5. In the Set Selection dialog box, type in the note you added in first action, such as "select."

When you create an object that you wish to select again later, run the first action. Run the second action to select the objects again later.

A.3

Customizing Illustrator's Defaults

Many users want to customize Illustrator's default settings to include items they use frequently. Often, this means a specific series of colors, but it can go beyond that. Objects that are frequently used, such as a logo or styled type blocks can be added as well.

Items that you want to use frequently can be saved as libraries. Saved correctly, libraries give you easy access to swatches, brushes, styles, and symbols. *(For more information, see 42.1, Libraries.)* Libraries do not change Illustrator's defaults, though. If you want to have items available every time you open Illustrator, you will need to edit the start up documents. Follow these steps:

1. On your system, open the directory Adobe Illustrator 10: Plug ins. In that directory, find the files Adobe Illustrator Startup_CMYK and Adobe Illustrator Startup_RGB. These files store the default swatches, brushes, styles, and symbols. Each time a new document is created, Illustrator refers to these documents to tell it what should go in the palettes. The documents must have these names and live in this location.

2. Duplicate the documents and move the copies to a secure location on your computer. This will give you the opportunity to recall the factory defaults if needed.

3. Return to the Plug-ins directory and open the file for the color mode you most frequently use.

4. Change the document to set your defaults. Add or remove swatches, brushes, symbols, and styles from the palettes. To add swatches, they must be used on an object in the document as well as in the palette. Add objects you wish to have available in every document, such as prestyled text, to the Symbols palette. Changing the default style in this document will enable you to set Illustrator's default stroke width, color, and fill.

5. Set your document up as you want to work. Show or hide the rulers, grid, transparency grid, page tiling, and artboard. You can also change the document set up. Many users use this to set the Raster/Vector Balance higher than the default.

6. Repeat the process for the other color mode start up file if required. Save the document. The next document you make in that color mode will have the new defaults.

Issues to Consider

Stationary pads can serve a similar purpose. Some users build a series of start up documents and swap them in and out for each job. Since what most users want to save are document resources, it's usually easier to use a stationary pad. A stationary pad is a document that duplicates itself on open so that you work on a copy by default.

On the Mac, make a file a stationary pad by selecting it at the Finder level and choosing File: **Get Info**. Click the Stationary Pad option. Now when you open the file from the Finder it will duplicate itself first. To modify the stationary pad instead of a copy, open it from within Illustrator.

A.4
Using Symbol Libraries

Symbol libraries can be used to save commonly used items. Unlike patterns and brushes, which can also store objects, symbols retain the live features in objects. Patterns and brushes expand these features. This means that you can create a palette of commonly used objects that are highly editable. For example, you could warp a compound shape and convert it to a symbol. If the link to the symbol were broken for an instance of the symbol, you could still edit the envelope and the compound shape inside of it. More usefully, you can retain text. Follow these steps:

1. Create the objects that you want to use again. For example, you could set type to a corporate font at a specific size and place it in a bounding box next to the company logo. Select the objects.

2. Click the New Symbol button in the Symbols palette. Repeat the process for all the symbols you wish to make.

3. Delete all the other symbols from the palette and save the file. If you want the files to be one of the choices in the Symbol Library menu, save it in the directory Adobe Illustrator 10: Presets: Symbols.

To use the symbols in another document, follow these steps:

1. Choose Window: Symbol Libraries: **Other Library**. If you saved the file into the Symbols presets directory, you can choose it directly from the Symbol Libraries menu.

2. The symbol palette of the saved document opens as a library. Click the symbols to add them to the current Symbols palette or drag instances directly into the document.

3. To convert the instances into editable objects, select the instances and click the Break Link to Symbol button in the Symbols palette.

A.5

Preparing a File for SWF

Illustrator is often used to prepare objects that will be animated in Flash or LiveMotion. Both applications support copying and pasting objects between applications. Since Illustrator doesn't have robust animation features, many users copy and paste rather than export. Copy and paste produces slightly different results than exporting. In general, you should copy and paste when you intend to continue editing in Flash. This provides greater object flexibility. If the appearance of objects varies greatly when pasted, or if you are producing animation directly from Illustrator, use the Export command instead.

Regardless of the way art is moved, Flash does not support all of Illustrator's features. This often results in the objects being converted to raster art. Raster art greatly increases the file size and transmission times of web animation. Work around these limitations as follows:

*   **Don't use gradient meshes.** Gradient meshes are not supported and must be rasterized. You cannot copy and paste gradient mesh objects.

*   **Apply transparency in Flash.** Objects with transparency, blend modes, and opacity masks are flattened when brought into Flash. Although Flash does not support blend modes or opacity masks, it does support transparency. When copying and pasting items into Flash or exporting incomplete animations, set the object's opacity to 100%. Apply transparency using Flash's Alpha setting. This makes for a more flexible, truer transparency experience.

*   **Expand or reset strokes with nonrounded caps and joins.** Flash only supports rounded joins on strokes. If a mitered and beveled stroke is important to your design, you should consider expanding it. Illustrator

can correctly convert joins by choosing Object: Expand. However, it fails to expand dashed lines and rounded or projecting caps. Work around this by setting the opacity of the stroke to 99% and choosing Object: **Flatten Transparency**. This expands the stroke while retaining its appearance.

Exporting a dashed line to SWF produces a series of independent dash shapes. This retains the visual appearance of the art but destroys the ability to edit it as a stroke. Copying and pasting a dashed line produces a group of solid lines. The lines can be reset to dashes using the stroke function in Flash.

- **Avoid affects that require leading, kerning, and tracking.** These features are not supported in Flash. When exported, type is converted to separate objects to reproduce these features. When pasted, the features are discarded.

- **Avoid using patterns.** When you copy and paste, patterns are discarded. When you export, objects with patterns are rasterized.

- **Keep gradients under eight sliders.** If you have more than eight stops in a gradient, Flash will have difficulty with it. When exporting, the gradients will rasterize. If you copy and paste, the gradient will either turn black or discard the last sliders.

- **Keep your eye on nested groups in Flash.** Some Illustrator features are retained in Flash, but hidden in nested groups. For example, clipping masks are retained when pasted into Flash, but they are converted into Flash's mask layer. To edit the items, you will need to edit through several redundant groups Keep double-clicking on groups in Flash until you find the actual content.

A.6

Setting Up to Begin Web Work

When you get ready to build or convert art for the web, you will want to set up Illustrator to best forecast the results you'll see online. Here are some settings to consider:

- **Set the document color mode to RGB when you create it.** Convert a CMYK document by choosing File: Document Color Mode: **RGB**.

- **Choose an appropriate artboard size.** Some users take screen captures of the various browser default windows and place them as template layers and then set artboard size to match. This helps give a sense of scale and continuity. To see the art against different browsers, you can show and hide the templates.

- **Set the preference to pixels.** To set the preferences, (Control) [Right]-click on the rulers or choose Edit: Preference: **Units & Undo**.

- **Choose View: Proof Setup: Custom.** In the dialog box, choose sRGB IEC1966-2.1. This is representative of a wide range of PC monitors and will help you forecast how the bulk of your audience will see your work. If your Color Settings are set to Emulate Illustrator 6, you will not be able to use this command. Change the Color Settings model to anything else and you will be able to.

- **Unless you are producing SWF or SVG graphics, choose View: Pixel Preview.** This will give you a better sense of how edges will appear in your work when it is converted to pixels. You may want to turn this on and off as you work as it can slow down performance.

- **Work at 100% view depth as much as possible.**

- **Choose Window: Swatch Libraries: Web.** This opens the web safe color palette as a library. Since these colors produce a consistent color experience among almost all users, you should use these colors as often as possible. You could also set the Color palette to this set of colors by choosing Web Safe RGB from the Color Palette menu.

- **Find out as much as you can about the use of the graphics.** In most cases, Illustrator will not be the final authoring tool for the web site. This will help you answer questions like what color to matte transparency against and how large to make graphics.

A.7

Reducing Colors in a GIF

Images for online viewing should be prepared with a web safe palette in mind. The web safe colors are the 216 colors that can be shown reliably on most monitors. Files saved in the GIF and PNG format are limited to a specific set of colors. The set of colors that can be included in the file is called the Color Table. When saving files in these formats, you can edit which colors in the table are web safe and which are not. This enables you to preserve important colors while reducing the occurrence of browser dithering. To prepare a color table for a GIF (or PNG):

1. Choose File: **Save for Web**. Click the 2-Up tab and set the format to GIF. Set the Color Reduction Method to Perceptual.

2. Set the number of colors to Auto. The actual number of colors used is displayed in the lower left of the Color Table.

3. Identify important colors in the image. Select the Eyedropper tool and click directly on the color in the preview pane. The swatch corresponding to the color becomes highlighted in the table. To protect the color from being changed or removed when colors are reduced, click the Lock button at the base of the palette.

4. Inspect the image for dithering. Click with the Eyedropper tool on dithered areas in the preview pane. Click the Snap to Web Safe button to switch pixels in the image to their nearest web safe color. This should cause colors to shift. Be certain that this does not cause too much damage to the quality of the image overall.

5. Reduce the number of colors used to lower than the current usage. Compare the processing time gained with the file quality and repeat as needed.

A.8

Setting Up an SVG File

When setting up a document that will be saved as an SVG file, keep the following considerations in mind:

- **Layers in Illustrator become groups in SVG.** Use this to organize your document. A document prepared for SVG output should use layers extensively. Each logical group of objects should be its own layer. For example, a button would be a layer, rather than an entire navigation bar. This will make it easier for developers to identify and affect objects.

- **Layer visibility is preserved but layer transparency is ignored.** If a layer's visibility is turned off, it is recorded in the SVG. Opacity settings applied by targeting a layer are ignored. You must apply transparency to objects to have it carry over to the SVG file.

- **Raster data can live in an SVG file, but it can't be scaled when viewed in the SVG viewer.** Raster data also cannot be edited as other objects can and dramatically increases file size. Avoid using raster art and elements that become raster art, such as gradient meshes, Effect: Rasterize, **Effect**: Stylize: **Inner Glow** and **Outer Glow**, Effect: Stylize: **Drop Shadow** with the Blur option, soft-edged opacity masks, and all Effects from Artistic to Video.

- **Use Symbols and SVG effects instead of standard techniques and objects wherever possible.** For example, instead of using Effect: Stylize: Drop **Shadow**, use Effect: SVG Filters: **AI_Shadow_1**. SVG filters are text instructions in the file, rather than pixels attached to a graphic. This reduces file size overall and works around the limitations of raster art. Keep in mind that Illustrator will display a pixel preview of objects that use SVG Filters. Set the resolution of the display by choosing Effect: **Document Raster Effects Settings**.

- **Links can be added to SVG art the same ways that it can be added to any other document.** Use image maps, slices, or scripts to add interactivity to the SVG file produced.

A.9

Adding SVG Interactivity

Adding interactivity to an SVG file is done through JavaScripting. Space prohibits a full discussion of JavaScript workflow here. In brief, a .js file containing a series of JavaScript commands is attached to the file (choose JavaScript Files from the SVG Interactivity palette). This gives the document access to a library of JavaScript commands. Then specific objects are given interactivity by selecting them and keying JavaScript into the SVG Interactivity palette. For several good examples of these commands in action, see *http://www.adobe.com/svg*. From there you can also download a .js file containing many commands.

A.10

Preparing a File for Handoff

There are great opportunities for error when a file is passed from one party to another in a production chain. To minimize the risk, make sure that when you are handing off a file the work is complete and the communication is clear. Your files should be elegant in their simplicity and pleasing in their completeness. Follow these steps:

1. Check your Layers palette for hidden items. Show and unlock everything. If there are unneeded items consider deleting them now. If you need to keep nonprinting items in the document for some reason, save the document, delete the items and perform a Save As to create a new file for handoff.

2. Choose Type: **Check Spelling**. Correct any errors and then visually inspect the document for words that are spelled correctly but are incorrect in the document.

3. Choose Object: Path: **Clean Up**. In the Clean Up dialog box, select the items you want to remove. In most cases, you will want to select all items in the dialog box. You should be careful about any unpainted boxes you may be using to control object placement, though. When compositing files together in another application, such as QuarkXPress, empty bounding boxes are sometimes used to assist in positioning files correctly.

4. In the Styles palette menu, choose Select All Unused, then press Delete. Repeat the process for the Brushes, Symbols, and Swatches palettes. Delete styles before brushes since one of default styles uses a brush. This will prevent errors when attempting to delete brushes. When deleting unused items, make sure each palette is set to Show All.

5. Decide what to do about fonts. You may choose to embed fonts when you save the file or convert them to outlines. If you have a paragraph or

more of type in the document you will likely want to embed rather than outline. Outlining a large amount of type may create problems for other people handling your file. If the person receiving your file is going to work on it more in Illustrator, you will want to send them all of the font files you used as well. If you have a small amount of type and do not want to embed fonts, first make sure you do not have an active insertion point in type and then choose Edit: **Select All**. Next choose Type: **Create Outlines**. All of the text is converted to shapes.

6. Choose File: **Save As**. This will give you a chance to check the settings used when the filed was saved. *(For more information, see 7.7, File: Save As.)*

Examining a Client File

When you receive a file from someone else, you should inspect it right away to make sure you have what you need. Although some service bureaus have a file submission form that is used to confirm correct receipt of a file, most design shops do not. Frequently, files are passed around from client to client with little certainty about the file's lineage and purpose. When you pick up a file, take a moment to inspect it. The things you are looking for will vary depending upon your role. Follow this general outline:

1. Before you open it, check the file's size. If it is very small (below 50k) or large (above 2MB) consider it a red flag. The file may be missing pieces, the wrong type, or containing a lot of pixel data.

2. If the file uses fonts that aren't active on your station, you will be alerted upon opening the file. If this happens, jot down the names of the fonts before proceeding. You will have other opportunities to get the names, but this is the best time.

3. Before you start looking through the file, open the Document Info palette. Make sure the palette is not set to Selection Only. Choose Objects from the Document Info palette menu. This will list the number of objects in the document by type. You are looking to see what kinds of elements that have been used in the document. For example, you can find out the color modes of objects in the document.

4. Learn more about objects of concern by choosing different categories from the Document Info palette menu. While all of these categories are important, links, spot colors, and fonts used in the document are often of special concern with files for print. Check for features that may print as rasters, such as opacity masks, gradient meshes, and transparency. Also look for complex features, such as symbol sets. The presence of these features may not be obvious when looking at the document. Knowing about them will give you places to look in the event that trouble happens.

5. Inspect the document visually. Zoom out far enough to see the whole thing and check the document in both Preview and Outline mode. You want to see how the client has constructed the art.

6. Check the Layers palette to see how the file was organized. You are looking for the gradient circles that indicates appearance or effects next to objects layers and groups and for clipping masks. Both of these items can make objects appear very different in Preview than in Outline mode.

If you find things that will cause problems, don't hesitate to contact the client. Frequently problems that are fixed but unreported repeat themselves. Eventually they don't get caught and cause a real problem. Most people are happy to learn so long if approached in a friendly manner.

One of the key things to look for in Illustrator 10 is the presence of complex symbol sets. Symbols sets with many objects and transparency can create printing problems, especially when in-rip trapping is involved. Remember that flattened transparency often becomes complex masked raster art. If you are experiencing or expect to experience difficulty printing these types of documents, lower the raster/vector balance. Rasters are not a bad thing.

A.12

Basic Short-Run XML

Illustrator's Variables are not limited to high-end developer solutions. They can be useful in smaller systems to recycle data you've already entered. You can create an XML library directly from Illustrator that you can use to populate later designs. The model is the same as it would be for a large run, except that in smaller amounts it becomes manageable for an individual to perform the tasks without a developer's script.

For example, a small firm is preparing business cards, letterhead, and web bio pages for each of a dozen employees. A user might enter the names and data for each employee in a document and export the information as an XML file. The user then builds template for the business card, letterhead, and web page. The XML is then imported and connected to each template. The user then (either manually or assisted by a basic action) saves off a file for each employee. To create an XML library, follow these steps:

1. Determine the data that should be in the file. This is the information that changes in each different version. In the previous example, it might be employee's name, email address, and work phone but not the company name and address.

2. Create the first set of changing data. In our example, that would be a different text block for each piece of info. One for employee name, one for email, and one for phone number. You shouldn't waste time styling the text, as it will take its style from the template it's attached to.

3. Select each object individually and click the Make Dynamic button in the Variables palette. There should be a different variable for each item.

4. Double-click on the variables to name them each. Give them names that will make sense to you a year from now. **A**

5. Click the Capture Data Set button to save the information attached to each variable. Put your cursor in the set name field and key in a new name for the set. For example, the employee's last name. **B**

A *A basic set of variables for*   **B** *Set the data and save it as a set.*
employee data.

6. Change the data attached to the variables. In our example, this would be keying in the next employee name, address, and phone number. As you do this, the data set's name will be italicized to indicate that a change has happened. **C**

7. Click the Capture Data Set button to create a second complete set of data. Rename the set as before. Repeat this process of changing all the data and then creating a new set for each employee. **D**

8. Choose Save Variable Library from the Variables palette menu.

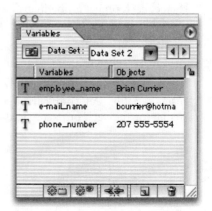

C *Key in new data. Once all the data has been changed, save the changes as a second data set.*

D *The new data is now a set. The old text can be recalled by switching to the previous set.*

Once you have saved a variable library as an XML document, you can apply it to other documents. To set up a template to use the library:

1. Create a design that you want to bring the data into. You should create an object for every variable. Of course, you can have other nondynamic objects in the design.

   Make sure you allow for different sizes of data. Some text strings may be longer than others. If the text is apt to be long, use area text instead of point text so that it will break to the next line instead of continuing off the page. You'll need to make a separate object for each variable. For example, you can't connect some characters in a text block to a variable and not others. **E**

2. In the Variables palette menu, choose Load Variable library and navigate to a valid XML file.

3. The variables in the library will fill in the palette. Click on a variable and select an object in the document that should be connected to it.

4. Click the Make Object dynamic button to connect the variable and the object. Repeat for all the variables needed. **F**

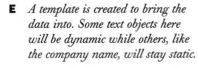

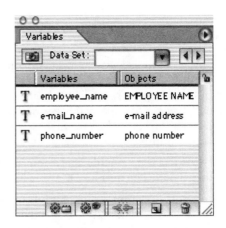

E *A template is created to bring the data into. Some text objects here will be dynamic while others, like the company name, will stay static.*

F *Text that will be changed is connected to the corresponding variables.*

5. To view the data sets, click the Data Set dropdown menu to choose one by name or click the forward and backward arrows to the right of the field. **G**

G *As the Data Sets change, the corresponding values populate the dynamic objects.*

Once data is connected to objects, you may need to produce a separate document for each set. This can be done by choosing File: **Save A Copy** (or **Save for Web**), advancing to the next data set and repeating.

A.13

Using Soft Proofing

Soft proofing is a way of forecasting print color onscreen rather than through printed "hard" proofs. This is intended to save money and turn-around time by providing more accurate display color. It works by creating descriptions, or "profiles," of the way devices reproduce color. By adjusting the display and printing of colors based on these profiles, color fidelity improves onscreen and in print.

While this is a laudable goal, there are a number of limitations to this process that should be considered:

- **Soft proofing assumes high monitor quality, and consistent working environments.** Even if you have a high-quality monitor to display color correctly, the changing light during the course of the day greatly impacts onscreen color. Professional color correctors work in the consistent light of windowless rooms.

- **Soft proofing is only as good as your profiles.** This model changes color onscreen based on information supplied about the devices in the print chain, including the monitor. If these are inaccurate, generic, or out-of-date, soft proofing will fail. Also, producing a print profile is not a trivial matter. It may take many rounds and a lot of money to produce an accurate color profile that works for all images. Newsprint output is notoriously hard to calibrate. Once produced, these extreme profiles can cause problems when switching color spaces and correcting color. The profiles used to describe newsprint output may produce horrible color spaces that are very difficult to correct in.

- **Profiles are not always consistently interpreted in different applications.** Profiles may be embedded in AI, PDF, JPEG, TIF, and PSD files. Placing art in a page layout application that uses color management may produce inconsistent color results when displaying and printing this art.

Some of these limitations apply to soft proofing, others to using profiles in an integrated color management scheme. Complete color management is one of the hottest, and most frustrating issues in the industry today. While complete color matching is currently not possible, Illustrator's soft proofing can still be useful. You should regard all onscreen displays as suspect. Soft proofed colors are only slightly less suspect. They may be wrong, but they will be wrong in a specific way. After a while you will be able to predict the differences and come to expect the resulting color better. To activate soft proofing:

1. Choose Edit: **Color Settings**. Make sure you are not set to Emulate Illustrator 6.

2. Check the profiles used in your working spaces. Set the RGB space to the profile that best matches your monitor. If you have not done so, consider using the Adobe Gamma utility to create a custom profile for your monitor. Set the CMYK working space to the output device used.

3. Choose View: **Proof Colors**. If soft proofing is active, a check mark will appear next to the command and the current profile will be displayed in the document title bar.

4. You may need to preview color in a different space than the document profile. For example, you may wish to see the image as printed to another local proofer or on a different monitor. To do this, choose View: Proof SetUp: **Custom**. Choose another profile from the list provided.

Coloring Techniques

Creating Shadows and Highlight Colors

Highlights and shadows can be added to art in a number of ways. The method you choose will be determined by the needs of the image and the level of time and sophistication the project calls for. In many cases, lighting can be added using several well-placed objects with simple fills. To add shadows or highlights to art in colors, begin by creating basic lighter and darker versions of the original color. Follow these steps:

1. Determine the color that the object should be with middle lighting. This will be your base color. The highlights and shadows will be lighter and darker than this color.

2. Make an object that uses this color as a fill. If viable, create the object in a document with colors that you will use with this color. Although you should never pick print colors from an onscreen display, many users do this as they audition colors from swatch books to get a sense of color's harmony with other colors.

3. Save the color as a swatch. Choose New Swatch from the Swatches palette menu.

4. Using the Color palette, click-drag the color sliders to create a lighter or darker version of the color. When you Shift-drag a color slider, all sliders move together.

5. If you are creating a shadow color, consider adding a small amount of black (if you are mixing in CMYK). This can be done before or after Shift-dragging the sliders. Black often helps dull colors while darkening them.

6. Some users mix colors by switching the color palette to the HSB sliders. This enables them to adjust the dark component (B) and the intensity of the color (S).

7. As you create new versions of the color, add new swatches to the document.

B.2

Creating Replaceable Shadows and Highlight Colors

Some workflows call for color families to be switched on a regular basis. For example, you may need to switch all of one process color with another. This would include the highlight and shadow versions of the color as well. If you anticipate that this may happen, consider a global swatch workflow:

1. Select the darkest version of the color: The color that will be the shadow side of the object.

2. Save this color as a swatch by choosing New Swatch from the Swatches palette menu. In the Swatch options dialog box, enable the Global option.

3. Use the swatch at 100% for shadows. For middle values, use it at 50% tints. Highlights may be lighter percentages. You can create additional swatches of these tints as required. **A**

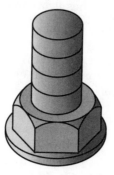

A *Different tints of the same global color are used for the highlight and shadow sides of the bolt.*

4. If you need to edit the colors used, open the Swatch Options dialog box for the color. Editing color sliders here will update them to all objects that use the swatch, all tints of swatch, and all swatches based on tints of the swatch. **B C**

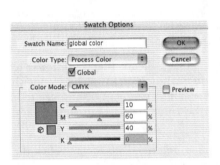

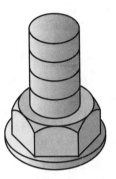

B *Edit the colors of the global swatch. Here a lighter color is used.*

C *Color changes throughout the document.*

Issues to Consider

It is hard to anticipate how middle values will look. Some trial and error will be involved to get a shadow swatch correct for the middle colors you want.

You can't edit the color values differently for different tints. Each tint has to be based on the same color values. So, for example, you can't add black to the dark swatch.

Blend modes and transparency open up color options. Although global colors are limited in their editing options, you can apply blend modes and opacity to objects that use the colors. This opens up some coloring options without destroying the connection to the global color.

B.3

Creating a Color Family Palette

When setting up a document, you may want to consider color choices up front. Some users decide upon several key colors in a design and then set about to creating related color swatches before creating and coloring art. They then lighten and darken the colors or create compliments. This technique creates a series of swatches based upon an initial, key color. To create related color swatches:

1. In the Swatches Palette menu, make sure the color swatches are showing and choose Select All Unused. From the same menu, choose Delete Swatches. This will clear the palette of unneeded items.

2. Create a square in the document with the rectangle tool. Give the square a stroke of none and a fill of a key color in your design.

3. Select the square and drag it horizontally to the other side of the document. Add the (Option) [Alt] key as you drag to create a copy.

4. Adjust the color in the duplicate square. For example, you could add black ink to the color or switch to HSB and reduce the saturation of the color. To create a series of colors blending to gray and then to the color's opposite, choose Compliment from the Color Palette menu.

5. Set the Blend Options (by choosing Object: Blend: **Blend Options**) to Specified Steps. Set a number based on the number of swatches you wish to create of each color variation. For example, you may wish to see four sequentially desaturated versions of the color. Select both squares and choose Object: Blend: **Make. A**

6. Select the Eyedropper and click upon an intermediate square. Click the New Swatch button in the Swatches palette to create a new color swatch from the color. **B**

7. Repeat the process to generate all the swatches for the variation. Next, adjust the color in either square and repeat.

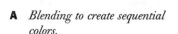

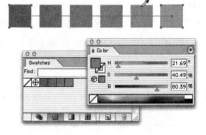

A *Blending to create sequential colors.*

B *Using the Eyedropper to sample each color to create swatches.*

B.4

Highlight and Shadow Masks

Positioning highlight and shadows within an object is often easier with a masking group. This enables you to position the highlight and shadow shapes without worrying about making the edges match the shape of the object.

1. Set up the middle, highlight, and shadow colors. Ideally, these should be swatches so that you can apply them easily. If the object to be shaded is complex (if it has more than one fill or stroke or uses effects), consider saving its appearance as a style by clicking the New Style button in the Styles palette.

2. Create simple objects for the highlight and shadow shapes. Position the shapes behind the object that will be colored by them. If the document is complex, you may want to hide objects not used in this technique. **A**

3. Select the object that will receive the highlight and shadow, and the lighting objects and choose Object: Clipping Mask: **Make**.

4. Select the masking shape and reset its appearance to what it was before it became a mask. **B**

A *The original art (left) and the shapes used in the mask isolated (right).*

B *The Clipping Mask (right) and the mask after a fill and stroke are added and the hidden objects shown (left).*

Issues to Consider

Masking increases complexity. If your lighting effects do not overlap the edges of the object, you can do this without needing to make a mask.

More complex lighting objects can also be masked. Gradients, blends, and meshes can also be used as lighting objects in this model.

B.5

Creating a Basic Bevel Shadow and Highlight

Frequently, you will want to make basic beveled shadow objects. For example, you may need to quickly create light and dark sides of an object to imply depth for a button. This method is fast and loose and requires some hand-eye coordination. If you need a more exact method, consider creating a bisecting object first and using Object: Path: **Divide Objects Below** to cut the beveled shape in two. Follow these steps:

1. Select the object that will get the shadow and choose Object: Path: **Offset Path**. Use a negative offset amount. This will create a new version of the path in front of the one selected. The distance of the offset you choose will be the size of the bevel. It may take several attempts to get the correct distance.

2. Select the original shape. It will be directly behind the shape you created with Offset Path. Choose the Knife tool. When objects are selected, the Knife tool will affect only those objects.

3. Hold down the (Option) [Alt] key before click-dragging completely across the selected object. Be sure to completely cross the object starting from outside the object. This will cut the object in half, enabling you to style each half differently.

4. Select the highlight side of the bevel and lighten the fill. If its a solid color fill, you can do this by shift-dragging color sliders in the color palette, or choosing Filter: Colors: **Saturate** and choosing a negative value. Complete by darkening the shadow side.

B.6

Shadow and Highlight Blend Modes

Blend modes are often used to create highlight and shadow colors automatically. The color of the top object and the colors of the items below are combined to produce the lighting effect. The colors are updated automatically as items are modified. This is often used in conjunction with masks and effects.

Blend modes offer ease of use, but give you little control over the final product. If you don't like the result, you have limited predictable recourses for adjusting colors. On the other hand, they work well for objects that have gradients, patterns, and styles or when dropping a lighting effect across multiple objects with different fills. To set up a shadow or highlight using blending modes, follow these steps:

1. Select the item that will receive the highlight or shadow. Note the color of the object's fill. If the fill is a gradient, pattern, or style, try to get a sense of the overall color. You'll use this color when creating the lighting effect objects. If the colors the lighting effect cover are too varied, consider using a representative color or gray. **A**

2. Create an object that outlines the highlight or shadow area. Set the fill to the color of the object beneath it, as noted in step 1. Many users click with the Eyedropper tool on the lower object to sample the lower object's fill. Do not apply a stroke to this object. **B**

A *The original artwork.*

B *Objects outlining the shadow and highlight areas. Here a 25% black was used for both objects.*

3. Set the lighting object's blending mode to Multiply to create a shadow version of the color. Set to Screen to create a highlight. In some cases, Soft Light or Hard Light will produce good results as well. **C**

4. If the lighting impact of the objects is too great, lower the Opacity of the blend. In the event that colors are incorrect, consider adjusting the colors of the top object.

c *The highlight object set to Soft Light, the shadow object set to multiply.*

In some cases, you may want to limit the impact of the lighting objects to only areas inside of a specific area. For example, you may be creating "hard cut" modeling within an object. *(For more information, see B.4, Highlight and Shadow Mask.)* Instead of using different colored objects for each highlight and shadow object, use objects with the same color and different blend modes.

Issues to Consider

Blend mode objects will affect each other by default. If you are creating coloring objects that overlap each other, their colors will affect each other where they intersect. One way to work around this to build objects that don't overlap. Another option is to group the shapes that are doing the lighting (by choosing Object: **Group**), select the group and activate the Knockout Group option in the Transparency palette. When this option is activated, the blend modes of groups do not affect each other.

B.7
___

Creating Tint Gradients

A tint gradient is one that goes between two related colors. Usually it will be a color and a darker or lighter version of that same color. This is used to create simple shading and lighting effects. For example, when working on a portrait, you may wish to create a shadow under the chin of your subject. This can be done by starting with the flesh color of the neck and then creating a darker tint gradient. The dark end of the gradient is set up under the chin, creating the falling shadow. To set up a tint gradient, follow these steps:

1. Choose a color to begin with. This may be an existing swatch or a color you have prepared with the Color Palette. **A**

2. Be sure you don't have anything selected and drag the starting color directly into the color ramp in the gradient palette. A gradient slider will be created in the ramp.

3. Drag the gradient slider you have just created to the right or left in the ramp. Hold down the (Option) [Alt] key as you drag. This creates a duplicate slider.

4. Delete all of the other sliders in the ramp by dragging them off the ramp. Only the two new sliders should remain, creating a one-color gradient. **B**

A *The original art. The same color is used in the neck, face, and arm.*

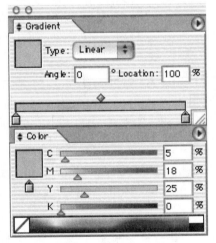

B *The flesh color (C:5 M:18 Y:25 K:0) is used as a both sliders in the gradient.*

5. Select one of the sliders to tint. To tint a process color, Shift-drag one of the sliders in the Color palette. All of the sliders will move together, creating a lighter or darker version of the color.

6. Save the gradient as a swatch by clicking the New Swatch button in the Swatches palette. The gradient may be linear or radial, depending upon how it is to be used. In many cases, linear gradients make better effects. **c**

c *K:25 is added to one of the gradient color sliders and the gradient is applied to the objects.*

Issues to Consider

Global (and spot) swatches can only get lighter. If you are using a global swatch as a gradient slider, you can only make it lighter in color. Further, you won't need any keyboard shortcuts since the color palette will only show tints of the global swatch.

A third slider is sometimes added for shadows. In dark-to-light gradients, you may want to add an even darker slider before the dark color. This is done to add a deeper shadow side to the gradient and to give more snap to the gradient. To do this, first position the dark slider closer to the light one. Then click behind the slider in the ramp to add a new color. Darken the slider by adding some black ink (CMYK) or reducing the Brightness (HSB).

Typically, the dark shadow and the dark slider are close to each other in the ramp. This creates a subtle transition.

The shapes of gradients you can make limit this technique. It will be difficult to create odd corners and three-dimensional shapes. For those techniques, consider object blends and gradient meshes, respectively.

B.8

Creating Tint Gradient Meshes

Usually, the intention with a mesh is to make an object look three-dimensional. Gradient meshes look the most natural when similar colors are used to create this effect. Typically, a solid color is applied to the object overall and then lighter and darker versions of the color are used as light falls across the item. To create this effect:

1. First trace the outline of the object that will become the mesh.

2. Set the fill of the outline object to the base color for the mesh. Be sure you do not use a gradient or pattern to fill the object. **A**

3. Using the Mesh tool, click in the fill to create mesh points. These should be positioned along areas of light and dark changes in the image. If the change is abrupt, you may wish to place a series of points to indicate the position the color changes stop and start. **B**

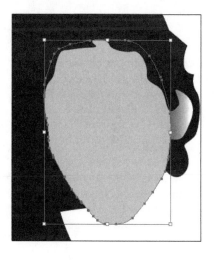

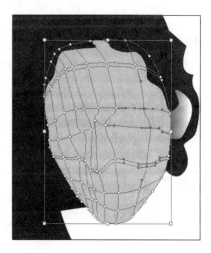

A *A basic shape outlining an object.*

B *Mesh points created. Note the proximity of the mesh points where the shadow of the nose will fall.*

4. Do not recolor mesh points until you have placed the bulk of them. If you recolor mesh points as you go, new mesh points will be given the color of the last mesh points. This often makes it harder to recover original colors than need be.

5. Use the Direct Lasso tool to select mesh points to be colored. Alternatively, use the Direct Selection tool and Shift-click mesh points to receive the same color.

6. Darken or lighten selected points by Shift-dragging sliders in the color palette to move them together. **C**

C *The mesh points colored and other objects added.*

Issues to Consider

If you need to have a stroke on the mesh, copy the object before turning it into a mesh. You will need a second shape for the stroke since meshes do not support them. Choose Edit: **Paste in Front** to add the stroke copy. Isolate the stroke copy by choosing Object: Lock: **Selection**, or hide it by choosing Object: Hide: **Selection**. Many users reposition the stroke object on its own layer. If your document is complicated, you should consider this option as well.

Shift-click with the Eyedropper tool to sample image object colors. If you are tracing a scanned image, you can sample colors directly from the object by Shift-clicking on it with the Eyedropper tool. Some users begin in this way and create a series of color swatches from the image to apply later.

Selected mesh points can be edited using color filters. Although somewhat slower, you can use filters to recolor selected mesh points. Both Filter: Color: **Saturate** and Filter: Color: **Adjust Colors** can be useful for editing color values. Typically, this happens when you need to change many points in the same overall way. Commonly, this may follow a round of proofing.

As with traditional illustration, observation is critical. Careful observation of form, light, and shadow is essential for illustration. Take the time to observe.

B.9

Gradients in Multiple Objects

To create the appearance that color changes across more than one object they can be given the same gradient. When the same gradient is applied to more than one object, it falls across each object from left to right be default. Reset the gradients by selecting the objects and click dragging with the Gradient tool. This can give the appearance that color is changing across multiple shapes. **A B**

A *The default appearance of gradients applied to multiple objects.*

B *The objects after resetting all gradients together.*

B.10

Blend Color Transitions

Object blends are often used to create color transitions in shapes other than the lines and ellipses available in gradients. This may be used to create vector versions of inner and outer glows. In this example, the blend will create a transition from a foreground color to a background color. To create color transitions:

1. Select the edge line segment on the foreground object and copy it. **A**

2. Choose Edit: **Paste in Back**. Set the stroke to 1 point and color it the same as the fill of the object in front.

3. (Option) [Alt] drag a copy of the line segment to where you want the transition to end.

4. Color the copied stroke the same as the background color.

5. Select both strokes and choose Object: Blend: **Make. B**

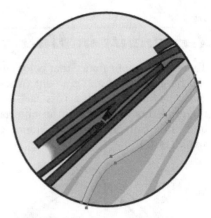

A *The edge of the object selected.*

B *The edge segment duplicated and offset. The offset shape is colored the darker gray.*

6. Measure the distance you dragged the copy stroke using the Measure tool. Set the Blend options to specified steps and create one step for each point of distance between the strokes. **C**

C *The final blend.*

Issues to Consider

This transition is not "live." Unlike the Inner and Outer Glow Effects, this transition does not update as the foreground object changes. Be certain that the objects are set the way you want before creating this effect.

For encompassed shapes, use Offset Path. If the foreground or background completely surrounds the other color, you will need to blend shapes and not segments. Instead of (Option) [Alt] dragging a copy in step 3, use Object: Path: **Offset Path** instead. This will create a complete shape for blending instead of a segment.

B.11
_____

Creating Custom Gradient Shapes

Illustrator has only two gradient shapes, linear and radial. Create additional gradient shapes using a combination of object blends and masks. This is often used to create custom lighting effects. For example, diamond gradient shapes are often used in metal objects. Follow these steps:

1. Create a perfect square by Shift-dragging with the Rectangle tool. Color the square the outside color of the gradient. Do not apply a stroke.

2. Rotate the square 45°. To open the rotate dialog box, double-click the Rotate tool in the toolbox.

3. Leave the square selected and switch to the Scale tool. Position the cursor to the right of the square and drag horizontal toward the center of the square. Add your Shift key as you drag to constrain the height of the object and your (Option) [Alt] key to create a copy. Release the mouse before you release your modifier keys.

4. Color the second shape the interior color of the gradient. **A**

5. Select both shapes and choose Object: Blend: **Make.**

6. Measure the distance you dragged the copy stroke using the Measure tool. Set the Blend options to specified steps and create one step for each point of distance between the strokes.

7. Position the path that will be filled with the "gradient" atop the blend. Make sure the object is completely surrounded by blend shapes.

8. Choose Object: Clipping Mask: **Make. B**

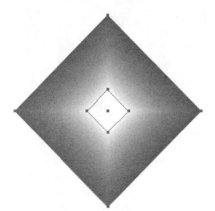

A *Two squares rotated and turned into blend.*

B *The same blend fills the front panel and top plate of the scanner.*

Issues to Consider

Different gradient require different shapes. To create custom gradient shapes, you will need to build different blending shapes. As you do this, consider the shapes of the objects blended.

Some tinkering may produce a better gradient shape. Offsetting the position of the smaller diamond or the adjusting the position of anchor points may give the gradient a less "perfect" look and do a better job of recreating light. Since the blend updates automatically, you can experiment.

B.12

Creating Soft Highlights

A soft highlight is sometimes used to add an element of realism to an illustration. A simple, diffuse highlight can be created by:

1. Creating a shape for the highlight. Often this is done with the Pencil tool to create an organic, smooth shape. **A**

2. Create a radial gradient that goes from white, or some light color, to the color behind the highlight. If there are multiple colors behind, choose the predominant one. **B**

A *The initial graphic.*

B *A white shape is added, to become the highlight area.*

3. Apply the gradient to the highlight object. To soften the highlight object, set the Blend mode of the object to Soft Light and apply a small Gaussian Blur (using the Effects: Blur: **Gaussian Blur** command). You may also consider lightening the opacity of the object. **C**

C *The highlight object with a Gaussian Blur and the Soft Light blend mode.*

B.13

Creating Transparent Blends for Lighting Effects

Intermediate objects in blends record the transparency of objects in the blend. This can be used to create ghosting effects, to set up animations and to create lighting effects. To set up a transparent blend for a lighting effect, use simple shapes. For example, you could create a spotlight effect:

1. Select the item that will be the rear object in the blend. Sets its transparency and colors as required. In the spotlight example, the opacity of the object would be 0% and it would have a yellow or white fill with no stroke. **A**

2. Create the second object. Set the opacity of this object to a higher value than the first. Although it may not be 100%, it should be larger than the first. In the spotlight example, the circle would be smaller than the first and offset from it. The fill would be the same as the first circle. To soften the edge of the circle, you could also apply Effect: Blur: **Gaussian Blur**.

3. Select both objects and create an object blend between them (Object: Blend: **Make**).

4. Set the blend options (by choosing Object: Blend: **Blend Options**) to Specified Steps. Set the number of steps to the number of points of distance between the two shapes. **B**

5. The shapes and positions of the objects relative to each other will determine the type of effect created. For example, if the second circle were
atop the first instead of offset from it, the effect would be a soft light
instead of a spotlight.

A *Both circles have white fills. The*
larger circle is 15% opaque, the
smaller is 100% opaque.

B *The blend between the circles.*

B.14

Coloring Expanded Blends

Once a blend is expanded, the intermediate objects do not automatically
change colors as the ends are adjusted. In the event that you've expanded a
blend and wish to recolor the items in it, follow these steps:

1. Use the Direct Selection tool to select one of the end shapes. Recolor the
   item as required. If you are adjusting more than one object, repeat the
   process.

2. Select all the items in the former blend. This should be easy since the
   items are grouped by default.

3. Choose Filter: Colors: **Blend Front to Back**.

Issues to Consider

**If the blend contained more than two objects, you may need to repeat the
process.** If you are coloring an intermediate object in the blend, you will
want to do this in two passes. First select the object and all those behind
it and apply the filter. Then select the object and those in front of it and
apply the filter.

The Blend Colors filters do not work on gradients. If you are adding a
gradient object, delete the intermediate objects and create the blend
again. Blends (Object: Blend) can handle gradient-to-solid blending, but
the filter cannot.

B.15

Creating Spot Color Meshes

Although Gradient Meshes support spot colors, it is easy to accidentally cause them to print with process colors. To ensure that they print as spot colors:

1. Select the object that will become the mesh and fill it with a spot color. Make sure that if more than one fill is used, the spot color is the cardinal fill. Do not give the object a stroke. **A**

2. Click with the Mesh tool to add points to the mesh. As points are added, color them only with tints of the original spot color. Do this by dragging the tint slider for the spot color in the Color palette when a mesh point is selected. Keep the following advice in mind: **B**

   – Do not add white. For white, use a 0% tint of the spot color. Do not add process colors.

   – Do not add other spot colors. Meshes cannot support more than a single spot color.

   – Do not give the mesh a blend mode or make it transparent against other objects.

   – Do not apply effects to the mesh.

A *A shape is given a solid spot color fill and no stroke.*

B *Each mesh point is given tints of the spot color.*

B.16

Creating Process Color Duotones from Imported Grayscale Art

Adding process color to an imported grayscale image makes it appear as a monotone. It looks as though all the tones are printed with a single color. Depending upon the colors you add, you could inject up to three other printing inks. This will darken the image overall. Remember, this technique adds color to a grayscale file. Follow these steps:

1. Select an embedded grayscale image object. Embed linked objects by choosing Embed Image from the Links palette menu. **A**

2. Choose Filter: Colors: **Adjust Colors**. Choose the document color mode (RGB or CMYK) from the Color Mode menu and click the Convert button. **B**

3. Add colors to the object by dragging the color sliders. This is adding a flat color build to the object. If the image darkens considerably, you may consider removing black, but be careful. Removing too much black will destroy detail in the image.

A *The original embedded grayscale pixel art.*

B *After applying Adjust Colors, the art prints with two inks (here, magenta is added).*

B.17

Creating Monotones from Imported Grayscale Art

Coloring grayscale images with spot colors requires that a path object carry the spot color. This technique marries the tones in an image with a percentage of a swatch color. This could be a process or spot color swatch. Follow these steps:

1. Place a grayscale file into the document (by choosing File: **Place**). The image may be linked or embedded. **A**

2. Create a rectangle the exact size of the image. You may note the size by selecting the object and checking the Info palette. **B**

A *The raster art. It will be used as an opacity mask on a simple rectangle.*

B *A rectangle is placed over the image and then sent to the back. Here, the rectangle has a spot color gradient.*

3. Color the rectangle as you wish the image to be and align it with the imported image.

4. Copy the rectangle.

5. Send the rectangle behind the image by choosing Object: Arrange: **Send Backwards**.

6. Select both the rectangle and the image and choose Make Opacity Mask from the Transparency palette menu.

7. Select the Clip and Invert Mask options in the Transparency palette. **C**

8. To matte the transparent image against white, choose Edit: **Paste in Back** to paste the copied rectangle behind the image, and fill it with white.

C *The raster art becomes an opacity mask for the rectangle. Inverted, the mask shows the image detail correctly.*

B.18

Creating Duotones from Imported Grayscale Art

Duotones traditionally combine a spot color with black to create a custom ink effect on press. Illustrator doesn't have a multi-ink color mode or the ability to create true duotones. You can fake the process in a pinch, though. To create a duotone from imported grayscale art, follow the same procedure as for creating a monotone except for the following:

• **After importing your art, copy it.** Do not copy the rectangle, as described in step 4.

• **After converting the art to an opacity mask, paste the copied grayscale image in back, instead of pasting the rectangle.** This mattes the transparent version against a solid version.

B.19

Coloring Imported Grayscale Art

Coloring imported art differently in different places is, ideally, a job for Photoshop. There are stronger tools there and better support for the procedure. In the event that you need to do it in Illustrator, follow these steps:

1. Set the document's color mode to RGB.

2. Create a new layer atop the one with the grayscale art. Target the layer and set its blending mode to Overlay.

3. Trace the outlines of the objects you wish to color and fill the objects appropriately. Since the Layer holds the blend mode, the color of these objects does not affect each other unless you apply blend modes to the objects.

4. If the color looks nondescript, consider switching the layer's blending mode to Color. This sometimes produces harsh, saturated color, but may work better for some images. **A B**

A *A path is traced around the area to be colored.*

B *The Layer is set to Overlay to blend the color to the object below.*

If you need to work in CMYK, you may experience difficulties with grayscale art and blend modes. Follow these steps:

1. Set the document's color mode to CMYK.

2. Select the imported grayscale art and choose Filter: Colors: **Convert to CMYK**.

3. Switch the document's color mode to RGB and then back to CMYK. This will make the grayscale file a rich black with tones in all the channels. Since blend modes work on channels, they will function more as anticipated.

B.20

Colorizing Line Art Scans

Line art is a one-bit raster image. It may also be called "bit map" art. You will know it because all of the pixels must be solid black, or they will be transparent. Line art is the only kind of imported raster art that can have color applied directly to it. Follow these steps:

1. Select the line art to be colored. Use any selection tool to do this.

2. The fill and stroke of the art will be set to None. Although you cannot apply a stroke to the line art, you can apply a fill.

3. Select a Fill for the line art by setting a color in the Color palette or by choosing one directly in the Swatches palette.

In some instances, you may need to color different parts of the same line art with different colors. Line art cannot accept gradients or patterns, but you can work around the problem:

1. Place the image on its own layer and copy the image. If you need to, apply a solid color fill to the line art. **A**

2. Copy the layer by choosing Duplicate Layer from the Layers palette menu.

3. Draw a path around the area in the image that should have the second color. Be sure the path that does the outlining is on top and choose Make Clipping Mask from the Layer palette menu. **B**

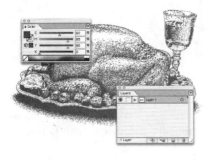

A *Line art with a fill applied.*

B *The duplicated layer, masked to isolate part of the image. The artwork mask receives its own fill.*

4. Twirl down the new layer's triangle to see the contents of the layer. Select the image object by (Option) [Alt] clicking on its name.

5. Apply a new fill color to the line art.

6. If it's appropriate, edit the points or reposition the Clipping Path object on the layer to reveal a new section of the image. If it isn't, drag the clipping path object into the trash of the Layers palette to delete it and create a new one.

7. Repeat steps 3 through 6 to create additional color areas for the image. **C**

C *The two layers together.*

B.21

Coloring Auto-Traced Line Art Scans

Although it is ideal to manually trace line art, many users do not have the time or inclination to create every path by hand. Especially when existing line art is complicated, users turn to an automatic pixel to vector conversion utility. Both Photoshop and Illustrator have an auto trace function that does a fair-to-poor job. Adobe Streamline does a better job than both of them, but it is still limited.

One of limits of the tools is that they generally cannot create negative space on their own. This ends up causing problems when it comes to adding color to the art. A strategy many users employ is to rely on the line art to provide solid black outlines and to add colors as secondary objects, rather than trying to color the vectors created by the auto tracing. This same general principal is also used when adding color to line art that hasn't been traced. To set up the file, follow these steps:

1. Make sure the traced line art is on its own layer. Double-click the layer to set its options. Name the layer something descriptive, like "Black Line Vector." **A**

2. Select all the objects on the layer. Choose Object: Compound Paths: **Make**. This will convert all the black line shapes to a large, single path. This may cause overlapping parts of the path to turn black. You will need to correct this. **B**

A *After running through Streamline, the art (shown here against gray) has some white areas and some transparent areas.*

B *After being converted to a Compound Path, some paths need to be reversed to correct the image.*

3. You may be able to correct negative space in the compound path by opening the Attributes palette and clicking the Even-Odd rule button. If this doesn't work, you may need to correct the compound path by selecting individual paths with the Direct Select tool and reversing their direction. To reverse paths, open the Attributes palette and select Reverse Path Direction (on or off). After reversing several paths, you should be able to recover the appearance of the path. Once you have, lock the layer by clicking the Lock column in the layers palette. **C**

4. Create a new layer by choosing New Layer button in the Layers palette menu. This will be the flat color layer and it should be named descriptively as well.

5. Drag the new layer below the Black Line Vectors layer in the Layers palette. Be sure you do not nest the layer inside the Black Line layer.

6. Set the fill to None so that you can trace without your view being obstructed.

7. Create basic shapes that describe the "hollow" parts of the path. You can be somewhat sloppy as you do this as long as the line art layer obscures the edges. As you complete shapes, add fills to indicate the areas you have completed. **D**

C *The corrected compound path.*

D *Color is added as separate shapes on their own layer.*

8. If your work calls for adding shading or gradients to the color, duplicate the Flat Color Layer. Rename the layer "shading layer" and hide the Flat Color Layer. The Flat color layer will provide a fallback in the event that objects become scrambled or incorrect. Some users also make the shading layer partially transparent and blend it with the flat color layer.

9. Color the art on the shading layer as desired. The kind of shading you create will depend on the intent of the art. You may use any of the lighting techniques noted previously. **E**

E *The completed image.*

B.22

Applying Color Screens to Objects

In some cases, you may need to create an object that retains its overall colors, but is tinted toward another color. For example, you may want two versions of a house, one normal and one bathed in yellow morning light. Further, gradients and patterns should be affected and the effect ought to be editable. To do this:

1. Create the art that will be tinted. The art can contain anything: gradients, meshes, patterns, envelopes, and raster images. **A**

2. Select the art and click the New Symbol button in the Symbols palette to save the art as a symbol. Once you have done this, delete the art in the document. It is no longer needed and may be recalled at any time if it were.

3. Click the Place Symbol Instance button in the Symbols palette to add a version of the art back into the document as a symbol. Position the art as required by dragging it with the Selection tool. **B**

A *The original art.*

B *After being converted to a symbol, the original art is deleted and an instance of the symbol is placed on the page.*

4. Select a solid fill color to tint the art with in the Color palette.

5. Choose the Symbol Stainer tool and click directly on the instance you placed. Click again to add more of the color to the instance or click and hold to add a progressive amount. If you have added too much color overall, (Option) [Alt] click to reduce the amount. **C**

c *The instance is colored with the Symbol Stainer.*

Applying Gradient Screens to Objects

In some cases you may need to add a screened gradient to objects. This can be done to add a fading color change to an object. Just as you added flat colors to objects, you can also add gradients and styles. This technique will not apply gradients to raster symbols.

1. Make sure nothing is selected in the document. Create or select a gradient. With nothing selected, set the fill swatch to the gradient and the stroke to None.

2. Click the New Style button in the Styles palette to save the fill and stroke combination as a style.

3. Create the art that will be tinted. The art cannot contain raster images but may contain gradients, meshes, patterns, and envelopes.

4. Select the art and click the New Symbol button in the Symbols palette to save the art as a symbol. Once you have done this, delete the art in the document. It is no longer needed and may be recalled at any time if it were.

5. Click the Place Symbol Instance button in the Symbols palette to add a version of the art back into the document as a symbol. Position the art as required by dragging it with the Selection tool.

6. Select the Style you created in step 2 from the Styles palette.

7. Choose the Symbol Styler tool and click directly on the instance you placed. Click again to add more of the color to the instance or click and hold to add a progressive amount. If you have added too much color overall, (Option) [Alt] click to reduce the amount. **A**

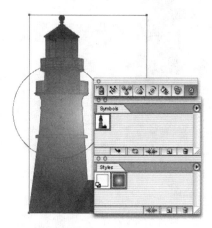

A *A gradient style applied to a symbol instance with the Symbol Styler.*

B.24

Staining Part of an Instance

Staining affects an instance overall. You cannot stain part of an instance with one color and another with a different color. Work around the problem with multiple objects:

1. Create a symbol instance (as described in *B.22, Applying Color Screens to Objects*).

2. In the Layers palette, find the stained instance. If it is selected, you may choose Locate Object in the Layers palette menu to make that section of the layers palette visible.

3. Select the item in the Layers palette by clicking on its name and duplicate it by dragging it onto the New Layer Button or choosing Duplicate from the Layers palette menu. **A**

4. Stain the newly created (top) instance.

5. Draw a rectangle atop the instance and fill it with a gradient.

6. Select both the gradient and the stained instance and choose Make Opacity Mask from the Layers palette menu. If required, click on the opacity mask thumbnail to adjust the opacity mask. **B**

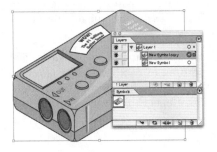

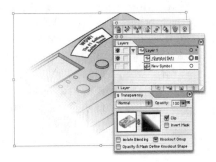

A *Two symbol instances directly atop each other.*

B *The top instance stained and masked. The bottom instance is hidden.*

7. The top, stained, instance should blend into the lower, unstained instance. Repeat the process as required to add more colors to the items. **C**

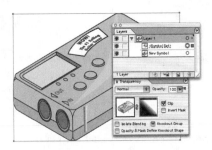

C *The two instances shown together.*

B.25

Creating Seamless Patterns

Patterns repeat in a noticeable way. In some cases, this is the intention and it looks correct. In other cases, the patterns should be created so that the repeating (or "tiling") is not noticeable. To set this up, we'll copy repeating objects around the bounding box. This will work around the squared-up bounding box and make it less noticeable. Follow these steps:

1. Shift-drag with the Rectangle tool to create a perfect square. Set the fill and stroke to None.

2. Arrange the items for the pattern around the square. Items should overlap the square on some sides. It is better if a single object doesn't cross

two sides of the square and if objects do not cross directly across from each other. Also, try to keep objects from crossing the square entirely, as this will be hard to work around. **A**

3. Select all of the objects, including the square. Position your cursor on one of the anchor points of the square and drag to another anchor point on the square. Add the (Option) [Alt] key as you drag. This makes a duplicate of the square and the pattern tiles. Repeat this process for all four sides of the rectangle. **B**

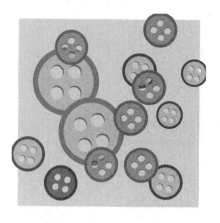

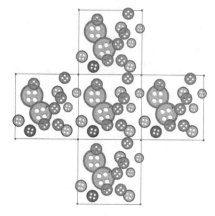

A *Objects arranged atop the pattern's bounding square (shown in gray).*

B *Objects copied around will provide the opposite halves of objects cropped by the bounding box.*

4. Check for objects that crash into each other on the sides of the center square. Reposition them as needed.

5. At this point, you could create a pattern and be done. It is good tradecraft, though, to delete any objects that are not needed. Delete all the squares except the first one and any objects that do not cross the first square. **C**

6. Drag all the objects into the Swatches palette or choose Edit: **Define Pattern**. If you dragged in, double-click the new swatch to name the pattern. **D**

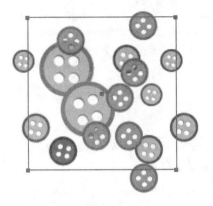

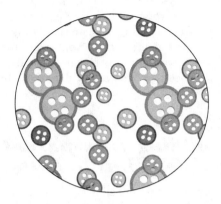

C *Only objects inside or on the bounding box are needed.*

D *A C:100, Y:100 monotone.*

B.26

Creating Variations on Patterns

Once a pattern is established, you can create variants of it to adjust particulat items within it. This might be done to create the impression of transparency, to change spot color definitions in the pattern, or to reuse patterns in a new way. To create a variation on a pattern:

1. Drag an existing pattern out of the Swatches palette into the document.

2. The objects in the pattern will be placed in the document in the current layer as a group. A bounding box with a fill and stroke of None will be the lowest pattern object in the stacking order.

3. Select the items to be edited. This will often mean deselecting all of the items in the pattern first and then selecting the items you require. For example, you may need to select only the spot color items to be modified. Since the items are grouped, you will want to use the Direct Selection tool to select the items to edit.

4. Select all of the items in the pattern group. Drag the items directly into the Swatches palette to create a new pattern.

Issues to Consider

Pattern variants are often applied to objects atop each other. This is done to create optical illusions or to change the colors of parts of a pattern fill. This works when pattern fills have not be transformed independently of their objects. Since the patterns tile like wallpaper, placing pattern fills based on the same bounding box size tile together seamlessly. For example, you could create a pattern variation with one object a different color than the original pattern. Placing items with these patterns atop each creates an area of color difference bound by the path the pattern is in. Since the other colors are the same, the impression is that a colored object has been inserted below the other objects in the pattern.

B.27

Adding Transparent Gradients and Color Tints to Pattern Fills

Gradients are not allowed to be part of a pattern fill. Commonly, users expand gradients into objects to add them to a fill. In the even that the gradient covers the entire pattern fill, rather than being a component of it, it can be added as a second fill.

1. Create the object you wish to have the pattern and gradient combination. Be sure you have the gradient and pattern you want to use saved as swatches.

2. Fill the object with the pattern you want to use and leave the object selected.

3. Open the Appearance palette and select the fill attribute by clicking directly on its name. This will ensure that the new fill is below the stroke.

4. Choose Add New Fill from the Appearance palette menu or click the Duplicate Selected Item button on the face of the palette.

5. The new fill will have the same pattern as the old fill. Switch it to a gradient by clicking the gradient you want in the Swatches palette.

6. Leave the gradient highlighted in the Appearance palette and open the Transparency palette. Set the opacity of the gradient fill in the transparency palette to less than 100%. This will let you see the pattern below. Alternatively, set a Blend mode for the fill. Note in the Appearance palette that the transparency is being added to the second fill only. **A**

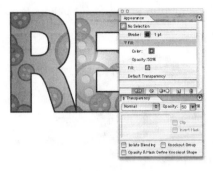

A *A transparent second fill adds a gradient appearance to a pattern fill.*

7. Use the gradient tool to reposition the start and end of the gradient in the object.

8. Click the New Style button in the Styles palette to save the pattern and gradient combination for later use.

Issues to Consider

This same technique is used to add flat color tints to patterns. Although you can include a transparent flat color in a pattern fill, this method allows you more flexibility to change the color and opacity (tint) of the color on-the-fly.

B.28

Adding Gradients to Strokes

A gradient cannot be applied to a stroke. Although you cannot apply a gradient as a true stroke, you can work around the problem on open paths as follows:

1. Make sure you have the gradient you wish to use saved as a swatch.

2. Select the object to receive the gradient and apply the gradient as a fill. Open the Appearance palette.

3. Make sure the fill is highlighted in the Appearance palette and choose Effects: Path: **Offset Path**. In the Offset Path dialog box, choose the width of the "stroke" and the joins options. Many users employ the Round joins to avoid the odd caps that can occur with this technique.

4. Click the New Style button in the Styles palette to save for later use. **A**

A *Offset Path applied only to the Fill of an open path.*

If you need to apply a gradient stroke to a closed path, use the following variation.

1. Make sure you have the gradient you wish to use saved as a swatch.

2. Select the object to receive the gradient and set the Fill as it should be. Set the stroke of the object to none. Open the Appearance palette.

3. Select the Fill in the palette and click the Duplicate Selected item button.

4. The top fill will be selected in the palette. Select the lower fill in the palette by clicking on it. Set the fill to the gradient you want for the stroke. Choose Effects: **Offset Path**. In the Offset Path dialog box, chose the width of the "stroke" and the joins options. Now the offset is applied to just the top object and the bottom fill retains its standard appearance.

5. Click the New Style button in the Styles palette to save the pattern and gradient combination for later use. **B**

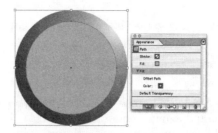

B *The lower fill is offset, giving it the appearance of a stroke.*

B.29

Adding Gradients to Text

Gradients cannot be added to type objects normally. You can work around the problem by adding an extra fill to the type object and applying a gradient to that.

1. Select the type object with one of the selection tools.

2. In the Appearance palette menu, choose Add New Fill.

3. Select a gradient from the Swatches palette or create a new one in the gradient palette to apply.

4. Use the Gradient tool to adjust the start and end of the gradient as desired. **A**

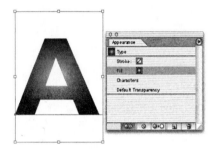

A *A gradient fill added to a type object.*

Path & Object Techniques

Selecting Objects for Alignment

Often, you may wish to position two objects such that their anchor points are directly on top of each other. This may be done when you are aligning objects and when you are creating art with continued lines. The Align palette positions things about bounding boxes but may not position anchor points exactly together. To reposition one object so an anchor point is directly atop another. Follow these steps:

1. Make sure that the View: **Snap to Point** option is activated.

2. Using the Direct Select tool (Option) [Alt] click on the object to be moved to select it. If the object is a compound path or part of a group that you want to move, you may need to (Option) [Alt] click again to completely select the items.

3. Position the cursor directly over an anchor point. The cursor will display a white box to the right of it when are on the point. **A**

4. Click-drag the object until the cursor is directly over another anchor point. The cursor will turn white when you are directly over another anchor point. **B**

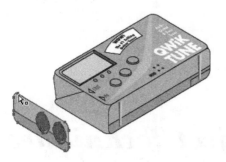
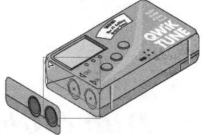

A *The cursor is placed directly atop an anchor point before dragging the selection.*

B *When the points are aligned, the transformation arrowhead turns white.*

C.2

Selection Strategies

The most versatile selection tool is the Direct Selection tool. It can be used to the exclusion of other selection tools for everyday selecting. The main reasons to use other selection tools are as follows:

- **To select mesh points.** Mesh points are often located in positions to each other that make it difficult to use the Direct Selection tool. The Direct Selection Lasso is most commonly used in these cases.

- **To make basic transformations to selected objects without switching tools.** If you need to scale, move, or rotate a series of objects, the Selection tool is a good choice. Used in conjunction with View: **Show Bounding Box**, the Selection tool can make easy work of selecting and transforming objects.

- **When you are very inexperienced with Illustrator.** The Direct Selection tool can be confusing. If you are very new to Illustrator, you might consider starting with the Selection tool and working your way to the Direct Selection.

For most other circumstances, the Direct Selection tool is an excellent choice. Use the following tips:

- **Select the tool once, and then select another tool you want to use.** Hold down the (Command) [Ctrl] key to temporarily return to the Direct Selection tool.

- **Click directly on anchor points, segments, and direction points, to select them.** This enables you to edit the basic shape of paths.

- **(Option) [Alt]-click paths to select them.** If you have accessed the Direct Selection tool with the (Command) [Ctrl] keys, you will need to keep those keys down as well. These modifiers switch you to the Group Selection tool. Use this tool to select sequentially through items in a group. This also works for compound paths and other objects that are comprised of multiple paths. For example, the word "be" converted to outlines consists of four paths connected as two grouped compound paths. The outside shapes for each letter and their counters combine to make compound paths that are then grouped together. (Option) [Alt]-click on a shape, such as the outside of the "b", to select it. Click again to select the next item, such as the inside of the "b."

- **To select multiple items, (Shift) click them.** To select complete paths as you do this, (Option) [Alt]-click the objects. Shift-clicking actually toggles a selection, or turns it on or off. This can get in the way of sequential group selecting. To add items in a group with the group selection you can Shift-click directly on the additional items or release the Shift key and click again on the first object. This does not deselect objects that were already selected, even if they are not part of the initial group. For example, selecting an object and then the expanded letter "b" in the previous example might go like this. (Option) [Alt]-click on the first object with the Direct Selection tool. (Option-Shift) [Alt-Shift]-click on the outside shape of the "b." (Option) [Alt]-click again on the "b" to select the inside path in the object. Note that there is no Shift in the third selection. Once objects are selected, you do not need to continue holding down modifier keys.

C.3

Drawing a Basic Path

The easiest path to create is made entirely out of straight lines—just click around the image without dragging. Most paths require a little curving, though, but many people try to get around that by clicking hundreds of tiny straight lines, hoping they're small enough to escape detection (a technique that never works as well as you hope). Getting the most out of the Pen tool suite does require a bit of experience, but you can use the following technique to start drawing simple curves with a minimum of effort. In this example, the Pen tool is used to trace a basic shape:

1. To start the path, click once with the Pen tool (without dragging) to place a single point.

2. Move the cursor a small distance along the shape you're tracing, making sure the next segment you place won't have to curve too steeply.

3. As you click to place the next point, hold the mouse button down and drag in the same direction as the path. This reveals the handles, enabling you to curve the segment. **A**

4. Move the handle until the segment matches the edge of the shape. (Take your time; as you get accustomed to the handles, it may take a moment or two to get it right.) Release the mouse button.

5. Hold down the (Option) [Alt] key and click the point you just placed. This hides the second curve handle, preventing it from adding curve to the next segment. **B**

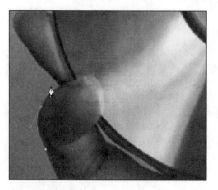

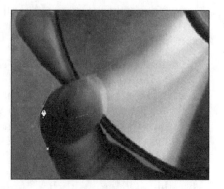

A *After placing the initial point, click-drag to place a point with curve handles.*

B *Remove the forward curve handle by clicking on the anchor point.*

6. Repeat steps 2 through 5 until you complete the path. **C**

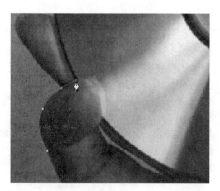

C *Continuing the process.*

The advantage of this technique is that each segment is controlled by only one curve handle, making it much easier to shape the path as you create it. The disadvantage is that curves tend to be less smooth with this method. As you get experience with the Pen tool, you will learn when to remove the forward direction point and when to leave it.

Mistakes to Avoid

Positioning anchor points poorly. Anchor points should be positioned in places where the curve is changing directions. A change in direction could be where the slope begins to curve more steeply, or at a corner, or where a curve begins to change angle. Positioning anchor points in other places usually results in too many or too few points.

Confusing direction points with anchor points. Many users click too rapidly and accidentally place anchor direction points thinking that they are making anchor points. This makes it difficult to anticipate the shape of curves and causes confusion. Click slowly and deliberately when learning the Pen tool.

Using very large direction segments. A common maxim holds that direction segments should be no longer than one third of the length of the line segment they are attached to. This is a good one to keep in mind, even if you wind up discarding it as you become handier with the tools. Try to limit the size of the direction segments.

Dragging in the wrong direction. As you drag out direction points, you should be moving in the direction the path is going. If you are dragging in the opposite direction, your path will cross itself, creating a knot and making the path harder to work with.

Issues to Consider

Closing a path. If you've determined that you need a closed path, remember to end on the first point you placed.

Leaving a path open. The Pen tool makes it difficult to leave a path open. If you decide to leave a path open, the fastest way to stop drawing a path is to (Command) [Ctrl]-click away from the path. These modifier keys switch you to either the Selection or Direct Selection tool (whichever you used last), enabling you to deselect by clicking off the path.

Editing a path. Don't try to get the path perfect the first time around. Just try to get as close as you can. When you've completed the path, you can always tweak it as necessary with the Direct Selection tool.

Be ready to undo. If you click in error, don't try to repair the path on-the-fly (if you're new to the Pen tool, your path can quickly spin out of control). Instead, press (Command) [Ctrl]-Z to undo the last action, then try again.

Placing the path when tracing an image element. When tracing an element for a clipping path, try to place the path just inside the element's edge, shaving off a couple of pixels. This way, you reduce the chances of including any unwanted background pixels in the outline. When intending to use the path as an object, for redrawing an item, try to place the path precisely along the edge of the element.

C.4

Continuing an Existing Open Path

It's possible for a path to become deselected as you're creating it. To reactivate a deselected path, click either end of it with the Pen tool. This can be done whether or not the path is selected. The Pen tool cursor will display a forward slash when you are over an open anchor point. From there, continue placing new points.

Issues to Consider

Forward direction points are lost. Forward direction points on open paths are removed when the path is continued. You can redraw the points by click-dragging on the end point, but there is no way to preserve it.

C.5

Transformation Strategies

When transforming objects using the Scale, Rotate, Reflect, and Shear tools, preciseness counts. Keep the following issues in mind:

- **It matters when you hold down the modifier keys.** Hold down the (Option) [Alt] key before you click with these tools and it sets the point of transformation and opens the dialog box. Hold (Option) [Alt] down after you begin dragging to transform a copy.

- **When drag transforming, give yourself plenty of room.** Many users click drag directly atop an object with a transformation tool. This makes it hard to see what you are doing and forces your movements to be more acute. Select the object to be transformed and then move your cursor well away from the object.

- **The Shift key constrains differently depending on the direction you're dragging.** This is another reason to give yourself plenty of room when transforming. For example, when scaling, Shift-dragging horizontally constrains the height of the object. Shift-dragging vertically constrains the width and Shift-dragging diagonally with the scale tool locks the proportions of the object.

Many users prefer the Scale, Rotate, Reflect, and Shear tools to other methods because they offer more ways to transform. Here are some examples that illustrate the ways the tools might be used.

- **Create longitude and latitude lines on a globe with the Scale tool.** Starting with a circle, click-drag horizontally toward the center of the circle with the Scale tool. Add the (Option-Shift) [Alt-Shift] keys as you drag. Release your mouse before releasing the modifier keys. Repeat the process to make several longitude lines. Then select the initial circle again and click-drag vertically toward the center of the circle with the Scale tool. Add the (Option-Shift) [Alt-Shift] keys as you drag. Style the art as needed. **A**

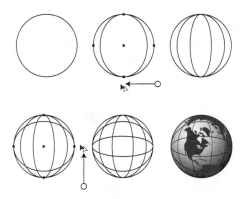

A *Adding the (Option) [Alt] and Shift keys as you drag to constrain the width and/or height as you drag and create a copy.*

- **Change the inner radius of an existing star with the Scale tool.** Use the Direct Selection tool to select only the inner anchor points of a star. Do this by shift-selecting the points. Alternatively, if the star is isolated from other objects and the radii of the star permits, click drag a marquee around the inner anchor points. Once selected, switch to the Scale tool. Position your cursor away from the star and drag diagonally toward the center of the star to reduce the radius. Drag diagonally away from the center of the star to increase the radius. **B**

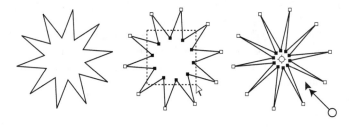

B *Scaling anchor points to change the inner radius of a star.*

- **Create a series of objects disappearing to a vanishing point with the Scale tool.** Select the object to be scaled and switch to the Scale tool. Click once on the "vanishing point" the objects will be scaled toward. The point of transformation will be reset to that position. If you change your mind about the position, click-drag directly on the point of transformation to move it. If you click-drag anywhere else, you will begin scaling the object. Position your cursor so that the object to be scaled is between the cursor and the vanishing point. Click-drag toward the point of transformation. Add the (Option) [Alt] keys as you drag to create a copy. Repeat manually or choose Object: Transform: **Transform Again.** **C**

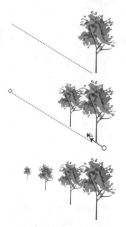

C *Choosing a "vanishing point" to scale toward.*

- **Create a deco border with basic polygons.** Create a circle and place a horizontal and vertical guide on the circle's center point. Create a series of rectangles centered along the vertical guide below the circle. Select the rectangles and (Option) [Alt]-click in the center of the circle with the Rotate tool. Enter a degree in the Rotate dialog box and choose Copy. The number of degrees to rotate will be 90° divided by the number of copies you want. For example, to create 6 rectangle sets, rotate 15°. Leave the new rectangles selected and repeat the transformation (by choosing Object: Transform: **Transform Again**) until you have all the rectangle sets you need. **D**

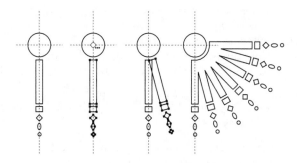

D   *Using Repeat Transformation to create a repeating pattern.*

C.6

Isometric Perspective

Isometric perspective is sometimes used in technical drawings. Unlike traditional perspective, objects in isometric perspective do not approach a vanishing point at different angles. Instead, object sides are parallel. This shows parts of objects not visible in normal perspective. This makes it unsuitable for natural drawing, but useful for technical drawing. Further, you can create isometric perspective by performing a series of repeatable transformations on an object. **A**

A   *Isometric perspective (left) enables you to see parts of objects not usually visible in traditional perspective (right).*

This series of transformations is usually recorded as a series of actions. This makes it easy to perform the scaling and prevents you from having to remember the steps involved. Different actions are needed for the top, left, and right sides of an object.

To create the appearance of three-dimensional object, start by creating the sides of the object straight. Picture taking a cereal box apart and laying it flat. You'll create each side of the box flat and square to the page and then run the action to create the perspective. Once each side is distorted as needed, the pieces are aligned and positioned to create the object. Follow these steps:

1. Create an object you can dispose of to apply the actions to. A simple rectangle will do. You'll use this only to build the action and then delete it. Leave the object selected.

2. In the Actions palette menu, click the Create New Set button to begin the process. Name the set "isometric actions."

3. Click the Create New Action button. Make sure the action is saved in the set you have just built and name it "right side isometric." The Begin Recording light should be on.

4. Double-click the Scale tool to open the Scale dialog box. Choose Non Uniform scaling: Horizontal 100% and Vertical 86.6%.

5. Double-click the Shear tool to open the Shear dialog box. Choose Shear 30° and angle 0°. A 0° angle is the same as Horizontal.

6. Double-click the Rotate tool to open the Rotate dialog box. Choose 30°.

7. Click the Stop Recording button.

8. Repeat the process to create two more actions: one for the left side and one for the top. Use the same scaling percentage but change the reference, shear and rotate to the following settings: **B**

   – Left side: -30° shear, -30° rotate.

   – Top: -30° shear, 30° rotate.

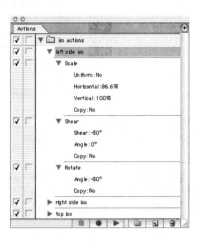

B *An action set for isometric scaling.*

Once you've built all three actions, you are ready to apply them to objects. Remember to build the complete object flat first. You can add objects to the design later, but it will be easier to make things match up if you build them complete the first time. **c**

c *The "flat" design for a simple package (left). Each side transformed using the isometric actions (right).*

When you are ready to position the scaled objects, take the following steps:

1. Make sure the View: **Snap to Point** option is activated.

2. Select all objects in the side of an object to be moved. Usually, there will be corresponding anchor points on two sides. These points will match up in the same spot when the sides are repositioned. Identify one of those points in the objects you have selected. Switch to the Direct Selection tool and position your cursor directly atop that anchor point. The cursor will display a white box next to it when you are over the point.

3. Drag the objects from that point to the corresponding point. The cursor will indicate you are atop the anchor point by turning white.

After you have created objects in isometric perspective you may want to edit them. Commonly, this involves repositioning and resizing. The default snap-to angles are 45°. This makes it hard to drag things and maintain the angle of the drawing. Switch the Constrain Angle by choosing Edit: Preferences: General. The scaling model given here is based on 30°. If you set the constrain angle to 30° and then hold down Shift while dragging, you'll constrain correctly when dragging upper right and lower left. This won't work when dragging upper left and lower right. To snap to that angle, you'll need to reset the preference to 60°.

When you reset the constrain angle, the entire document is affected. The Grid is reset to the constrain angle and that can be very helpful for repositioning items. Also the Rectangle tool will create angled boxes. The boxes created will need to be sheared to fit the perspective. When the Constrain angle is at 30°, shear objects –30° and Axis: Horizontal. When it's 60°, shear –30° and Axis: Vertical to fit them into the perspective.

Changing the default angles of the document can be frustrating. It takes time to do and makes some tasks more difficult. It's often easier to reposition items using the Move command. Double-click on the Selection or Direct Selection tools to open the Move dialog box. Enter values in the Distance and Angle fields only to reposition the object.

Another option is to use Smart Guides. Set the Angles field of the Smart Guides & Slices preference to the 30° Angles options. Next, activate smart guides by choosing View: **Smart Guides**. Although this won't make things snap to the correct angle, it will display a guide when you are dragging something at the correct angle. This is often the fastest way to transform at the required orientation.

Issues to Consider

Saving selections saves time. When resizing isometric objects, many users employ the Direct Selection Lasso to pick up the part of an object for repositioning. For example, you may need to select just the right side anchor points and legs of a table. As more objects populate the drawing, this becomes more difficult. Save complex selections for use later by choosing Select: **Save Selection**.

Use Symbol instances. Often in these kinds of drawings, you'll be using the same objects again and again. Saving them as a Symbols and then dragging individual instances into the document makes the objects easy to select and saves file size.

C.7

Creating Transparent Blends for Animation

With or without transparency, object blends are useful for creating basic sequential animation. Typically, this involves an object, like type or a logo, fading in, morphing, or changing position. This work is usually done in Illustrator when the end result is an SWF file and Flash or LiveMotion is not part of your toolkit.

To prepare an object for sequential, "fade-in" animation, follow these steps:

1. Group the objects to be animated. Choose Object: **Group**. Without this step blends may not work correctly.

2. Set the opacity of the Group to 0%.

3. Copy the Group and choose Edit: **Paste in Front**. Set the Opacity of the pasted group to 100%. If the animation involves motion as well as the fade effect, reposition the pasted group to the position the animation ends in.

4. Select both copies of the group and choose Object: Blend: **Make**.

5. Determine the amount of time the animation should take. By default in Flash, movies play at 12 frames per second. Set the Blend Options (by choosing Object: Blend: **Blend Options**) to the number of frames you want the animation to be. So if your fade should take a half of a second and you are working 12 frames per second, you want 6 steps. Since you already have the first and last object, set the blend to the number of frames you want minus two. **A**

6. Expand the blend (by choosing Object: Blend: **Expand**) and ungroup (by choosing Object: **Ungroup**). If your blend was created from groups, do not ungroup those as well.

7. Select the Layer in the Layers palette by clicking on its name. Choose Release to Layers (Sequence) from the Layers palette submenu. **B**

8. Choose File: **Save for Web** and set the sequence to save as an SWF file. Choose the Layers to Fames option to create a self-contained animation. If the animation is not part of a more elaborate page to be saved, or you will be building pages in another application, you may also consider choosing File: **Export** and choosing SWF.

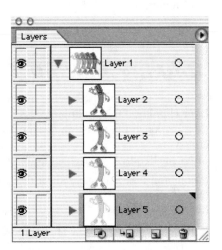

A *Set to 2 steps, this blend would take a third of a second to play at 12 frames per second.*

B *An expanded and ungrouped blend released to layers.*

Issues to Consider

Art brushes are often used in setting up animation. Since you can easily alter the appearance of brushes, they are often used to create the steps in an animation. For example, you can apply an art brush on an open path, duplicate it and then edit the path's shape with the Direct Selection tool. After selecting both paths, you can create an object blend between them to make the intermediate steps. From there, you can expand the blend and release the objects to layers. You can then either export to Photoshop to make an animated GIF or export to SWF.

Illustrator is not an animation application. Although Illustrator can do a lot, to create anything other than the most basic sequences you will need another application, such as Flash, LiveMotion, Premiere, or ImageReady.

Blending symbols instances reduces file size. In this workflow, first convert the object to be blended into a symbol by selecting it and choosing New Symbol from the Symbols Palette menu. Next, place two instances of the symbol by choosing Place Symbol Instance from the Symbols Palette menu twice. Instances can be made transparent using the transparency palette or the Symbol Screener. The remaining steps are the same.

Preparing Animated GIFs. Illustrator has no tool to create animation internally. You'll need to export to Photoshop to create animated fade GIFs. Fade and motion animation, such as those found commonly in banner ads are easy to prepare in ImageReady. Export the Illustrator file to the Photoshop format. Be sure to include layers. Set the resolution to 72 and the color mode to RGB. Open the file in ImageReady and prepare the animation there.

C.8

Masking Multiple Layers

There are two models for clipping objects in Illustrator: object clipping and layer clipping. Object clipping sets specific objects to be masked; layer clipping masks all the items on a layer. You should use object clipping when you are trying to create a specific image effect or work around complex stacking order problems. Use layer clipping when you want to crop images overall.

A common task is to crop all of the objects in a document into a single area. Object clipping creates a group and can disrupt the organization of objects on different layers. Follow these steps:

1. Create a new layer by choosing New Layer from the Layers palette menu. This layer will provide a mask for all the other layers. Name the layer something that you will recognize, like "Master Clip." **A**

2. Put the object that will do the masking in this layer. You may create a new object or drag an existing item to this layer. If the item that you want to do the clipping isn't the only object on the layer, make sure it's on top. Some objects may not be used as masks. *(For more information, see 9.69, Object: **Clipping Mask**.)*

3. From the Layers palette menu, choose Make Clipping Mask. The top item becomes the clipping mask for the layer. This will be indicated by the object being underlined in the Layers palette and the lines between objects on the layer being dashed.

4. Select the layers you wish to mask in the Layers palette. Selected layers will be highlighted in the palette.

5. Drag the layers into the Master Clip layer. The master layer clips the layers in it while the sub-layers retain their independence and stacking order. **B**

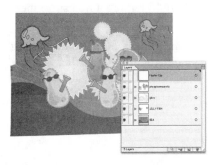

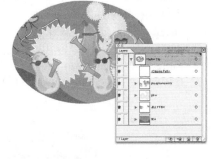

A *The Master Clip layer added to an existing document.*

B *Layers in the Master Clip layer are masked by the clipping object on the layer, but stay independent layers.*

C.9

Basic Trapping

Although it is less widespread as a responsibility than it once was for designers, trapping is still an important consideration when preparing a file for print. If you are responsible for preparing a trap manually, consider the following technique. Although the specific steps you will take may vary from job to job, the basic process remains the same. Do not undertake this responsibility unless you need to do so and you are sure that trapping is required. *(For more information, see 18.2, Overprint Fill.)*

There are two models for creating trap objects: trap with strokes or trap with fills. Trapping with fills uses thin overprinting closed paths. Trapping with strokes uses the stroke of an object to create the overprinting area. Each has its advantages. Trapping with a stroke enables you to easily adjust the thickness and direction of the trap. To change the trap size, you need only adjust the stroke width. To change the direction of the trap, you switch the color of the stroke. Fills enable you to trap with a gradient.

In this technique, we will create strokes initially, and then convert to fills as required. Follow these steps:

1. Determine the need for trapping. This may be the hardest part of the technique, especially if you weren't the one who prepared the file. Trapping is usually needed whenever spot colors abut other colors or where process colors with no common components are next to each other. A 20% common ink component is often enough in process colors to avoid the need for trapping. For example, C:40, Y:60 abutting M:60 Y:35 would not require trapping since they have yellow in common. However, C:40, K:10 next to M:60, Y:35 would require a trap since there is no commonality. **A**

    Determining trapping objects can be confusing, especially in complex documents. The presence of masks and gradients can further confuse things. Stay calm and focus on abutting color areas and don't be distracted by the contents of the file.

A *The commonality of yellow prevents the need for trapping where the square on the left overlaps. With no commonality on the right, trapping is required.*

2. Determine which colors will be used in the trap. The lighter color is always used to trap since it less noticeable. For example, in process trapping, yellow is used when possible. Lighter refers to ink density, not just visual appearance. If you have questions about which of two colors to trap with, touch base with your printer.

3. Locate and select the objects that will be involved in the trapping. Make sure the entire objects are selected and choose Edit: **Copy**.

4. Create a new layer and name it "trapping." Put traps on their own layer so that they can be identified and isolated quickly. As different traps are required for different paper/press combinations, traps on their own layers are easier to find and adjust.

5. Hide all of the layers except the trapping layer by (Option) [Alt] clicking on the visibility icon for the trapping layer.

6. Choose Edit: **Paste in Front** to paste the trapping objects into the trapping layer in the positions they were copied from. **B**

7. Leave the objects selected and click the Outline button in the Pathfinder palette. A new, open path with no fill and a 0 point stroke replace are created wherever paths intersect. **C**

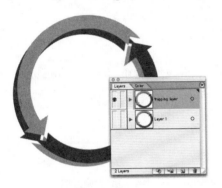

B *Objects required for trapping duplicated onto their own layer.*

C *Using Pathfinder Outline to create the segments that will provide the traps.*

8. Delete the paths you don't need. You may need to refer to the original layer to remind yourself where the traps will be. This is usually easiest if you lock the original layer and set the trapping layer to Outline mode by (Command) [Ctrl]-clicking on the visibility icon for the layer in the layers palette. Make sure you don't delete object's you'll need for the traps. **D**

9. Set the remaining strokes to the color and width of the trap needed. If you don't know and cannot find someone to tell you, set the strokes to .3 points. This is a liberal trap that works in most situations.

10. In the Attributes palette, click on Overprint stroke. **E**

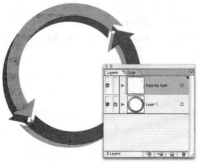
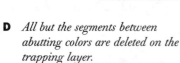
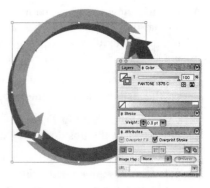

D *All but the segments between abutting colors are deleted on the trapping layer.*

E *The trapping objects given a stroke and set to overprint.*

11. Choose View: **Overprint Preview** and inspect all the layers to together. The traps should appear slightly darker than the underlying objects.

C.10
Trapping Gradients

In the event that you are trapping a gradient, follow the same steps described under *C.9, Basic Trapping*. After you have an overprinting stroke of the desired width, follow these steps:

1. Choose Object: Path: **Outline Stroke**. This will convert the stroke to a fill and transfer the overprinting value to the fill as well.

2. Fill the object with the gradient. Many users do this by clicking on the trapped object with the Eyedropper tool to sample the gradient. Be careful when doing this, since the Eyedropper samples overprinting status by default as well. Double-click the Eyedropper tool to change its options or reset the overprinting value manually.

C.11
Using the Trap Pathfinder

Some users prefer to use the Trap Pathfinder command when preparing traps. This has the advantage that Illustrator determines the need for trapping rather than the user and it sets the overprinting automatically. As with most automatic processes, this doesn't always work correctly and should be regarded with some suspicion. Also, the Trap Pathfinder makes traps in a specific direction, using filled shapes. Because of this, you cannot reset the width or direction of the trap easily. Make sure you know the correct width and color to trap with before applying this technique. Follow these steps:

1. Copy the objects that need to be trapped.

2. Create a new layer and name it "trapping." Hide the other layers by (Option) [Alt]-clicking on the trapping layer's visibility icon.

3. Choose Edit: **Paste in Front.**

4. Select the objects of one set of colors and fill them all with 100% cyan. Select the remaining objects and fill them with 100% magenta.

5. Select all the objects and choose Trap from the Pathfinder palette menu. *(For more information, see 29.14, Trap.)*

6. Once you've applied the Trap Pathfinder, you'll want to delete all of the non-trapping objects from the layer. The newly created trapping objects will be selected. Leave them selected and choose Select: **Inverse** or Shift-drag across all the objects with the Selection tool. Press the Delete key to remove the objects.

7. Recolor the trapping objects as required. The traps will be set to overprint automatically. Inspect the layers with View: **Overprint Preview** activated.

Mistakes to Avoid

Using the Trap effect. The Trap pathfinder may be applied as an effect. This is generally a poor idea and should be avoided. It may not be applied to individual objects and its effects are hard to anticipate.

C.12

Using an Envelope as an Opacity Mask

As an envelope changes the shape of an object, you may also want to use it to adjust the object's opacity. This is often used in transitional color effects or to create a fade. For example, warped text may fade to transparent in the same shape that it is warped. To convert an existing envelope into an opacity mask for the object it distorts:

1. Select the envelope and locate it in the Layers palette.

2. In the Layers palette drag the envelope directly onto the Create New Layer button or choose Duplicate <Envelope> from the Layers palette menu. **A**

3. Hide the original envelope (click on its visibility icon in the Layers palette) and select the newly created one.

4. Choose Object: Envelope Distort: **Release**. A mesh will be created and the formerly enveloped objects will be behind it. The mesh will be gray. Delete the original objects. **B**

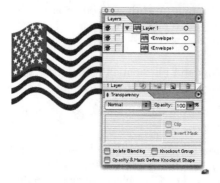
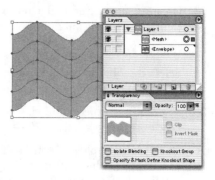

A *The envelope duplicated in place.*

B *The duplicate envelope released to a gradient mesh.*

5. Show the first enveloped object. Select it and the mesh you created from the copy. The mesh should be the same as the envelope on the first object.

6. Choose Create Opacity Mask from the Transparency palette submenu.

7. Click the opacity mask thumbnail in the Transparency palette to begin editing the mask. Select mesh points with Direct Selection or Direct Selection Lasso tools to begin to recolor them. Unless inverted, the darker the mesh points, the more transparent the envelope will be in that area. **C**

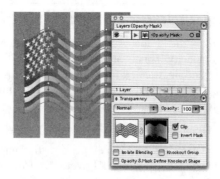

C *The mesh used as an Opacity Mask.*

Issues to Consider

You cannot edit an object and its opacity mask at the same time. This means that if you edit the shape of the envelope, you may need to edit the opacity mask as well afterward. Try to set the envelope the way you want it before making the mask.

C.13

Gradient Mesh Strategies

There are four ways to create a gradient mesh. Each has its advantages:

- **Select an object and choose Object: Create Gradient Mesh.** This option is good when you want to create an evenly spaced mesh. Often this is used to create smoother color transitions. For example, you might want color to change at the same rate in different directions.

- **Select an object with a gradient fill and choose Object: Expand and choose the Gradient Mesh option.** This option turns the gradient object into a mask for a gradient mesh. It produces a very faithful version of the original gradient, not a mesh that follows the outline of the shape. It also retains any stroke that may have been on the gradient by applying it to the mask. This is often used when you like the source gradient but want to curve it or create a shape that standard gradients do not support. It is not commonly used to create a three-dimensional appearance.

- **Click in an object with the Mesh tool.** This option creates a custom mesh. It is most often used when using meshes to draw organic things, such as tracing a scan.

- **Release an envelope.** When an envelope is released, it becomes a gradient mesh. By default all of the mesh points are gray, but they can be recolored. This is often used to take advantage of the prebuilt shapes available in the Make with Warp command. For example, you could make a warp using the Arc shape, release it and use the arc as a gradient mesh.

When you set about to create a mesh, first think about the shape of the mesh you wish to create. If you want to make an object appear rounded or to get started on a mesh by making a series of points, use Object: **Create Gradient Mesh.** If you want to add a specific color adjustment based on an object's shape, use the mesh tool. If you want to make a mesh but leave the outline of the shape, apply a gradient and expend to a mesh.

Typically, the hardest task with meshes is tracing scans for realistic color and appearance. Consider the following guidelines:

- **Keep your task in mind.** You are using vectors. If you want a perfect reproduction of the art, use the art. No matter how well you trace or how accurate your mesh is, you are still making a different version of the art. Give yourself permission to take some liberties with the image.

- **Set the art you are tracing on a template layer.** *(For more information, see 25.6, Template Layer.)*

- **Create a new layer to do your tracing on.** Target the layer and set its opacity to 50%. You may need to experiment with opacity to set it correctly.

- **Trace the outline of the shape first.** If your trace will involve multiple items, trace the one in the back first. This will make it easier to resolve the stacking order later. It is more important to get the overall shape of the object than to follow lines exactly. If you can't see the entire object, try to create a path that follows where the shape would go. For example, if you are tracing a head with hair, don't follow the hairline; trace the round shape of the top of the skull. This will make for more accurate mesh points. **A**

- **Set the fill of the object to a middle tone of the image you are tracing.** Some users Shift-click on the image they are tracing with the Eyedropper tool to sample the colors used in the original.

- **Click with the Mesh tool inside the path to add mesh points.** Try to click in areas that show the overall contour of the shape you are tracing. In the example of a head, you might click on the cheekbone.

- **Watch for areas of changing color and place mesh points there.** Be careful about placing two mesh points very close together. This is often reserved for hard color changes. Try to minimize the number of points by clicking on existing mesh lines to make crossing lines. **B**

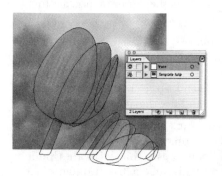

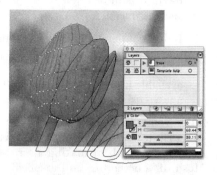

A *Basic shapes outlining color areas.*

B *Mesh points added and color applied.*

- **After you have made a few points, begin the process of coloring.** If you rough in the light and dark areas first, mesh points added later will start in the correct color family.

- **Adjust the mesh points positions and curves as needed.** You should avoid dragging points too far away from other points. If color needs to change in a different location, add new mesh points.

- **Don't try to do it all with one mesh.** Use additional meshes or paths as needed. Take your time and be sure to observe the original closely.

- **Reset the layer opacity to 100% and check your work.** Many users duplicate the tracing image and place it to the side so that they can see the trace and the original at the same time. Adjust your colors as needed. The Direct Select Lasso is a good tool for selecting mesh points. You can make color adjustments manually, or by using Filter: Color: **Adjust Color** and Filter: Colors: **Saturate**. Depending on your intention, Filter: Colors: **Convert to Grayscale** can also be useful. **c**

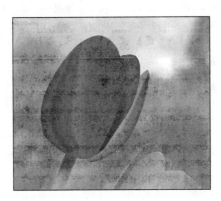

c *Meshes completed.*

C.14

Converting a Gradient Mesh to a Path

Once an object has been converted to a gradient mesh, you cannot convert it back with a single click. This causes an issue when a user changes their mind about a complex mesh or needs the shape to use as a mask or type bounding area. To convert an existing mesh to a path, follow these steps:

1. Select the mesh.

2. Choose Object: Path: **Offset Path**. Set the distance to -1 point and the Joins to Miter. This will create a new path in front of the mesh offset a point. This is a temporary path that you will delete later. To make it easier to select and delete it, consider choosing Select: Save Selection.

3. Choose Object: Path: **Offset Path** again. This time, set the distance to 1 point. A new path is created directly on top of the mesh.

4. Go back and delete the first Offset Path. You may choose to delete the original gradient mesh as well, depending upon your needs.

C.15

Isolating Objects in Complex Documents

After working on a document for a while, you may yourself cramped by the documents contents. For example, you may want to use the Knife tool to cut a copy of an object into several pieces to create objects for shadows and then pathfinder the shapes together. This would be easier if you could see only the object that you wanted to work on without the other objects in the document. In cases where it is not convenient to create new layers to isolate elements, consider the following steps:

1. If you've repositioned the zero point of the rulers, reset them by double clicking in the ruler origin position.

2. Select the objects you want to work on and choose Edit: **Cut**. In cases where you want to edit a copy instead of the original, choose Copy instead.

3. Create a new document.

4. Choose Edit: **Paste in Front**. The objects are pasted into the document. It's important not to choose Edit: **Paste**, which will position the new objects in the center of the document window. Paste in Front (or Back) will retain the same X Y position of the original objects.

5. Once you have edited the objects as required, select them and copy them.

6. Return to the original document. Select an object behind the original object's position and choose Edit: **Paste in Front**. The edited objects are returned to their original position.

C.16

Creating Banners

Deciding how to go about creating a specific shape, even a simple one, is an important choice in Illustrator. There are many ways to create the same shapes, but some will make more sense depending upon the needs and mindset of the user. This example is intended to outline several models for creating the same basic shape, a curved rectangle, like those used in banners. Consider the following options:

*   **Convert a curved stroke.** Create an ellipse. Leave it selected and choose Object: Path: **Add Anchor Points**. You could also add anchor points manually with the Add Anchor Point tool. Use the Direct Selection tool to select all but the top three anchor points on the path. Press the Delete key. You are left with an open path. Stroke the path the width you want the banner shape to be. Choose Object: Path: **Outline Stroke**. This will convert the stroke into a fill, enabling you to add a stroke to the shape.

If the original ellipse had a fill, a filled open path will be left beneath the stroke shape after you outline the stroke. You may bring this to the front and use it as a baseline for type if needed.

Instead of outlining a thick stroke, you could also offset the open path. Choose Object: Path: **Offset Path**. This produces the same results as outlining a thick stroke. The key difference is that by applying a stroke you are given as chance to see the width before you outline it. Offset Path has no preview option.

- **Knock out shapes with a Pathfinder.** Create an ellipse. Using the Selection or Direct Selection tool, (Option) [Alt]-drag the circle straight down to create a second ellipse in front of the first. Position it so that the distance between the tops of each ellipse makes the width of the banner you want to create. Create a rectangle on the left side of the ellipse. Switch to Outline mode and (Option) [Alt]-click in the center of the first ellipse with the reflect tool. In the Reflect dialog box, choose Vertical and click the Copy button. Select all of the objects you have just created. In the Pathfinder palette, (Option) [Alt]-click on the Subtract from Shape button. The rectangles and second ellipse are knocked out of the first ellipse, leaving the curved banner shape. If other shapes are created as well, select them with the Direct Selection tool and delete them.

  If you need a baseline for type, you could select the bottom anchor points of the oval and (Option) [Alt]-drag a copy of the segments into the position for the type.

- **Warp a rectangle.** Create a rectangle. Optionally, set type for the banner as well. Select the items and choose Object: Envelope Distort: **Make with Warp**. Choose options to your liking. The Arc style is often used to make banners. Many users continue by choosing Object: Envelope Distort: **Expand** to create basic path shapes. If you used text, be aware that expanding envelopes converts type to outlines.

C.17

Adding Objects to Envelopes

Objects can be added to envelopes. This may need to be done to add something you left out or just to change an existing design. For example, after turning a rectangle into a banner shape with an envelope you decide to add an inset version of the rectangle shape. Selecting the enveloped shape and choosing Object: Path: **Offset Path** does not add the object to the envelope. It creates a new shape atop the envelope. To add an object to an envelope, follow these steps:

1. Select the Envelope you want to add items to.

2. Choose Object: Envelope: **Edit Contents**.

3. Locate the object in the Layers palette and click its turn down arrow. The enveloped objects will appear under the envelope object in the palette. **A**

4. Click drag the item you want to add to the envelope into position above or behind one of the enveloped shapes. The envelope will affect the new shape. **B**

A *The enveloped object available for editing.*

B *Additional objects dragged into the envelope group.*

Depending upon your goal, it may make more sense to change the enveloped objects rather than adding additional shapes. For example, in the previous example of an inset path you could do the following:

1. Select the Envelope you want to add items to.

2. Choose Object: Envelope: **Edit Contents**.

3. Select the object that you would like to apply the offset path to.

4. In the Appearance palette menu, choose Add New Stroke.

5. Make sure the new stroke is highlighted in the Appearance Palette and choose Effect: Path: **Offset Path**. Set the options that you want. The offset path is applied to a second stroke inside the already-enveloped path and is distorted automatically.

C.18

Creating an Emboss Style

Illustrator has no default emboss style or effect. At its most basic, an emboss consists of a highlight and shadow effect on the same object. The light play creates the impression that the object is raised off the surface. To create a basic emboss style:

1. Select an object to begin the emboss process. You do not need to select all of the objects because the effects will be saved as a style that you can apply to the other objects later.

2. Choose Effect: Stylize: **Drop Shadow**. Choose the shadow options that look best to you, but use a dark color. Note the offset amounts before closing the dialog box. Many users set the Blur value to 0 to create a hard-edged effect. This may also keep the effect from flattening to pixels when printed. **A**

3. Choose Effect: Stylize: **Drop Shadow** again. This time, you'll create the highlight side. Use the offset numbers that you choose for the shadow, but reverse the positive and negative values. For example, if you offset the shadow –3 X and 3 Y, offset this one 3 X and –3 Y. Set the Color to White and the Mode to Screen. Leave the other options the same as with the shadow. **B**

4. Click the New Style button in the Styles palette to save the current Appearance as a style. Apply the new style as required to other objects in the document.

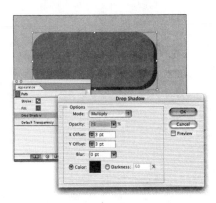

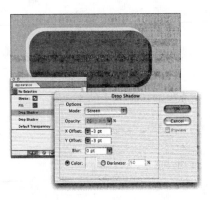

A *The first drop shadow effect creates the shadow side of the emboss effect.*

B *The second drop shadow creates the highlight side.*

There are other options for embossing. Some users prefer to use fills to create the effect. Follow these steps:

1. Select a representative object to begin the process of creating the style.

2. In the Appearance palette, highlight the object's fill and then click on the Duplicate Selected Item button.

3. Select the lower of the two fills. This will become the shadow. Choose Effect: Distort & Transform: **Transform**. Set an offset amount for the object. Typically, a small distance produces fine results.

4. Set the blend mode of the fill to Multiply. You may also consider darkening the fill color and or reducing the opacity.

5. Duplicate the shadow fill by clicking the Duplicate Selected Item button. This will be the highlight side.

6. In the Appearance palette, twirl down the contents of new fill and double-click on the Transform effect. Change the distance values from positive to negative and vice versa to reverse the offset direction.

7. Reset the blend mode of highlight fill to Screen. Many users also reset the color to white. **C**

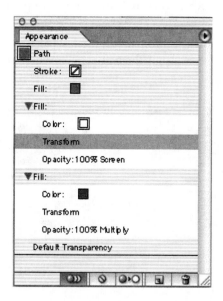

C   *The appearance palette for an emboss effect.*

C.19

Group Effects

In some instances, it will be useful to apply an effect to a group of objects rather than individual items. This may because you want a series of individual objects to have the same effect or because the group collectively describes the image. For example, you may have a group of objects that collectively make up a specific object, such as a screwdriver or a basketball.

Some effects work better if you add a fill to the group first. For example, you may want to apply a freely distorted shadow to a group of objects. Adding a fill to a group provides a home for the effect so that it does not disturb the contents of the group. Commonly, the fill will be behind the group's original contents. To apply an effect to a group fill, follow these steps:

1. Select the entire group. Alternatively, target the group in the Layers palette.

2. Choose Add New Fill from the Appearance palette menu. A new fill appears in the palette. If your intention is to add an effect that uses strokes, you should choose Add New Stroke instead.

3. Drag the fill under the word Contents in the Appearance palette. This puts the new fill behind the objects in the group. This step may be optional, depending upon the effect you apply and the opacity of the fill. By default, though, the new fill will be on top of the current contents of the group, obscuring them.

4. Make sure the new fill is highlighted in the Appearance palette. Apply the effect that you intend. For example, you might apply Effect: Distort & Transform: **Free Distort** to create a perspective shadow.

5. With the new fill still selected in the Appearance palette, adjust the color and opacity as required.

Some common effects applied to groups using additional fills and strokes are as follows:

- Create a thick outline for the group by giving the group an additional stroke with a large width. Be sure the stroke is below the Contents of the group in the Appearance palette. **A**

- Create a filled box for the group by adding a new fill in the back and applying Effect: Convert to Shape: **Rectangle**. **B**

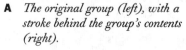

A *The original group (left), with a stroke behind the group's contents (right).*

B *The original group (top), with a new fill behind the group's contents (right). The box resizes with the group's contents automatically.*

- Create an offset stroke for the group by adding a new stroke and then applying Effect: Pathfinder: **Add** and Effect: Path: **Offset Path** to the stroke. You must apply the effects to the stroke in that order. **C**

- Create stylized effects by adding a new fill to the group, sending it to the back, choosing Effect: Path: **Offset Path** and then applying the Effect: **Stylize** commands. For example, you might apply a white inner glow to a dark fill to create a rounded appearance. **D**

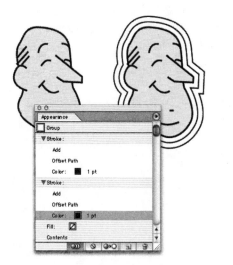

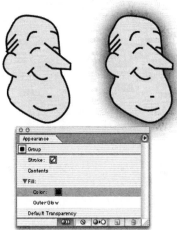

C *The original group (left), with offset strokes added (right).*

D *The original group (left), with a stylized fill added to the back (right).*

Type Techniques

Type on a Circle

Path type placed on the top and bottom of a circle is a common effect. Since type may run in one direction or the other, you must use two objects to make type right side up on both the top and bottom of the circle. Unfortunately, type in Illustrator always aligns the baseline of letters to the path, so you will need to offset it from the path for it to appear correct on the bottom half of the circle. Follow these steps:

1. Use the Ellipse tool to create the path that will serve as a baseline for the type. To create a perfect circle, hold down the shift key as you drag out the ellipse. The fill and stroke of the path are not important.

2. Position the Type tool so that the crossbar of the icon is directly on the path. The Type tool converts to the Area Type tool automatically. Hold down the (Option) [Alt] key to convert to the Path Type tool and click the mouse. This type will be the top half of the circle.

3. Enter the desired text. Use the Character and Paragraph palettes to set the

options for the type. Many users center align the type to simplify positioning. Apply the fill and stroke you want as well. It is best to style your type completely since you will be copying it in a moment. **A**

4. Switch to the Direct Selection tool. An "I-beam", or hot point, will be displayed in the position on the ellipse you clicked. If you need to, click drag the hot point to reposition the type about the ellipse. You may also use the Selection tool, but often the presence of the bounding box makes it difficult to position type. **B**

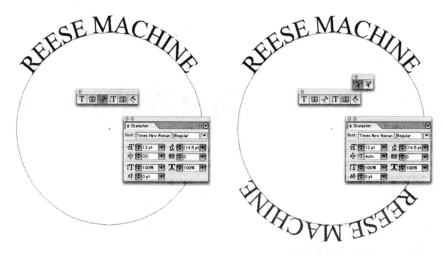

A *Type set onto a circle*

B *The type copied around to the bottom of the circle*

5. To create a copy of the path type for the bottom half of the circle, click-drag the hot point with the Direct Selection tool. As you drag, hold down the (Option) [Alt] key. Drag the text down to the bottom of the circle and position your cursor on the inside of the path. A duplicate text path is created with text on the inside of the circle. It may be difficult to drag the text inside the circle. If you have this problem, drag the text to the bottom of the circle and release your mouse. Double-click on the top or bottom crossbars of the hot point to switch the type to the inside of the path.

6. To align the ascenders of the type with the path, locate the baseline shift option in the Character palette. If it is not visible, choose Show Options from the Character Palette menu.

7. Apply a negative baseline shift to push the type below the path. Typically, letterforms make up about 80% of a typeface's size. Typefaces vary, though, so some trial and error will be involved. For example, if you have 10-point type you might try a −8-point baseline shift to begin with. **c**

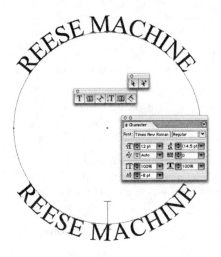

c *The lower text given a negative baseline shift.*

Issues to Consider

Both top and bottom type can be baseline shifted. Some users shift both the top and bottom type the same negative amount so that the type is in the middle of the path. This can be useful if you are using an ellipse with a thick stroke behind the type objects as a design element. For example, you could copy the ellipse before placing type on it, complete your text wrapping and then paste the ellipse in back. After applying a thick stroke, to the ellipse you could choose Object: Path: **Outline Stroke** to create a closed path to which you could apply a stroke.

Two objects are created. Remember that when you duplicated the type to create the bottom half, you duplicated both the type and the circle. This can create some difficulty when selecting individual paths. For best results, click directly on the characters with the Direct Selection tool. The type with the hot point is the type that is selected.

D.2

Strokes Outside of Type

When strokes are applied to text, they often disturb the letterforms. By default, strokes are in front of fills. This means that half of the stroke overlaps the fill. This can cause the letters to look odd and may disrupt the appearance of text, especially small type.

This can be remedied by placing the fill in front of the stroke. This must be done to a text object, not to individual characters. Often, this will also be saved as a style. Follow these steps:

1. Select the type object to be edited with the Selection tool. Do not select the characters with the Type tool. You may want to take a moment and save the fill color in the object as a swatch. **A**

2. In the Appearance palette menu, choose Add New Fill. It should be above the word Characters in the palette. Apply the same fill to the text object that was applied to the characters. The fill should sit atop the character attributes, obscuring the inside half of the stroke. **B**

3. In the Styles palette, click the New Style button to save the Appearance settings.

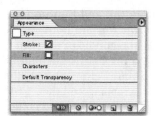

A *The original type. Strokes cut into the letterforms.*

B *The text with an additional fill to obscure the inside of the stroke.*

Issues to Consider

The Default Fill & Stroke button the toolbox applies to characters only. You can't apply the default fill and stroke attributes to a type object. It only applies attributes to characters.

Type attributes are atop character attributes. The characters still have their attributes, but they are beneath the type object characteristics. This means you can return the characters to their original settings if need be. Select the type with the Text tool to edit the characters' attributes.

You can also apply a stroke to the type. For this particular technique, this is redundant. In other techniques, in may be useful to include the stroke as well.

When applying to paths, move the stroke below the fill. Simple path objects may also have strokes appear on the outside only. To do this, drag the stroke below the fill in the Appearance palette. There is no need to add additional fills or strokes.

D.3

Creating a Hanging Indent

Hanging indents are commonly used with bulleted or numbered lists to separate the paragraph from the bullet or number. There are two ways to do this. In one model, the bullet falls inside the bounding text area, in the other the bullet hangs outside the box. If type can fall outside the text block, it's easier to create an indent. In cases, where type must fit inside a specific area, such as a text column, you will have to do more work. Follow these steps:

1. Be sure that a tab character is between the bullet or number and the first word in the paragraph. Choose Type: **Show Hidden Characters** to inspect for tab characters. They will appear as right arrows when the Show Hidden Character option is activated. Add tab characters as needed.

2. Click somewhere in a paragraph within an area type block. All the type in the block need not be selected, but you may select through multiple paragraphs to set more than one paragraph at a time.

3. In the Tab Ruler palette, set a position for the first tab. Typically, this is a left-aligned tab. Note the position of the tab in the X field of the palette.

4. In the Paragraph palette, set the left indent to the same value as the tab position.

5. Set the first line indent to the same value as the left indent, only in a negative direction. For example, if the left indent is 10 points, set the first line indent to –10 points. **A**

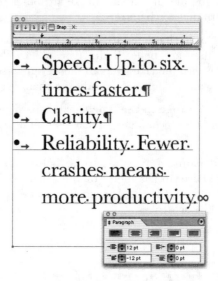

A *The basic structure of a hanging indent.*

If the bullet or number can fall outside of the paragraph area, the procedure is simpler:

1. Make sure that there is a tab between the bullet and the start of the rest of the paragraph.

2. Set the first line indent to a negative amount. The tab takes the rest of the text to the beginning of the text block automatically. You do not need to set a custom tab to make this happen. **B**

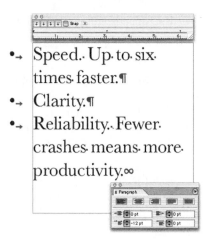

B   *A hanging indent outside of the type block. Note that no custom tab is set.*

Issues to Consider

Hanging indents use the paragraph alignment by default. This is not an issue with bullets, but it does create concern when creating numbered lists. For example, if you are creating a numbered list that goes beyond nine, the second digit will create a ragged margin in the bullets. This can be corrected when the indents are inside the text block but not when outside.

To set right alignment for a hanging numbered list, add tabs before the numbering characters. Set the tabs to be right aligned and position them where you want the end of the numbers to fall. The left and first line indents may be set as before.

D.4

Type Wrap Offset

Illustrator's type wrap command has no offset distance. In many cases, this causes type to come to close to objects. Further, type wrap ignores effects applied to objects and only obeys the actual path position. This means that if you apply an Offset Path or Convert to Shape Effect to an object that is used in a text wrap, the wrap will invariably be wrong. For this reason and to enable you to finesse a text wrap without adjusting the source object, many users apply wraps to invisible objects. Follow these steps:

1. Select the path that text should wrap around. Make sure it is in front of the text blocks that will wrap.

2. Choose Object: Path: **Offset Path**. Enter an amount of distance for the text to be offset from the original object. In most cases, this will be a positive number. In the event that it is a negative number, you will have a stacking order issue to resolve later. Negative numbers are typically only used when the wrapped object is partially opaque, so that the text may be seen through it.

3. A new path will be created in back of the original object. If you used a negative number in the offset path dialog box, choose Object: Arrange: **Step Backward** to position the object behind the original. Set the fill and stroke of the path to None.

4. Shift-select the text blocks so that they are added to the offset path selection. Choose Type: Wrap: **Make**.

5. The invisible, offset version of the path will be grouped with the type objects to create a wrap. Using the Direct Selection tool, adjust it as needed to create the best text wrap for your object. **A**

A   *Type is wrapped to an offset version of the art, instead of the original.*

6. Select the text-wrap group and the original object and choose Object: **Group**. This will keep the objects together as they are moved and selected. Do not add the original object to the text wrap group by dragging it into the group in the layers palette. This will cause the path to make text wrap as well, defeating the purpose of this technique.

D.5

Linking Text Blocks

Although it is not a common technique, there are occasions where linking type is invaluable in Illustrator. For example, when creating a calendar template that will be used to create multiple months. Without linking, text would need to be reset for every day each month. Follow these steps:

1. Decide on the area that all the linked text will occupy. Click-drag with the Type tool over the entire area the blocks should sit in.

2. Without setting any type, set the attributes the text should have in the Character and Paragraph palettes.

3. Switch to the Selection tool and choose Type: Rows & Columns. Fill in the fields as needed. For example, to create a calendar template you would create 5 rows and 7 columns to account for the longer months. You would also set the height of the boxes small enough that could only hold a single line of type. The type in this example would flow by rows, left to right.

4. Set type in the boxes to check the sizing. In the calendar example, you should be able to enter the dates and then break to the next box by pressing the Return key. You would then enter all of the dates 1 to 31 into the boxes. As you need to adjust the start of the month to a different day, add additional hard returns before the first to move it through the days of the week. To move the beginning back, delete the returns.

D.6

Actions for Type Style

Unlike page layout applications, Illustrator does not feature paragraph or character styles. Styles are used to apply a collection of type attributes to a selection in a single click. In these applications, text is dynamically linked to a style; as a style is redefined, text that uses the style is updated to match. Illustrator has no way to link text to a definition, but there are several options for applying a series of text characteristics to text.

A common way to do this is through Actions. This is useful when you are preparing text the same way many times in a row in different documents. For example, you may need to reset the default text in graphs for a series of different documents. Actions are useful since they are stored with the application and not the document. Follow these steps:

1. Decide on the character attributes that the text will have. Many users start with the body text first and then create variations on the action to apply bold and italic versions of the type.

2. Create a block of dummy type to begin creating the action. Set all of the characteristics for the type you want in the Character and Paragraph palette except one. For example, set the type with the correct size, leading and tracking but the wrong font. Likewise set the Paragraph palette to all but one setting correct. Since actions record the entire contents of a palette, setting one wrong enables you to set many attributes in a single click.

3. Click the Create new Set button on the face of the Actions palette. Name the new set in a way that will make sense later, such as "quarterly graph type styles."

4. Click the New Action button. Name the action in a way that will identify it easily, such as "value axis type gill sans 10pt."

5. In the Character palette, rectify the one incorrect setting that you made in step 2. Press Enter or Return to accept the change. The entire contents of the Character palette are written as a step in the Actions palette.

6. Repeat the process for the Paragraph palette. If you are setting tabs as part of a style, they must be added individually as steps in the action.

7. Click the Stop Recording button in the palette.

8. To make variations on the style, drag the action onto the Create New Action button in the front of the palette. Name the new action appropriately.

9. Delete the Character step in the action by dragging it onto the Delete Step button in the front of the palette.

10. Repeat step 5 and click the stop recording button. Repeat to create additional character style variations.

Use the actions by selecting type and playing the action. Select an entire text object or individual characters to change with this action.

Importing Text

In general, Illustrator does an excellent job of importing text from popular word processing applications. Text documents can be opened, placed, or pasted. Pasting retains the least of the character formatting and should only be used to move small amounts of text that you intend to style manually.

Placing should be used when you need to pick up a block of text for use in an existing design. Text will be placed in a large, single block the size of the page. Opening Microsoft Word and RTF documents produces a similar experience. Opened documents are usually in RGB mode. The following features are translated correctly:

- Font, size, alignment, and most character attributes

- Text colors are converted to global process swatches

- Tab position and kind

- Tabs are added for indent and outdent

- Subscript and superscript are translated to baseline shifts

The following features are not understood by Illustrator and are omitted:

- Unsupported character styles, such as shadow and outline

- Tab leaders or fill characters

- Page breaks

- Headers, footers, and footnotes

- Comment fields

- Tables are converted to tab-delimited text

- Hyperlinks

You should be aware that these features are not translated and plan around this accordingly.

D.8

Rebuilding Broken Paragraphs

Illustrator is often used to edit pages saved as EPS files from QuarkXPress or PDF files. Due to the way these files are constructed, text blocks are often broken into many individual text objects. For example, the first two letters of a word may be one object and the remainder of the word another. This makes it difficult to edit words and impossible to edit paragraphs. The individual objects no longer flow as a paragraph and must be set manually.

Paragraphs can be reformed, but this may cause text to break in different places and will create additional work. Be sure you need to rebuild the paragraph before attempting this technique. To build a series of text objects into a paragraph:

1. Place guides on the page to identify the area the paragraph occupies. *(For more information, see 14.24, View:* **Guides**.*)*

2. Select all of the text objects that make up the paragraphs to be rebuilt.

3. Choose Edit: **Cut**.

4. Using the Type tool, draw a box for area type to fit the guides you placed in step 1.

5. Choose Edit: **Paste** to insert all of the cut text into the area type box.

6. Inspect the type for areas where spacing is incorrect and adjust accordingly. Many users do this by choosing Type: **Check Spelling**.

D.9

Pathfinder Type Techniques

Commonly, visual effects require that type characters be combined to create a single shape. For example, you may want all of the type letters to touch each other and have the stroke run around the contour of the objects. There are two models for doing this, as a Compound Shape and as an Effect. Use an Effect when you want to create a Style that you can apply to other objects later. When combining multiple text paths it is easier to use Compound Shapes.

To combine text paths as an Effect, follow these steps:

1. Group the text paths. This is not required if only one text block is being used. Select all the text paths with the Selection tool and choose Object: **Group**.

2. Target the Group in the Layers palette. Locate the Group you have created and click the target circle to the right of the Group's name in the palette.

3. Choose Effect: Pathfinder: **Add**. The text areas will unite where they overlap.

4. Adjust the type as you see fit. Many users track type together when using this technique so that characters crash into each other. You may also consider using the Appearance palette to place the stroke of the objects behind the fills. Do this by targeting the Group and choosing Add Fill from the Appearance palette menu. **A**

A *Grouped text objects with the Add Pathfinder Effect applied.*

To combine text paths as a Compound Shape, follow these steps:

1. Select the items to be used using the Selection or Direct Selection tool.

2. If you are using a single text path for the technique, choose Make Compound Shape from the Pathfinder palette menu. The text will become a Compound Shape using the Add mode.

3. If you are using multiple text paths, click one of the Shape Mode buttons on the face of the palette. Commonly, this will be the Add button.

4. Adjust the type as you see fit. Since the object is now a Compound Shape (and not a type object), you can position the stroke behind the fill in the Appearance palette directly. **B**

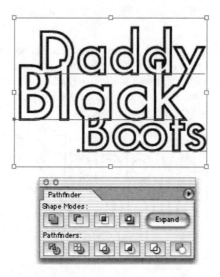

B *Multiple type objects converted to a single compound shape.*

D.10

Adding an Expanding Box for Type

Use this technique to put text inside a basic geometric shape that adjusts to fit the type as it changes. This is often used to make web buttons or callout boxes for text. The boxes may be complex, but must be either a rectangle, a rounded rectangle, or an ellipse.

1. Set the type you want to work on. Style it at this time if you want, but you will be able to change the attributes later.

2. Select the text block with one of the Selection tools. You can do this by switching from the Text tool to a Selection tool.

3. Choose Add New Fill from the Appearance palette menu. Drag the new fill that appears below the word Characters in the palette. This places the new fill that you have created in back of the letters in the type.

4. Be sure that the new fill that you have created is selected in the Appearance palette by clicking on it.

5. Choose one of the three commands under Effect: **Convert to Shape**. Set the options that you want. Many users choose the Relative option to create a box that expands with the type. The added space here will be about the object's bounding box. Since type includes white space, the distance to the characters may change if the type is later converted to outlines.

6. To create a stroke around the offset box, (Option) [Alt] drag the Effect you added to the fill onto the stroke attribute in the Appearance palette. This offsets the stroke to match the fill, outlining the box. The stroke need not be behind the characters for this to work. Many users create multiple inset boxes by duplicating the fill (select the fill in the Appearance palette and choose Duplicate Item from the Appearance palette menu), and then changing its color and offset amounts. **A**

A   *A type object with two new fills added. Each fill is converted to a rectangle and colored.*

Keyboard Shortcuts

Tool Shortcuts

Action	Mac OS	Windows
Selection	V	V
Direct Selection	A	A
Group Selection		
Magic Wand	Y	Y
Direct Lasso	Q	Q
Pen	P	P
Add Anchor Point	=	=
Delete Anchor Point	-	-
Convert Anchor Point	Shift-C	Shift-C
Type	T	T
Line Segment	\	\
Rectangle	M	M
Ellipse	L	L
Brush	B	B
Pencil	N	N

Action	Mac OS	Windows
Rotate	R	R
Reflect	O	O
Scale	S	S
Warp	Shift-R	Shift-R
Free Transform	E	E
Symbol Sprayer	Shift-S	Shift-S
Column Graph	J	J
Mesh	U	U
Gradient	G	G
Eyedropper	I	I
Paint Bucket	K	K
Blend	W	W
Slice	Shift-K	Shift-K
Scissors	C	C
Hand	H	H
Zoom	Z	Z
Toggle Fill/Stroke	X	X
Default	D	D
Swap Fill/Stroke	Shift-X	Shift-X
Color	,	,
Gradient	.	.
None	/	/
Toggle Screen Mode	F	F
Show/Hide All Palettes	Tab	Tab
Show/Hide All But Toolbox	Shift-Tab	Shift-Tab
Symbolism Tools: Increase Diameter	]	]
Decrease Diameter	[	[
Increase Intensity	Shift-]	Shift-]
Decrease Intensity	Shift-[	Shift-[

File Menu Shortcuts

Action	Mac OS	Windows
New	Command-N	Ctrl-N
Open	Command-O	Ctrl-O
Revert	F12	F12
Close	Command-W	Ctrl-W
Save	Command-S	Ctrl-S
Save As	Shift-Command-S	Shift-Ctrl-S
Save a Copy	Option-Command-S	Alt-Ctrl-S
Save For Web	Option-Shift-Command-S	Alt-Shift-Ctrl-S
Document Setup	Option-Command-P	Alt-Ctrl-P
Page Setup	Shift-Command-P	Shift-Ctrl-P
Print	Command-P	Ctrl-P
Quit	Command-Q	Ctrl-Q

Edit Menu Shortcuts

Undo	Command-Z	Ctrl-Z
Redo	Shift-Command-Z	Shift-Ctrl-Z
Cut	Command-X	Ctrl-X
Copy	Command-C	Ctrl-C
Paste	Command-V	Ctrl-V
Paste in Front	Command-F	Ctrl-F
Paste in Back	Command-B	Ctrl-B
Keyboard Shortcuts	Option-Shift-Command-K	Alt-Shift-Ctrl-K
Preferences General	Command-K	Ctrl-K

Object Menu Shortcuts

Transform Again	Command-D	Ctrl-D
Move	Shift-Command-M	Shift-Ctrl-M
Transform Each	Option-Shift-Command-D	Alt-Shift-Ctrl-D
Bring to Front	Shift-Command-]	Shift-Ctrl-]
Bring Forward	Command-]	Ctrl-]

Action	Mac OS	Windows
Send Backward	Command-[	Ctrl-[
Send to Back	Shift-Command-[	Shift-Ctrl-[
Group	Command-G	Ctrl-G
Ungroup	Shift-Command-G	Shift-Ctrl-G
Lock Selection	Command-2	Ctrl-2
Unlock All	Option-Command-2	Alt-Ctrl-2
Hide Selection	Command-3	Ctrl-3
Show All	Option-Command-3	Alt-Ctrl-3

Path Shortcuts

Join	Command-J	Ctrl-J
Average	Option-Command-J	Alt-Ctrl-J
Blend Make	Option-Command-B	Alt-Ctrl-B
Release	Option-Shift-Command-B	Alt-Shift-Ctrl-B
Make with Warp	Option-Command-W	Alt-Ctrl-W
Make with Mesh	Option-Command-M	Alt-Ctrl-M
Make with Top Object	Option-Command-C	Alt-Ctrl-C
Edit Contents	Shift-Command-V	Shift-Ctrl-V
Clipping Mask: Make	Command-7	Ctrl-7
Clipping Mask: Release	Option-Command-7	Alt-Ctrl-7
Compound Path: Make	Command-8	Ctrl-8
Compound Path: Release	Option-Command-8	Alt-Ctrl-8
Create Outlines	Shift-Command-O	Shift-Ctrl-O
Select All	Command-A	Ctrl-A
Deselect	Shift-Command-A	Shift-Ctrl-A
Reselect	Command-6	Ctrl-6
Next Object Above	Option-Command-]	Alt-Ctrl-]
Next Object Below	Option-Command-[	Alt-Ctrl-[

Filter Shortcuts

Action	Mac OS	Windows
Apply Last Filter	Command-E	Ctrl-E
Last Filter	Option-Command-E	Alt-Ctrl-E

Effects Shortcuts

Apply Last Effect	Shift-Command-E	Shift-Ctrl-E
Last Effect	Option-Shift-Command-E	Alt-Shift-Ctrl-E

View Shortcuts

Toggle Outline/Preview	Command-Y	Ctrl-Y
Overprint Preview	Option-Shift-Command-Y	Alt-Shift-Ctrl-Y
Pixel Preview	Option-Command-Y	Alt-Ctrl-Y
Zoom In	Command- =	Ctrl- =
Zoom Out	Command- -	Ctrl- -
Fit In Window	Command-0	Ctrl-0
Actual Size	Command-1	Ctrl-1
Show/Hide Edges	Command-H	Ctrl-H
Show/Hide Template	Shift-Command-W	Shift-Ctrl-W
Show/Hide Rulers	Command-R	Ctrl-R
Show/Hide Bounding Box	Shift-Command-B	Shift-Ctrl-B
Show/Hide Transparency Grid	Shift-Command-D	Shift-Ctrl-D

Guides Shortcuts

Show/Hide Guides	Command-;	Ctrl-;
Lock/Unlock Guides	Option-Command-;	Alt-Ctrl-;
Make Guides	Command-5	Ctrl-5
Release Guides	Option-Command-5	Alt-Ctrl-5
Smart Guides	Command-U	Ctrl-U
Show/Hide Grid	Command-'	Ctrl-'
Snap To Grid/Pixel	Shift-Command-'	Shift-Ctrl-'

Action	Mac OS	Windows
Snap To Point	Option-Command-'	Alt-Ctrl-'
Align	Shift-F7	Shift-F7
Appearance	Shift-F6	Shift-F6
Attributes	F11	F11
Brushes	F5	F5
Color	F6	F6
Gradient	F9	F9
Layers	F7	F7
Pathfinder	Shift-F9	Shift-F9
Stroke	F10	F10
Styles	Shift-F5	Shift-F5
Symbols	Shift-F11	Shift-F11
Transform	Shift-F8 Shift-F8	
Transparency	Shift-F10	Shift-F10
Character	Command-T	Ctrl-T
Paragraph	Command-M	Ctrl-M
Tab Ruler	Shift-Command-T	Shift-Ctrl-T
Illustrator Help	Shift-Command-/	Shift-Ctrl-/
First Object Above	Option-Shift-Command-]	Alt-Shift-Ctrl-]
First Object Below	Option-Shift-Command-[	Alt-Shift-Ctrl-[
Switch Selection Tools	Command-Tab	Ctrl-Tab

Other Text Shortcuts

Insert Hyphen	Shift-Command- -	Shift-Ctrl-Hyphen (-)
Point Size Up	Shift-Command-.	Shift-Ctrl-.
Point Size Down	Shift-Command-,	Shift-Ctrl-,
Font Size Step Up	Option-Shift-Command-.	Alt-Shift-Ctrl-.
Font Size Step Down	Option-Shift-Command-,	Alt-Shift-Ctrl-,
Kern Looser	Shift-Command-]	Shift-Ctrl-]
Kern Tighter	Shift-Command-[	Shift-Ctrl-[
Tracking	Option-Command-K	Alt-Ctrl-K

Action	Mac OS	Windows
Clear Tracking	Option-Command-Q	Alt-Ctrl-Q
Spacing	Option-Command-O	Alt-Ctrl-O
Highlight Font	Option-Shift-Command-F	Alt-Shift-Ctrl-F
Highlight Font (Secondary)	Option-Shift-Command-M	Alt-Shift-Ctrl-M
Uniform Type	Shift-Command-X	Shift-Ctrl-X
Left Align Text	Shift-Command-L	Shift-Ctrl-L
Center Text	Shift-Command-C	Shift-Ctrl-C
Right Align Text	Shift-Command-R	Shift-Ctrl-R
Justify Text	Shift-Command-J	Shift-Ctrl-J
Justify All Lines	Shift-Command-F	Shift-Ctrl-F

Other Object Shortcuts

Lock Others	Option-Shift-Command-2	Alt-Shift-Ctrl-2
Hide Others	Option-Shift-Command-3	Alt-Shift-Ctrl-3
Repeat Pathfinder	Command-4	Ctrl-4
Average & Join	Option-Shift-Command-J	Alt-Shift-Ctrl-J

Other Palette Shortcuts

Show Color Palette (Secondary)	Command-I	Ctrl-I
Show Attributes (Secondary)	F11	F11
Add New Fill	Command-/	Ctrl-/
Add New Stroke	Option-Command-/	Alt-Ctrl-/
New Layer	Command-L	Ctrl-L

Miscellaneous Shortcuts

Switch Units	Option-Shift-Command-U	Alt-Shift-Ctrl-U
New File (no dialog box)	Option-Command-N	Alt-Ctrl-N

Index

Symbols

3-D image simulation
Plaster effect, 329
Texturizer effect, 330

A

absolute links, 381
Accented Edges effect, 324
Action Options command (Actions palette), 358
actions. *See also* Actions palette
adding commands to, 355-356
adding paths to, 357
button mode versus list view, 360-361
changing name, F-key, and color, 358
common uses for, 350
copying, 354
creating, 353-354
defined, 349
deleting, 354-355, 359
Illustrator versus Photoshop, 350
isometric perspective, 642
loading from file, 360
pausing, 356-357
playback options, 359
playing, 355
re-recording, 355
replacing current list, 360
replacing with defaults, 359-360
selecting objects in, 358
selecting objects with, 580
sets, 349
creating, 354
saving, 360

styling text with, 673-674
versus scripts, 349
Actions palette.
See also actions
Action Options command, 358
Button Mode command, 360-361
Clear Actions command, 359
control buttons, 350-352
Delete command, 354-355
Duplicate command, 354
Insert Menu Item command, 356
Insert Select Path command, 357
Insert Stop command, 356-357
Load Actions command, 360
New Action command, 353-354
New Set command, 354
Play command, 355
Playback Options command, 359
Record Again command, 355
Replace Actions command, 360
Reset Actions command, 359-360
Save Actions command, 360
Select Object command, 358
Start Recording command, 355
Actual Size command (View menu), 339
Add Anchor Point tool, 11

Add New Fill command (Appearance palette), 374
Add New Stroke command (Appearance palette), 374
Add to Shape Area button (Pathfinder palette), 478
adding anchor points to paths, 223
adjustable boxes for text, 678-679
Adobe Illustrator documents (.ai), saving files as, 101, 103
Adobe PDF, saving files as, 104-105, 107
Affected Linked EPS Files button (Flattening Preview palette), 422
.ai (Adobe Illustrator documents), saving files as, 101, 103
Align palette. *See also* alignment
Align to Artboard command, 368
Cancel Key Object command, 368
Distribute Spacing Distance command, 367
Distribute Spacing Horizontal command, 367
Distribute Spacing Vertical command, 367
Horizontal Align Center command, 364
Horizontal Align Left command, 364
Horizontal Align Right command, 365

X-Z

Solutions from experts you know and trust.

www.informit.com

OPERATING SYSTEMS

WEB DEVELOPMENT

PROGRAMMING

NETWORKING

CERTIFICATION

AND MORE...

**Expert Access.
Free Content.**

New Riders has partnered with

InformIT.com to bring technical

information to your desktop.

Drawing on New Riders authors

and reviewers to provide additional

information on topics you're

interested in, **InformIT.com** has

free, in-depth information you

won't find anywhere else.

- **Master the skills you need,
  when you need them**

- **Call on resources from
  some of the best minds in
  the industry**

- **Get answers when you need
  them, using InformIT's
  comprehensive library or
  live experts online**

- **Go above and beyond what
  you find in New Riders books,
  extending your knowledge**

As an **InformIT** partner, **New Riders**
has shared the wisdom and knowledge
of our authors with you online.
Visit **InformIT.com** to see what
you're missing.

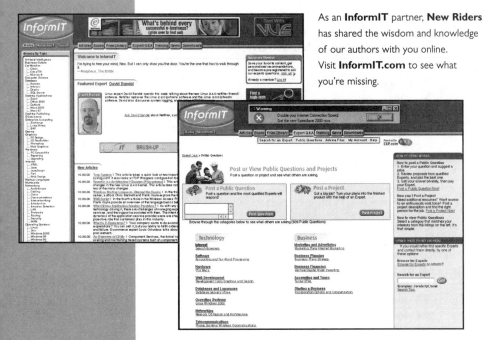

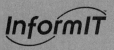

Publishing
the Voices
that Matter

OUR AUTHORS

PRESS ROOM

| web development | design | photoshop | new media | 3-D | server technologies |

EDUCATORS

ABOUT US

CONTACT US

You already know that New Riders brings you the **Voices that Matter**.

But what does that mean? It means that New Riders brings you the

Voices that challenge your assumptions, take your talents to the next

level, or simply help you better understand the complex technical world

we're all navigating.

Visit **www.newriders.com** to find:

▶ *Discounts* on specific book purchases

▶ Never before published chapters

▶ Sample chapters and excerpts

▶ Author bios and interviews

▶ Contests and enter-to-wins

▶ Up-to-date industry event information

▶ Book reviews

▶ Special offers from our friends and partners

▶ Info on how to join our User Group program

▶ Ways to have your Voice heard

WWW.NEWRIDERS.COM

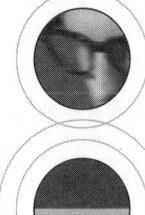
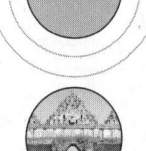

VISIT OUR WEB SITE

WWW.NEWRIDERS.COM

On our Web site you'll find information about our other books, authors, tables of contents, indexes, and book errata. You will also find information about book registration and how to purchase our books.

EMAIL US

Contact us at this address: **nrfeedback@newriders.com**

- If you have comments or questions about this book
- To report errors that you have found in this book
- If you have a book proposal to submit or are interested in writing for New Riders
- If you would like to have an author kit sent to you
- If you are an expert in a computer topic or technology and are interested i n being a technical editor who reviews manuscripts for technical accuracy

- To find a distributor in your area, please contact our international department at this address. **nrmedia@newriders.com**

- For instructors from educational institutions who want to preview New Riders books for classroom use. Email should include your name, title, school, department, address, phone number, office days/hours, text in use, and enrollment, along with your request for desk/examination copies and/or additional information.
- For members of the media who are interested in reviewing copies of New Riders books. Send your name, mailing address, and email address, along with the name of the publication or Web site you work for.

BULK PURCHASES/CORPORATE SALES

The publisher offers discounts on this book when ordered in quantity for bulk purchases and special sales. For sales within the U.S., please contact: Corporate Government Sales (800) 382-3419 or **corpsales@pearsontechgroup.com** Outside of the U.S., please contact: International Sales (317) 581-3793 or **international@pearsontechgroup.com**.

WRITE TO US

New Riders Publishing
201 W. 103rd St.
Indianapolis, IN 46290-1097

CALL US

Toll-free (800) 571-5840 + 9 + 7477
If outside U.S. (317) 581-3500. Ask for New Riders.

FAX US

(317) 581-4663

New Riders

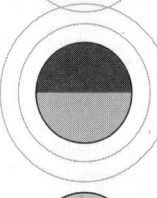

VOICES THAT MATTER

PHOTOSHOP® 7

Photoshop 7 Killer Tips
Scott Kelby
0735713006
$39.99

**Photoshop 7
Down & Dirty Tricks**
Scott Kelby
0735712379
$39.99

Photoshop 7 Magic
Sherry London,
Rhoda Grossman
0735712646
$45.00

Photoshop 7 Artistry
Barry Haynes,
Wendy Crumpler
0735712409
$55.00

Inside Photoshop 7
Gary Bouton, Robert Stanley,
J. Scott Hamlin, Daniel Will-Harris,
Mara Nathanson
0735712417
$49.99

**Photoshop Studio with
Bert Monroy**
Bert Monroy
0735712468
$45.00

**Photoshop Restoration
and Retouching**
Katrin Eisemann
0789723182
$49.99

**Photoshop Type Effects
Visual Encyclopedia**
Roger Pring
0735711909
$45.00

**Creative Thinking in
Photoshop**
Sharon Steuer
0735711224
$45.00

New Riders

VOICES
THAT MATTER™